SEBASTIAN O/THE MYSTERY PLAY
BY GRANT MORRISON

SEBASTIAN O/ THE MYSTERY PLAY

BY GRANT MORRISON

Grant Morrison...Writer

Steve Yeowell and Jon J Muth...Artists

Tatjana Wood.. Colorist

John Workman and Todd Klein.. Letterers

Steve Yeowell and Jon J Muth.. Cover Art

Steve Yeowell and Dave Stewart...SEBASTIAN O Original Cover Art

Jon J Muth..THE MYSTERY PLAY Original Cover Art

SEBASTIAN O created by Grant Morrison and Steve Yeowell

THE MYSTERY PLAY created by Grant Morrison and Jon J Muth

ART YOUNG..Editor – Original Series
TIM PILCHER...Assistant Editor – Original Series
JAMIE S. RICH...Group Editor – Vertigo Comics
JEB WOODARD..Group Editor – Collected Editions
SCOTT NYBAKKEN...Editor – Collected Edition
STEVE COOK..Design Director – Books
AMIE BROCKWAY-METCALF   LOUIS PRANDI...Publication Design

BOB HARRAS...Senior VP – Editor-in-Chief, DC Comics
MARK DOYLE..Executive Editor, Vertigo

DIANE NELSON .... President
DAN DiDIO.. Publisher
JIM LEE.. Publisher
GEOFF JOHNS...President & Chief Creative Officer
AMIT DESAI......................................Executive VP – Business & Marketing Strategy, Direct to Consumer & Global Franchise Management
SAM ADES...Senior VP & General Manager, Digital Services
BOBBIE CHASE..VP & Executive Editor, Young Reader & Talent Development
MARK CHIARELLO... Senior VP – Art, Design & Collected Editions
JOHN CUNNINGHAM...Senior VP – Sales & Trade Marketing
ANNE DePIES ....Senior VP – Business Strategy, Finance & Administration
DON FALLETTI .... VP – Manufacturing Operations
LAWRENCE GANEM ....VP – Editorial Administration & Talent Relations
ALISON GILL .... Senior VP – Manufacturing & Operations
HANK KANALZ... Senior VP – Editorial Strategy & Administration
JAY KOGAN... VP – Legal Affairs
JACK MAHAN ....VP – Business Affairs
NICK J. NAPOLITANO.. VP – Manufacturing Administration
EDDIE SCANNELL.. VP – Consumer Marketing
COURTNEY SIMMONS...Senior VP – Publicity & Communications
JIM (SKI) SOKOLOWSKI...VP – Comic Book Specialty Sales & Trade Marketing
NANCY SPEARS .... VP – Mass, Book, Digital Sales & Trade Marketing
MICHELE R. WELLS...VP – Content Strategy

SEBASTIAN O / THE MYSTERY PLAY BY GRANT MORRISON

Compilation published by DC Comics © 2017. Originally published in single magazine form as
SEBASTIAN O 1-3 and as the graphic novel THE MYSTERY PLAY. SEBASTIAN O Copyright
© 1993 Grant Morrison and Steve Yeowell. SEBASTIAN O and all related characters and
elements © & ™ Grant Morrison and Steve Yeowell. THE MYSTERY PLAY Copyright © 1994
Grant Morrison and Jon J Muth. THE MYSTERY PLAY and all related characters and elements
© & ™ Grant Morrison and Jon J Muth. VERTIGO is a trademark of DC Comics. All Rights
Reserved. The stories, characters and incidents featured in this publication are entirely fictional.
DC Comics does not read or accept unsolicited submissions of ideas, stories or artwork.

DC Comics
2900 West Alameda Avenue
Burbank, CA 91505
Printed in the USA. First Printing.
ISBN: 978-1-4012-7419-1

Library of Congress Cataloging-in-Publication Data is available.

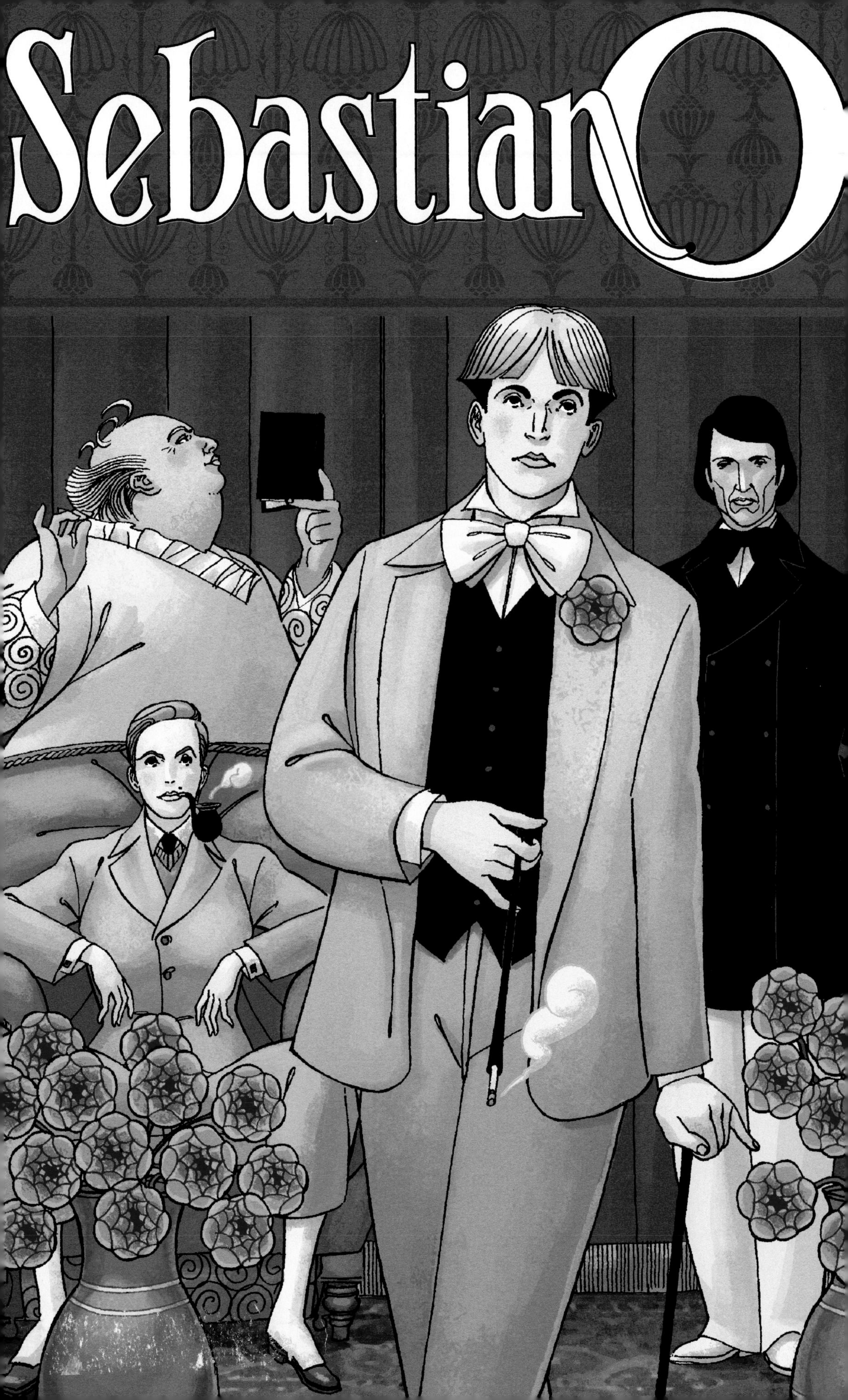
SebastianO

Sebastian O

WRITTEN BY
Grant Morrison

ILLUSTRATED BY
Steve Yeowell

COLORED BY Tatjana Wood
LETTERED BY John Workman

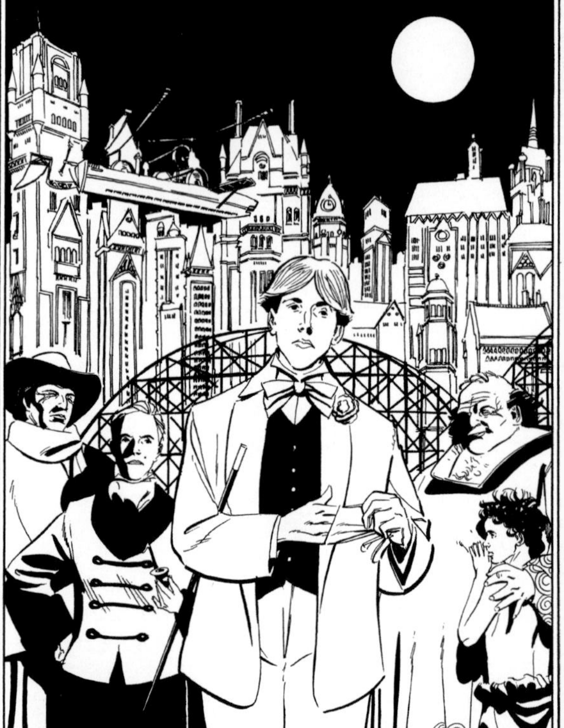

Sebastian O
CREATED BY Grant Morrison
AND Steve Yeowell

A Sebastian O
Chronology

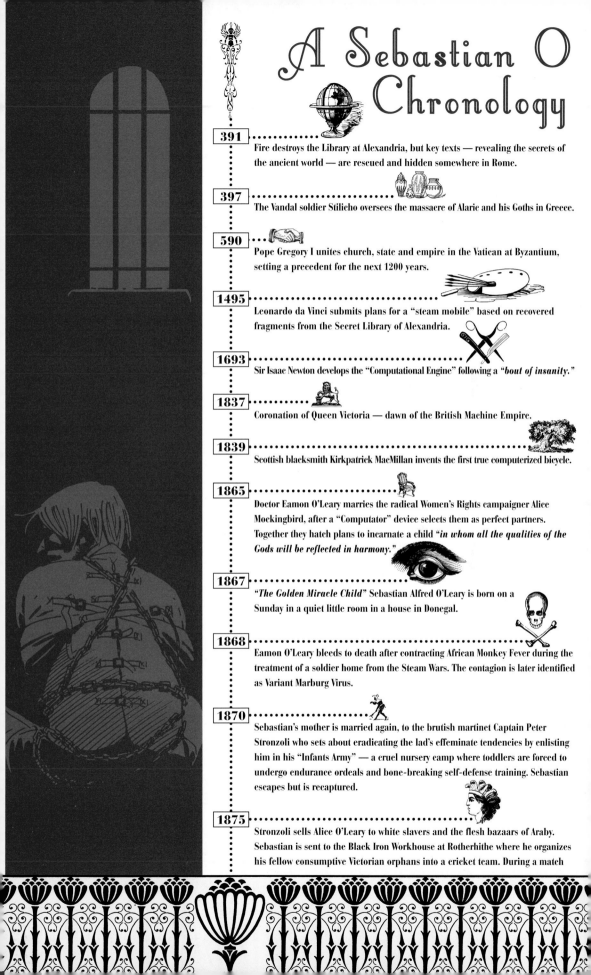

391
Fire destroys the Library at Alexandria, but key texts — revealing the secrets of the ancient world — are rescued and hidden somewhere in Rome.

397
The Vandal soldier Stilicho oversees the massacre of Alaric and his Goths in Greece.

590
Pope Gregory I unites church, state and empire in the Vatican at Byzantium, setting a precedent for the next 1200 years.

1495
Leonardo da Vinci submits plans for a "steam mobile" based on recovered fragments from the Secret Library of Alexandria.

1693
Sir Isaac Newton develops the "Computational Engine" following a *"bout of insanity."*

1837
Coronation of Queen Victoria — dawn of the British Machine Empire.

1839
Scottish blacksmith Kirkpatrick MacMillan invents the first true computerized bicycle.

1865
Doctor Eamon O'Leary marries the radical Women's Rights campaigner Alice Mockingbird, after a "Computator" device selects them as perfect partners. Together they hatch plans to incarnate a child *"in whom all the qualities of the Gods will be reflected in harmony."*

1867
"The Golden Miracle Child" Sebastian Alfred O'Leary is born on a Sunday in a quiet little room in a house in Donegal.

1868
Eamon O'Leary bleeds to death after contracting African Monkey Fever during the treatment of a soldier home from the Steam Wars. The contagion is later identified as Variant Marburg Virus.

1870
Sebastian's mother is married again, to the brutish martinet Captain Peter Stronzoli who sets about eradicating the lad's effeminate tendencies by enlisting him in his "Infants Army" — a cruel nursery camp where toddlers are forced to undergo endurance ordeals and bone-breaking self-defense training. Sebastian escapes but is recaptured.

1875
Stronzoli sells Alice O'Leary to white slavers and the flesh bazaars of Araby. Sebastian is sent to the Black Iron Workhouse at Rotherhithe where he organizes his fellow consumptive Victorian orphans into a cricket team. During a match

with the Bedlam Youth 11, he makes his escape from this "inescapable" fortress of soul-crushing child labor, but his freedom is once again short-lived.

1878

Florence Babbins, Sebastian's beloved nanny, rescues him from the Workhouse. They escape down the Thames in a prototype Water-Oscillator submersible machine, then journey by balloon, steam monorail train and waterbus twice around the globe.

1880

When Florence Babbins dies under the wheels of an oil-carrying Juggernaut in Morocco, Sebastian is delivered into the care of Ali ibn Hazred, and tutored in the ways of the *Hasheesheen*, a sect of all-male ecstatic killers who view death as the Royal Road to Paradise and venerate the act of Murder as the Highest, most Divine of the Arts, which delivers souls unto Eternity.

1882

Using mysterious "funds" obtained on an expedition into the desert in search of the Lost City of God, Sebastian returns to his schooling and enrolls himself at Lycée Louis-le-Grand, where he is initiated once more into the "Uranian Brotherhood" by a group of sexually inquisitive schoolboys. He becomes obsessed by Poe's *"voluptuous macabre"* and dedicates himself to the aesthetic, decadent life.

1883

Using the *nom de plume* "Sebastian O," he embezzles school funds to publish *Hymns to Myself*, a scandalous collection of poetry with themes including suicide, sickness, hypochondria, putrefaction, live burial, spectres, madness, the love of Jesus and John, diabolism and dandyism. His proposals for the school Nativity Play offer scenes in which headmaster and staff engage in "symbolic" coprophilia, bestiality and transvestism, only to be devoured by pupils following a four-hour cannibal orgy *"culminating in a Black Mass."*

1884

Sebastian is asked not to return to his school and takes a garret room in the East End of London, whereupon his physical and intellectual misery are seen to increase to a point where he is unable even to produce a one-act drama without recourse to the ruby decanter. Yet no matter how extreme his Lucifer-like plunges into disgrace and penury, Sebastian always ensures that dressing well remains his priority. *"It is the duty of the Dandy to embody that Platonic ideal to which Nature ever aspires in Vain."*

1886

Emerging from his "Purple Period" with a book of unpublishable poems entitled *Breakfast With Beelzebub*, Sebastian takes up a new career as a light-fingered gentleman murderer. He becomes Public Enemy Number One for a brief time in two different countries.

1887

Eluding capture by the Peelers in their Aeropedes, Sebastian makes his way to Vienna, where he joins the Midnight Circus of Shadows as "the Incredible India Rubber Poet." Here he begins a passionate "Plutonian" affair with the perverse Ringmaster, Lazarus Tonnerre. The entire Circus is jailed in London after an

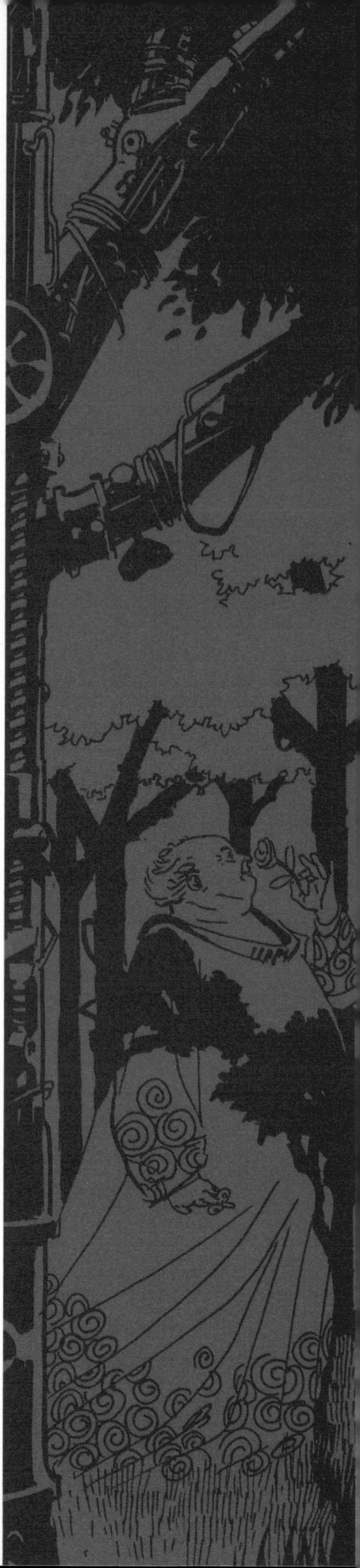

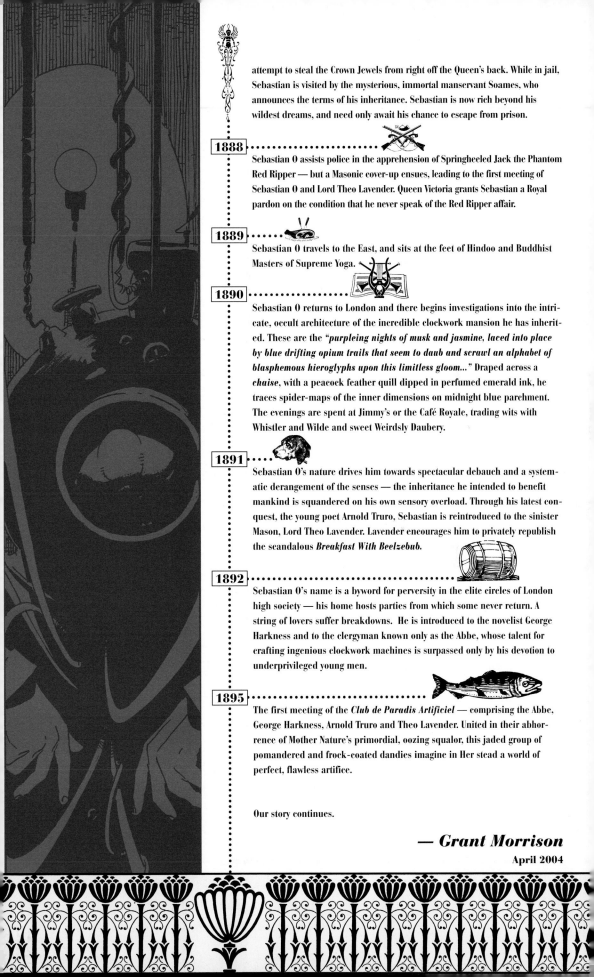

attempt to steal the Crown Jewels from right off the Queen's back. While in jail, Sebastian is visited by the mysterious, immortal manservant Soames, who announces the terms of his inheritance. Sebastian is now rich beyond his wildest dreams, and need only await his chance to escape from prison.

1888

Sebastian O assists police in the apprehension of Springheeled Jack the Phantom Red Ripper — but a Masonic cover-up ensues, leading to the first meeting of Sebastian O and Lord Theo Lavender. Queen Victoria grants Sebastian a Royal pardon on the condition that he never speak of the Red Ripper affair.

1889

Sebastian O travels to the East, and sits at the feet of Hindoo and Buddhist Masters of Supreme Yoga.

1890

Sebastian O returns to London and there begins investigations into the intricate, occult architecture of the incredible clockwork mansion he has inherited. These are the *"purpleing nights of musk and jasmine, laced into place by blue drifting opium trails that seem to daub and scrawl an alphabet of blasphemous hieroglyphs upon this limitless gloom..."* Draped across a *chaise*, with a peacock feather quill dipped in perfumed emerald ink, he traces spider-maps of the inner dimensions on midnight blue parchment. The evenings are spent at Jimmy's or the Café Royale, trading wits with Whistler and Wilde and sweet Weirdsly Daubery.

1891

Sebastian O's nature drives him towards spectacular debauch and a systematic derangement of the senses — the inheritance he intended to benefit mankind is squandered on his own sensory overload. Through his latest conquest, the young poet Arnold Truro, Sebastian is reintroduced to the sinister Mason, Lord Theo Lavender. Lavender encourages him to privately republish the scandalous *Breakfast With Beelzebub*.

1892

Sebastian O's name is a byword for perversity in the elite circles of London high society — his home hosts parties from which some never return. A string of lovers suffer breakdowns. He is introduced to the novelist George Harkness and to the clergyman known only as the Abbe, whose talent for crafting ingenious clockwork machines is surpassed only by his devotion to underprivileged young men.

1895

The first meeting of the *Club de Paradis Artificiel* — comprising the Abbe, George Harkness, Arnold Truro and Theo Lavender. United in their abhorrence of Mother Nature's primordial, oozing squalor, this jaded group of pomandered and frock-coated dandies imagine in Her stead a world of perfect, flawless artifice.

Our story continues.

— *Grant Morrison*
April 2004

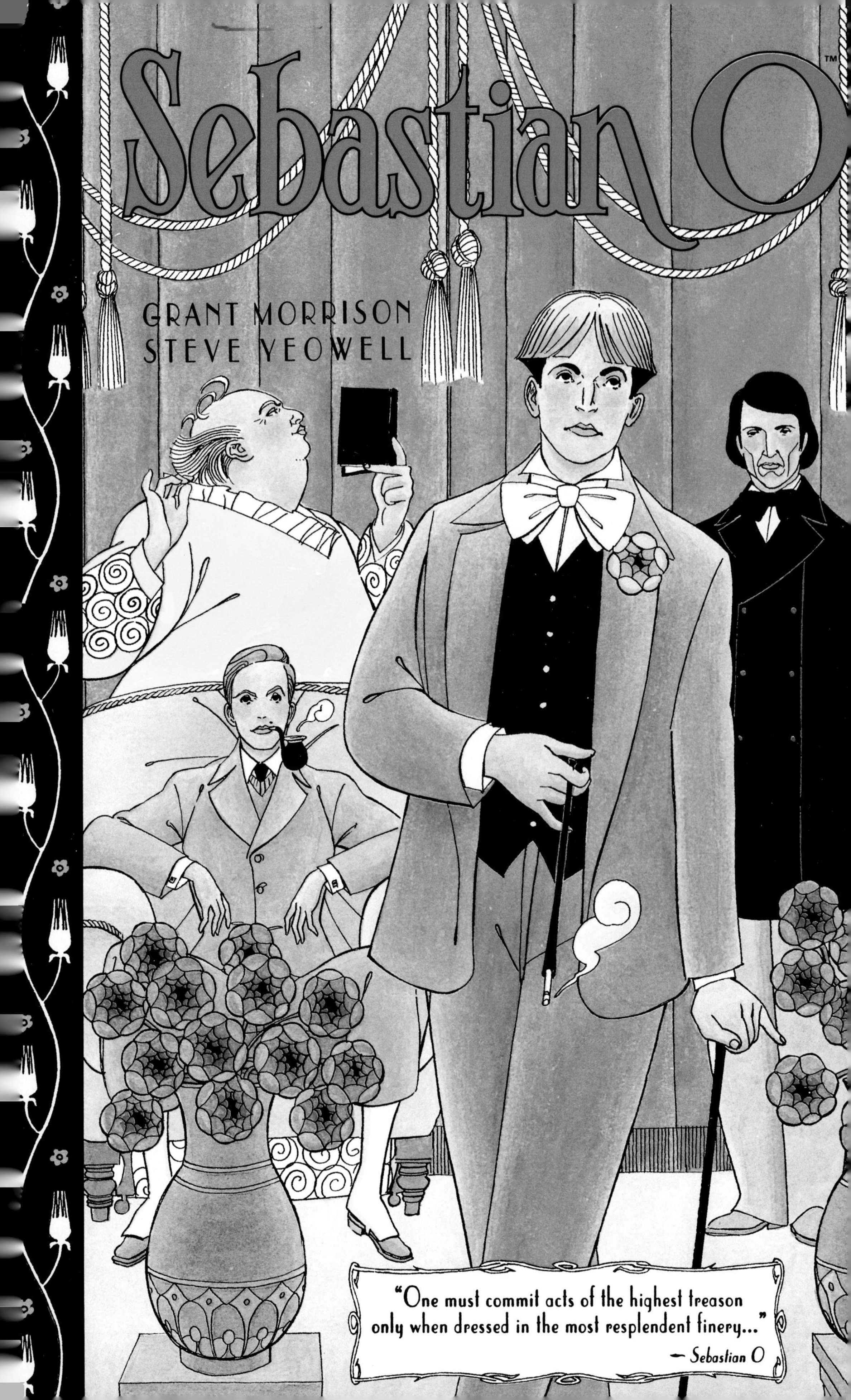
Sebastian O™
GRANT MORRISON
STEVE YEOWELL
"One must commit acts of the highest treason
only when dressed in the most resplendent finery..."
— Sebastian O

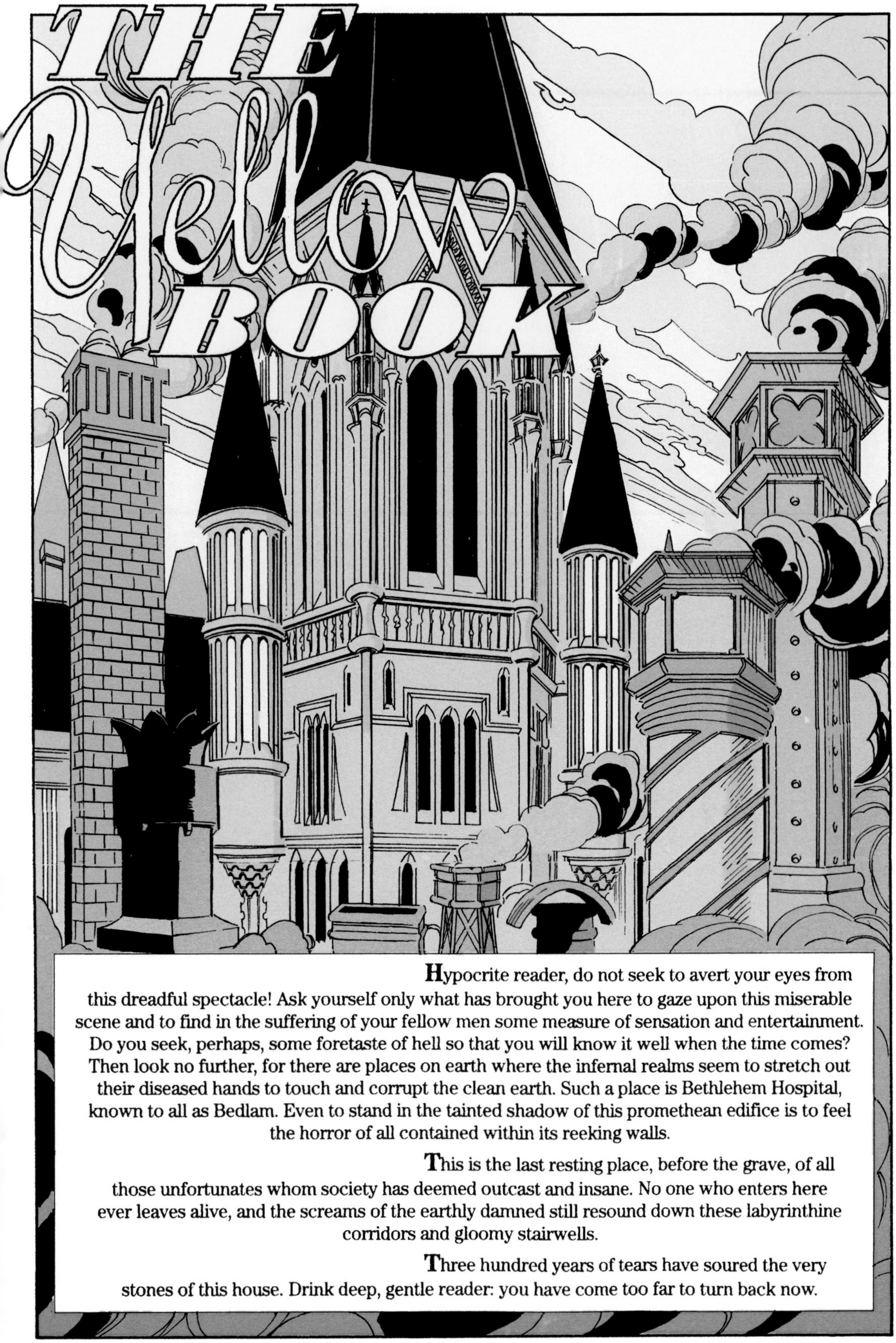
THE Yellow BOOK
Hypocrite reader, do not seek to avert your eyes from this dreadful spectacle! Ask yourself only what has brought you here to gaze upon this miserable scene and to find in the suffering of your fellow men some measure of sensation and entertainment. Do you seek, perhaps, some foretaste of hell so that you will know it well when the time comes? Then look no further, for there are places on earth where the infernal realms seem to stretch out their diseased hands to touch and corrupt the clean earth. Such a place is Bethlehem Hospital, known to all as Bedlam. Even to stand in the tainted shadow of this promethean edifice is to feel the horror of all contained within its reeking walls.
This is the last resting place, before the grave, of all those unfortunates whom society has deemed outcast and insane. No one who enters here ever leaves alive, and the screams of the earthly damned still resound down these labyrinthine corridors and gloomy stairwells.
Three hundred years of tears have soured the very stones of this house. Drink deep, gentle reader: you have come too far to turn back now.

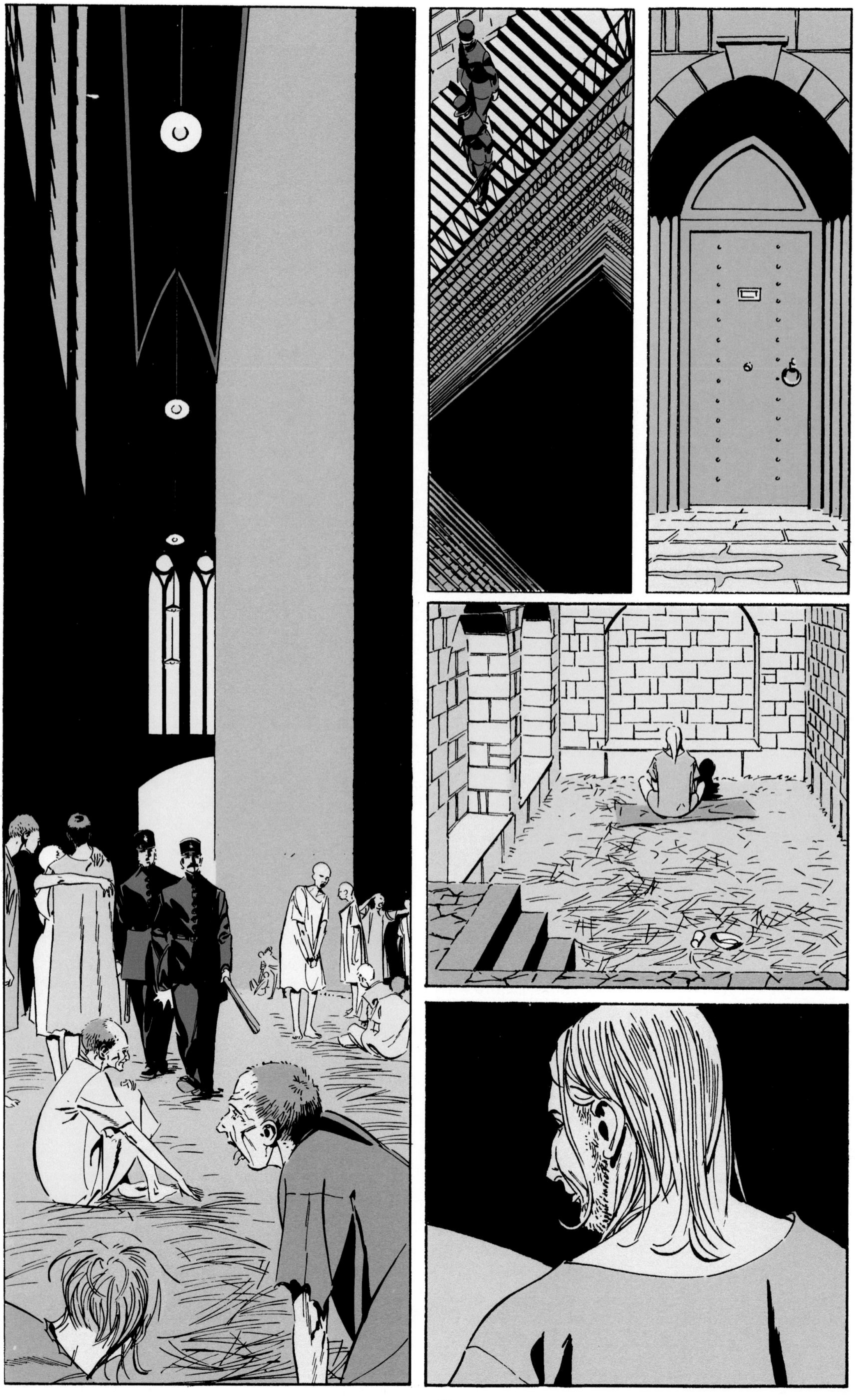

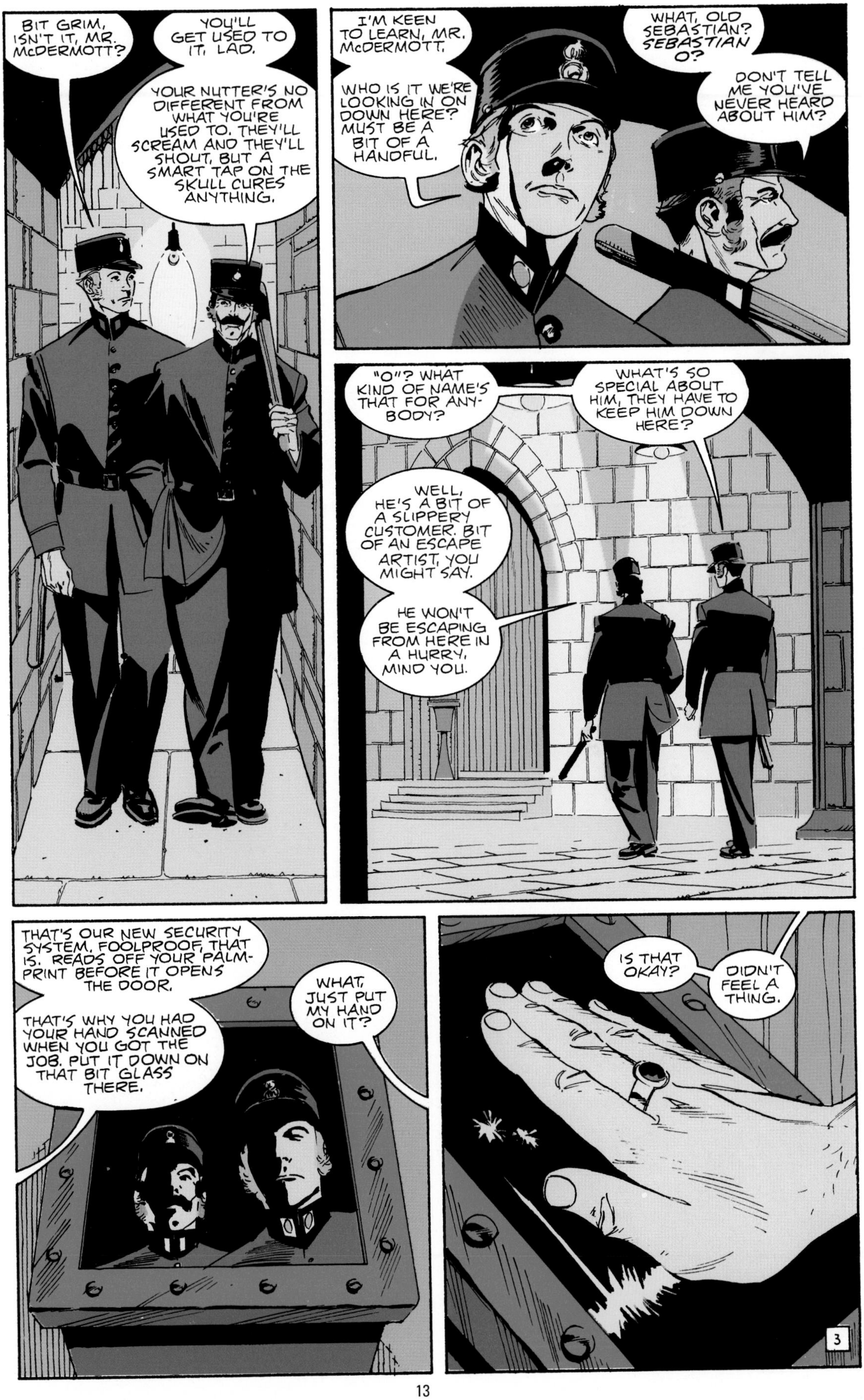

BIT GRIM, ISN'T IT, MR. McDERMOTT?
YOU'LL GET USED TO IT, LAD.
YOUR NUTTER'S NO DIFFERENT FROM WHAT YOU'RE USED TO. THEY'LL SCREAM AND THEY'LL SHOUT, BUT A SMART TAP ON THE SKULL CURES ANYTHING.
I'M KEEN TO LEARN, MR. McDERMOTT.
WHO IS IT WE'RE LOOKING IN ON DOWN HERE? MUST BE A BIT OF A HANDFUL.
WHAT, OLD SEBASTIAN? SEBASTIAN O?
DON'T TELL ME YOU'VE NEVER HEARD ABOUT HIM?
"O"? WHAT KIND OF NAME'S THAT FOR ANYBODY?
WHAT'S SO SPECIAL ABOUT HIM, THEY HAVE TO KEEP HIM DOWN HERE?
WELL, HE'S A BIT OF A SLIPPERY CUSTOMER. BIT OF AN ESCAPE ARTIST, YOU MIGHT SAY.
HE WON'T BE ESCAPING FROM HERE IN A HURRY, MIND YOU.
THAT'S OUR NEW SECURITY SYSTEM. FOOLPROOF, THAT IS. READS OFF YOUR PALM-PRINT BEFORE IT OPENS THE DOOR.
THAT'S WHY YOU HAD YOUR HAND SCANNED WHEN YOU GOT THE JOB. PUT IT DOWN ON THAT BIT GLASS THERE.
WHAT, JUST PUT MY HAND ON IT?
IS THAT OKAY?
DIDN'T FEEL A THING.
3

'COURSE YOU DON'T. IT'S SCIENCE, ISN'T IT?

COMPUTER READS OFF YOUR PRINT, CHECKS IT IN ITS BRAINBOX, AND OPENS THE DOOR.

AMAZING.

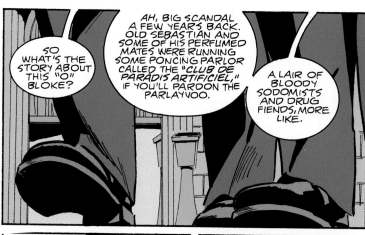

SO WHAT'S THE STORY ABOUT THIS "O" BLOKE?

AH, BIG SCANDAL A FEW YEARS BACK. OLD SEBASTIAN AND SOME OF HIS PERFUMED MATES WERE RUNNING SOME PONCING PARLOR CALLED THE *"CLUB DE PARADIS ARTIFICIEL,"* IF YOU'LL PARDON THE PARLAYVOO.

A LAIR OF BLOODY SODOMISTS AND DRUG FIENDS, MORE LIKE.

SO OUR BOY SEBASTIAN'S WRITTEN SOME SORT OF FILTHY, UNNATURAL BOOK AND THE LAW QUITE RIGHTLY COMES DOWN ON THE WHOLE BLOODY LOT OF THEM.

THEY COULDN'T PROVE ANYTHING ABOUT THE OTHERS, SO IT'S JUST SEBASTIAN AND YOUNG *ARNOLD TRURO* ENDED UP IN HERE.

YOU MUST HAVE SEEN IT ON THE TELLY.

I HATE THE NEWS.

I JUST WATCH THE WRESTLING.

HE SPENT A BIT OF TIME IN THE MYSTERIOUS EAST, SO I HEARD. LEARNED ALL SORTS OF TRICKS FROM THEM HINDOOS.

MAD AS A HATTER, THOUGH. IF HE WASN'T WHEN HE COME IN HERE, HE IS NOW. JUST SITS THERE ALL DAY.

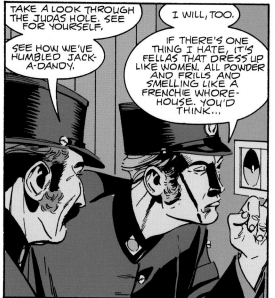

TAKE A LOOK THROUGH THE JUDAS HOLE. SEE FOR YOURSELF.

SEE HOW WE'VE HUMBLED JACK-A-DANDY.

I WILL, TOO.

IF THERE'S ONE THING I HATE, IT'S FELLAS THAT DRESS UP LIKE WOMEN, ALL POWDER AND FRILLS AND SMELLING LIKE A FRENCHIE WHORE-HOUSE. YOU'D THINK...

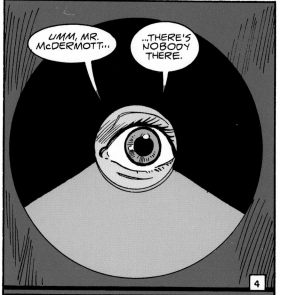

UMM, MR. McDERMOTT...

...THERE'S NOBODY THERE.

4

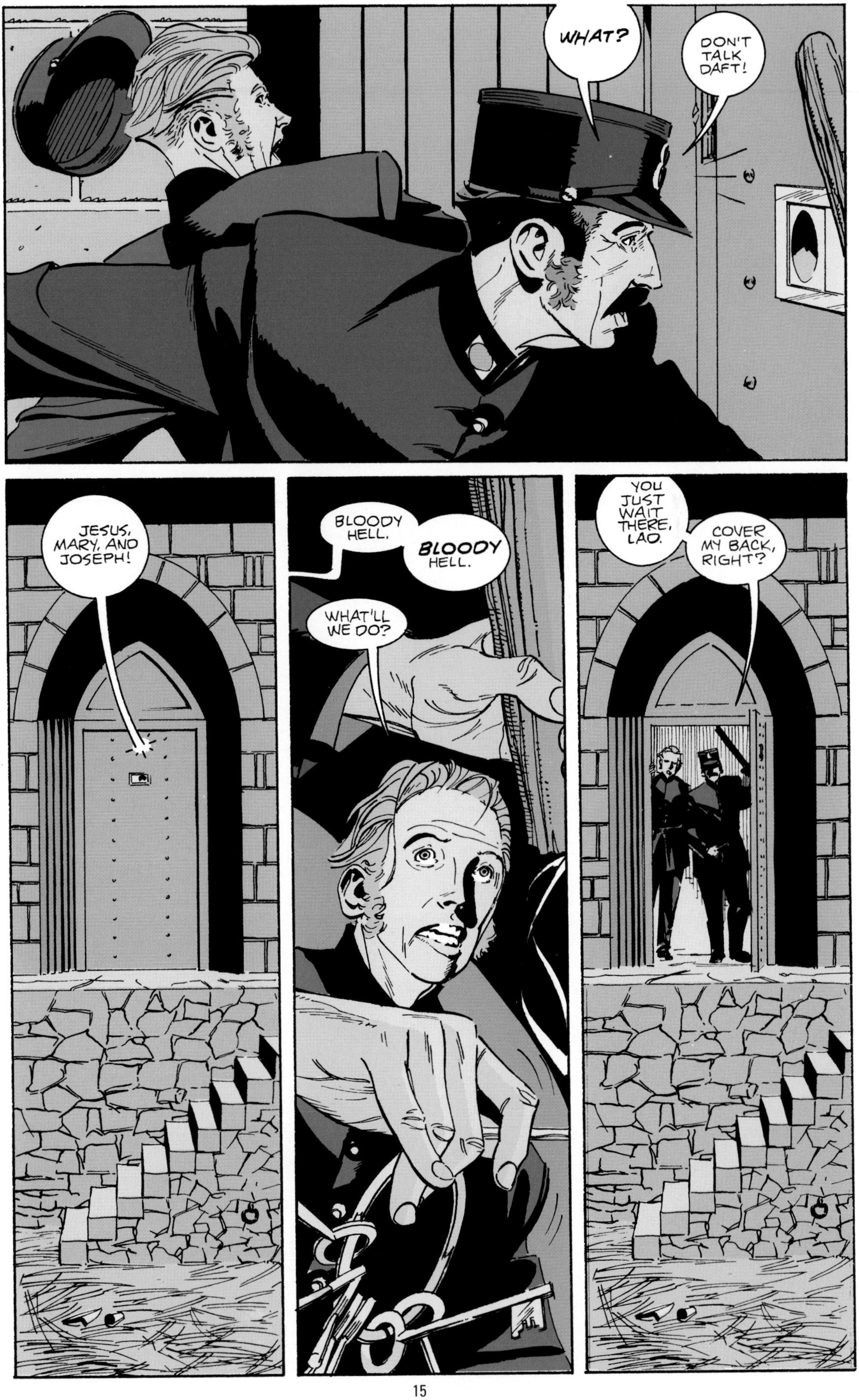
WHAT?
DON'T TALK DAFT!
JESUS, MARY, AND JOSEPH!
BLOODY HELL.
BLOODY HELL.
WHAT'LL WE DO?
YOU JUST WAIT THERE, LAO.
COVER MY BACK, RIGHT?

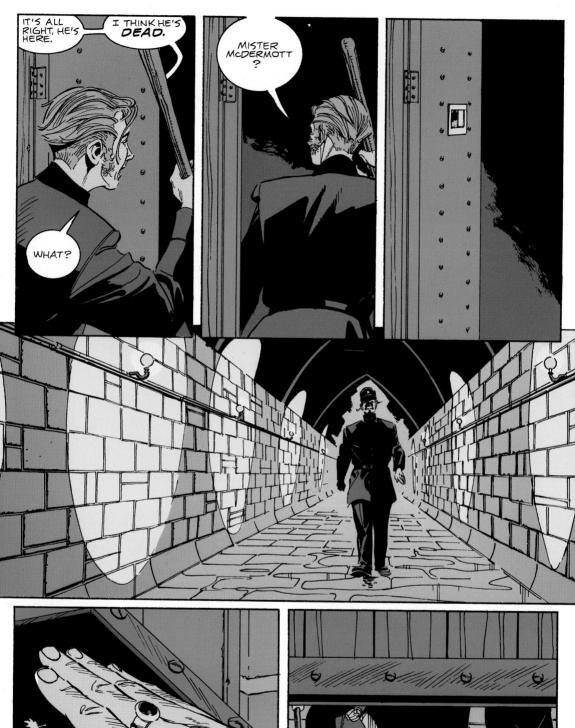

IT'S ALL RIGHT, HE'S HERE.

I THINK HE'S **DEAD.**

WHAT?

MISTER McDERMOTT?

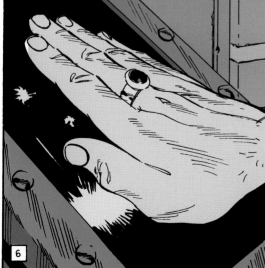

OI! WHERE THE BLOODY HELL ARE YOU GOING?

DIDN'T YOU HEAR THE ALARM GOING OFF? WE'VE GOT A RUNNER!

DON'T JUST STAND THERE, FOR CHRIST'S SAKE!

GIVE US A HAND!

DIDN'T YOU HEAR WHAT I...

AH.

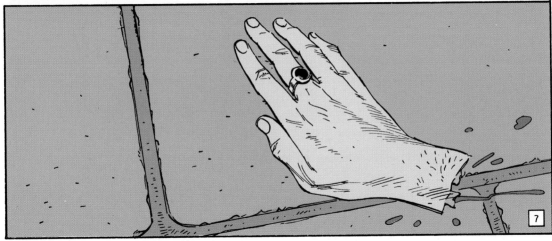

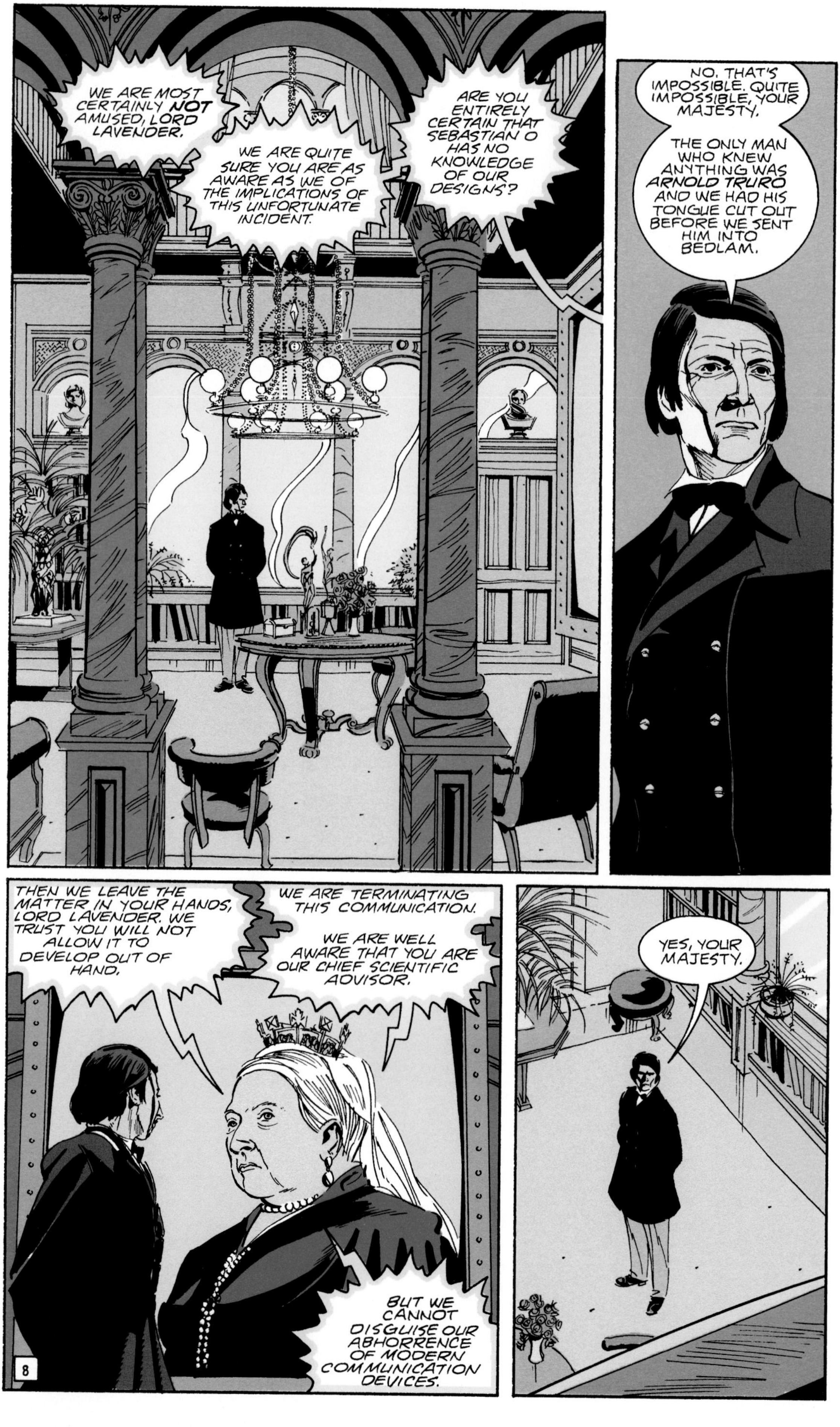
WE ARE MOST CERTAINLY NOT AMUSED, LORD LAVENDER.
WE ARE QUITE SURE YOU ARE AS AWARE AS WE OF THE IMPLICATIONS OF THIS UNFORTUNATE INCIDENT.
ARE YOU ENTIRELY CERTAIN THAT SEBASTIAN O HAS NO KNOWLEDGE OF OUR DESIGNS?
NO. THAT'S IMPOSSIBLE. QUITE IMPOSSIBLE, YOUR MAJESTY.
THE ONLY MAN WHO KNEW ANYTHING WAS ARNOLD TRURO AND WE HAD HIS TONGUE CUT OUT BEFORE WE SENT HIM INTO BEDLAM.
THEN WE LEAVE THE MATTER IN YOUR HANDS, LORD LAVENDER. WE TRUST YOU WILL NOT ALLOW IT TO DEVELOP OUT OF HAND.
WE ARE TERMINATING THIS COMMUNICATION.
WE ARE WELL AWARE THAT YOU ARE OUR CHIEF SCIENTIFIC ADVISOR.
BUT WE CANNOT DISGUISE OUR ABHORRENCE OF MODERN COMMUNICATION DEVICES.
YES, YOUR MAJESTY.

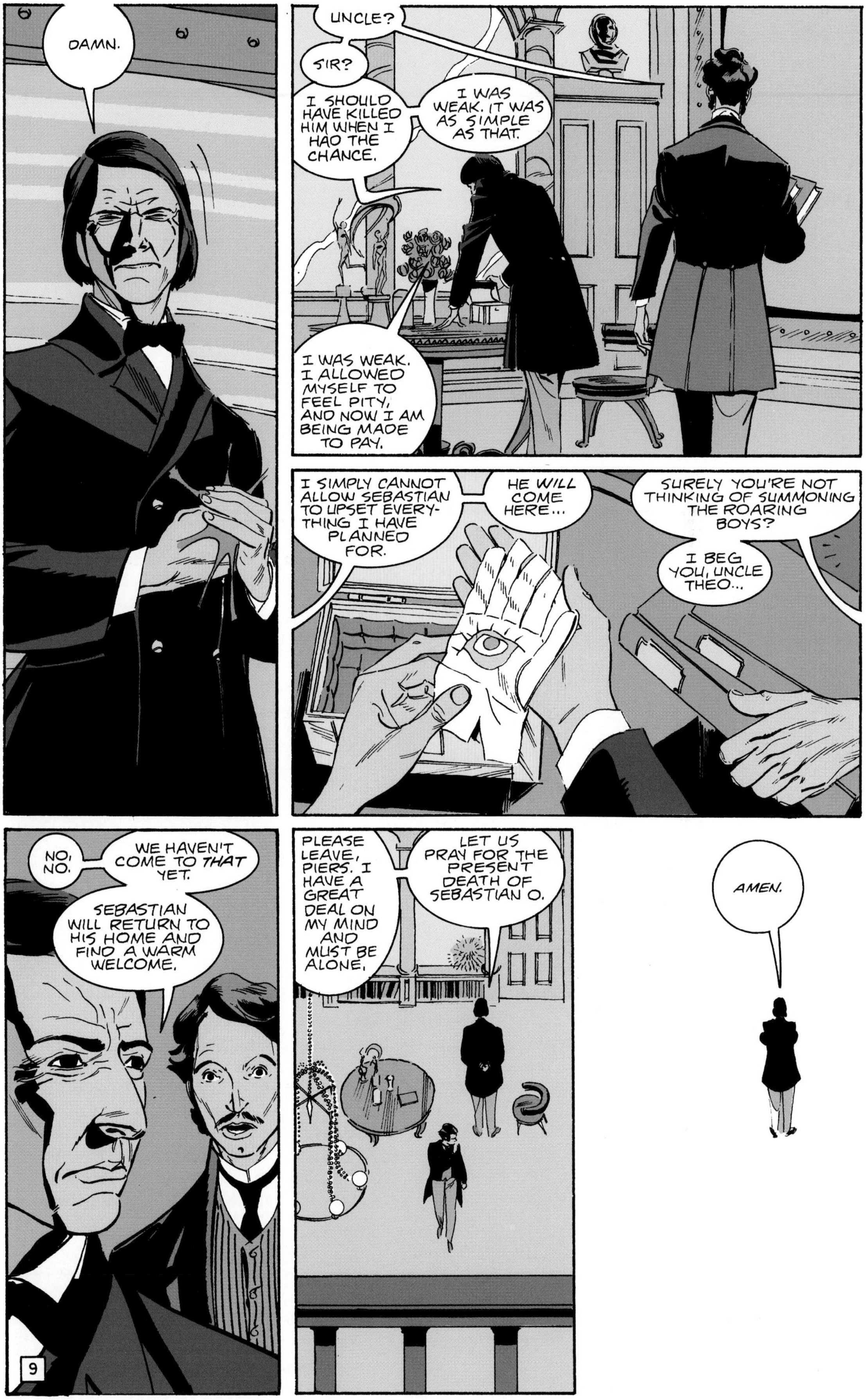
DAMN.
UNCLE?
SIR?
I SHOULD HAVE KILLED HIM WHEN I HAD THE CHANCE.
I WAS WEAK. IT WAS AS SIMPLE AS THAT.
I WAS WEAK. I ALLOWED MYSELF TO FEEL PITY, AND NOW I AM BEING MADE TO PAY.
I SIMPLY CANNOT ALLOW SEBASTIAN TO UPSET EVERYTHING I HAVE PLANNED FOR.
HE WILL COME HERE...
SURELY YOU'RE NOT THINKING OF SUMMONING THE ROARING BOYS?
I BEG YOU, UNCLE THEO...
NO, NO.
WE HAVEN'T COME TO THAT YET.
SEBASTIAN WILL RETURN TO HIS HOME AND FIND A WARM WELCOME.
9
PLEASE LEAVE, PIERS. I HAVE A GREAT DEAL ON MY MIND AND MUST BE ALONE.
LET US PRAY FOR THE PRESENT DEATH OF SEBASTIAN O.
AMEN.

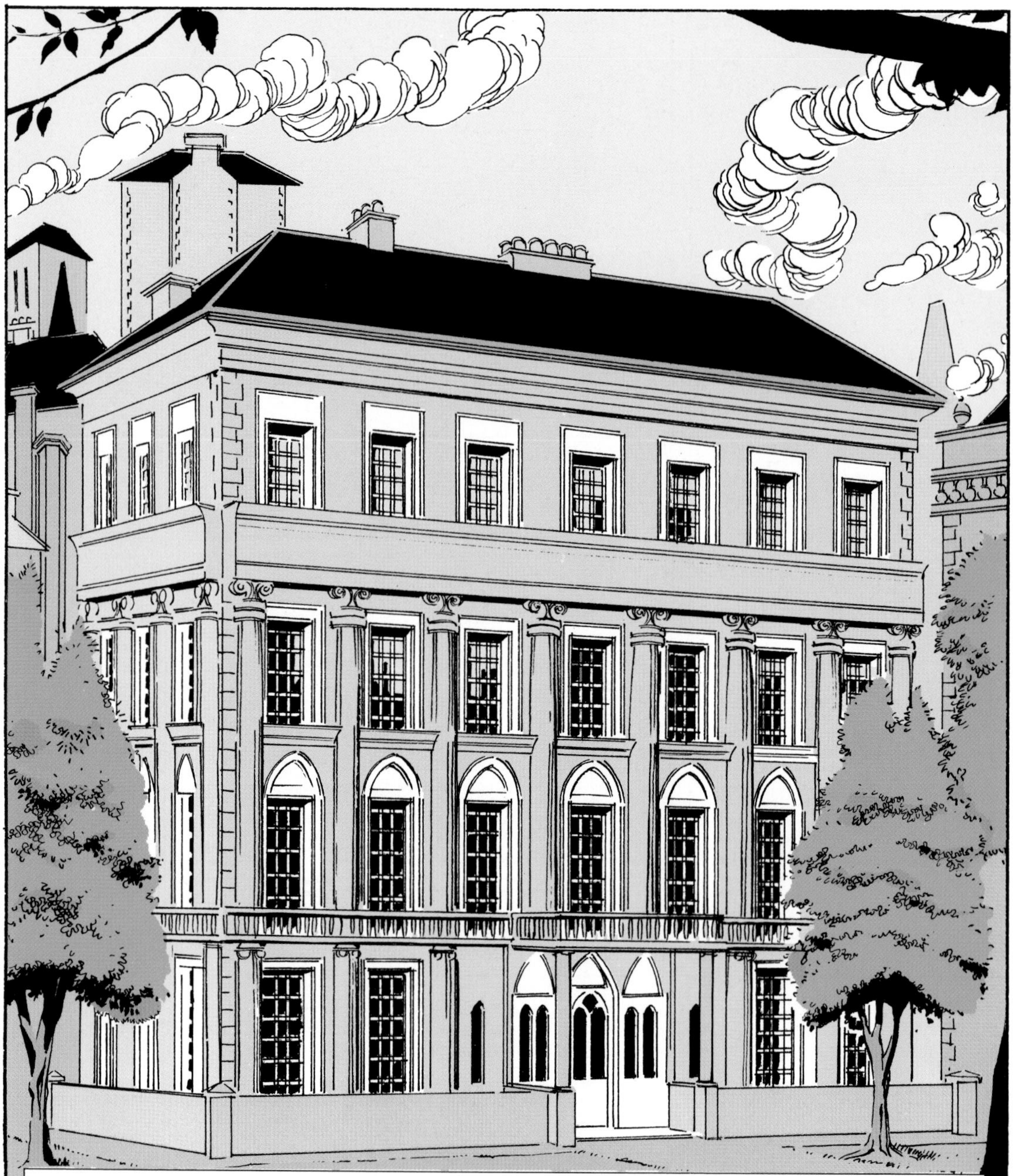

The house of Sebastian O stands in the heart of Bloomsbury, its walled garden deterring the curious eye. The house was designed and constructed by master Swiss craftsmen, now dead, their secrets long lost. It was built in 1780 by the scandalous Lord Carhaix, whose defiance of conventional morality outraged London society. A diabolist and member of Sir Francis Dashwood's infamous Hellfire Club, Lord Carhaix devised the eccentric architecture of the house as a means to add spice to his notorious orgies. Rumor had it that he even maintained a blasphemous zoo of human beings in the bowels of the house, and these he used for his own pleasure and occult experiments. Heaven had its revenge, however, when Carhaix and his mistress, a debauched nun named Eve Villon, died in a stupendous and mysterious fire in a small town near Pisa in Italy.

The house, like an exquisite Chinese cabinet, contains many secrets: hidden rooms and intricate mechanisms, sliding walls, moving stairs and strange passageways. Some, it is said, have entered the house and become lost, never to be seen again. One of the more extravagant claims made about the building is that its cellars open onto other worlds beyond our own, but such speculations we leave to the scientific romances of Monsieur Verne and Mr. Wells.

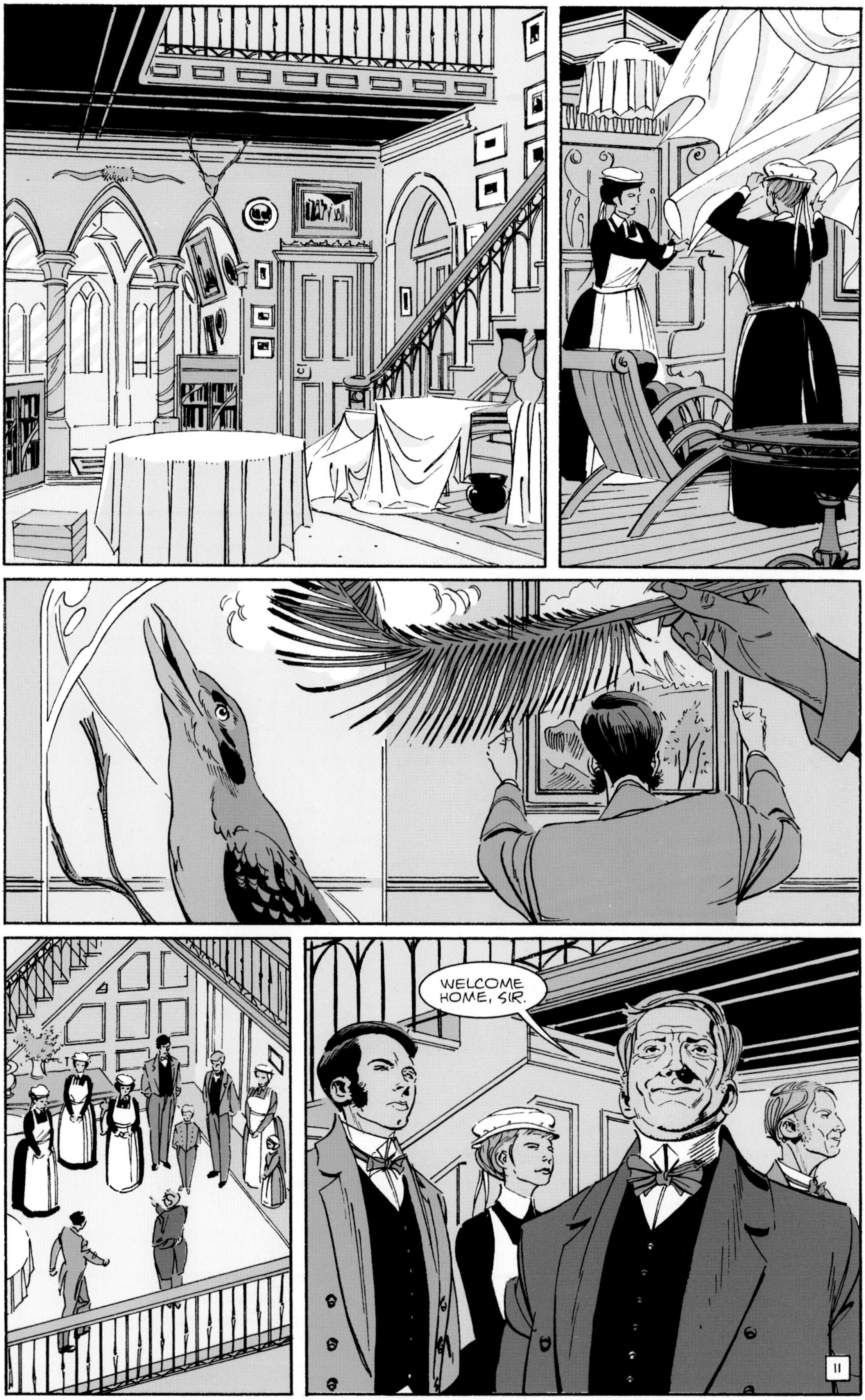
WELCOME HOME, SIR.
11

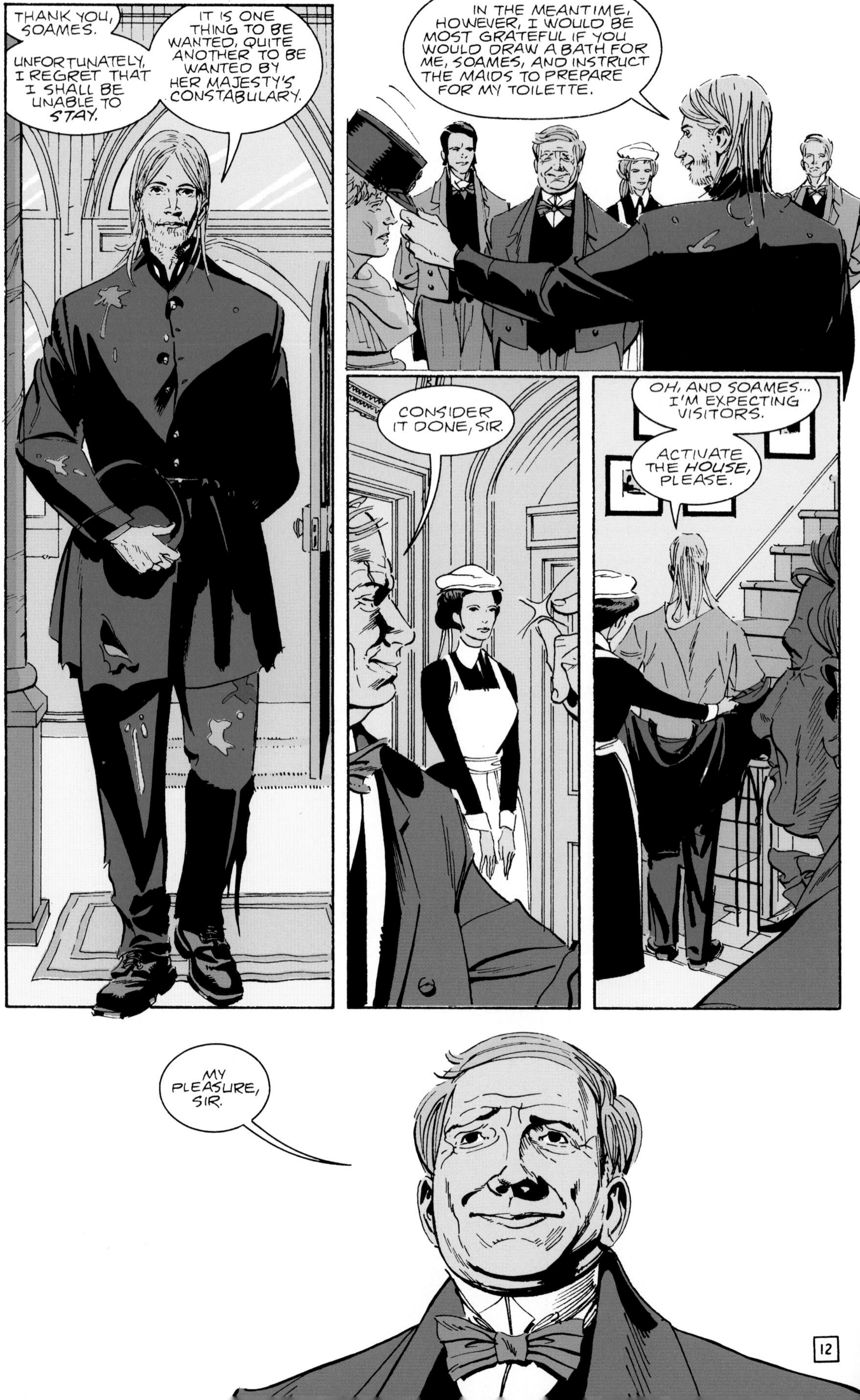
THANK YOU, SOAMES.
UNFORTUNATELY, I REGRET THAT I SHALL BE UNABLE TO STAY.
IT IS ONE THING TO BE WANTED, QUITE ANOTHER TO BE WANTED BY HER MAJESTY'S CONSTABULARY.
IN THE MEANTIME, HOWEVER, I WOULD BE MOST GRATEFUL IF YOU WOULD DRAW A BATH FOR ME, SOAMES, AND INSTRUCT THE MAIDS TO PREPARE FOR MY TOILETTE.
CONSIDER IT DONE, SIR.
OH, AND SOAMES... I'M EXPECTING VISITORS.
ACTIVATE THE HOUSE, PLEASE.
MY PLEASURE, SIR.

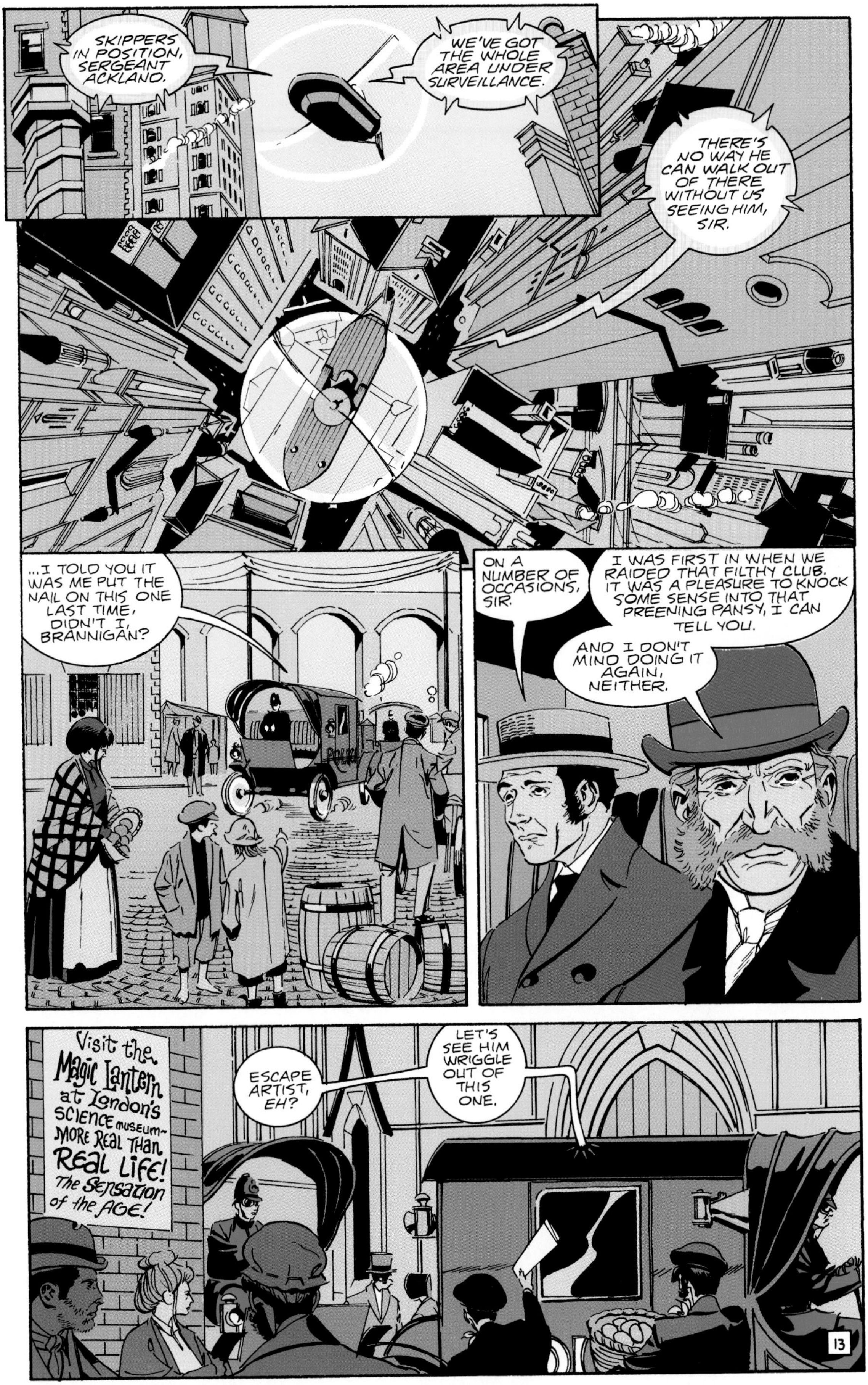

SKIPPERS IN POSITION, SERGEANT ACKLAND.
WE'VE GOT THE WHOLE AREA UNDER SURVEILLANCE.
THERE'S NO WAY HE CAN WALK OUT OF THERE WITHOUT US SEEING HIM, SIR.
...I TOLD YOU IT WAS ME PUT THE NAIL ON THIS ONE LAST TIME, DIDN'T I, BRANNIGAN?
ON A NUMBER OF OCCASIONS, SIR.
I WAS FIRST IN WHEN WE RAIDED THAT FILTHY CLUB. IT WAS A PLEASURE TO KNOCK SOME SENSE INTO THAT PREENING PANSY, I CAN TELL YOU.
AND I DON'T MIND DOING IT AGAIN, NEITHER.
Visit the Magic Lantern at London's SCIENCE MUSEUM~ MORE REAL THAN REAL LIFE! The Sensation of the AGE!
ESCAPE ARTIST, EH?
LET'S SEE HIM WRIGGLE OUT OF THIS ONE.
13

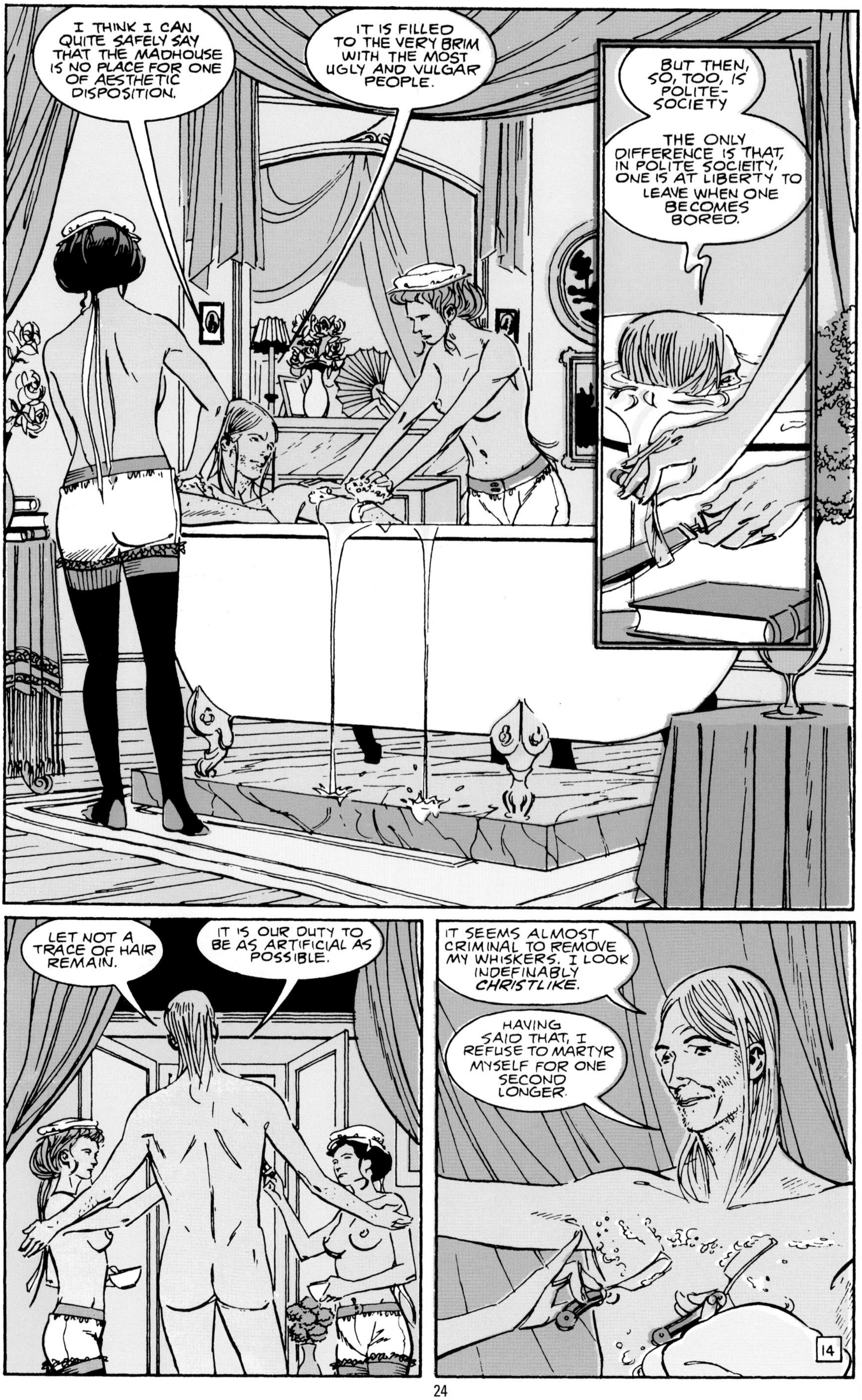
I THINK I CAN QUITE SAFELY SAY THAT THE MADHOUSE IS NO PLACE FOR ONE OF AESTHETIC DISPOSITION.
IT IS FILLED TO THE VERY BRIM WITH THE MOST UGLY AND VULGAR PEOPLE.
BUT THEN, SO, TOO, IS POLITE-SOCIETY
THE ONLY DIFFERENCE IS THAT, IN POLITE SOCIETY, ONE IS AT LIBERTY TO LEAVE WHEN ONE BECOMES BORED.
LET NOT A TRACE OF HAIR REMAIN.
IT IS OUR DUTY TO BE AS ARTIFICIAL AS POSSIBLE.
IT SEEMS ALMOST CRIMINAL TO REMOVE MY WHISKERS. I LOOK INDEFINABLY CHRISTLIKE.
HAVING SAID THAT, I REFUSE TO MARTYR MYSELF FOR ONE SECOND LONGER.
14

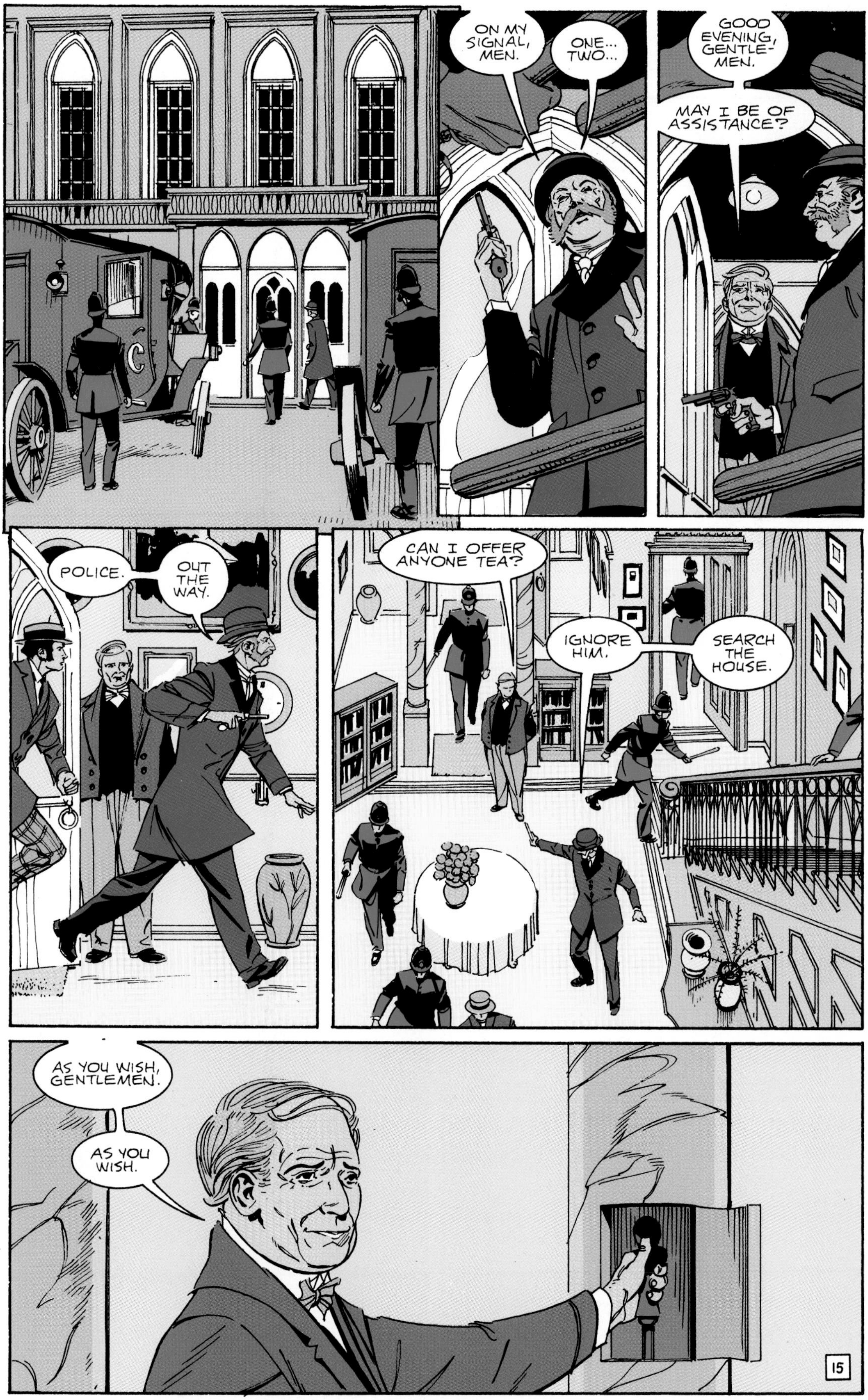

ON MY SIGNAL, MEN.
ONE... TWO...
GOOD EVENING, GENTLE-MEN.
MAY I BE OF ASSISTANCE?
POLICE.
OUT THE WAY.
CAN I OFFER ANYONE TEA?
IGNORE HIM.
SEARCH THE HOUSE.
AS YOU WISH, GENTLEMEN.
AS YOU WISH.
15

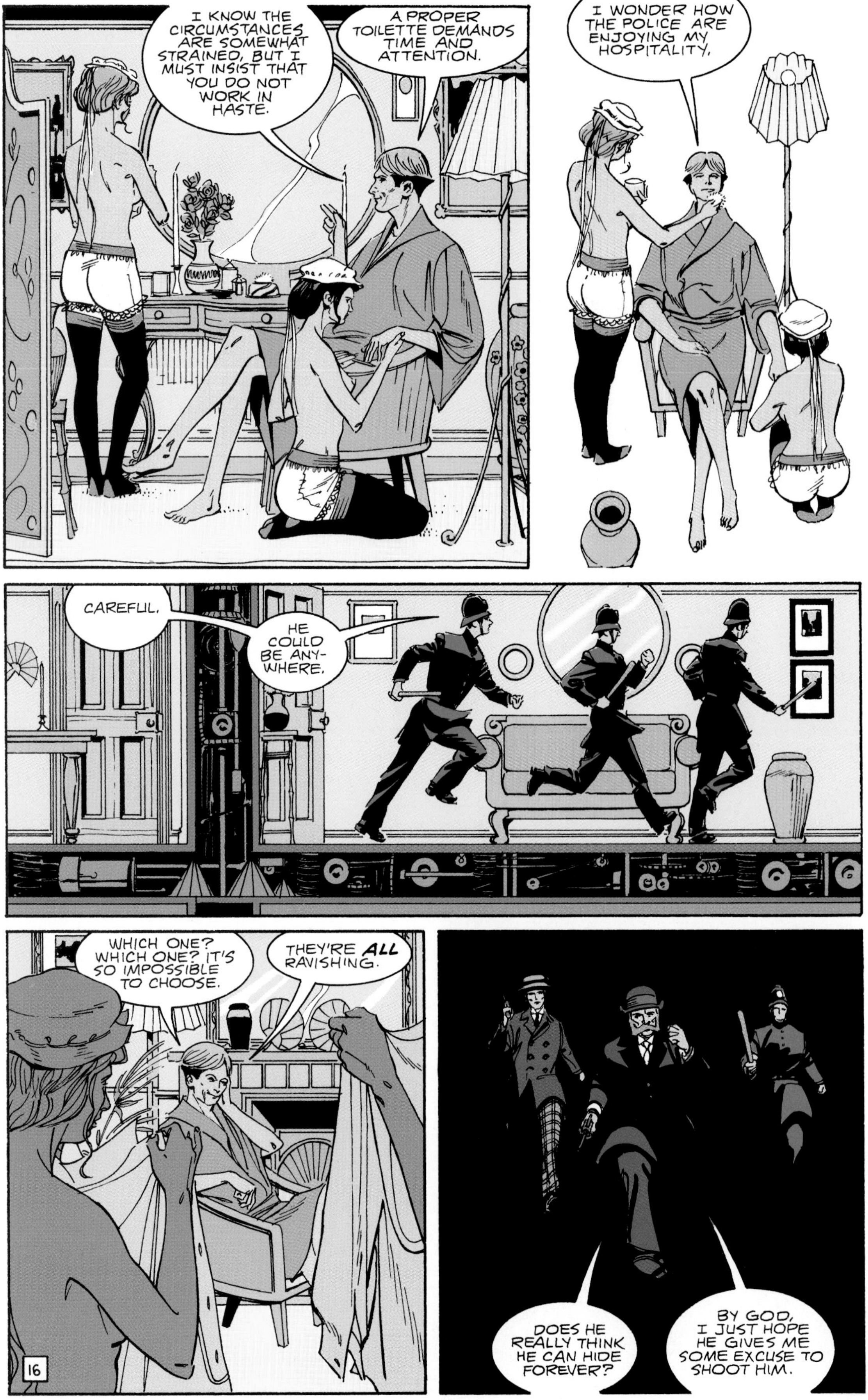
I KNOW THE CIRCUMSTANCES ARE SOMEWHAT STRAINED, BUT I MUST INSIST THAT YOU DO NOT WORK IN HASTE.
A PROPER TOILETTE DEMANDS TIME AND ATTENTION.
I WONDER HOW THE POLICE ARE ENJOYING MY HOSPITALITY.
CAREFUL.
HE COULD BE ANY-WHERE.
WHICH ONE? WHICH ONE? IT'S SO IMPOSSIBLE TO CHOOSE.
THEY'RE ALL RAVISHING.
16
DOES HE REALLY THINK HE CAN HIDE FOREVER?
BY GOD, I JUST HOPE HE GIVES ME SOME EXCUSE TO SHOOT HIM.

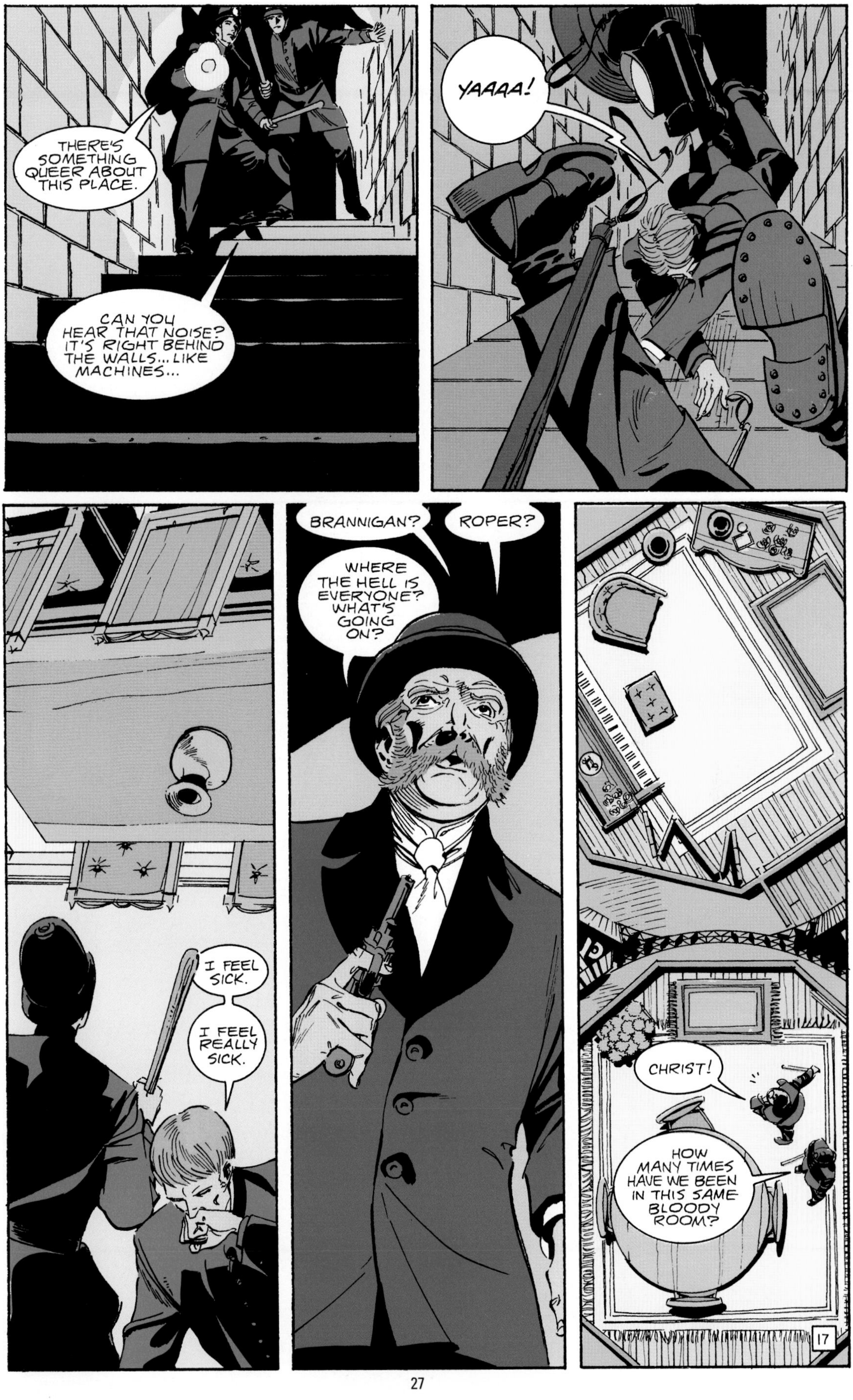
THERE'S SOMETHING QUEER ABOUT THIS PLACE.
CAN YOU HEAR THAT NOISE? IT'S RIGHT BEHIND THE WALLS...LIKE MACHINES...
YAAAA!
I FEEL SICK.
I FEEL REALLY SICK.
BRANNIGAN?
ROPER?
WHERE THE HELL IS EVERYONE? WHAT'S GOING ON?
CHRIST!
HOW MANY TIMES HAVE WE BEEN IN THIS SAME BLOODY ROOM?
17

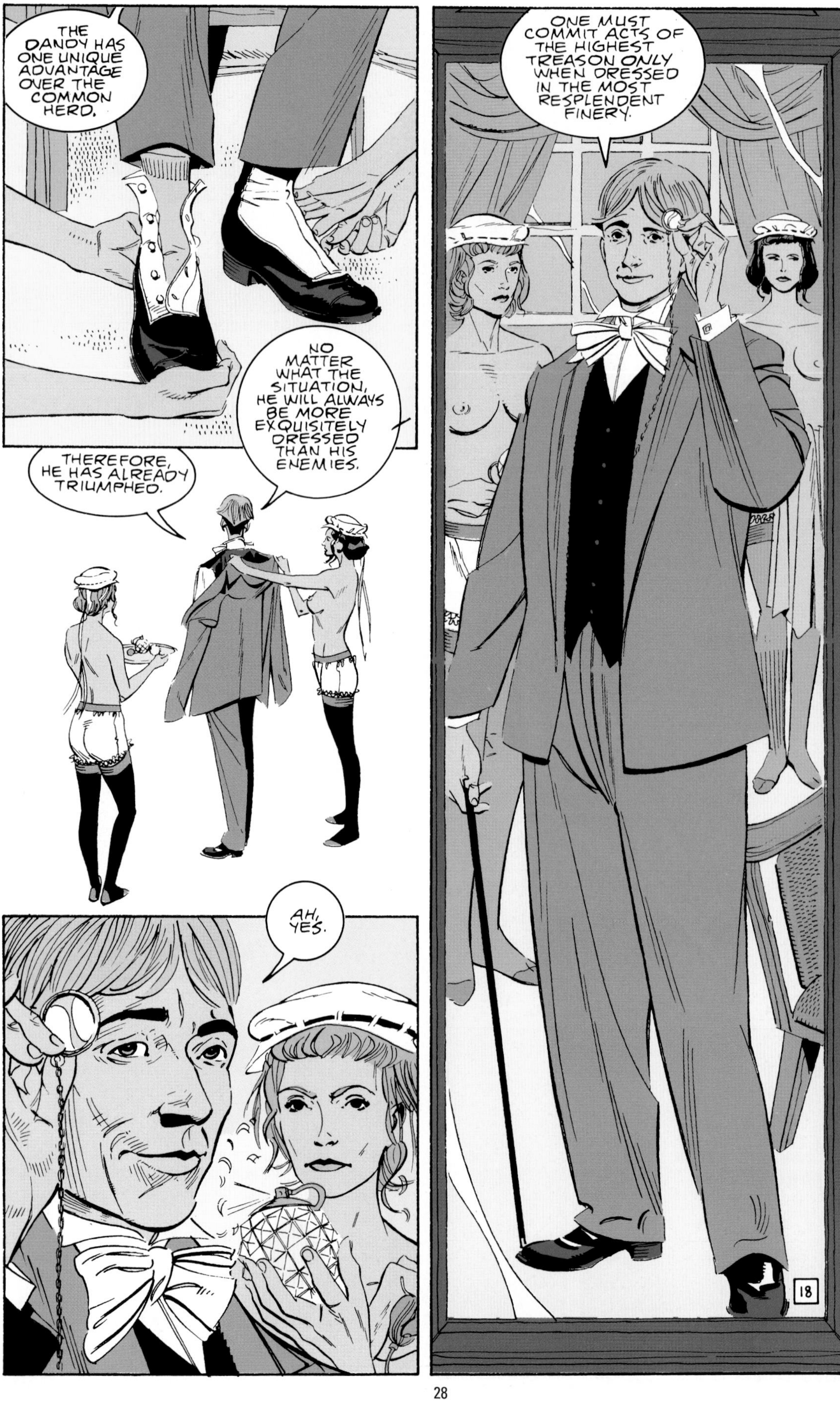
THE DANDY HAS ONE UNIQUE ADVANTAGE OVER THE COMMON HERD.
NO MATTER WHAT THE SITUATION, HE WILL ALWAYS BE MORE EXQUISITELY DRESSED THAN HIS ENEMIES.
THEREFORE, HE HAS ALREADY TRIUMPHED.
AH, YES.
ONE MUST COMMIT ACTS OF THE HIGHEST TREASON ONLY WHEN DRESSED IN THE MOST RESPLENDENT FINERY.
18

BLOOODY HELL!

THERE MUST BE A WAY...

SHITE!

AH.

DO JOIN US, SERGEANT ACKLAND. SO NICE TO SEE YOU AGAIN.

IT SEEMS YOU'VE ARRIVED JUST IN TIME FOR A SPOT OF TARGET PRACTICE.

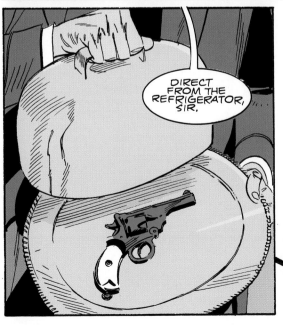

DIRECT FROM THE REFRIGERATOR, SIR.

CHILLED TO PERFECTION, SOAMES.

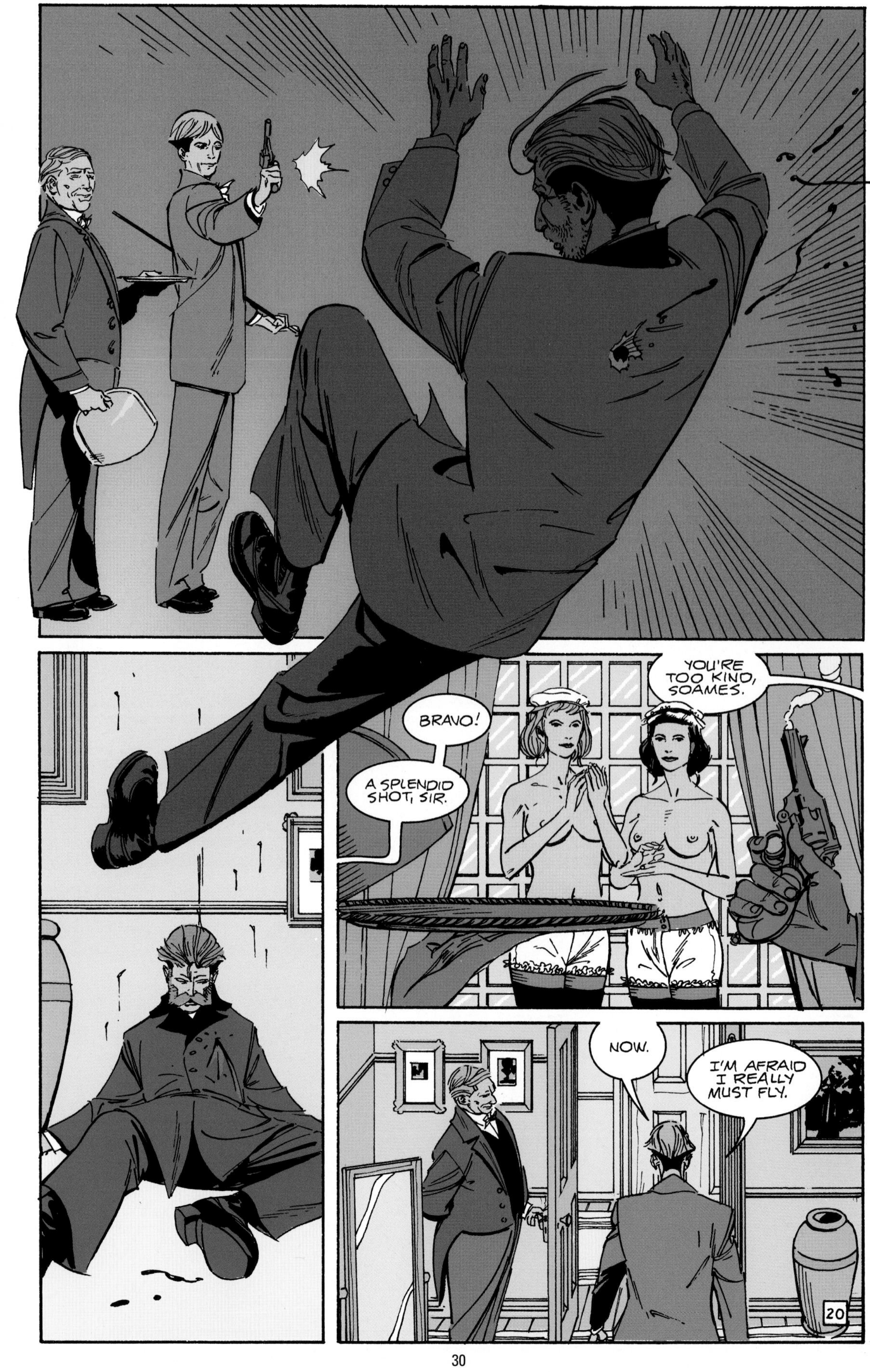
BRAVO!
A SPLENDID SHOT, SIR.
YOU'RE TOO KIND, SOAMES.
NOW.
I'M AFRAID I REALLY MUST FLY.
20

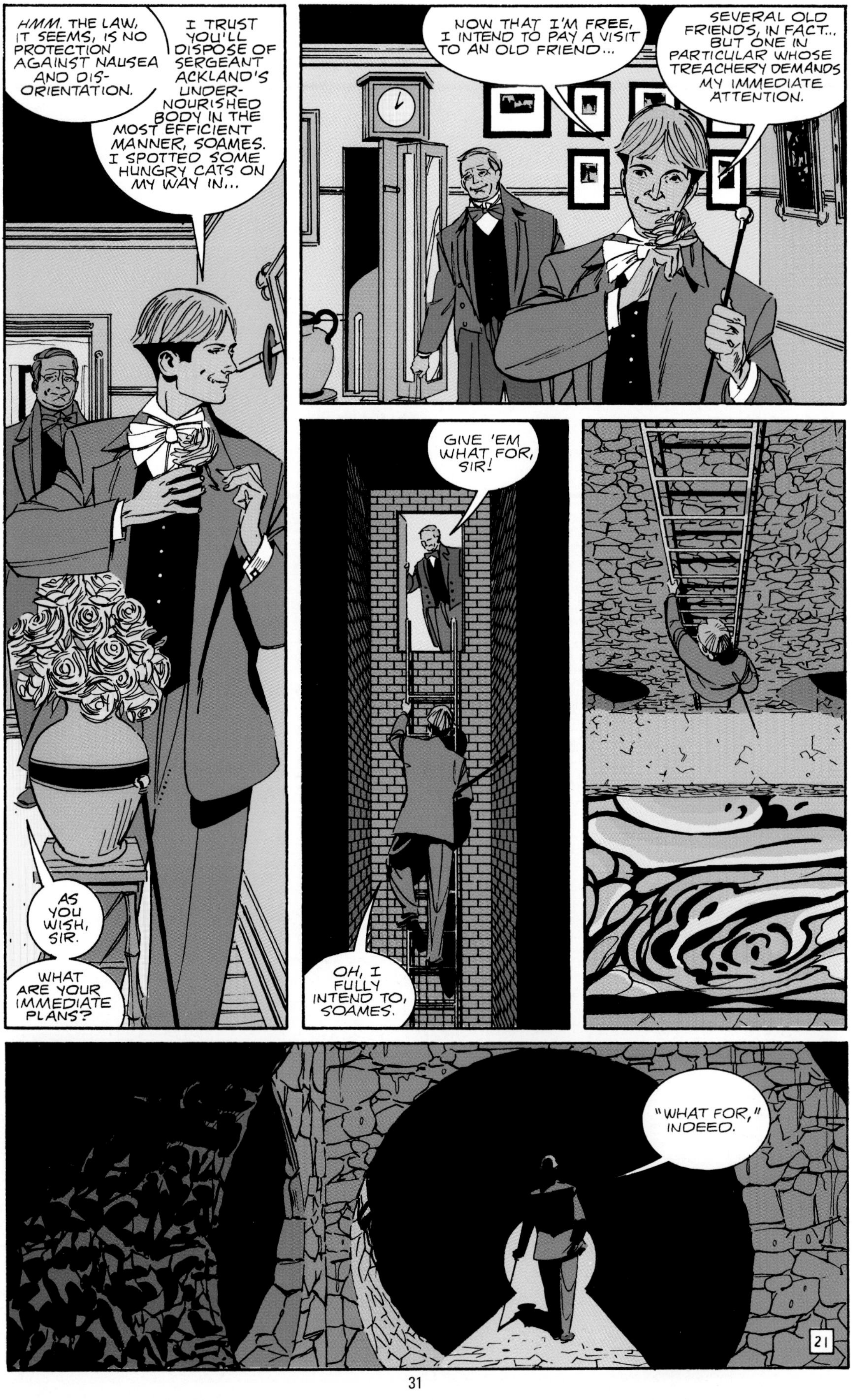

HMM. THE LAW, IT SEEMS, IS NO PROTECTION AGAINST NAUSEA AND DIS-ORIENTATION.
I TRUST YOU'LL DISPOSE OF SERGEANT ACKLAND'S UNDER-NOURISHED BODY IN THE MOST EFFICIENT MANNER, SOAMES. I SPOTTED SOME HUNGRY CATS ON MY WAY IN...
AS YOU WISH, SIR.
WHAT ARE YOUR IMMEDIATE PLANS?
NOW THAT I'M FREE, I INTEND TO PAY A VISIT TO AN OLD FRIEND...
SEVERAL OLD FRIENDS, IN FACT... BUT ONE IN PARTICULAR WHOSE TREACHERY DEMANDS MY IMMEDIATE ATTENTION.
GIVE 'EM WHAT FOR, SIR!
OH, I FULLY INTEND TO, SOAMES.
"WHAT FOR," INDEED.
21

...AND WE STILL HAVEN'T BEEN ABLE TO FIND SOME OF OUR LADS, SIR.

I'M SORRY.

YOU WILL BE SORRY.

I CAN PROMISE YOU THAT.

UNCLE?

I COULDN'T HELP BUT OVERHEAR.

YOU'RE NOT THINKING OF...

I SHOULD HAVE KILLED HIM.

THEY UNDER-ESTIMATED HIM.

THEY THOUGHT THEY WERE DEALING WITH A GENTLEMAN, BUT SEBASTIAN O IS A MAD, VICIOUS DOG.

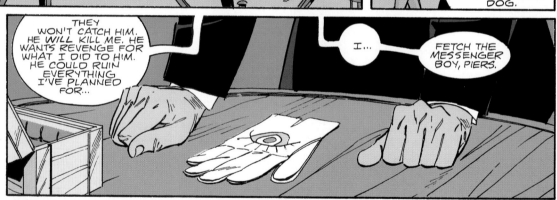

THEY WON'T CATCH HIM. HE WILL KILL ME. HE WANTS REVENGE FOR WHAT I DID TO HIM. HE COULD RUIN EVERYTHING I'VE PLANNED FOR...

I...

FETCH THE MESSENGER BOY, PIERS.

GOD FORGIVE ME.

OR DON'T.

WHAT DO I CARE?

22

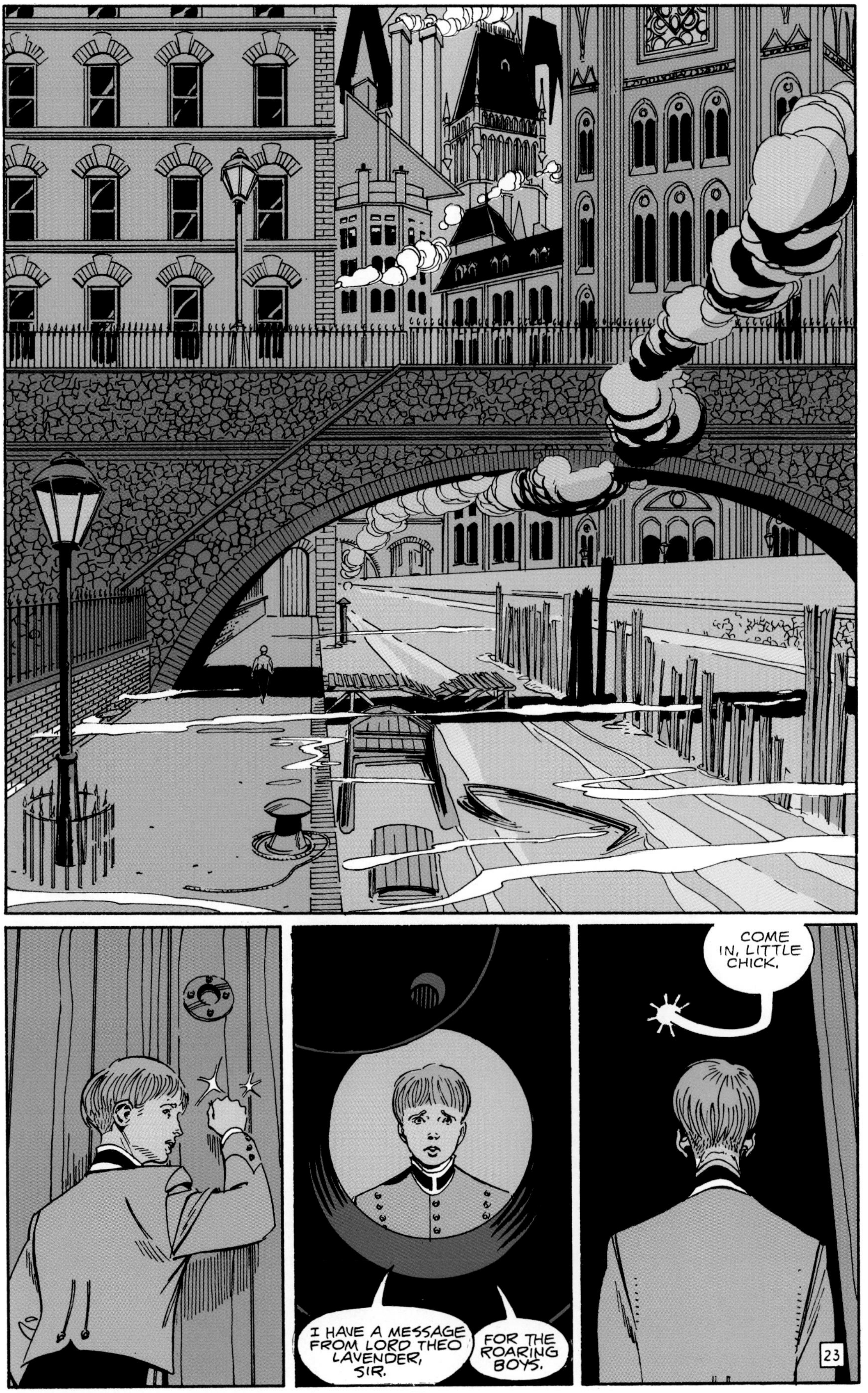
I HAVE A MESSAGE FROM LORD THEO LAVENDER, SIR.
FOR THE ROARING BOYS.
COME IN, LITTLE CHICK.
23

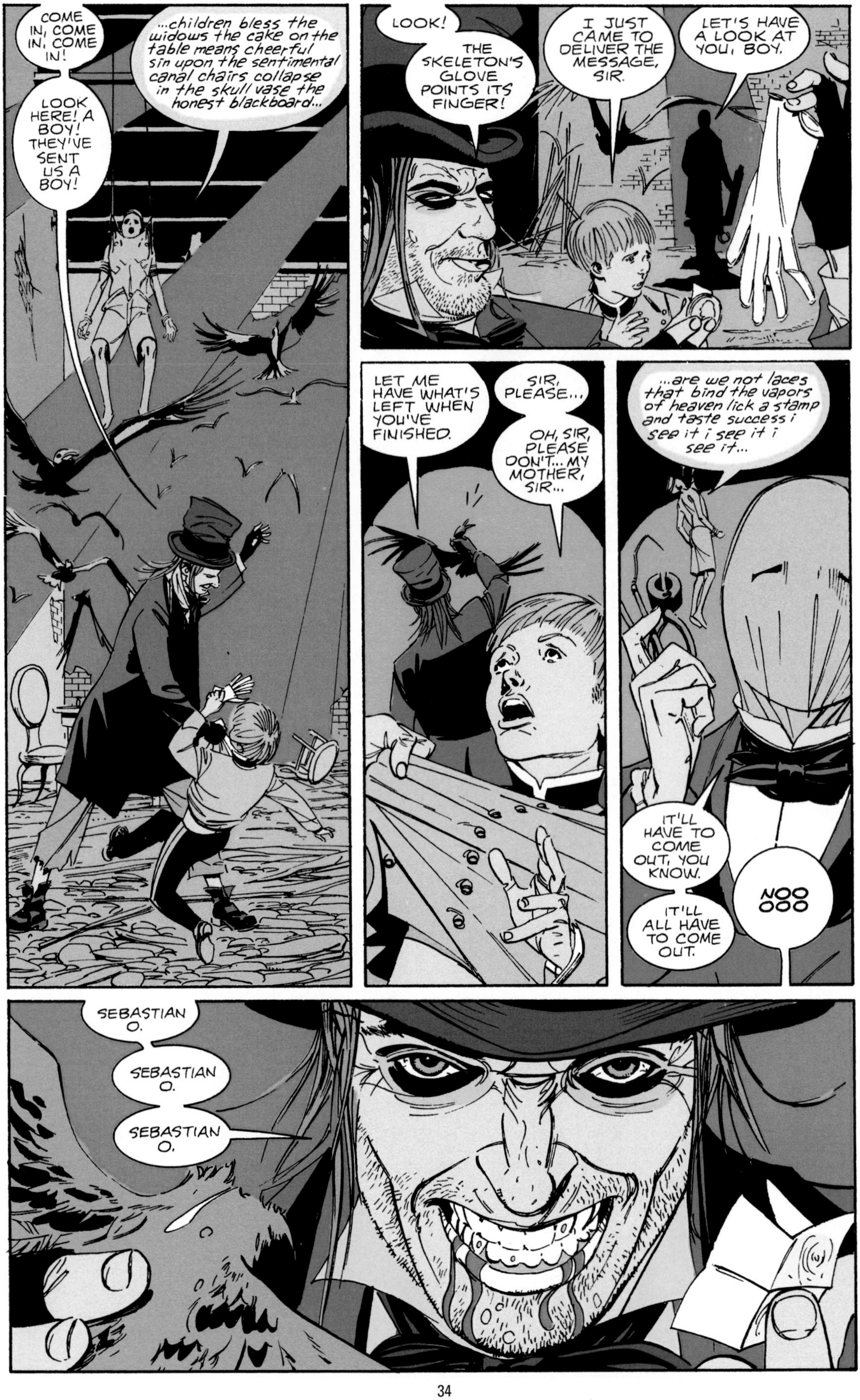

COME IN, COME IN, COME IN!
...children bless the widows the cake on the table means cheerful sin upon the sentimental canal chairs collapse in the skull vase the honest blackboard...
LOOK HERE! A BOY! THEY'VE SENT US A BOY!
LOOK!
THE SKELETON'S GLOVE POINTS ITS FINGER!
I JUST CAME TO DELIVER THE MESSAGE, SIR.
LET'S HAVE A LOOK AT YOU, BOY.
LET ME HAVE WHAT'S LEFT WHEN YOU'VE FINISHED.
SIR, PLEASE...
OH, SIR, PLEASE DON'T... MY MOTHER, SIR...
...are we not laces that bind the vapors of heaven lick a stamp and taste success i see it i see it i see it...
IT'LL HAVE TO COME OUT, YOU KNOW.
IT'LL ALL HAVE TO COME OUT.
NOOOOO
SEBASTIAN O.
SEBASTIAN O.
SEBASTIAN O.

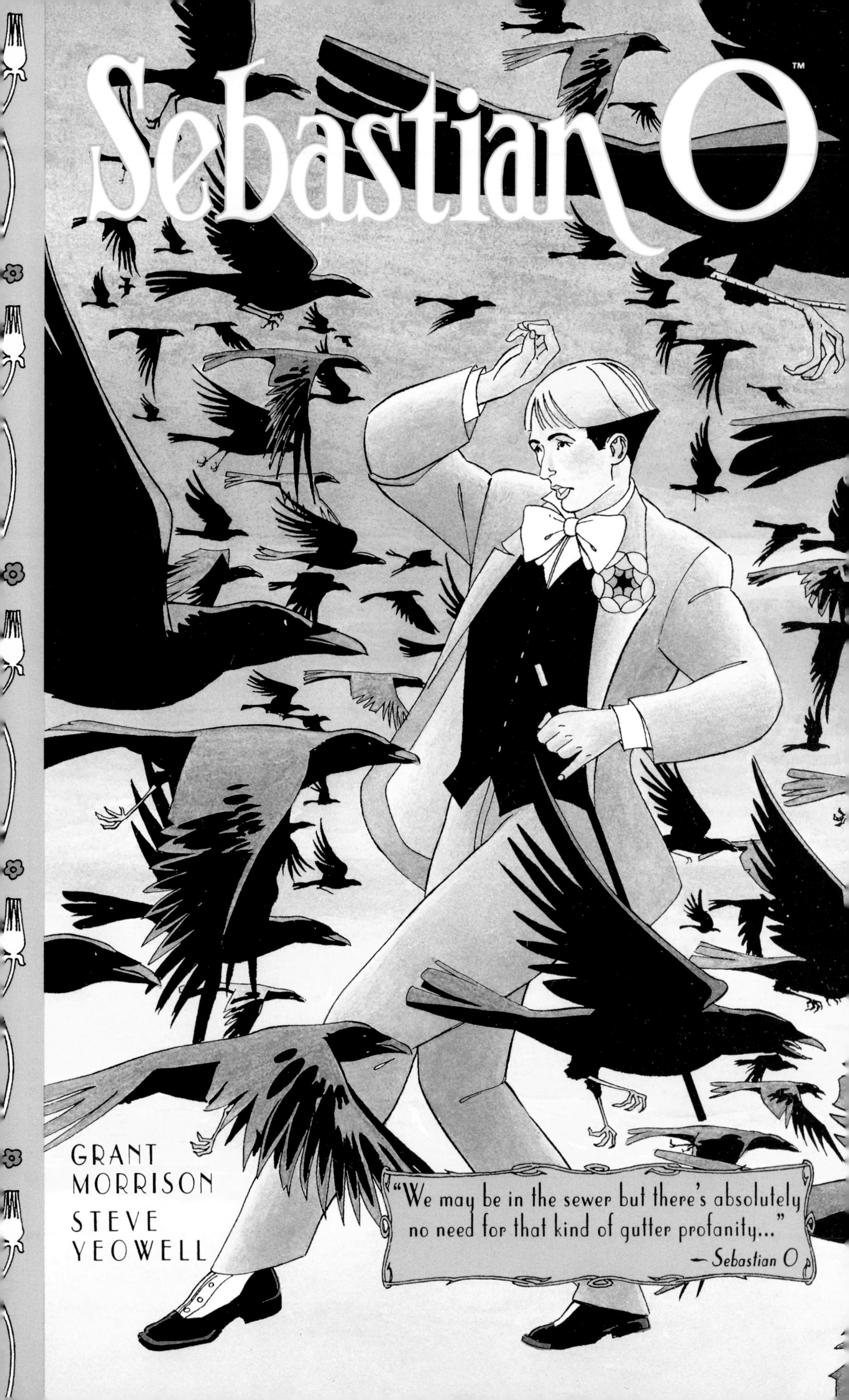
Sebastian O™
GRANT MORRISON
STEVE YEOWELL
"We may be in the sewer but there's absolutely no need for that kind of gutter profanity..."
— Sebastian O

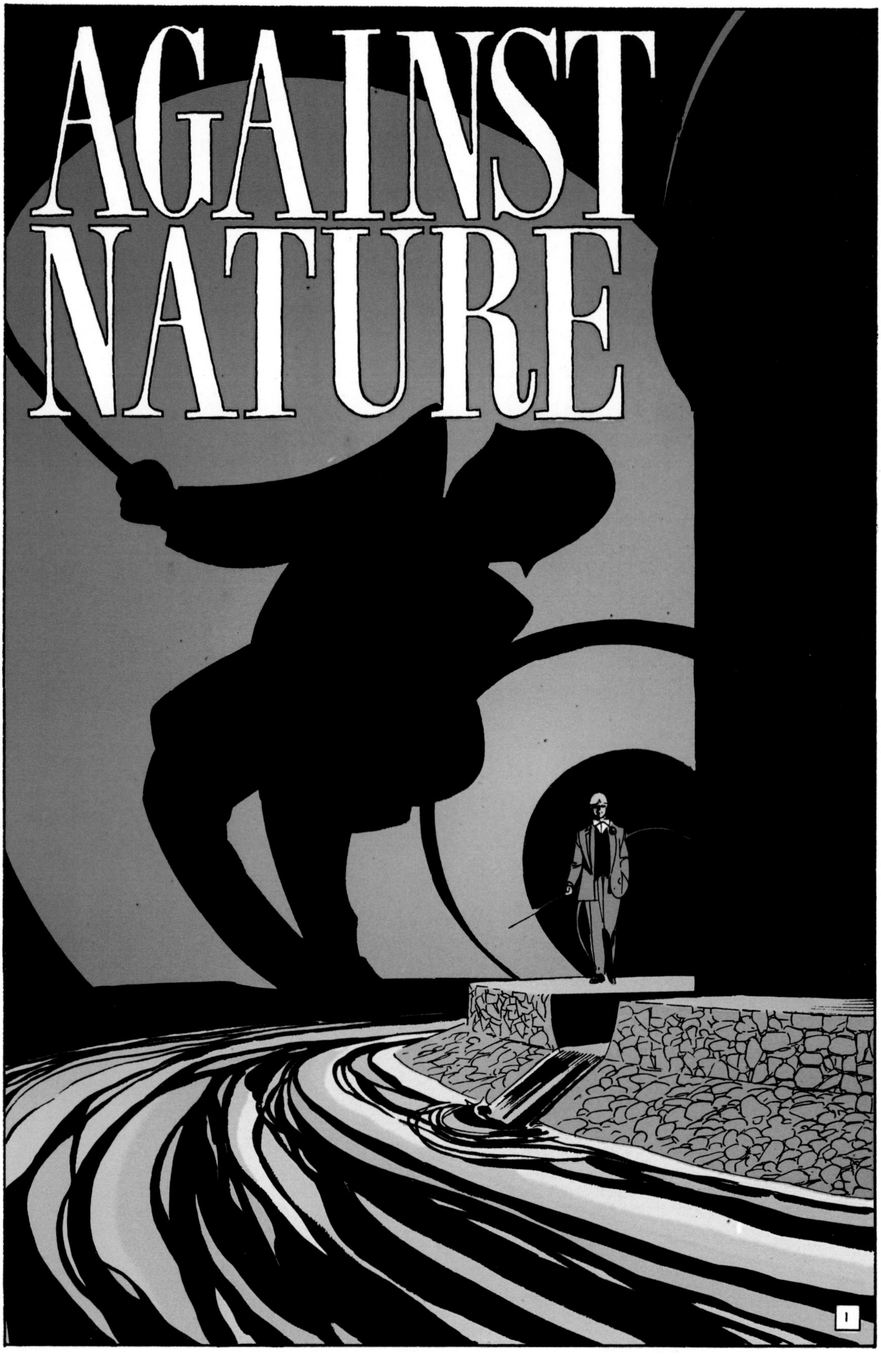
AGAINST NATURE
1

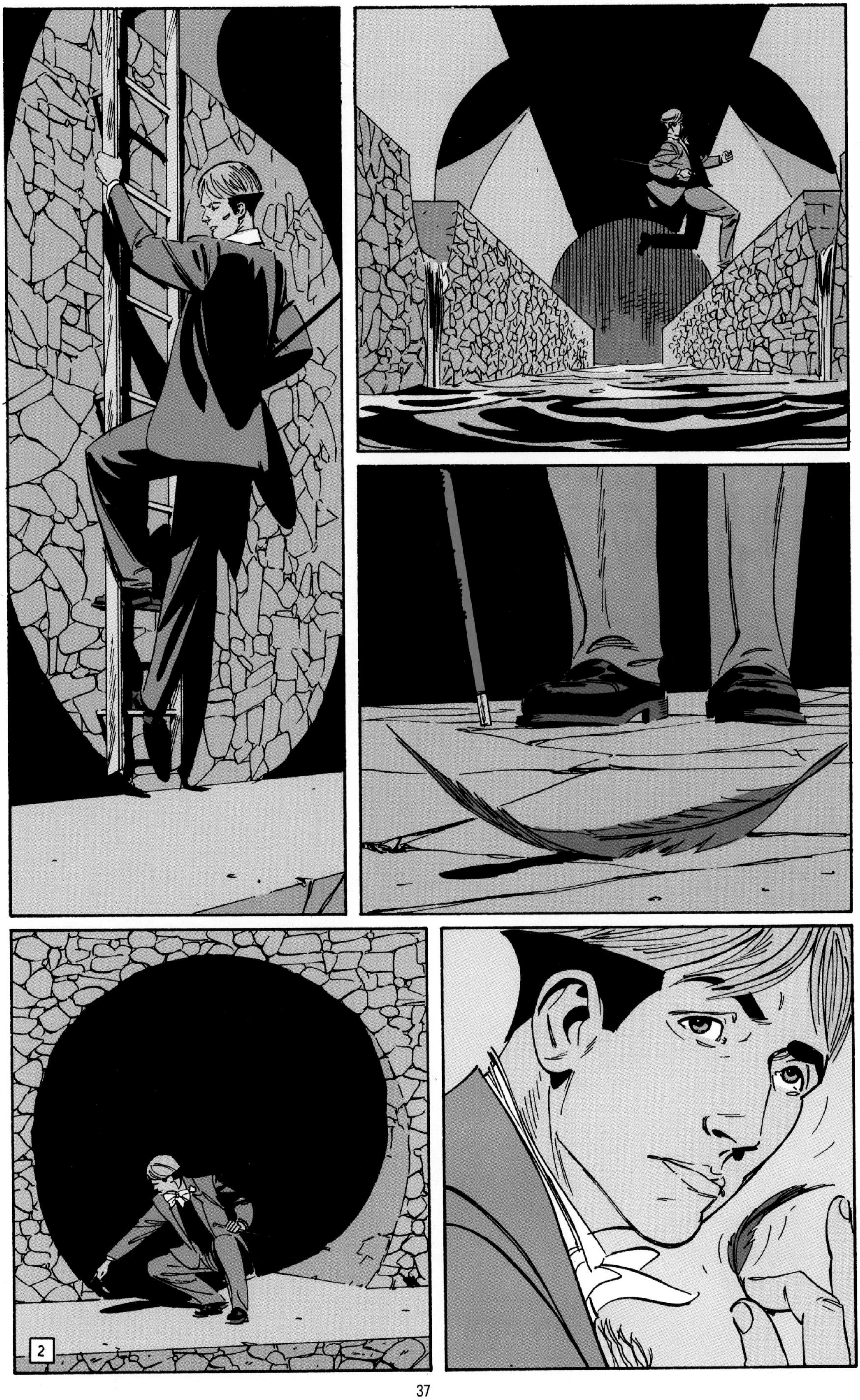
2

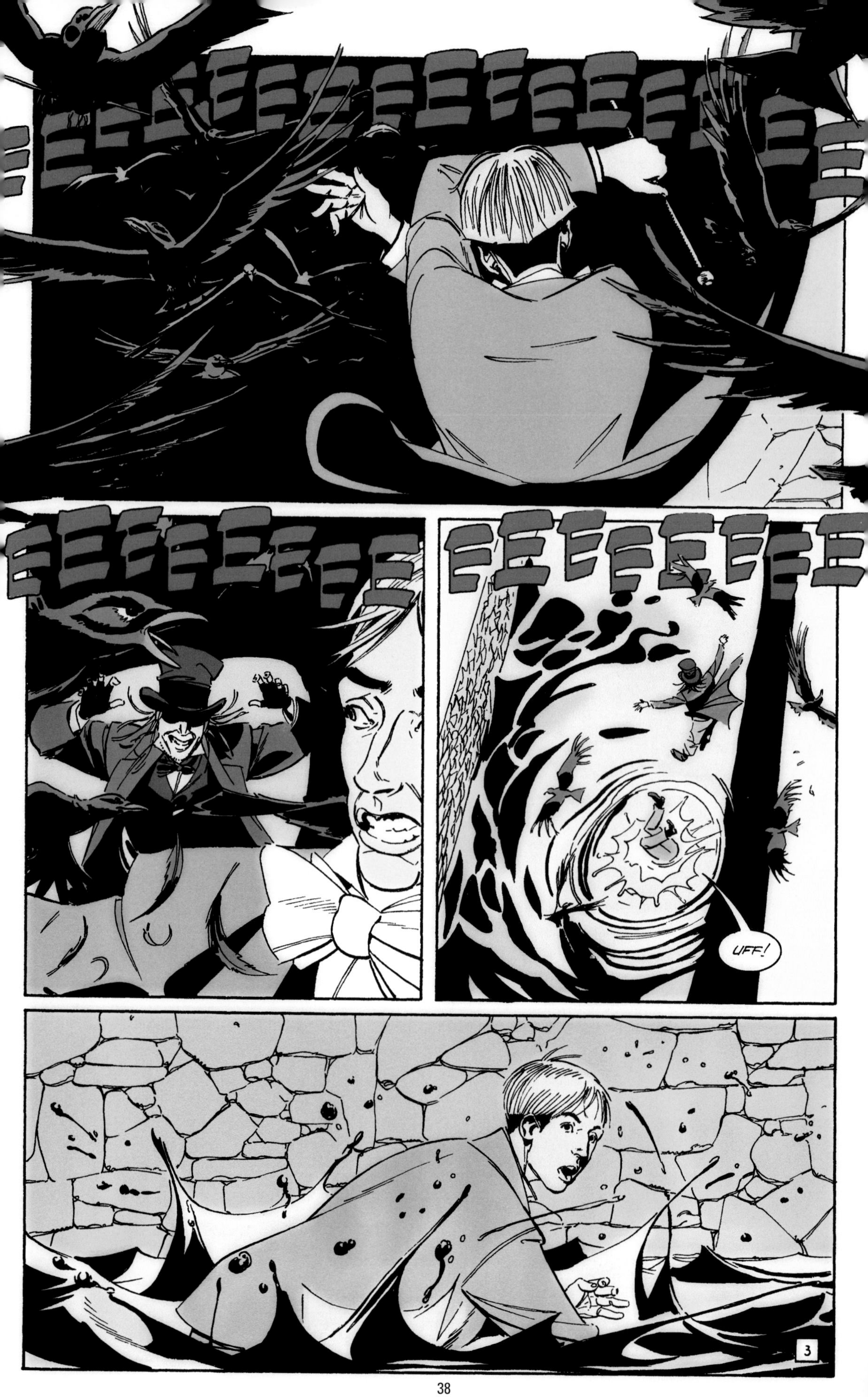
EEEEEEEEEEEEEEEEEEEE
EEEEEEEEEEE
EEEEEEEEEEE
UFF!
3

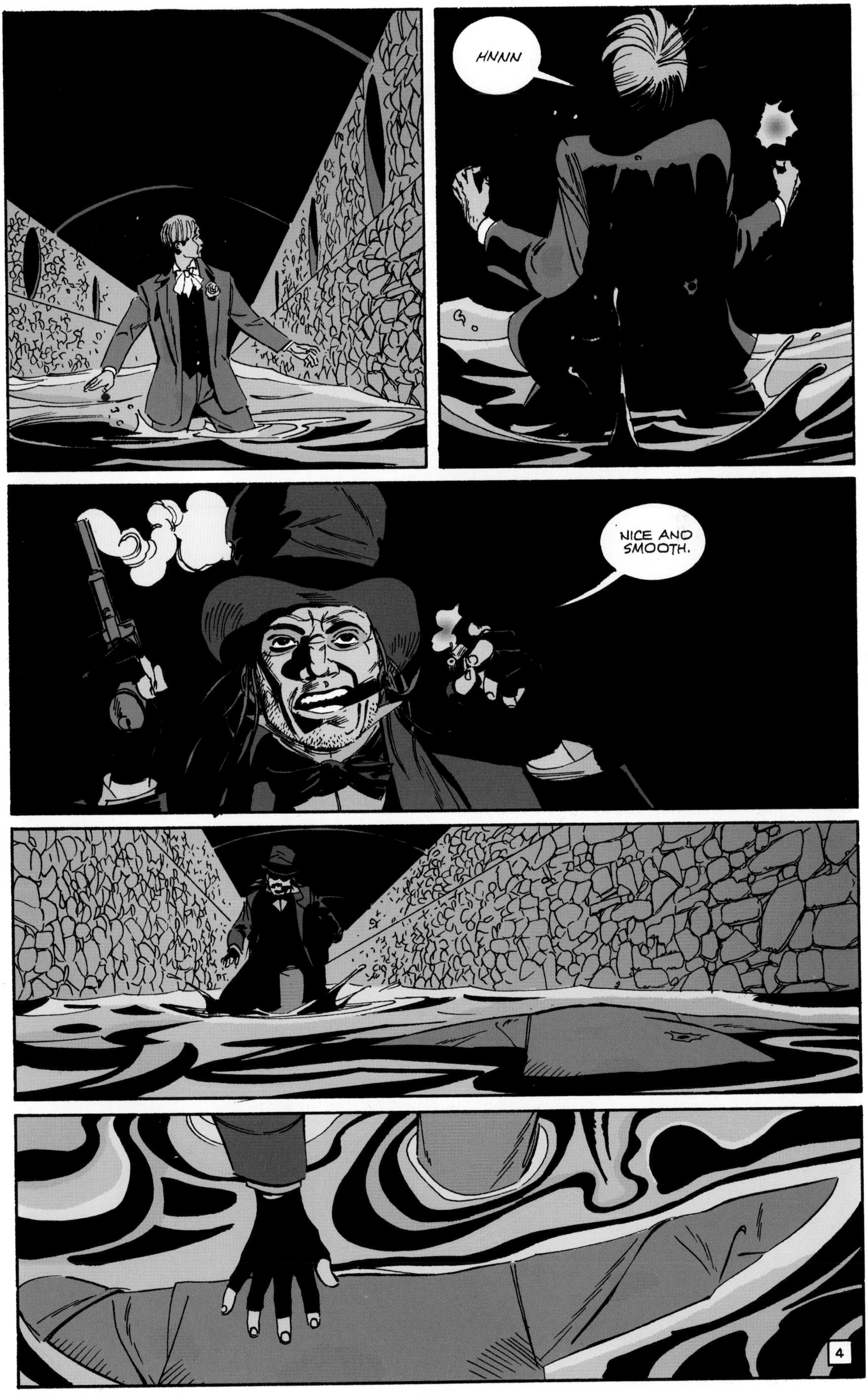
HNNN
NICE AND SMOOTH.
4

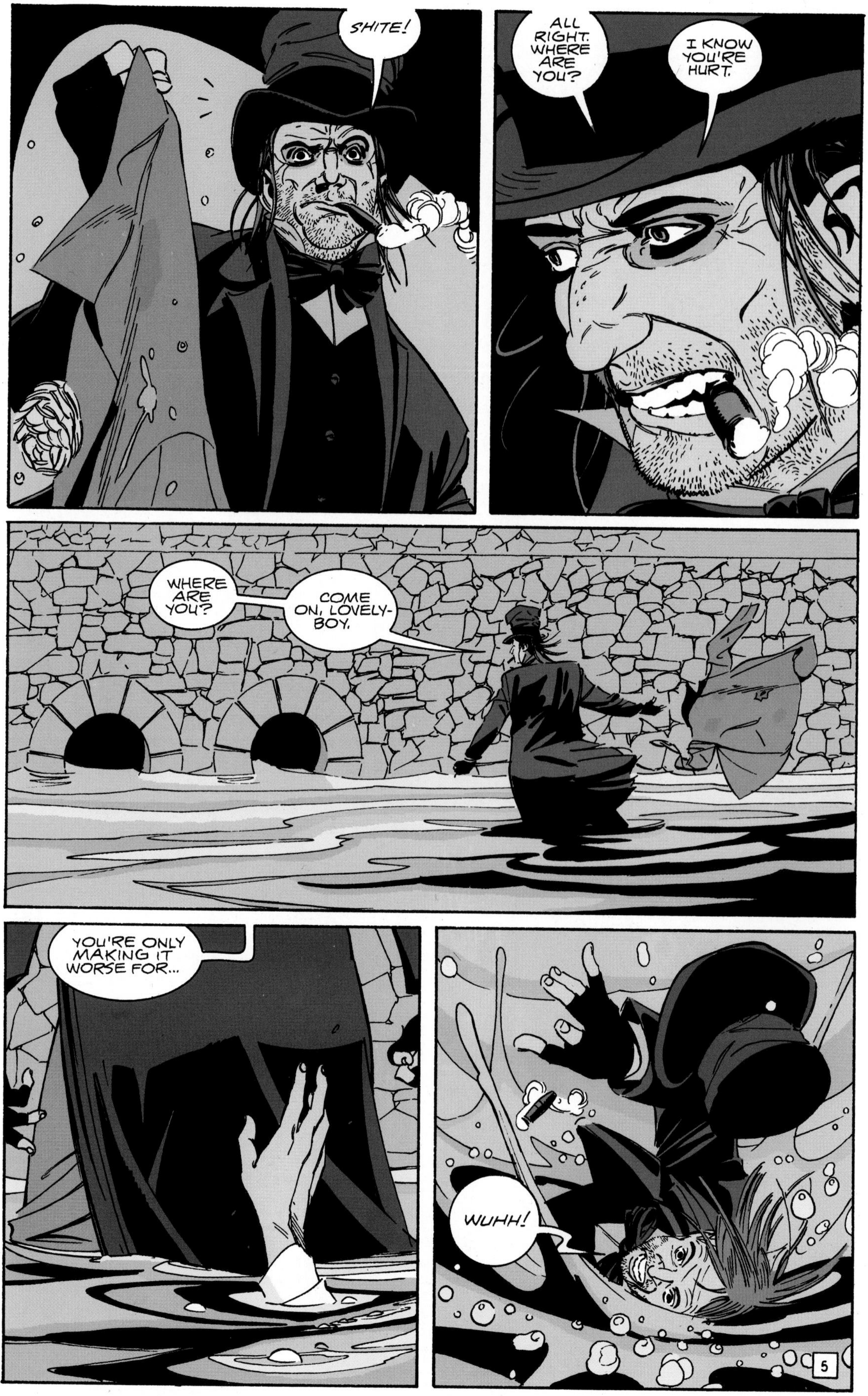
SHITE!
ALL RIGHT. WHERE ARE YOU?
I KNOW YOU'RE HURT.
WHERE ARE YOU?
COME ON, LOVELY-BOY.
YOU'RE ONLY MAKING IT WORSE FOR...
WUHH!
5

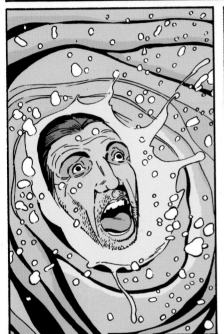

I DO BELIEVE YOU DROPPED YOUR CIGARETTE LIGHTER.

EEEAAAAAA

BASTARD! YOU'VE BLINDED ME, YOU BASTARD!

6

41

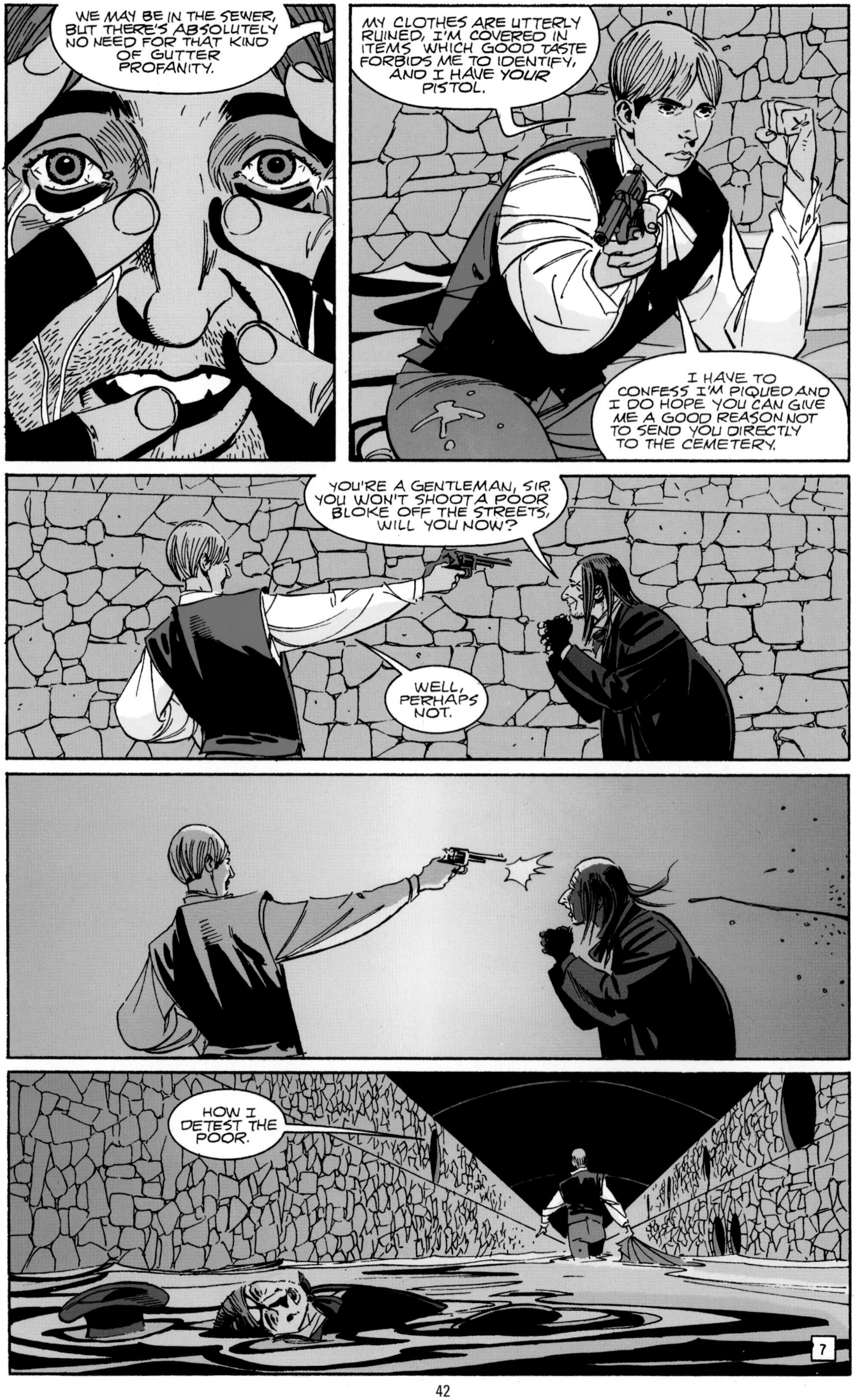
WE MAY BE IN THE SEWER, BUT THERE'S ABSOLUTELY NO NEED FOR THAT KIND OF GUTTER PROFANITY.
MY CLOTHES ARE UTTERLY RUINED, I'M COVERED IN ITEMS WHICH GOOD TASTE FORBIDS ME TO IDENTIFY, AND I HAVE YOUR PISTOL.
I HAVE TO CONFESS I'M PIQUED AND I DO HOPE YOU CAN GIVE ME A GOOD REASON NOT TO SEND YOU DIRECTLY TO THE CEMETERY.
YOU'RE A GENTLEMAN, SIR. YOU WON'T SHOOT A POOR BLOKE OFF THE STREETS, WILL YOU NOW?
WELL, PERHAPS NOT.
HOW I DETEST THE POOR.
7

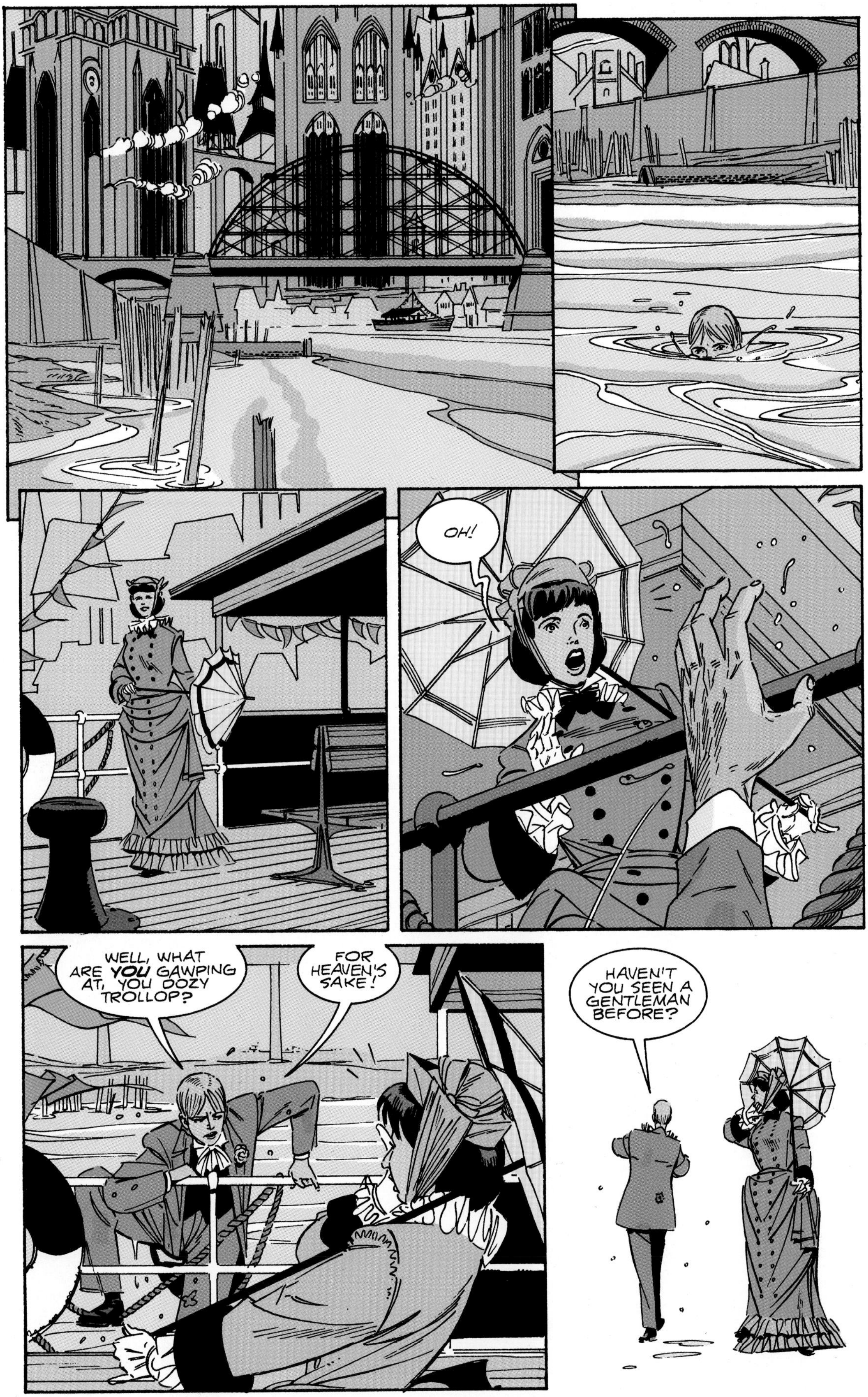
OH!
WELL, WHAT ARE YOU GAWPING AT, YOU DOZY TROLLOP?
FOR HEAVEN'S SAKE!
HAVEN'T YOU SEEN A GENTLEMAN BEFORE?

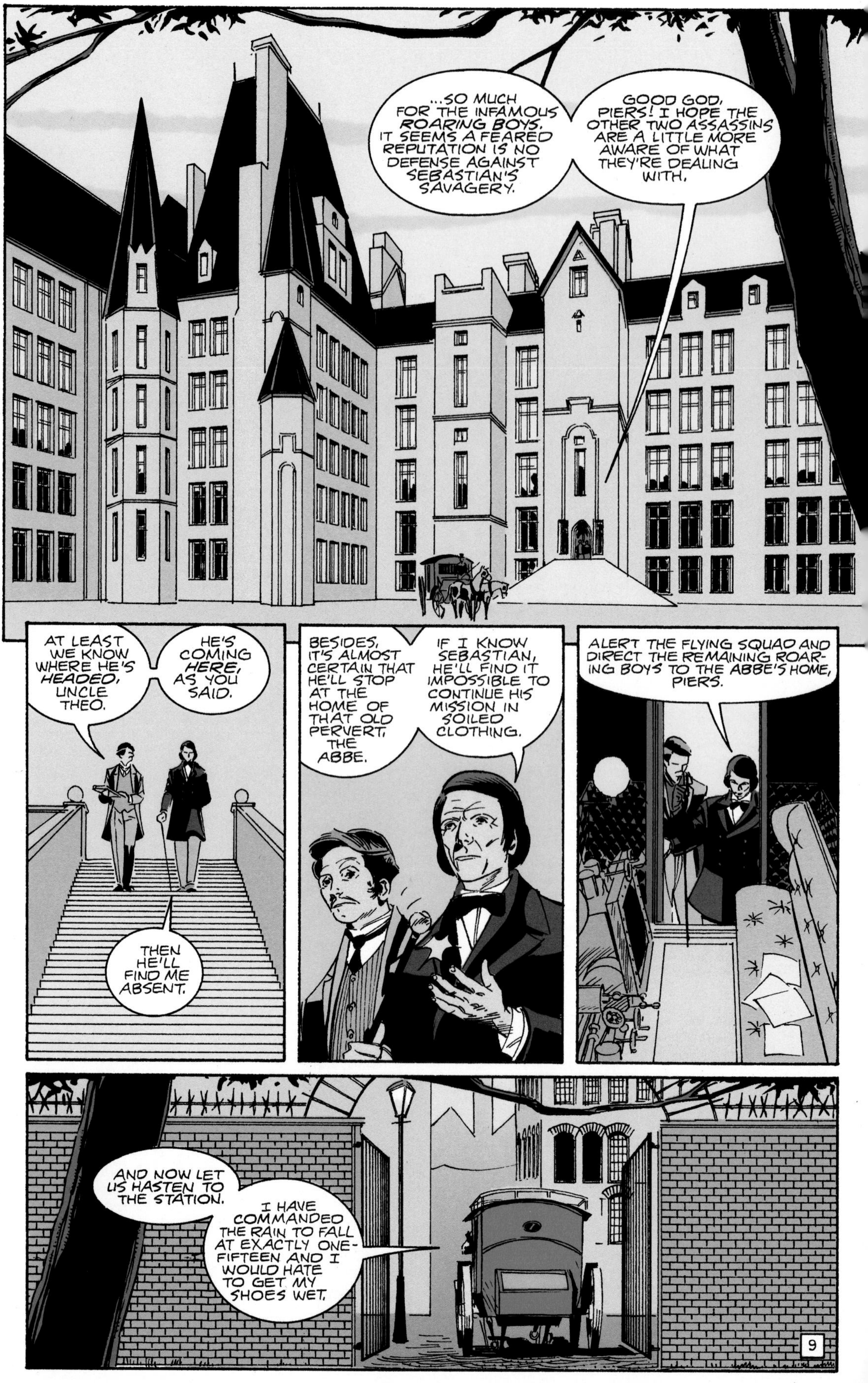

...SO MUCH FOR THE INFAMOUS ROARING BOYS. IT SEEMS A FEARED REPUTATION IS NO DEFENSE AGAINST SEBASTIAN'S SAVAGERY.
GOOD GOD, PIERS! I HOPE THE OTHER TWO ASSASSINS ARE A LITTLE MORE AWARE OF WHAT THEY'RE DEALING WITH.
AT LEAST WE KNOW WHERE HE'S HEADED, UNCLE THEO.
HE'S COMING HERE, AS YOU SAID.
THEN HE'LL FIND ME ABSENT.
BESIDES, IT'S ALMOST CERTAIN THAT HE'LL STOP AT THE HOME OF THAT OLD PERVERT, THE ABBE.
IF I KNOW SEBASTIAN, HE'LL FIND IT IMPOSSIBLE TO CONTINUE HIS MISSION IN SOILED CLOTHING.
ALERT THE FLYING SQUAD AND DIRECT THE REMAINING ROARING BOYS TO THE ABBE'S HOME, PIERS.
AND NOW LET US HASTEN TO THE STATION.
I HAVE COMMANDED THE RAIN TO FALL AT EXACTLY ONE-FIFTEEN AND I WOULD HATE TO GET MY SHOES WET.
9

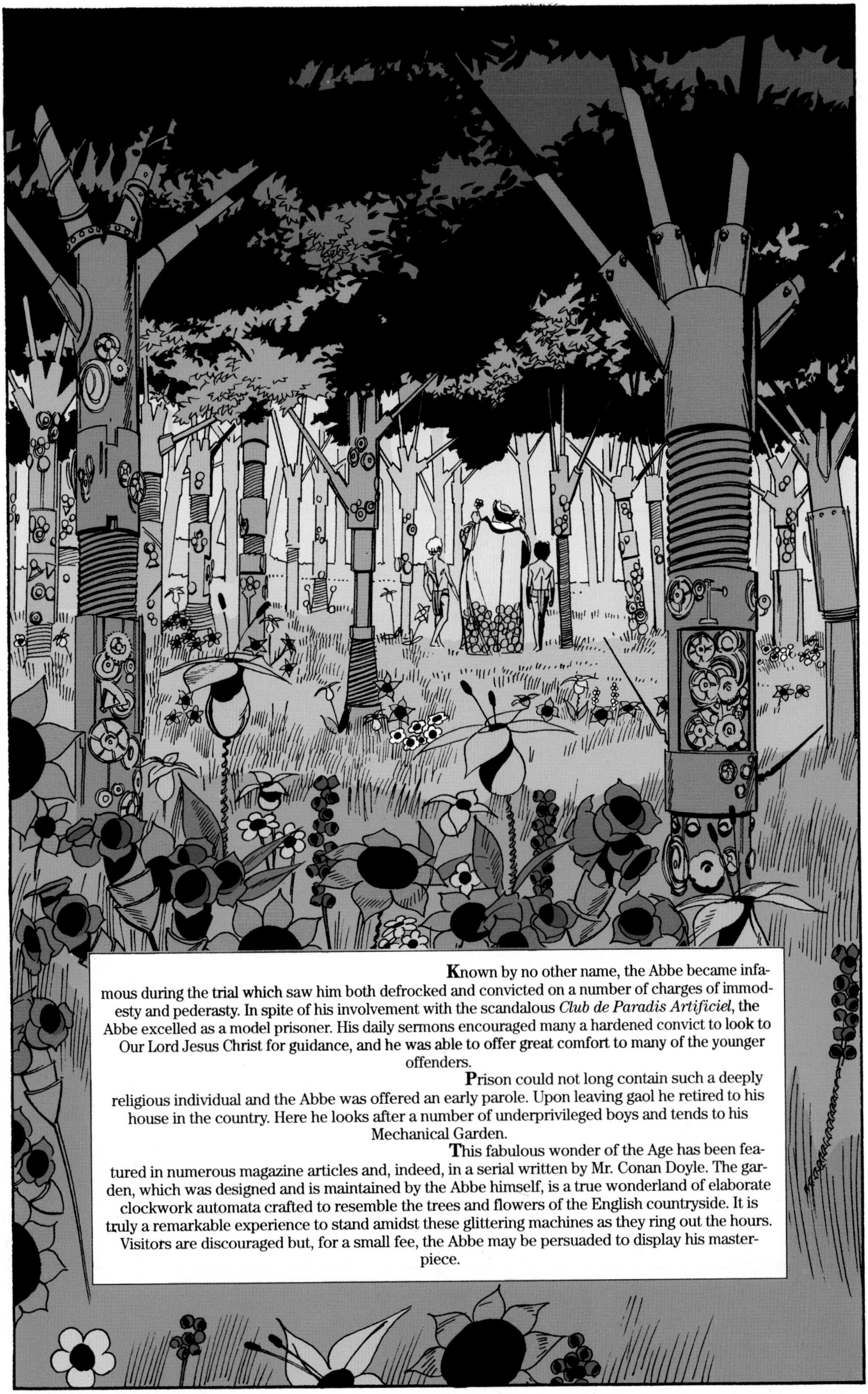
Known by no other name, the Abbe became infamous during the trial which saw him both defrocked and convicted on a number of charges of immodesty and pederasty. In spite of his involvement with the scandalous *Club de Paradis Artificiel*, the Abbe excelled as a model prisoner. His daily sermons encouraged many a hardened convict to look to Our Lord Jesus Christ for guidance, and he was able to offer great comfort to many of the younger offenders.
Prison could not long contain such a deeply religious individual and the Abbe was offered an early parole. Upon leaving gaol he retired to his house in the country. Here he looks after a number of underprivileged boys and tends to his Mechanical Garden.
This fabulous wonder of the Age has been featured in numerous magazine articles and, indeed, in a serial written by Mr. Conan Doyle. The garden, which was designed and is maintained by the Abbe himself, is a true wonderland of elaborate clockwork automata crafted to resemble the trees and flowers of the English countryside. It is truly a remarkable experience to stand amidst these glittering machines as they ring out the hours. Visitors are discouraged but, for a small fee, the Abbe may be persuaded to display his masterpiece.

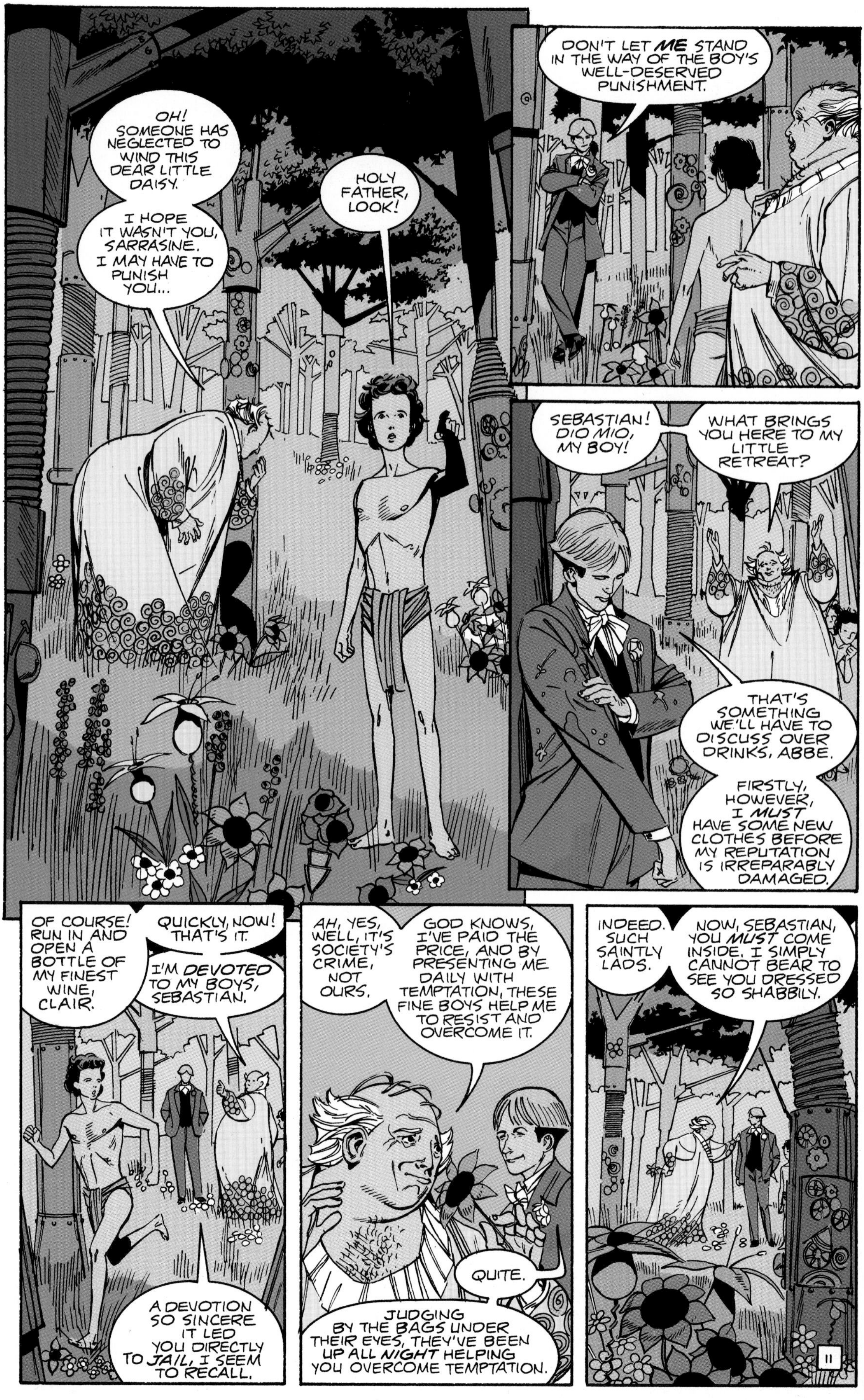
OH! SOMEONE HAS NEGLECTED TO WIND THIS DEAR LITTLE DAISY.
I HOPE IT WASN'T YOU, SARRASINE. I MAY HAVE TO PUNISH YOU...
HOLY FATHER, LOOK!
DON'T LET ME STAND IN THE WAY OF THE BOY'S WELL-DESERVED PUNISHMENT.
SEBASTIAN! DIO MIO, MY BOY!
WHAT BRINGS YOU HERE TO MY LITTLE RETREAT?
THAT'S SOMETHING WE'LL HAVE TO DISCUSS OVER DRINKS, ABBE.
FIRSTLY, HOWEVER, I MUST HAVE SOME NEW CLOTHES BEFORE MY REPUTATION IS IRREPARABLY DAMAGED.
OF COURSE! RUN IN AND OPEN A BOTTLE OF MY FINEST WINE, CLAIR.
QUICKLY, NOW! THAT'S IT.
I'M DEVOTED TO MY BOYS, SEBASTIAN.
A DEVOTION SO SINCERE IT LED YOU DIRECTLY TO JAIL, I SEEM TO RECALL.
AH, YES, WELL, IT'S SOCIETY'S CRIME, NOT OURS.
GOD KNOWS, I'VE PAID THE PRICE, AND BY PRESENTING ME DAILY WITH TEMPTATION, THESE FINE BOYS HELP ME TO RESIST AND OVERCOME IT.
QUITE.
JUDGING BY THE BAGS UNDER THEIR EYES, THEY'VE BEEN UP ALL NIGHT HELPING YOU OVERCOME TEMPTATION.
INDEED. SUCH SAINTLY LADS.
NOW, SEBASTIAN, YOU MUST COME INSIDE. I SIMPLY CANNOT BEAR TO SEE YOU DRESSED SO SHABBILY.

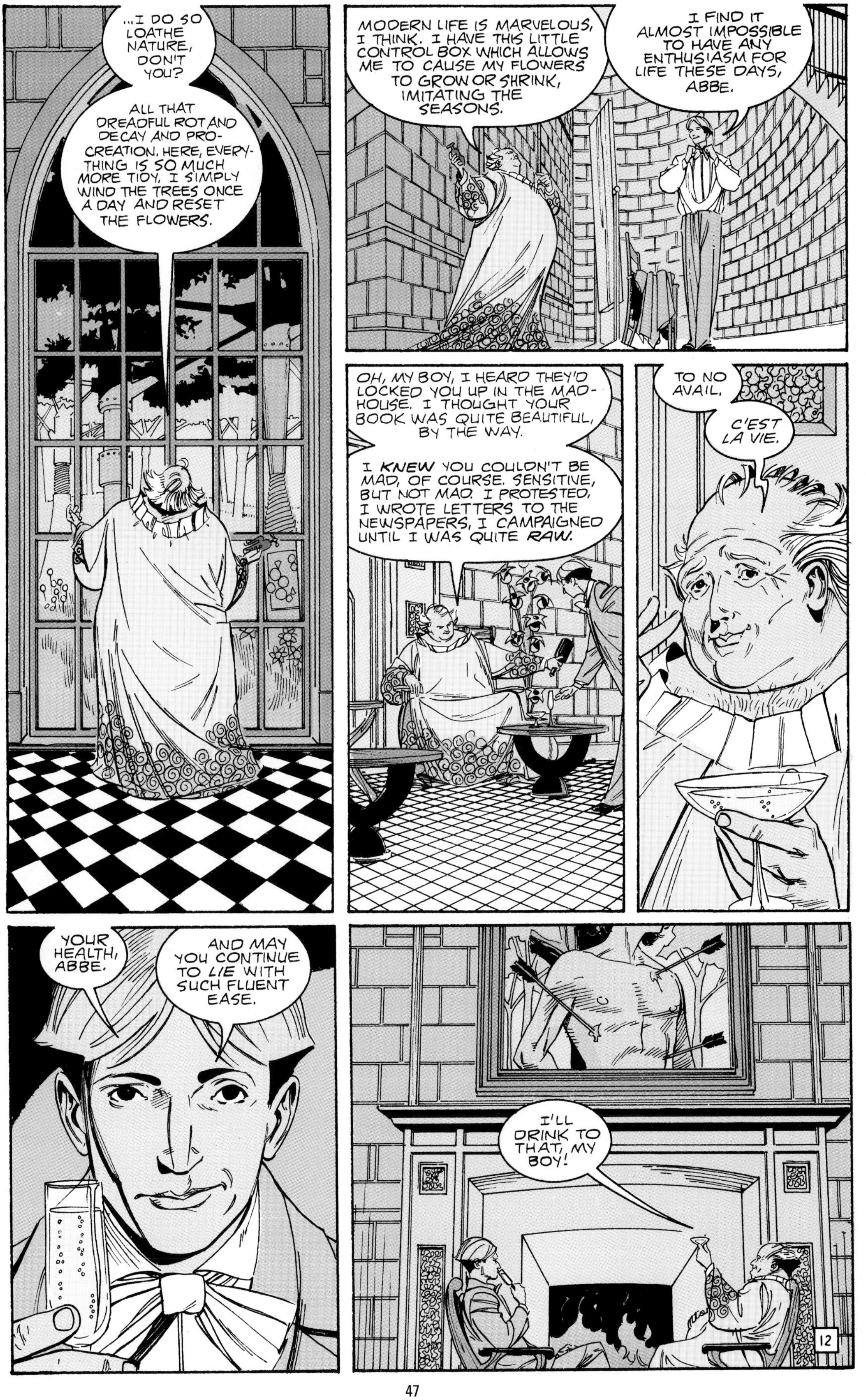
...I DO SO LOATHE NATURE, DON'T YOU?
ALL THAT DREADFUL ROT AND DECAY AND PRO-CREATION. HERE, EVERY-THING IS SO MUCH MORE TIDY. I SIMPLY WIND THE TREES ONCE A DAY AND RESET THE FLOWERS.
MODERN LIFE IS MARVELOUS, I THINK. I HAVE THIS LITTLE CONTROL BOX WHICH ALLOWS ME TO CAUSE MY FLOWERS TO GROW OR SHRINK, IMITATING THE SEASONS.
I FIND IT ALMOST IMPOSSIBLE TO HAVE ANY ENTHUSIASM FOR LIFE THESE DAYS, ABBE.
OH, MY BOY, I HEARD THEY'D LOCKED YOU UP IN THE MAD-HOUSE. I THOUGHT YOUR BOOK WAS QUITE BEAUTIFUL, BY THE WAY.
I *KNEW* YOU COULDN'T BE MAD, OF COURSE. SENSITIVE, BUT NOT MAD. I PROTESTED, I WROTE LETTERS TO THE NEWSPAPERS, I CAMPAIGNED UNTIL I WAS QUITE *RAW*.
TO NO AVAIL.
C'EST LA VIE.
YOUR HEALTH, ABBE.
AND MAY YOU CONTINUE TO *LIE* WITH SUCH FLUENT EASE.
I'LL DRINK TO THAT, MY BOY!
12

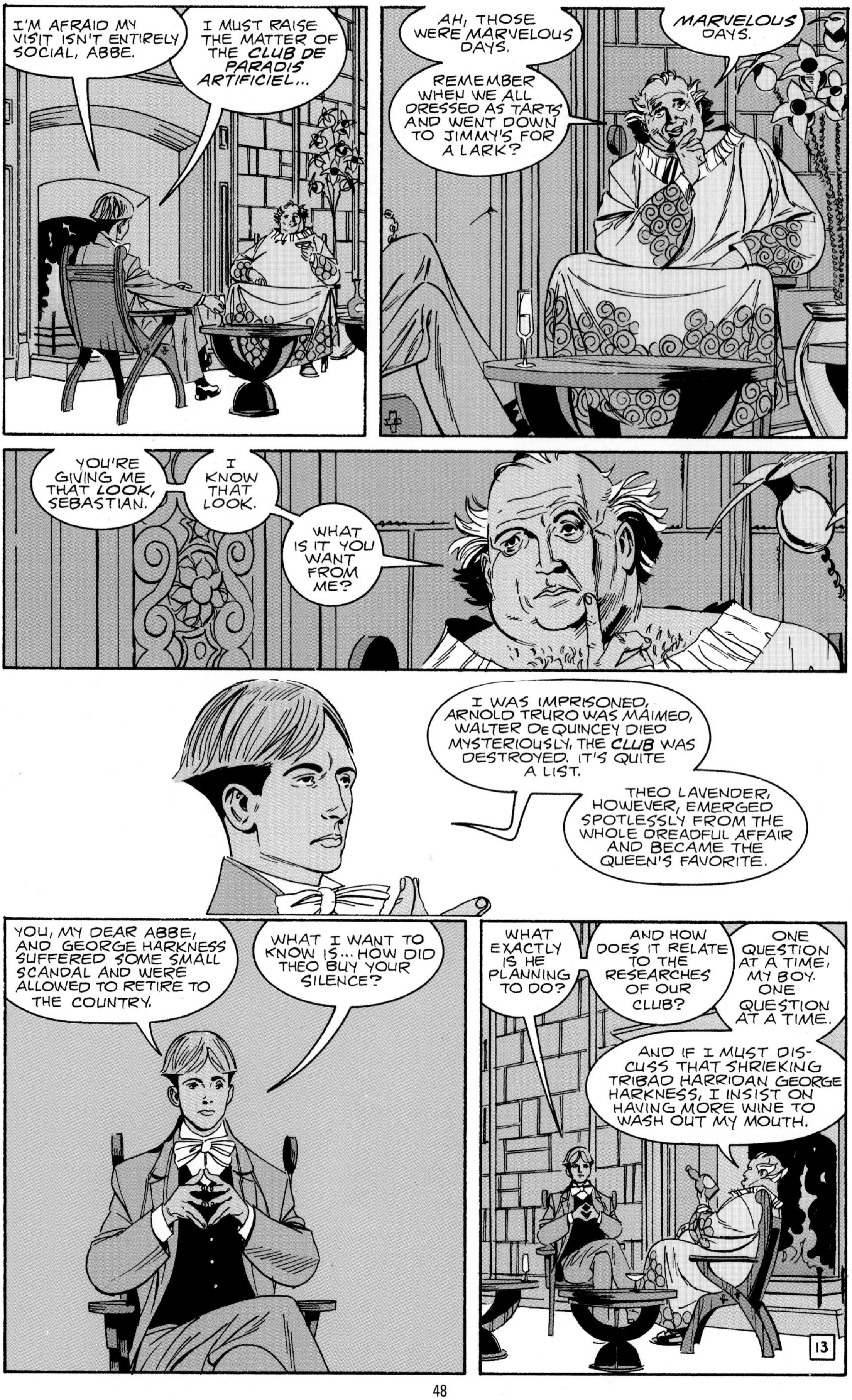
I'M AFRAID MY VISIT ISN'T ENTIRELY SOCIAL, ABBE.
I MUST RAISE THE MATTER OF THE CLUB DE PARADIS ARTIFICIEL...
AH, THOSE WERE MARVELOUS DAYS.
REMEMBER WHEN WE ALL DRESSED AS TARTS AND WENT DOWN TO JIMMY'S FOR A LARK?
MARVELOUS DAYS.
YOU'RE GIVING ME THAT LOOK, SEBASTIAN.
I KNOW THAT LOOK.
WHAT IS IT YOU WANT FROM ME?
I WAS IMPRISONED, ARNOLD TRURO WAS MAIMED, WALTER DeQUINCEY DIED MYSTERIOUSLY, THE CLUB WAS DESTROYED. IT'S QUITE A LIST.
THEO LAVENDER, HOWEVER, EMERGED SPOTLESSLY FROM THE WHOLE DREADFUL AFFAIR AND BECAME THE QUEEN'S FAVORITE.
YOU, MY DEAR ABBE, AND GEORGE HARKNESS SUFFERED SOME SMALL SCANDAL AND WERE ALLOWED TO RETIRE TO THE COUNTRY.
WHAT I WANT TO KNOW IS... HOW DID THEO BUY YOUR SILENCE?
WHAT EXACTLY IS HE PLANNING TO DO?
AND HOW DOES IT RELATE TO THE RESEARCHES OF OUR CLUB?
ONE QUESTION AT A TIME, MY BOY. ONE QUESTION AT A TIME.
AND IF I MUST DISCUSS THAT SHRIEKING TRIBAD HARRIDAN GEORGE HARKNESS, I INSIST ON HAVING MORE WINE TO WASH OUT MY MOUTH.
13

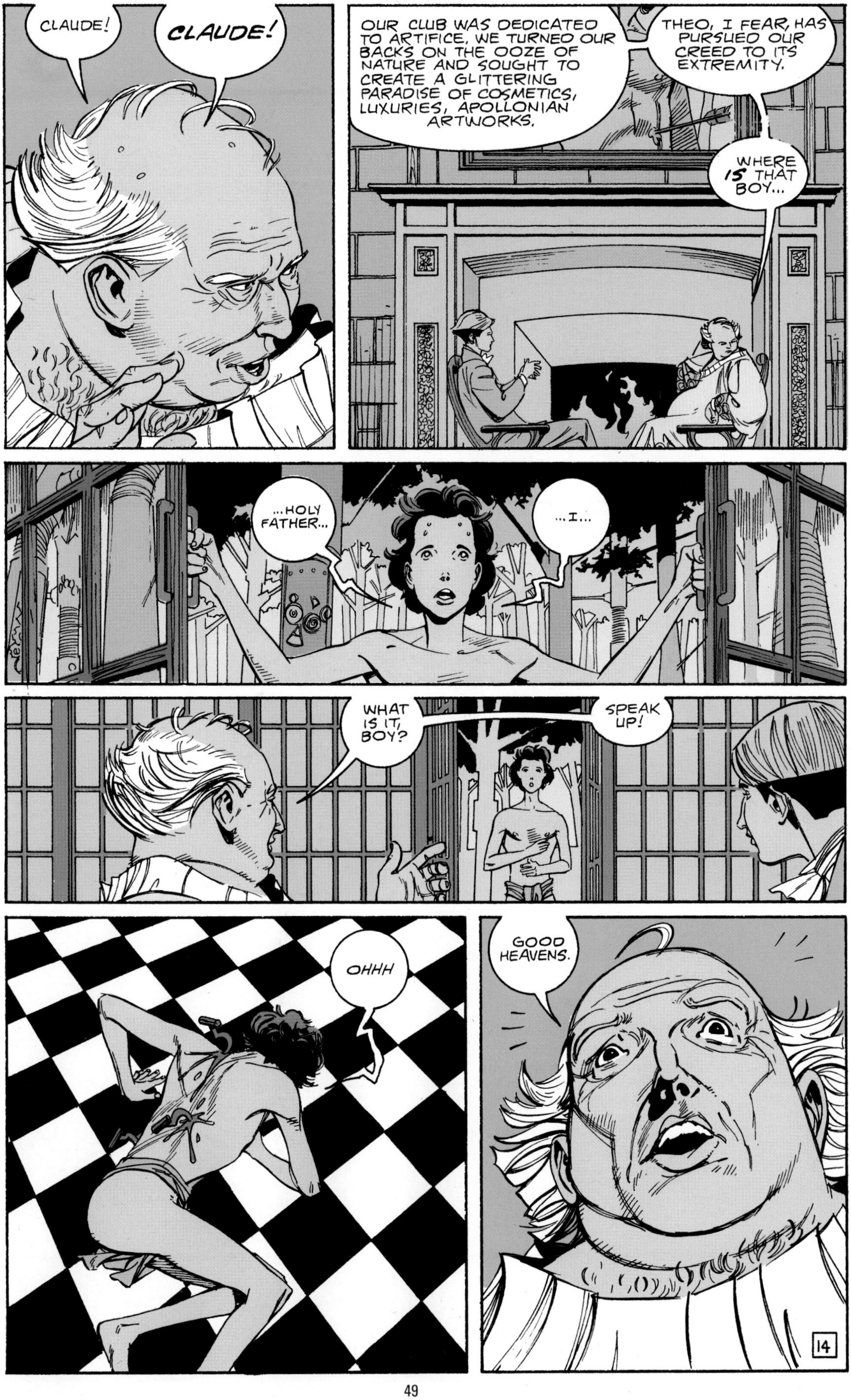

CLAUDE!
CLAUDE!
OUR CLUB WAS DEDICATED TO ARTIFICE. WE TURNED OUR BACKS ON THE OOZE OF NATURE AND SOUGHT TO CREATE A GLITTERING PARADISE OF COSMETICS, LUXURIES, APOLLONIAN ARTWORKS.
THEO, I FEAR, HAS PURSUED OUR CREED TO ITS EXTREMITY.
WHERE IS THAT BOY...
...HOLY FATHER...
...I...
WHAT IS IT, BOY?
SPEAK UP!
OHHH
GOOD HEAVENS.
14

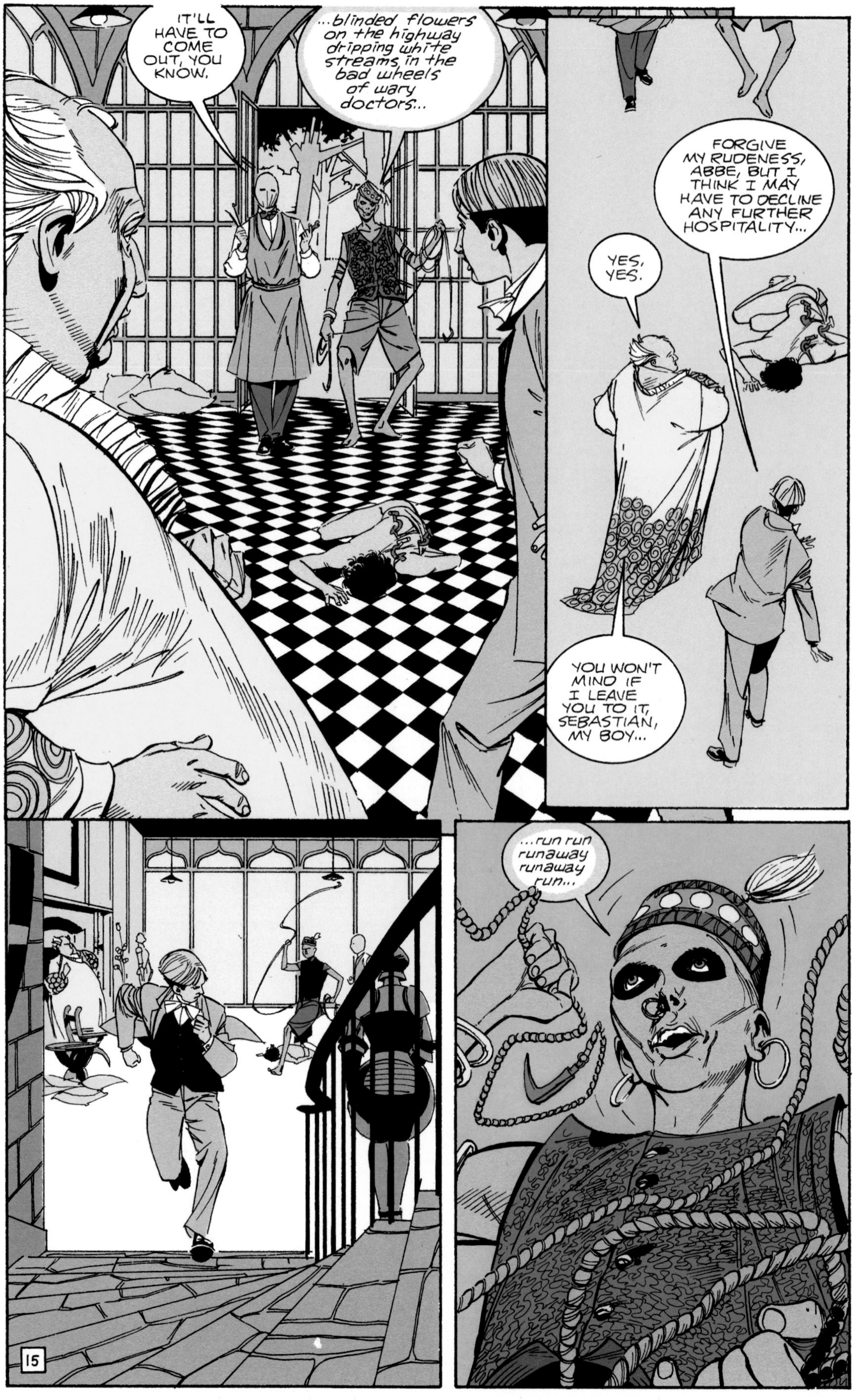
IT'LL HAVE TO COME OUT, YOU KNOW.
...blinded flowers on the highway dripping white streams in the bad wheels of wary doctors...
FORGIVE MY RUDENESS, ABBE, BUT I THINK I MAY HAVE TO DECLINE ANY FURTHER HOSPITALITY...
YES, YES.
YOU WON'T MIND IF I LEAVE YOU TO IT, SEBASTIAN, MY BOY...
...run run runaway runaway run...
15

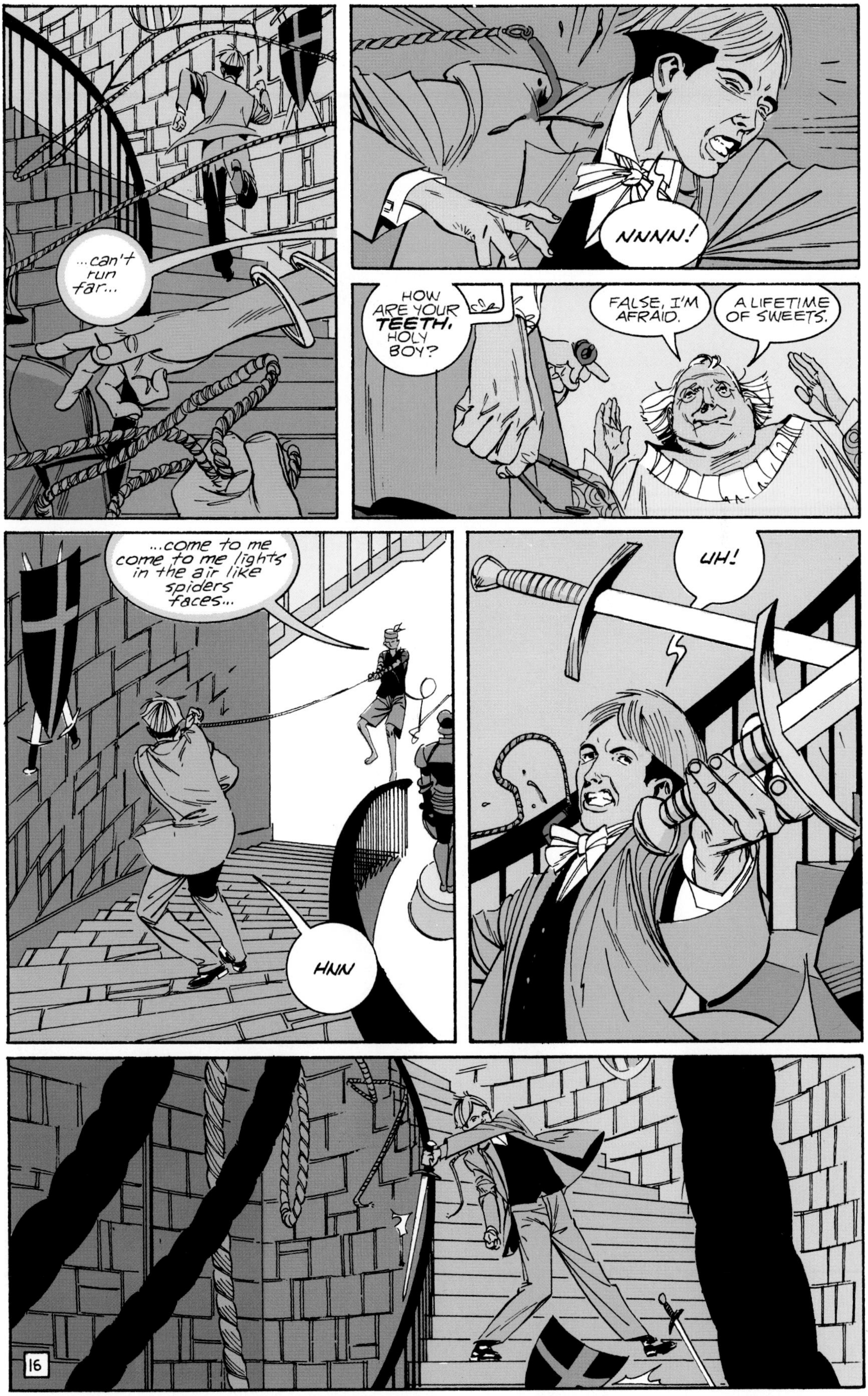
...can't run far...
NNNN!
HOW ARE YOUR TEETH, HOLY BOY?
FALSE, I'M AFRAID.
A LIFETIME OF SWEETS.
...come to me come to me lights in the air like spiders faces...
HNN
UH!
16

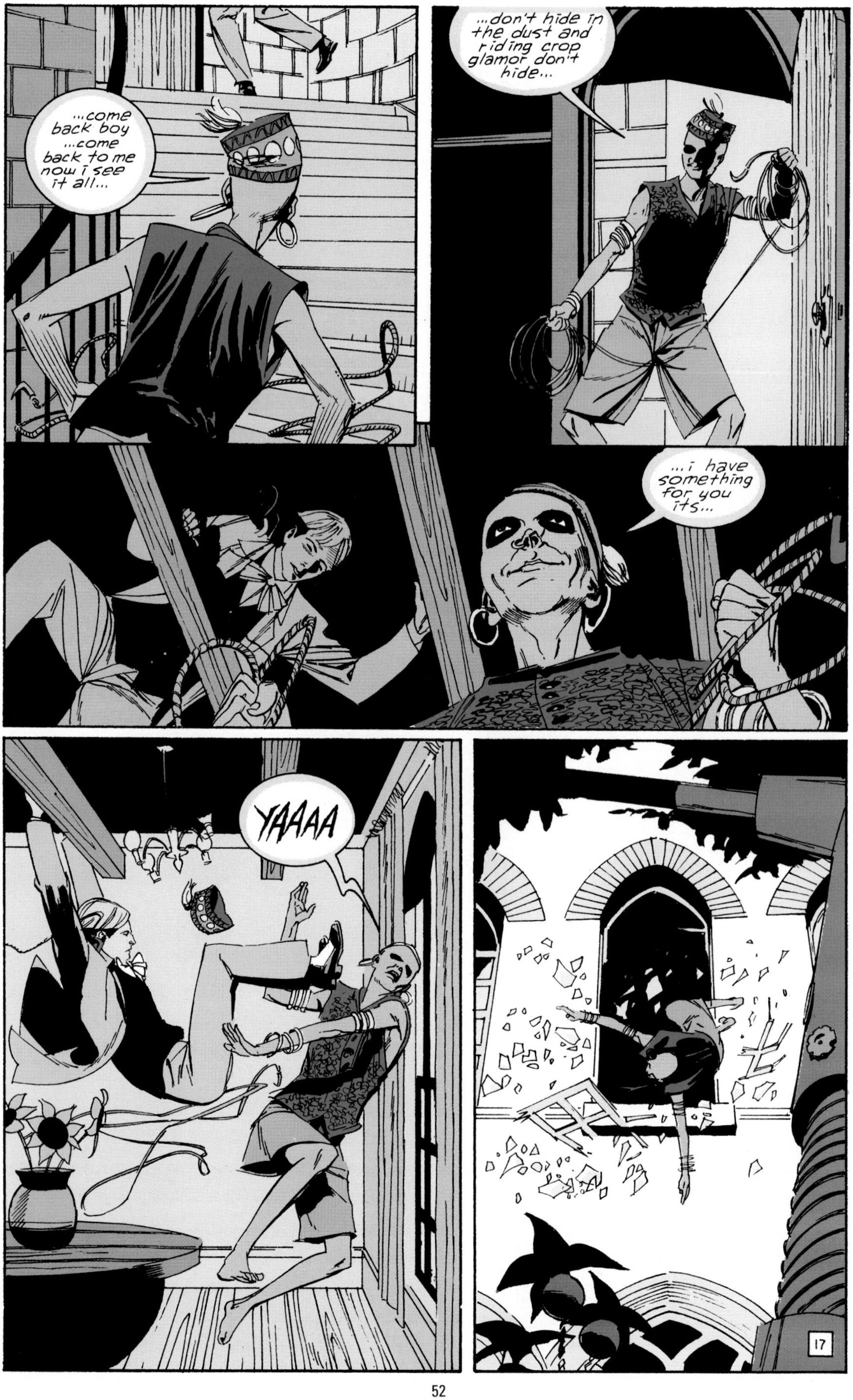
...come back boy ...come back to me now i see it all...
...don't hide in the dust and riding crop glamor don't hide...
...i have something for you its...
YAAAA
17

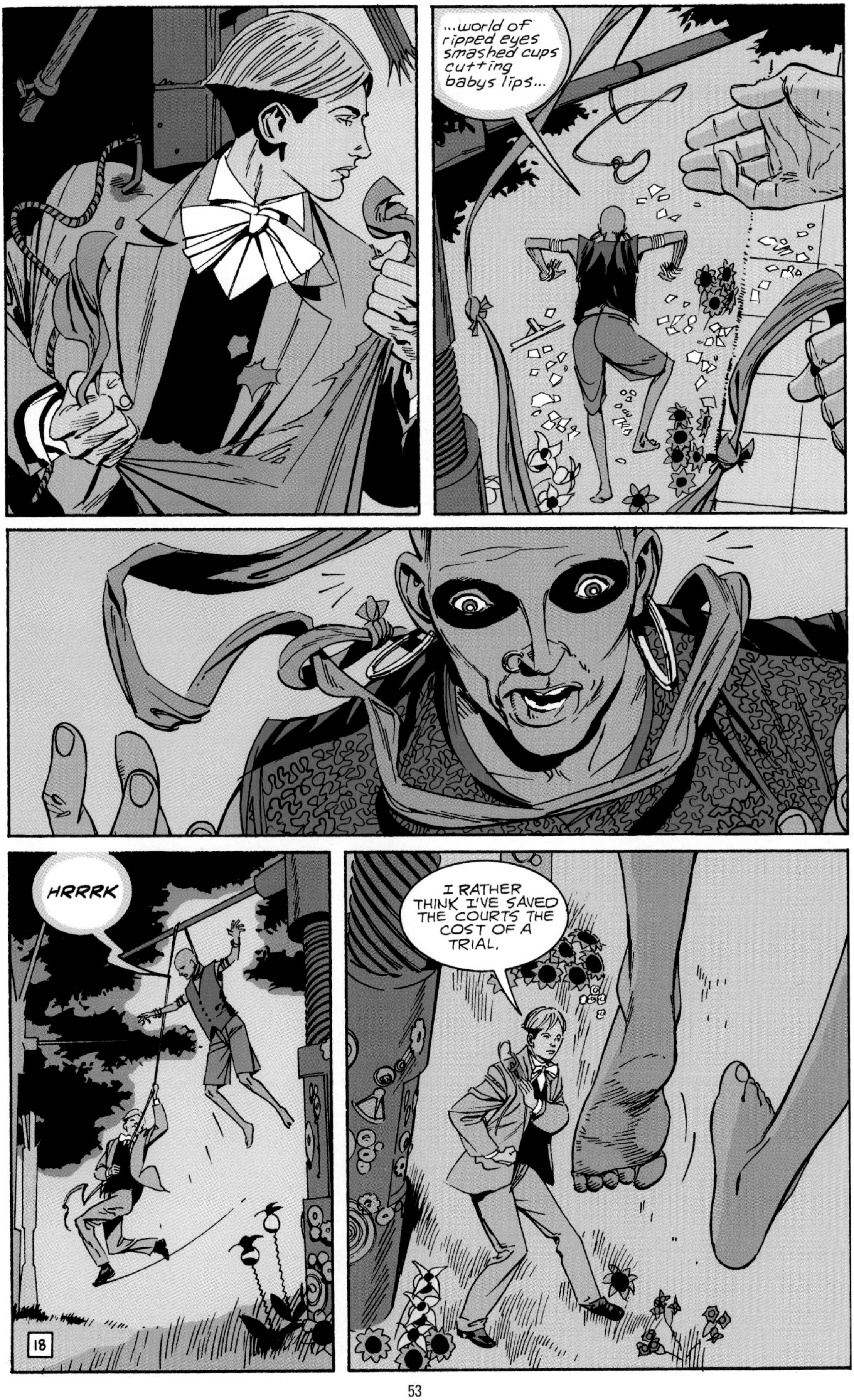
...world of
ripped eyes
smashed cups
cutting
babys lips...
HRRRK
I RATHER THINK I'VE SAVED THE COURTS THE COST OF A TRIAL.
18

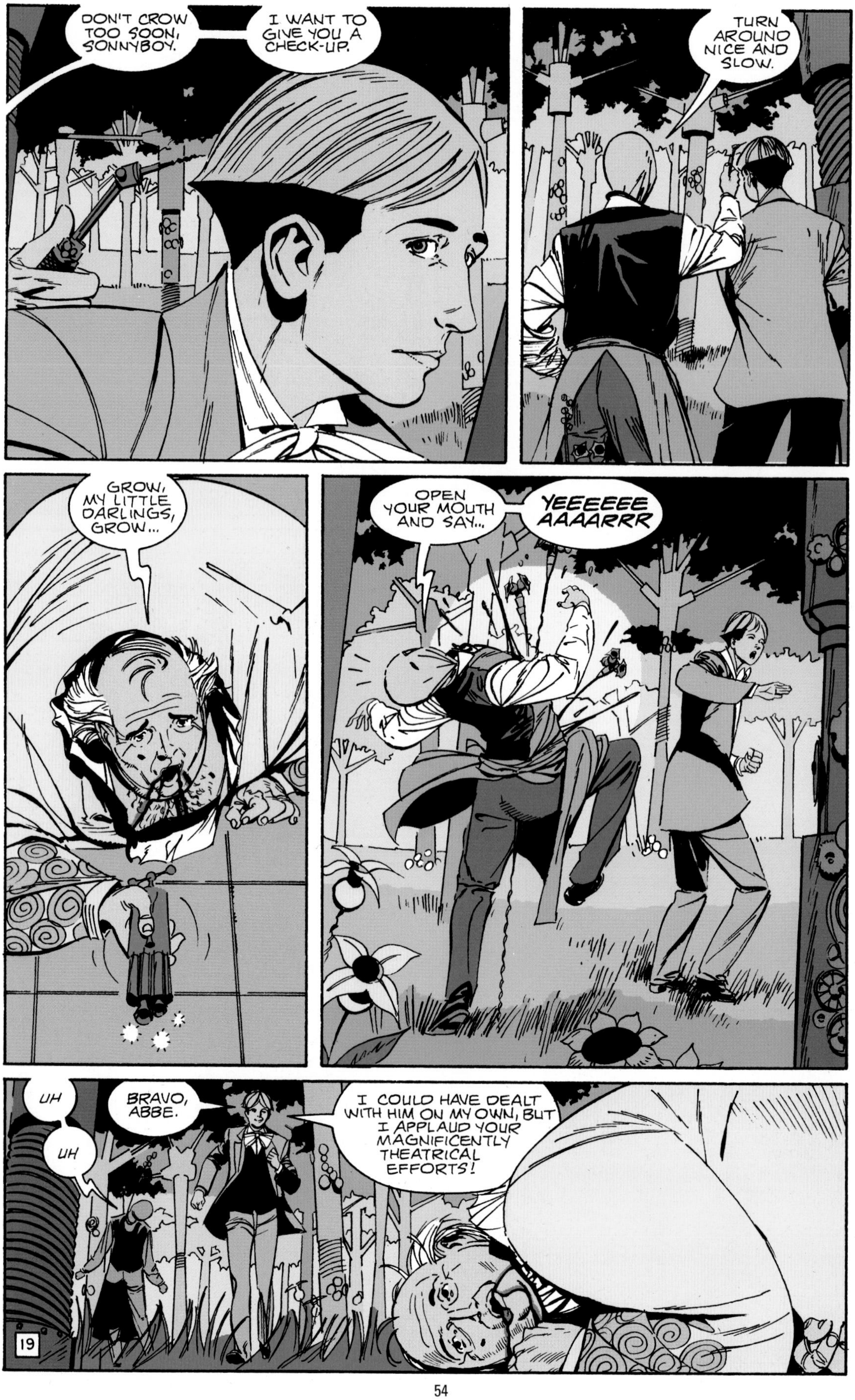
DON'T CROW TOO SOON, SONNYBOY.
I WANT TO GIVE YOU A CHECK-UP.
TURN AROUND NICE AND SLOW.
GROW, MY LITTLE DARLINGS, GROW...
OPEN YOUR MOUTH AND SAY...
YEEEEEE AAAARRR
UH
UH
BRAVO, ABBE.
I COULD HAVE DEALT WITH HIM ON MY OWN, BUT I APPLAUD YOUR MAGNIFICENTLY THEATRICAL EFFORTS!
19

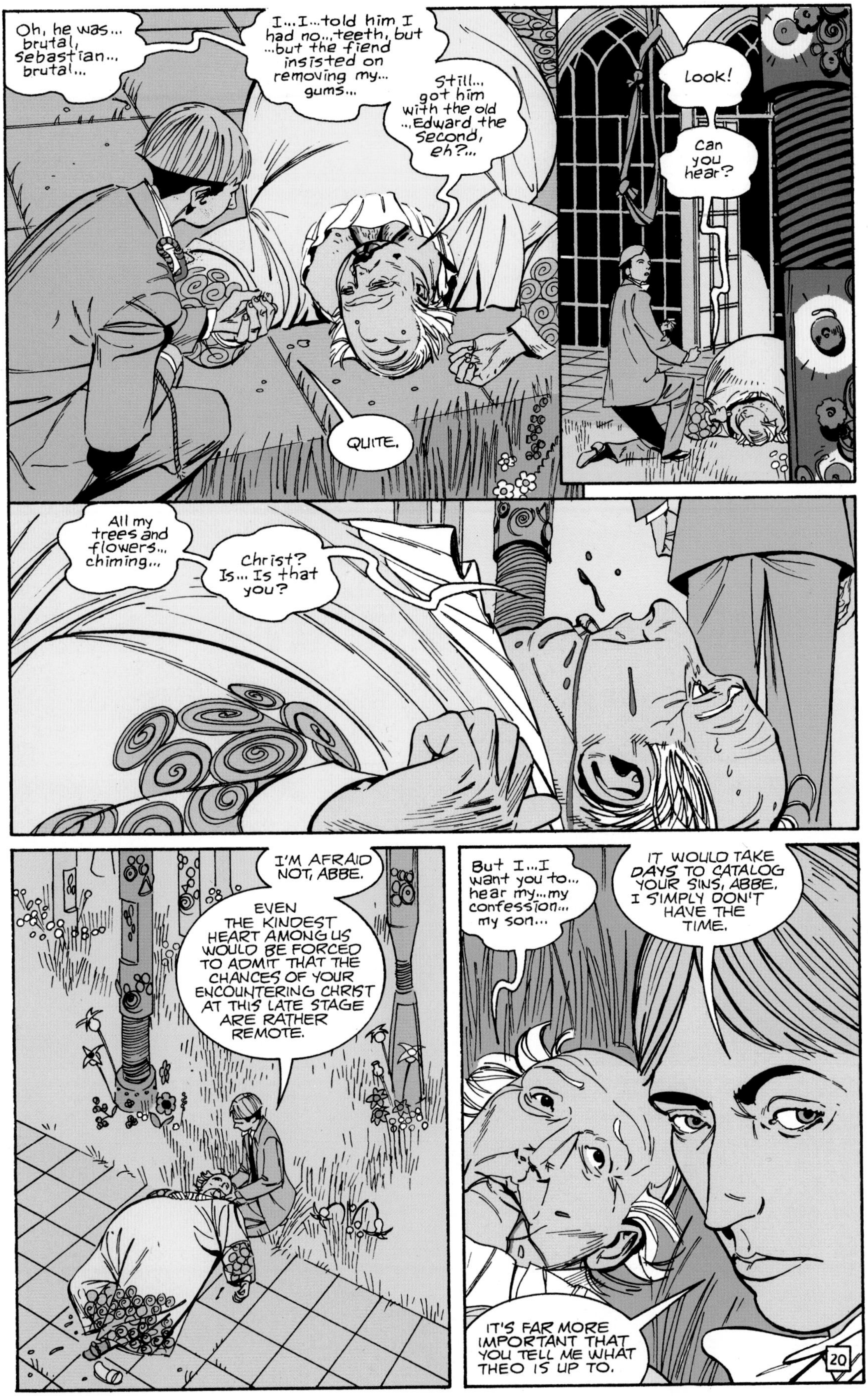
Oh, he was... brutal, Sebastian... brutal...
I...I...told him I had no...teeth, but ...but the fiend insisted on removing my... gums...
Still... got him with the old ...Edward the Second, eh?...
QUITE.
Look!
Can you hear?
All my trees and flowers... chiming...
Christ? Is... Is that you?
I'M AFRAID NOT, ABBE.
EVEN THE KINDEST HEART AMONG US WOULD BE FORCED TO ADMIT THAT THE CHANCES OF YOUR ENCOUNTERING CHRIST AT THIS LATE STAGE ARE RATHER REMOTE.
But I...I want you to... hear my...my confession... my son...
IT WOULD TAKE DAYS TO CATALOG YOUR SINS, ABBE. I SIMPLY DON'T HAVE THE TIME.
IT'S FAR MORE IMPORTANT THAT YOU TELL ME WHAT THEO IS UP TO.
20

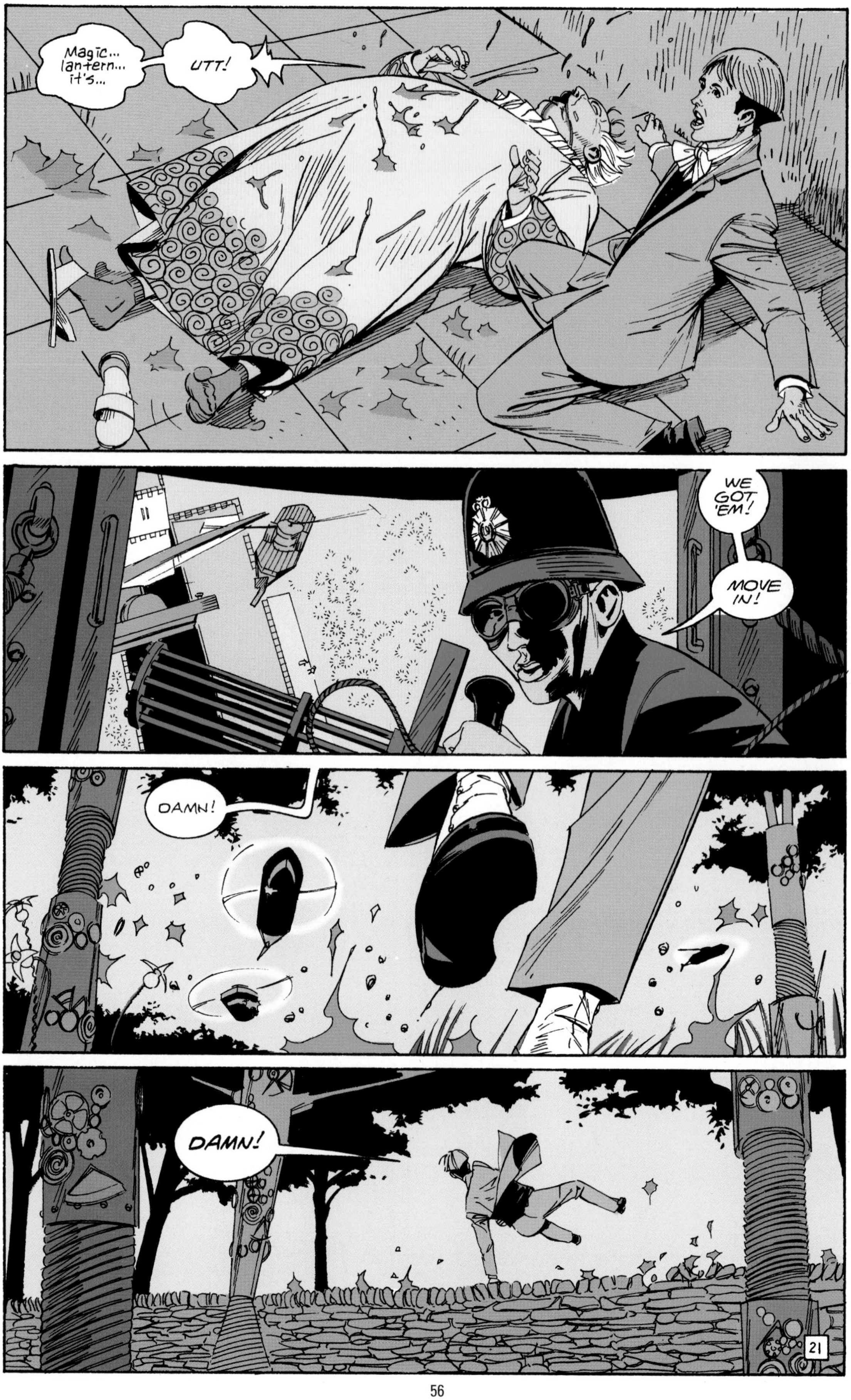

Magic... lantern... it's...
UTT!
WE GOT 'EM!
MOVE IN!
DAMN!
DAMN!
21

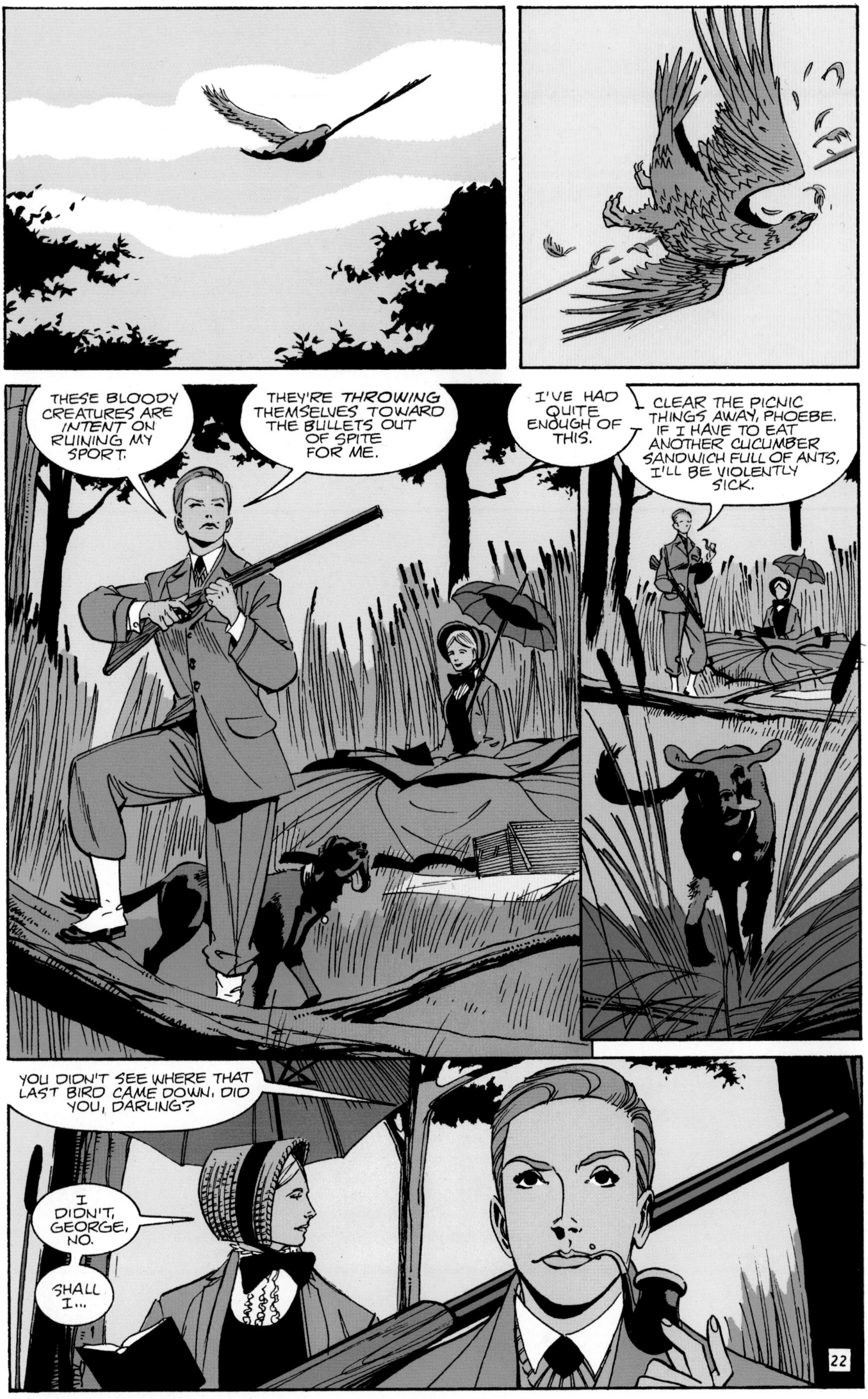
THESE BLOODY CREATURES ARE *INTENT* ON RUINING MY SPORT.
THEY'RE *THROWING* THEMSELVES TOWARD THE BULLETS OUT OF SPITE FOR ME.
I'VE HAD QUITE ENOUGH OF THIS.
CLEAR THE PICNIC THINGS AWAY, PHOEBE. IF I HAVE TO EAT ANOTHER CUCUMBER SANDWICH FULL OF ANTS, I'LL BE VIOLENTLY SICK.
YOU DIDN'T SEE WHERE THAT LAST BIRD CAME DOWN, DID YOU, DARLING?
I DIDN'T, GEORGE, NO.
SHALL I...
22

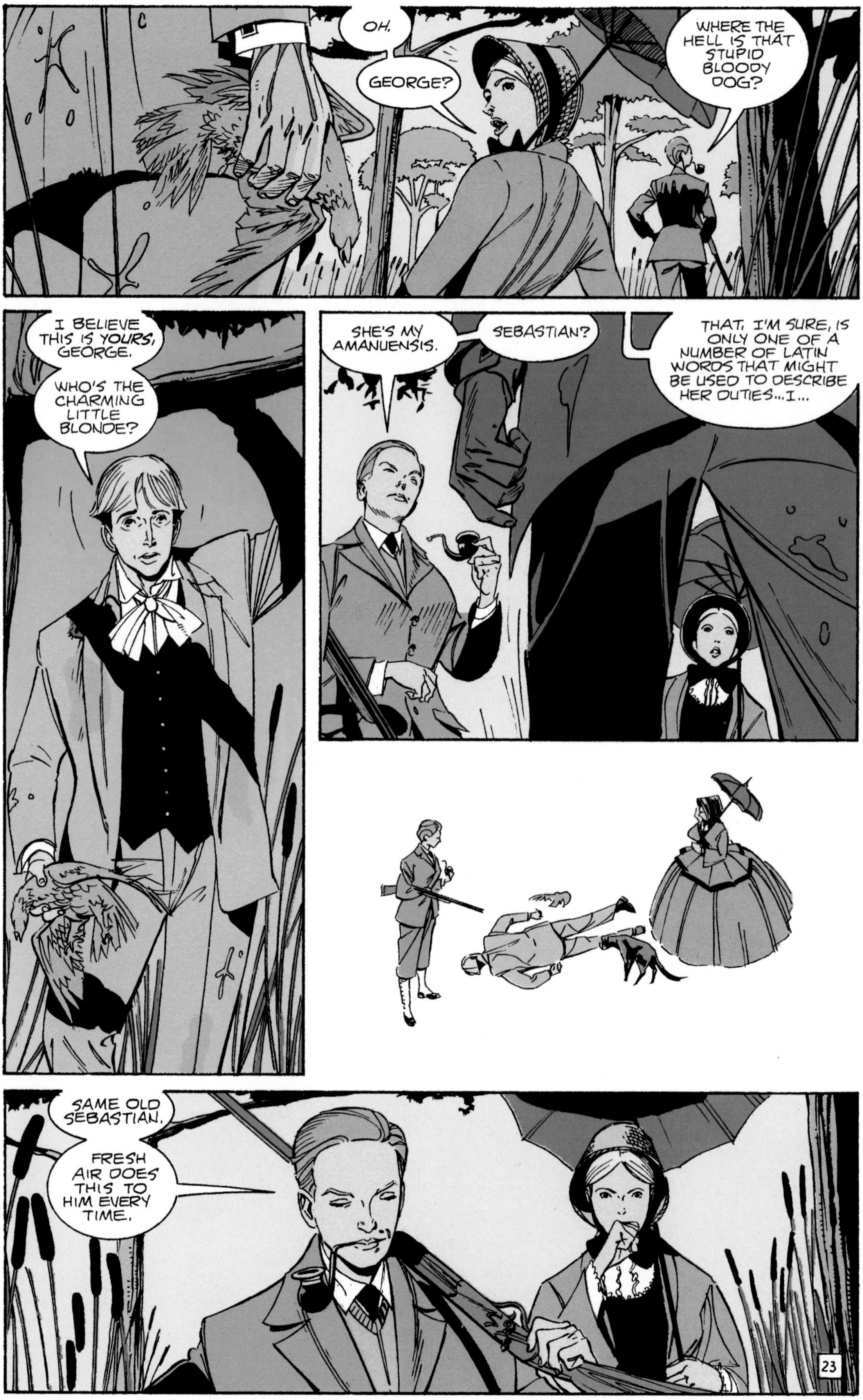
OH.
GEORGE?
WHERE THE HELL IS THAT STUPID BLOODY DOG?
I BELIEVE THIS IS YOURS, GEORGE.
WHO'S THE CHARMING LITTLE BLONDE?
SHE'S MY AMANUENSIS.
SEBASTIAN?
THAT, I'M SURE, IS ONLY ONE OF A NUMBER OF LATIN WORDS THAT MIGHT BE USED TO DESCRIBE HER DUTIES...I...
SAME OLD SEBASTIAN.
FRESH AIR DOES THIS TO HIM EVERY TIME.
23

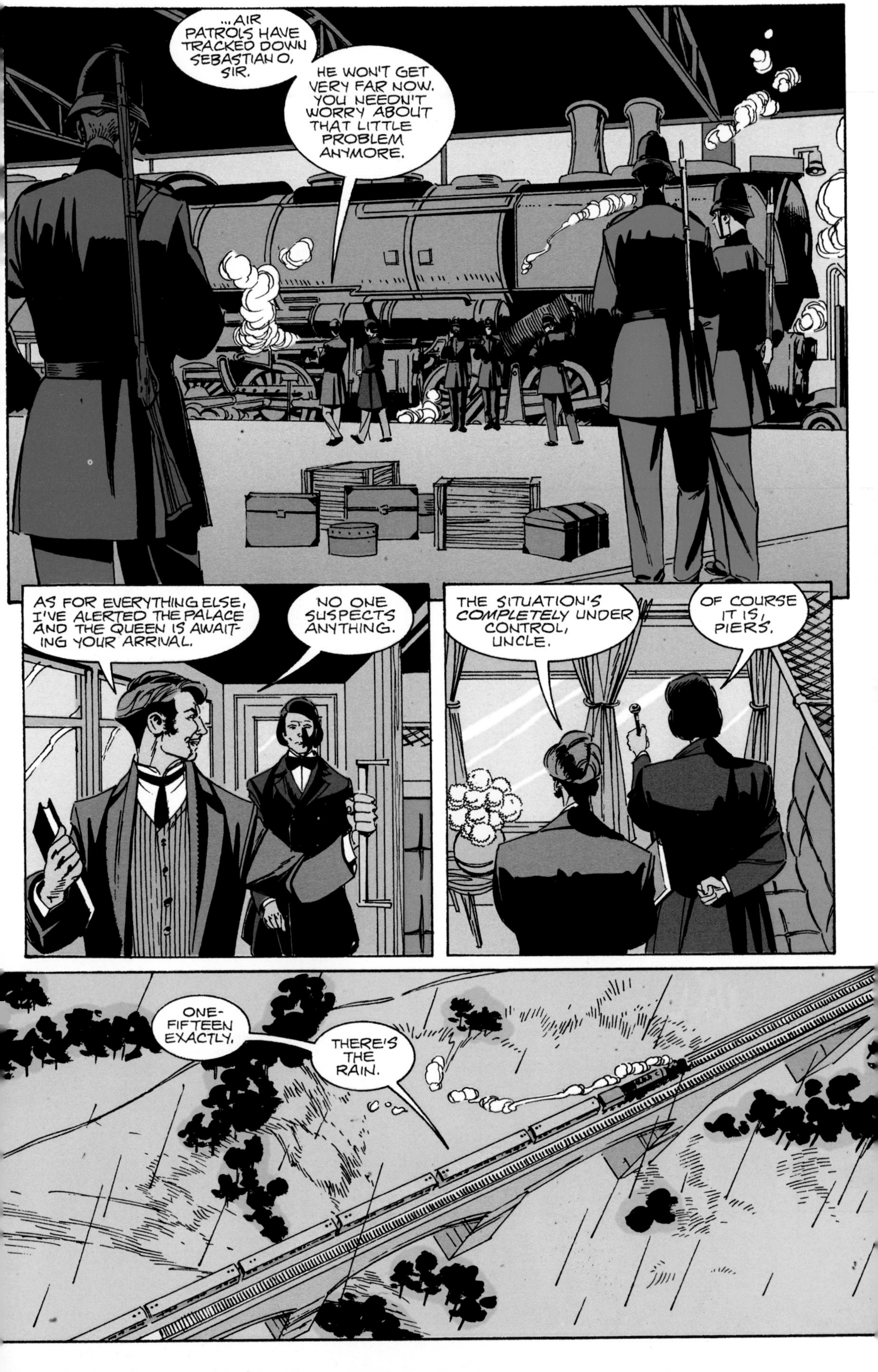
...AIR PATROLS HAVE TRACKED DOWN SEBASTIAN O, SIR.
HE WON'T GET VERY FAR NOW. YOU NEEDN'T WORRY ABOUT THAT LITTLE PROBLEM ANYMORE.
AS FOR EVERYTHING ELSE, I'VE ALERTED THE PALACE AND THE QUEEN IS AWAITING YOUR ARRIVAL.
NO ONE SUSPECTS ANYTHING.
THE SITUATION'S *COMPLETELY* UNDER CONTROL, UNCLE.
OF COURSE IT IS, PIERS.
ONE-FIFTEEN EXACTLY.
THERE'S THE RAIN.

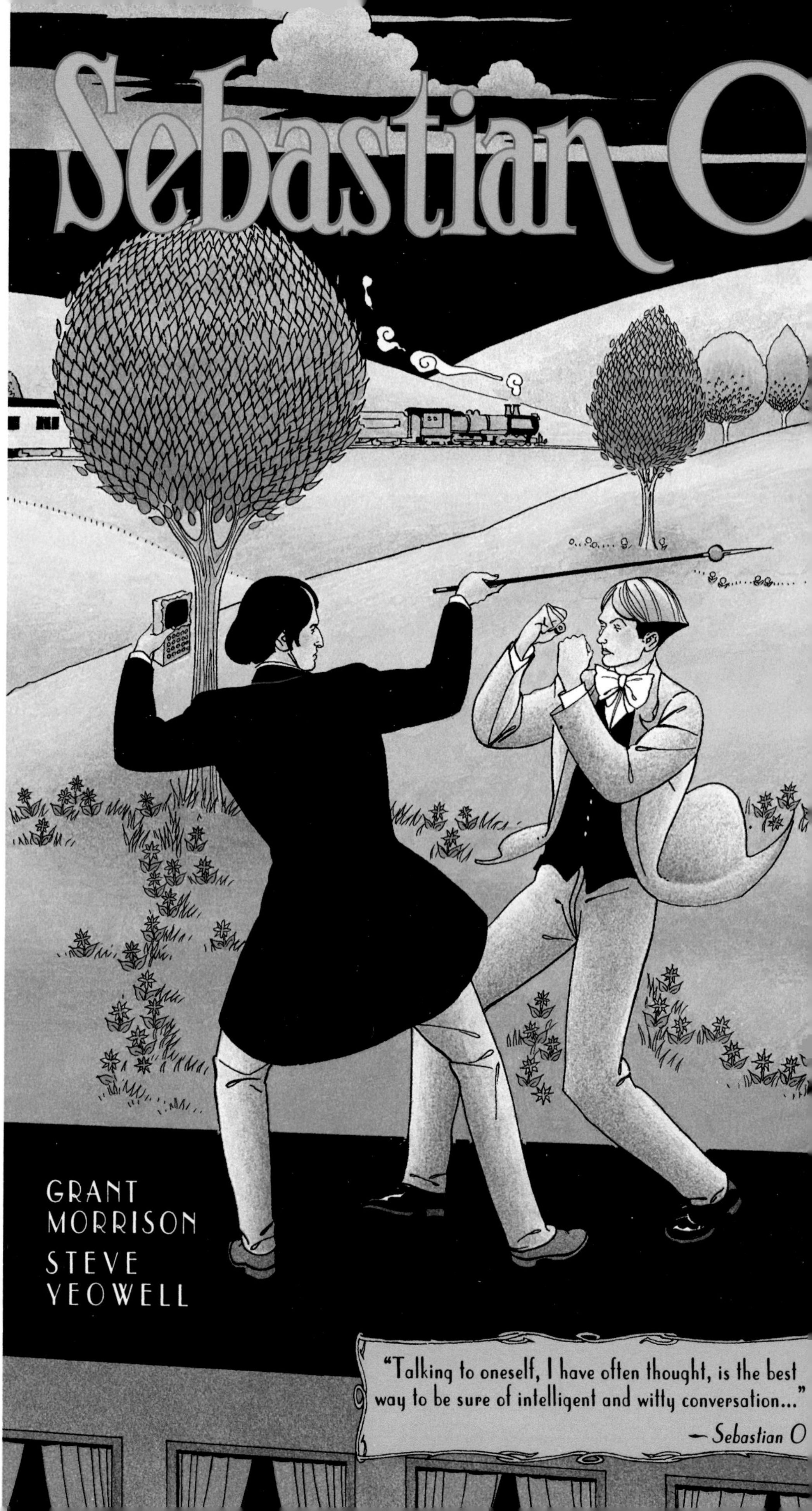
Sebastian O
GRANT MORRISON
STEVE YEOWELL
"Talking to oneself, I have often thought, is the best way to be sure of intelligent and witty conversation..."
— Sebastian O

The Queen Is DEAD

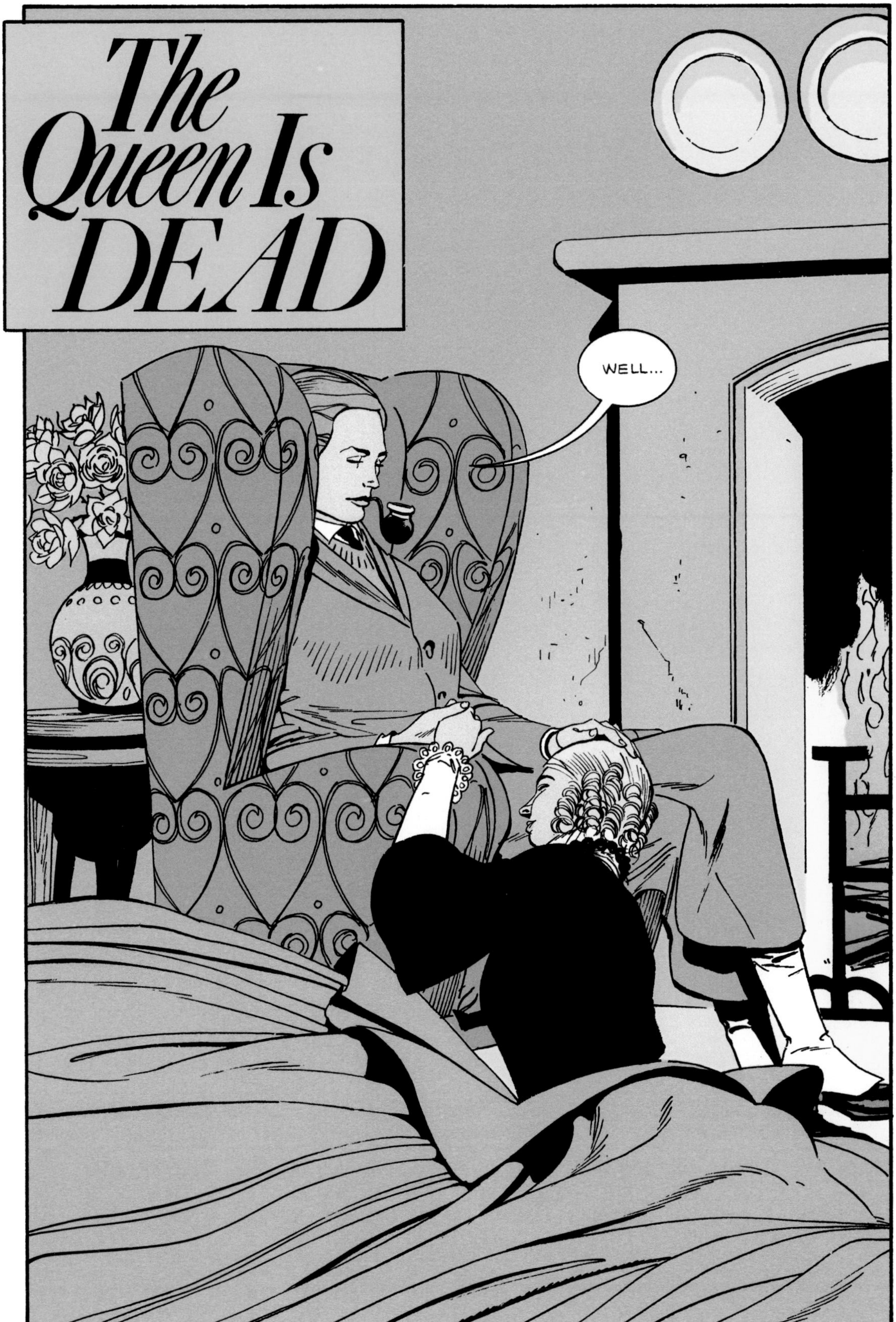
WELL...

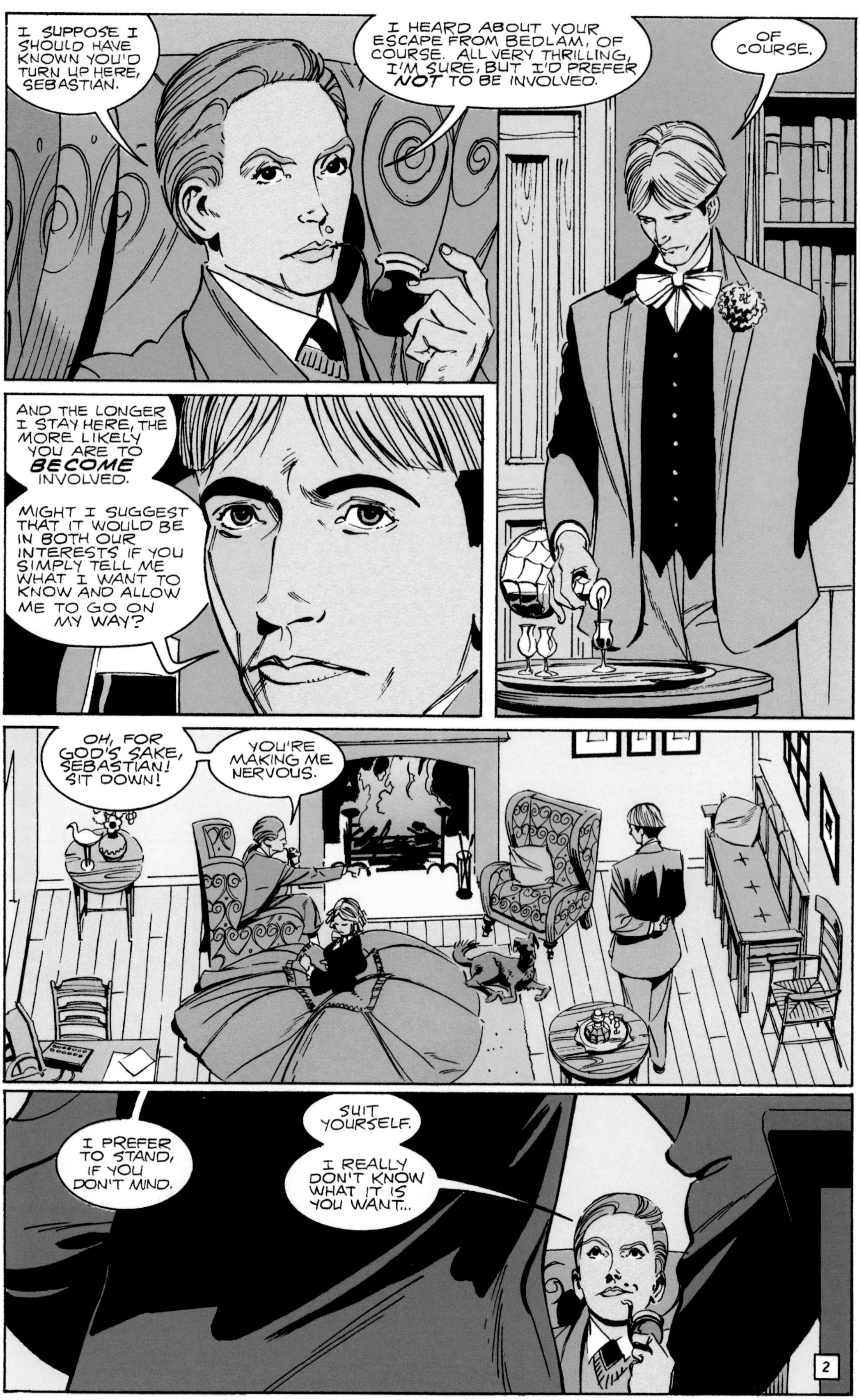
I SUPPOSE I SHOULD HAVE KNOWN YOU'D TURN UP HERE, SEBASTIAN.
I HEARD ABOUT YOUR ESCAPE FROM BEDLAM, OF COURSE. ALL VERY THRILLING, I'M SURE, BUT I'D PREFER *NOT* TO BE INVOLVED.
OF COURSE.
AND THE LONGER I STAY HERE, THE MORE LIKELY YOU ARE TO *BECOME* INVOLVED.
MIGHT I SUGGEST THAT IT WOULD BE IN BOTH OUR INTERESTS IF YOU SIMPLY TELL ME WHAT I WANT TO KNOW AND ALLOW ME TO GO ON MY WAY?
OH, FOR GOD'S SAKE, SEBASTIAN! SIT DOWN!
YOU'RE MAKING ME NERVOUS.
I PREFER TO STAND, IF YOU DON'T MIND.
SUIT YOURSELF.
I REALLY DON'T KNOW WHAT IT IS YOU WANT...
2

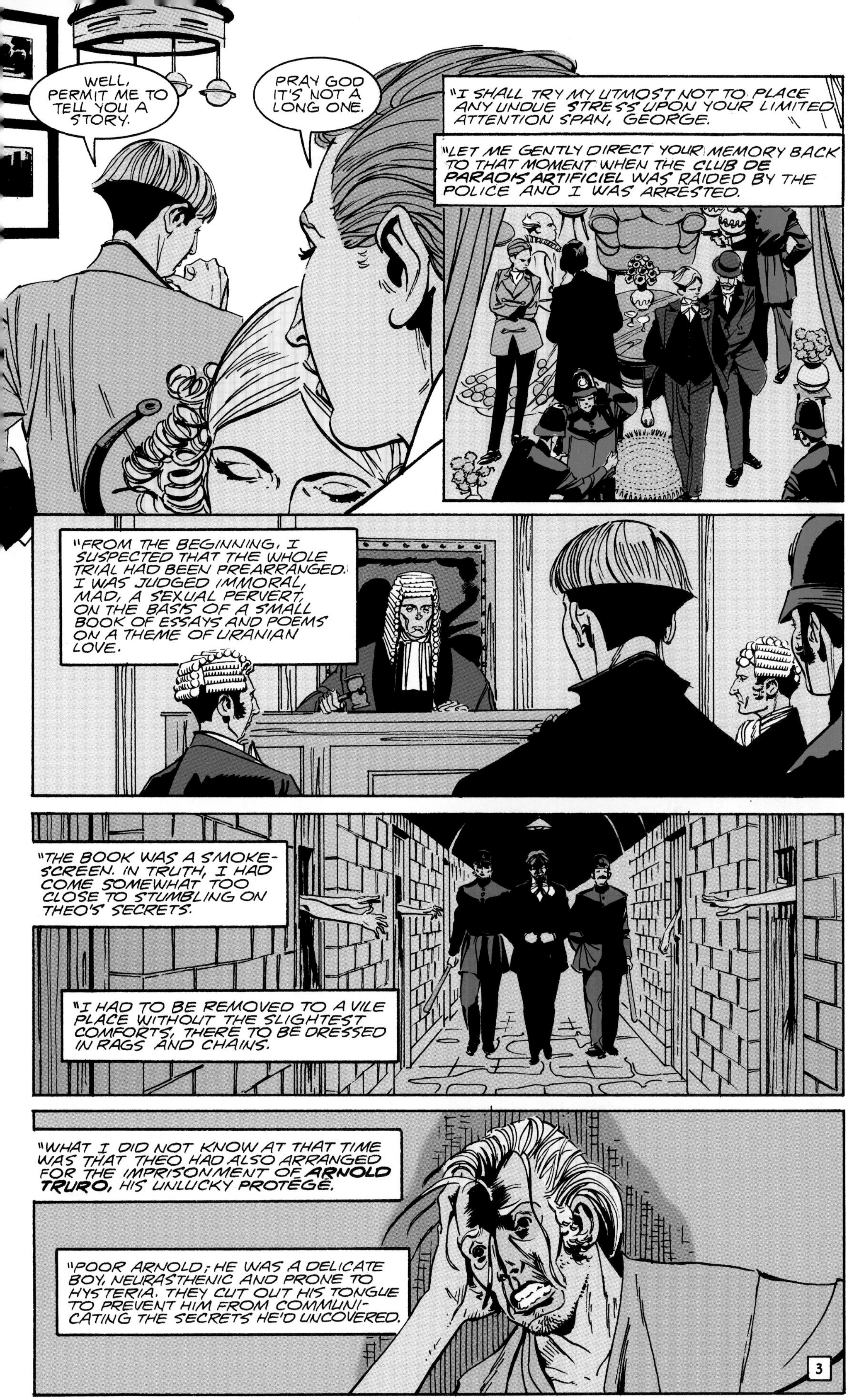
WELL, PERMIT ME TO TELL YOU A STORY.
PRAY GOD IT'S NOT A LONG ONE.
"I SHALL TRY MY UTMOST NOT TO PLACE ANY UNDUE STRESS UPON YOUR LIMITED ATTENTION SPAN, GEORGE.
"LET ME GENTLY DIRECT YOUR MEMORY BACK TO THAT MOMENT WHEN THE CLUB DE PARADIS ARTIFICIEL WAS RAIDED BY THE POLICE AND I WAS ARRESTED.
"FROM THE BEGINNING, I SUSPECTED THAT THE WHOLE TRIAL HAD BEEN PREARRANGED. I WAS JUDGED IMMORAL, MAD, A SEXUAL PERVERT, ON THE BASIS OF A SMALL BOOK OF ESSAYS AND POEMS ON A THEME OF URANIAN LOVE.
"THE BOOK WAS A SMOKE-SCREEN. IN TRUTH, I HAD COME SOMEWHAT TOO CLOSE TO STUMBLING ON THEO'S SECRETS.
"I HAD TO BE REMOVED TO A VILE PLACE WITHOUT THE SLIGHTEST COMFORTS, THERE TO BE DRESSED IN RAGS AND CHAINS.
"WHAT I DID NOT KNOW AT THAT TIME WAS THAT THEO HAD ALSO ARRANGED FOR THE IMPRISONMENT OF ARNOLD TRURO, HIS UNLUCKY PROTÉGÉ.
"POOR ARNOLD; HE WAS A DELICATE BOY, NEURASTHENIC AND PRONE TO HYSTERIA. THEY CUT OUT HIS TONGUE TO PREVENT HIM FROM COMMUNICATING THE SECRETS HE'D UNCOVERED.
3

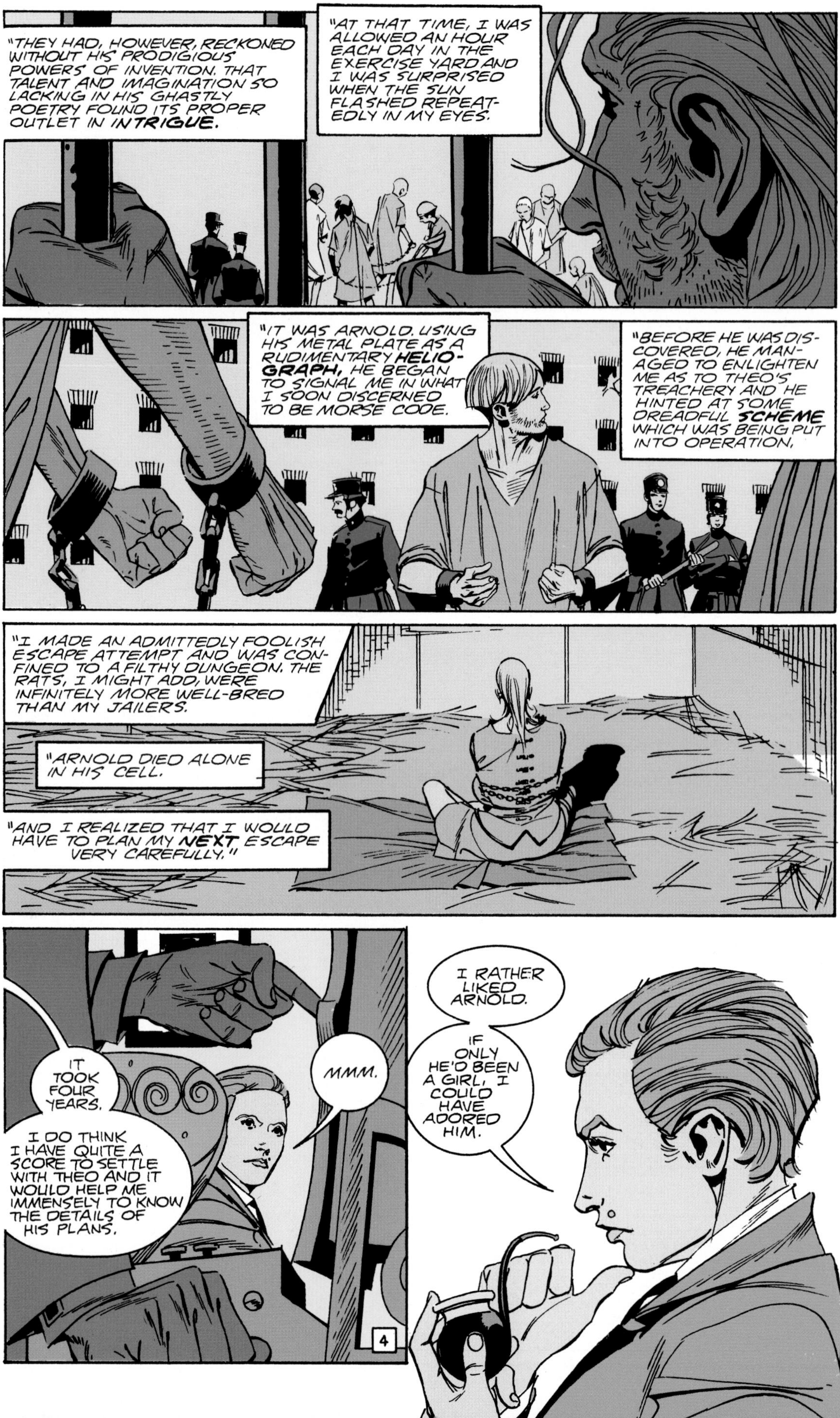
"THEY HAD, HOWEVER, RECKONED WITHOUT HIS PRODIGIOUS POWERS OF INVENTION. THAT TALENT AND IMAGINATION SO LACKING IN HIS GHASTLY POETRY FOUND ITS PROPER OUTLET IN INTRIGUE.
"AT THAT TIME, I WAS ALLOWED AN HOUR EACH DAY IN THE EXERCISE YARD AND I WAS SURPRISED WHEN THE SUN FLASHED REPEATEDLY IN MY EYES.
"IT WAS ARNOLD. USING HIS METAL PLATE AS A RUDIMENTARY HELIOGRAPH, HE BEGAN TO SIGNAL ME IN WHAT I SOON DISCERNED TO BE MORSE CODE.
"BEFORE HE WAS DISCOVERED, HE MANAGED TO ENLIGHTEN ME AS TO THEO'S TREACHERY AND HE HINTED AT SOME DREADFUL SCHEME WHICH WAS BEING PUT INTO OPERATION.
"I MADE AN ADMITTEDLY FOOLISH ESCAPE ATTEMPT AND WAS CONFINED TO A FILTHY DUNGEON. THE RATS, I MIGHT ADD, WERE INFINITELY MORE WELL-BRED THAN MY JAILERS.
"ARNOLD DIED ALONE IN HIS CELL.
"AND I REALIZED THAT I WOULD HAVE TO PLAN MY NEXT ESCAPE VERY CAREFULLY."
IT TOOK FOUR YEARS.
I DO THINK I HAVE QUITE A SCORE TO SETTLE WITH THEO AND IT WOULD HELP ME IMMENSELY TO KNOW THE DETAILS OF HIS PLANS.
MMM.
I RATHER LIKED ARNOLD.
IF ONLY HE'D BEEN A GIRL, I COULD HAVE ADORED HIM.
4

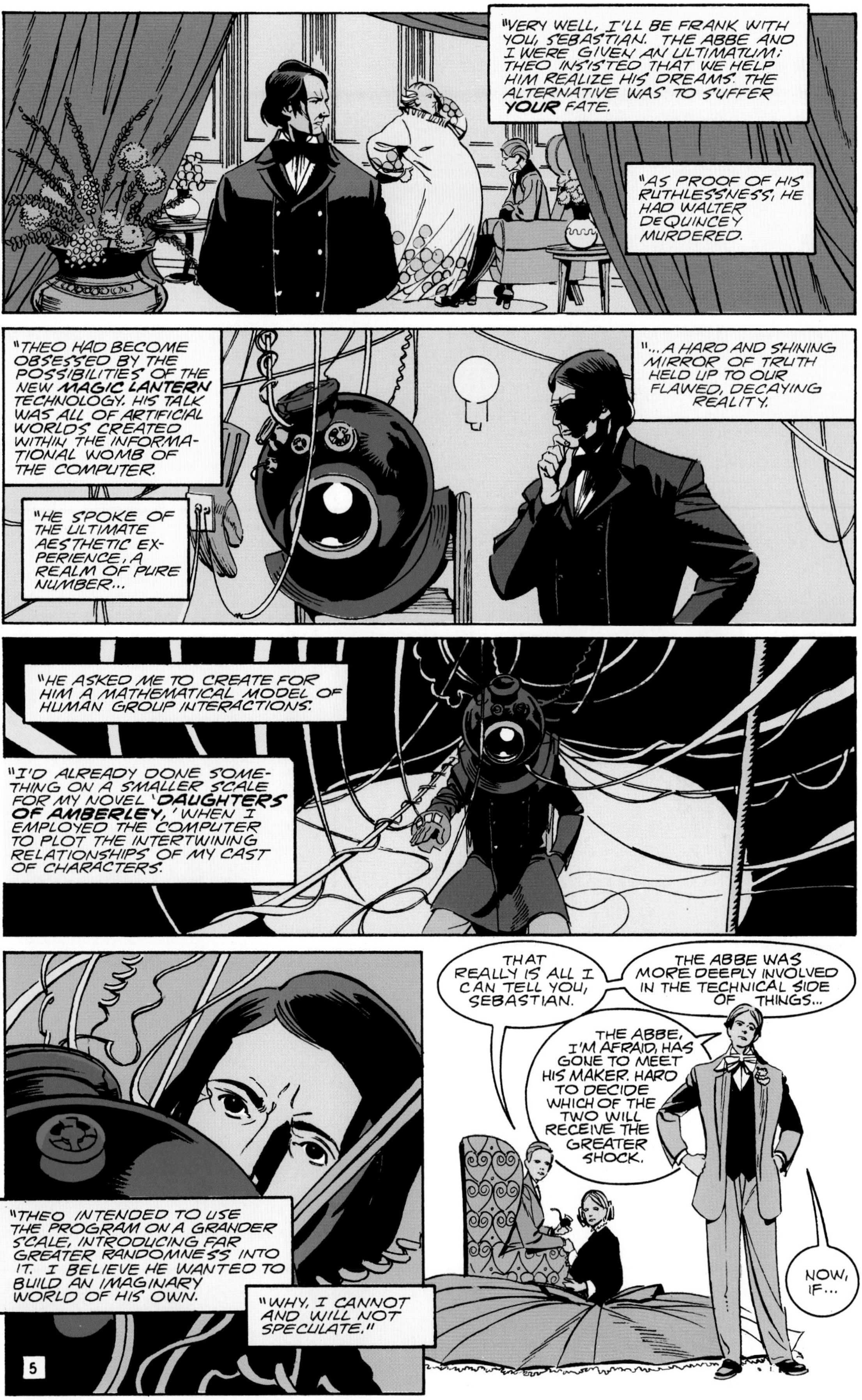

"VERY WELL, I'LL BE FRANK WITH YOU, SEBASTIAN. THE ABBE AND I WERE GIVEN AN ULTIMATUM: THEO INSISTED THAT WE HELP HIM REALIZE HIS DREAMS. THE ALTERNATIVE WAS TO SUFFER **YOUR** FATE.
"AS PROOF OF HIS RUTHLESSNESS, HE HAD WALTER DeQUINCEY MURDERED.
"THEO HAD BECOME OBSESSED BY THE POSSIBILITIES OF THE NEW **MAGIC LANTERN** TECHNOLOGY. HIS TALK WAS ALL OF ARTIFICIAL WORLDS CREATED WITHIN THE INFORMATIONAL WOMB OF THE COMPUTER.
"HE SPOKE OF THE ULTIMATE AESTHETIC EXPERIENCE, A REALM OF PURE NUMBER...
"...A HARD AND SHINING MIRROR OF TRUTH HELD UP TO OUR FLAWED, DECAYING REALITY.
"HE ASKED ME TO CREATE FOR HIM A MATHEMATICAL MODEL OF HUMAN GROUP INTERACTIONS.
"I'D ALREADY DONE SOMETHING ON A SMALLER SCALE FOR MY NOVEL '**DAUGHTERS OF AMBERLEY**,' WHEN I EMPLOYED THE COMPUTER TO PLOT THE INTERTWINING RELATIONSHIPS OF MY CAST OF CHARACTERS.
"THEO INTENDED TO USE THE PROGRAM ON A GRANDER SCALE, INTRODUCING FAR GREATER RANDOMNESS INTO IT. I BELIEVE HE WANTED TO BUILD AN IMAGINARY WORLD OF HIS OWN.
"WHY, I CANNOT AND WILL NOT SPECULATE."
THAT REALLY IS ALL I CAN TELL YOU, SEBASTIAN.
THE ABBE WAS MORE DEEPLY INVOLVED IN THE TECHNICAL SIDE OF THINGS...
THE ABBE, I'M AFRAID, HAS GONE TO MEET HIS MAKER. HARD TO DECIDE WHICH OF THE TWO WILL RECEIVE THE GREATER SHOCK.
NOW, IF...
5

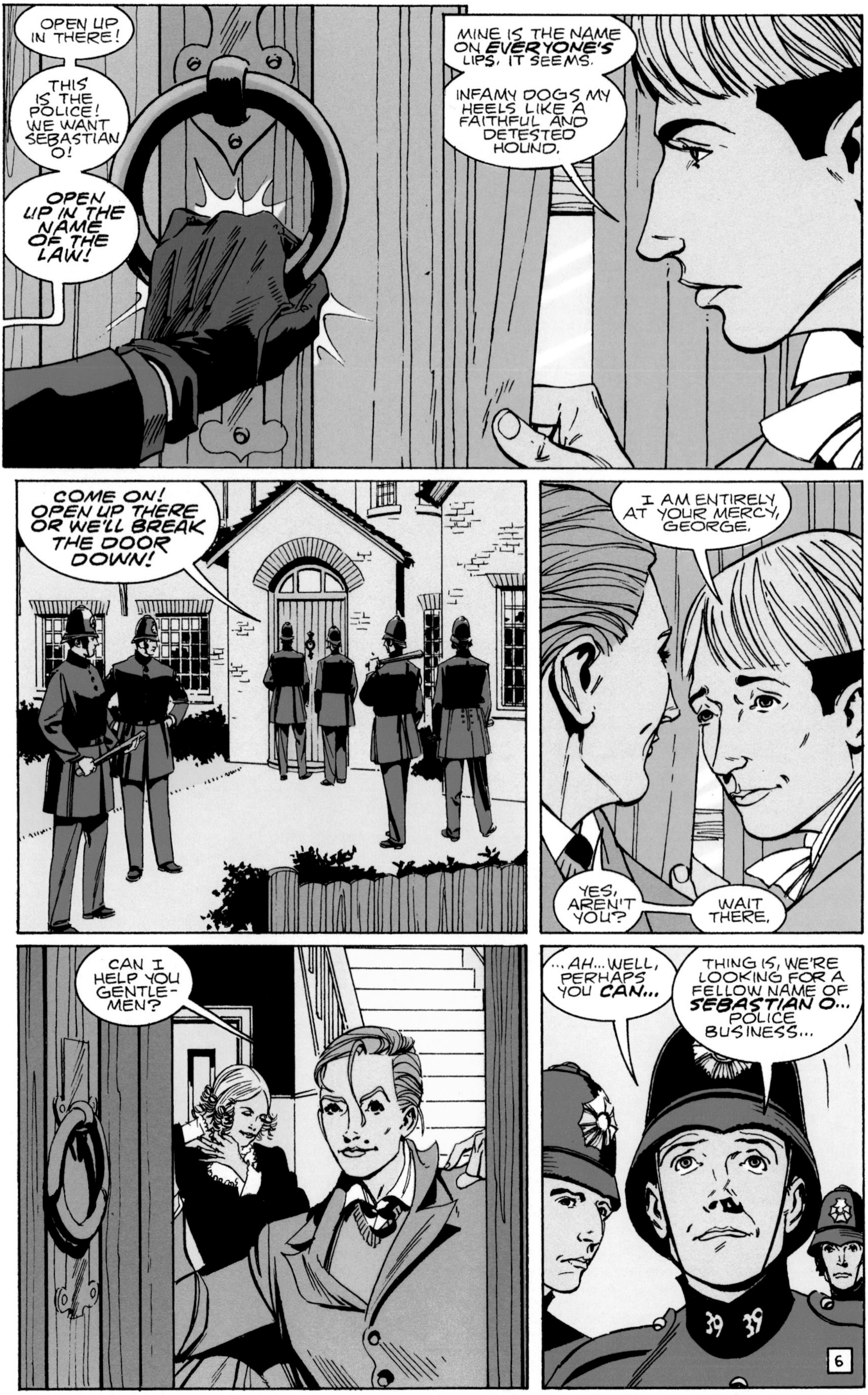

OPEN UP IN THERE!
THIS IS THE POLICE! WE WANT SEBASTIAN O!
OPEN UP IN THE NAME OF THE LAW!
MINE IS THE NAME ON EVERYONE'S LIPS, IT SEEMS.
INFAMY DOGS MY HEELS LIKE A FAITHFUL AND DETESTED HOUND.
COME ON! OPEN UP THERE OR WE'LL BREAK THE DOOR DOWN!
I AM ENTIRELY AT YOUR MERCY, GEORGE.
YES, AREN'T YOU?
WAIT THERE.
CAN I HELP YOU GENTLE-MEN?
...AH...WELL, PERHAPS YOU CAN...
THING IS, WE'RE LOOKING FOR A FELLOW NAME OF SEBASTIAN O... POLICE BUSINESS...
6

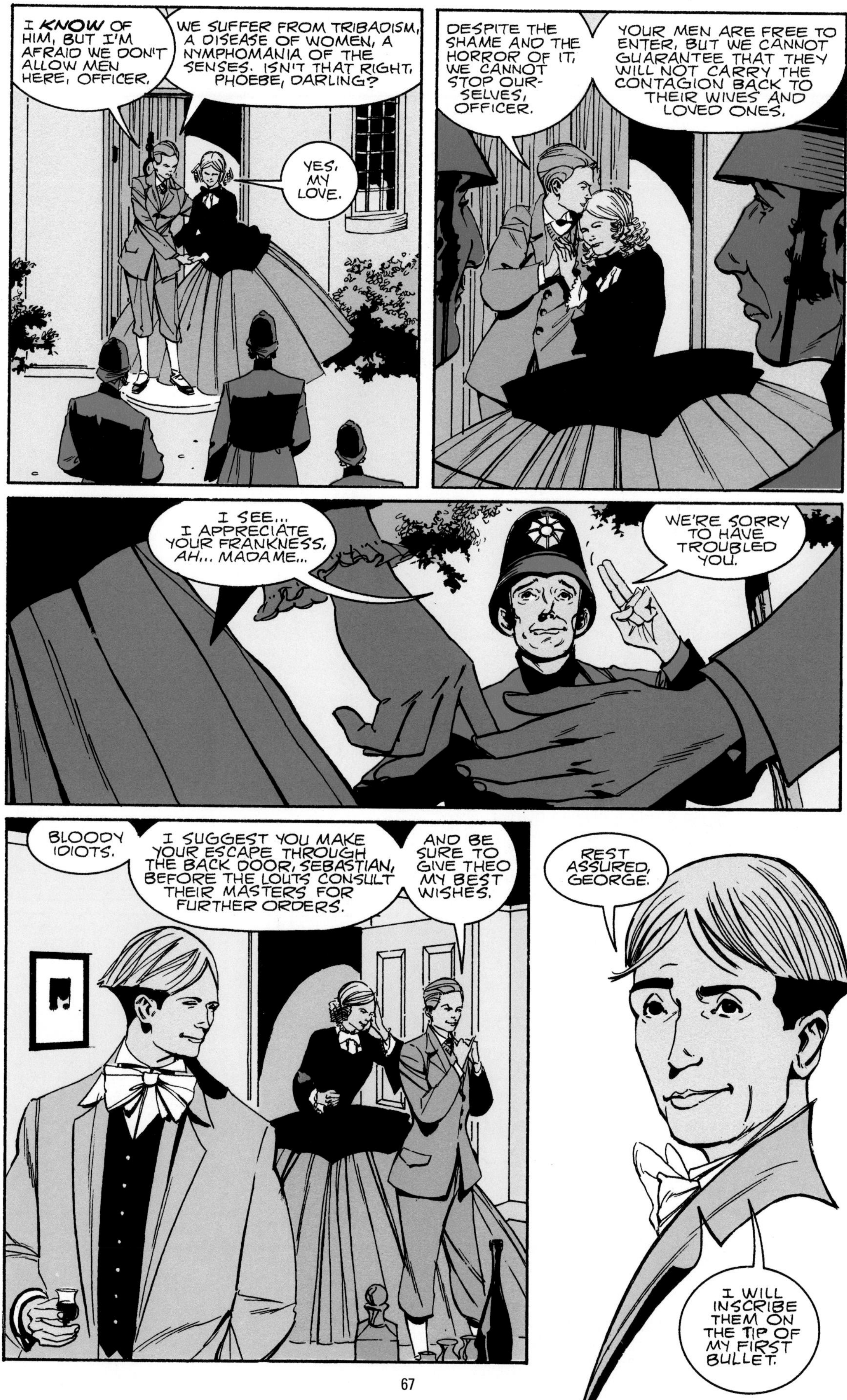
I KNOW OF HIM, BUT I'M AFRAID WE DON'T ALLOW MEN HERE, OFFICER.
WE SUFFER FROM TRIBADISM, A DISEASE OF WOMEN, A NYMPHOMANIA OF THE SENSES. ISN'T THAT RIGHT, PHOEBE, DARLING?
YES, MY LOVE.
DESPITE THE SHAME AND THE HORROR OF IT, WE CANNOT STOP OURSELVES, OFFICER.
YOUR MEN ARE FREE TO ENTER, BUT WE CANNOT GUARANTEE THAT THEY WILL NOT CARRY THE CONTAGION BACK TO THEIR WIVES AND LOVED ONES.
I SEE... I APPRECIATE YOUR FRANKNESS, AH... MADAME...
WE'RE SORRY TO HAVE TROUBLED YOU.
BLOODY IDIOTS.
I SUGGEST YOU MAKE YOUR ESCAPE THROUGH THE BACK DOOR, SEBASTIAN, BEFORE THE LOUTS CONSULT THEIR MASTERS FOR FURTHER ORDERS.
AND BE SURE TO GIVE THEO MY BEST WISHES.
REST ASSURED, GEORGE.
I WILL INSCRIBE THEM ON THE TIP OF MY FIRST BULLET.

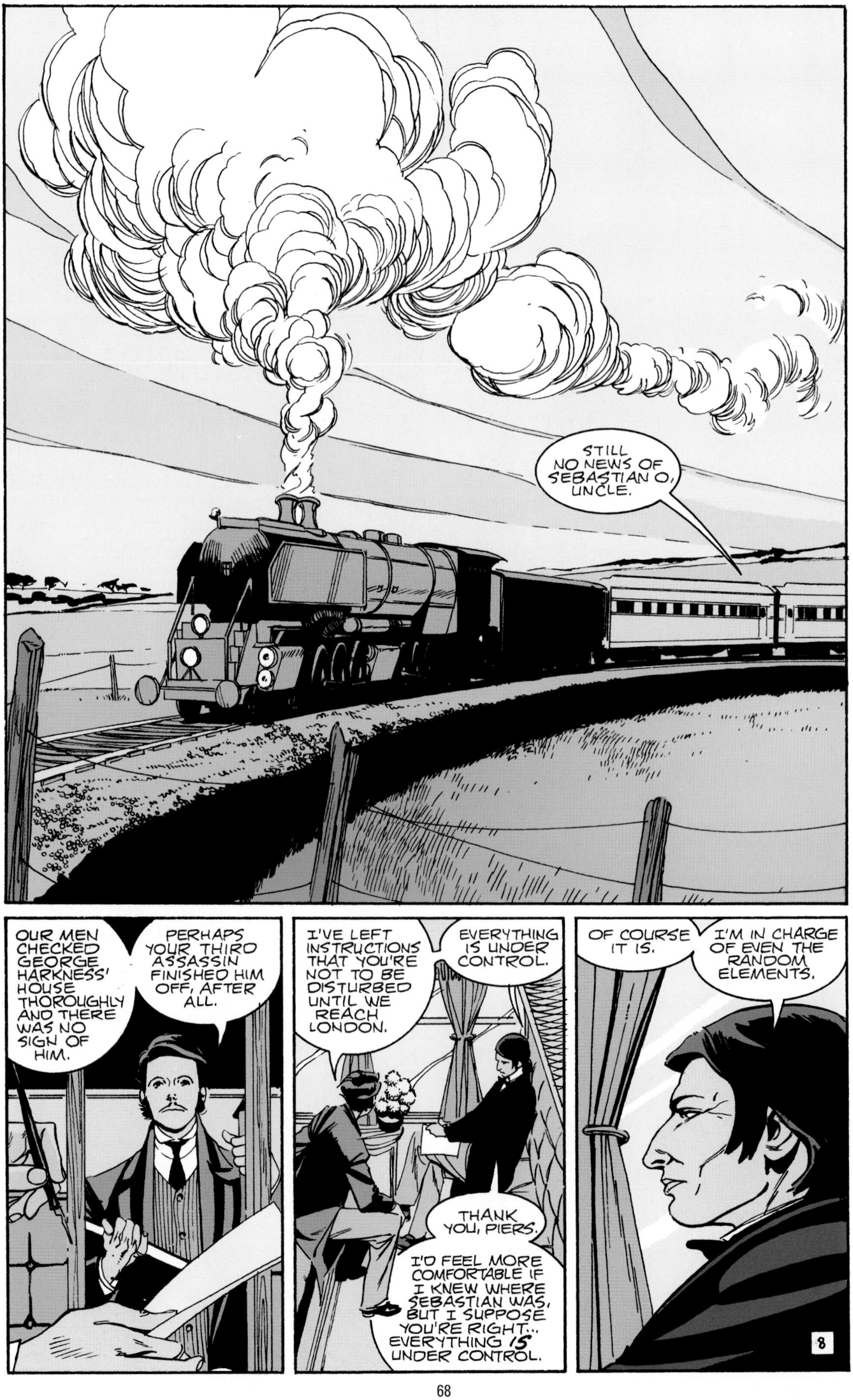
STILL NO NEWS OF SEBASTIAN O, UNCLE.
OUR MEN CHECKED GEORGE HARKNESS' HOUSE THOROUGHLY AND THERE WAS NO SIGN OF HIM.
PERHAPS YOUR THIRD ASSASSIN FINISHED HIM OFF, AFTER ALL.
I'VE LEFT INSTRUCTIONS THAT YOU'RE NOT TO BE DISTURBED UNTIL WE REACH LONDON.
EVERYTHING IS UNDER CONTROL.
THANK YOU, PIERS.
I'D FEEL MORE COMFORTABLE IF I KNEW WHERE SEBASTIAN WAS, BUT I SUPPOSE YOU'RE RIGHT... EVERYTHING IS UNDER CONTROL.
OF COURSE IT IS.
I'M IN CHARGE OF EVEN THE RANDOM ELEMENTS.
8

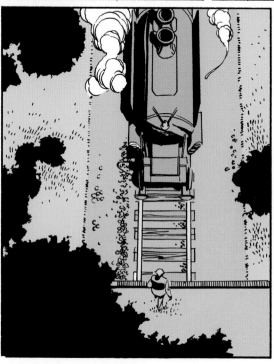

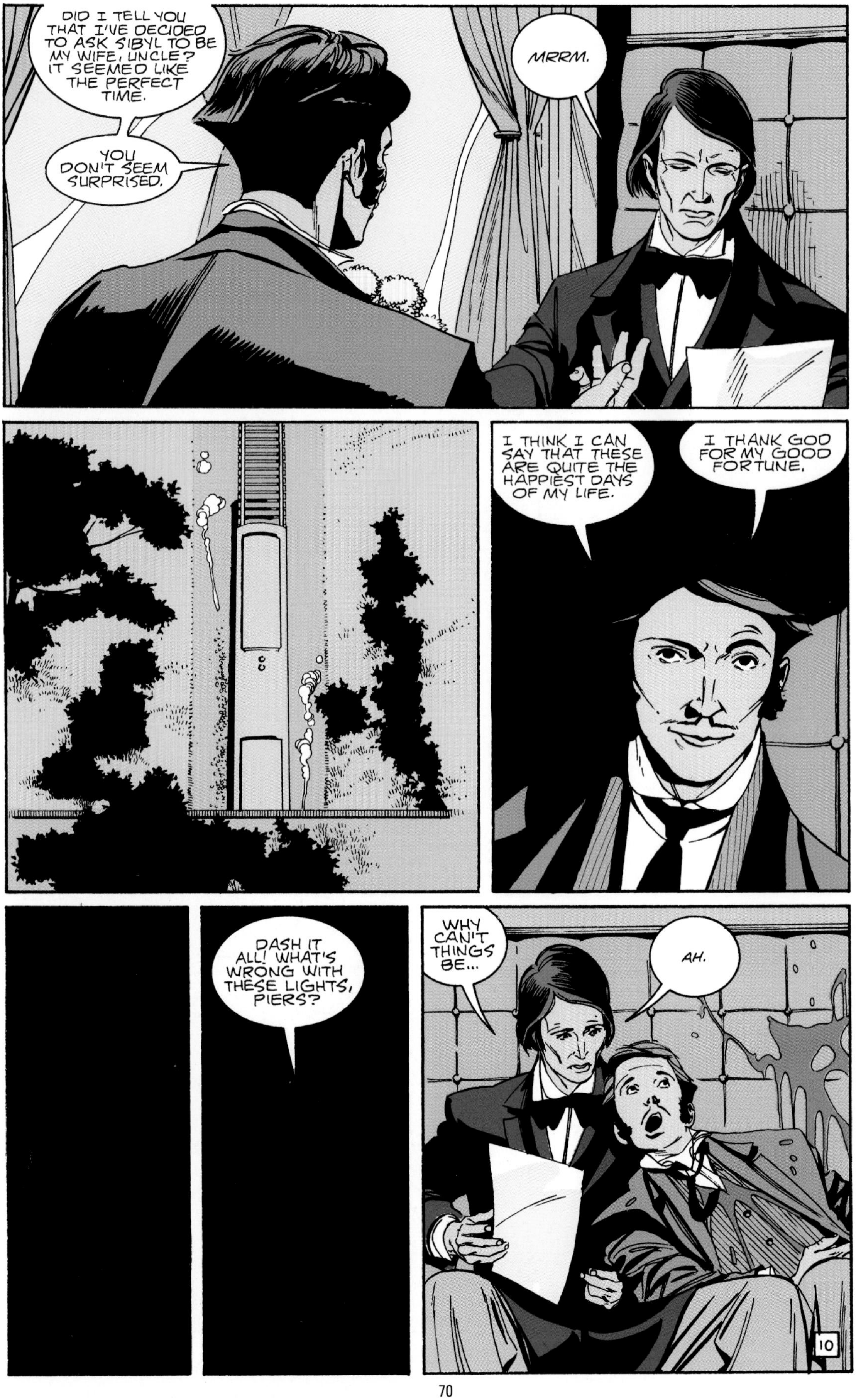
DID I TELL YOU THAT I'VE DECIDED TO ASK SIBYL TO BE MY WIFE, UNCLE? IT SEEMED LIKE THE PERFECT TIME.
YOU DON'T SEEM SURPRISED.
MRRM.
I THINK I CAN SAY THAT THESE ARE QUITE THE HAPPIEST DAYS OF MY LIFE.
I THANK GOD FOR MY GOOD FORTUNE.
DASH IT ALL! WHAT'S WRONG WITH THESE LIGHTS, PIERS?
WHY CAN'T THINGS BE...
AH.
10

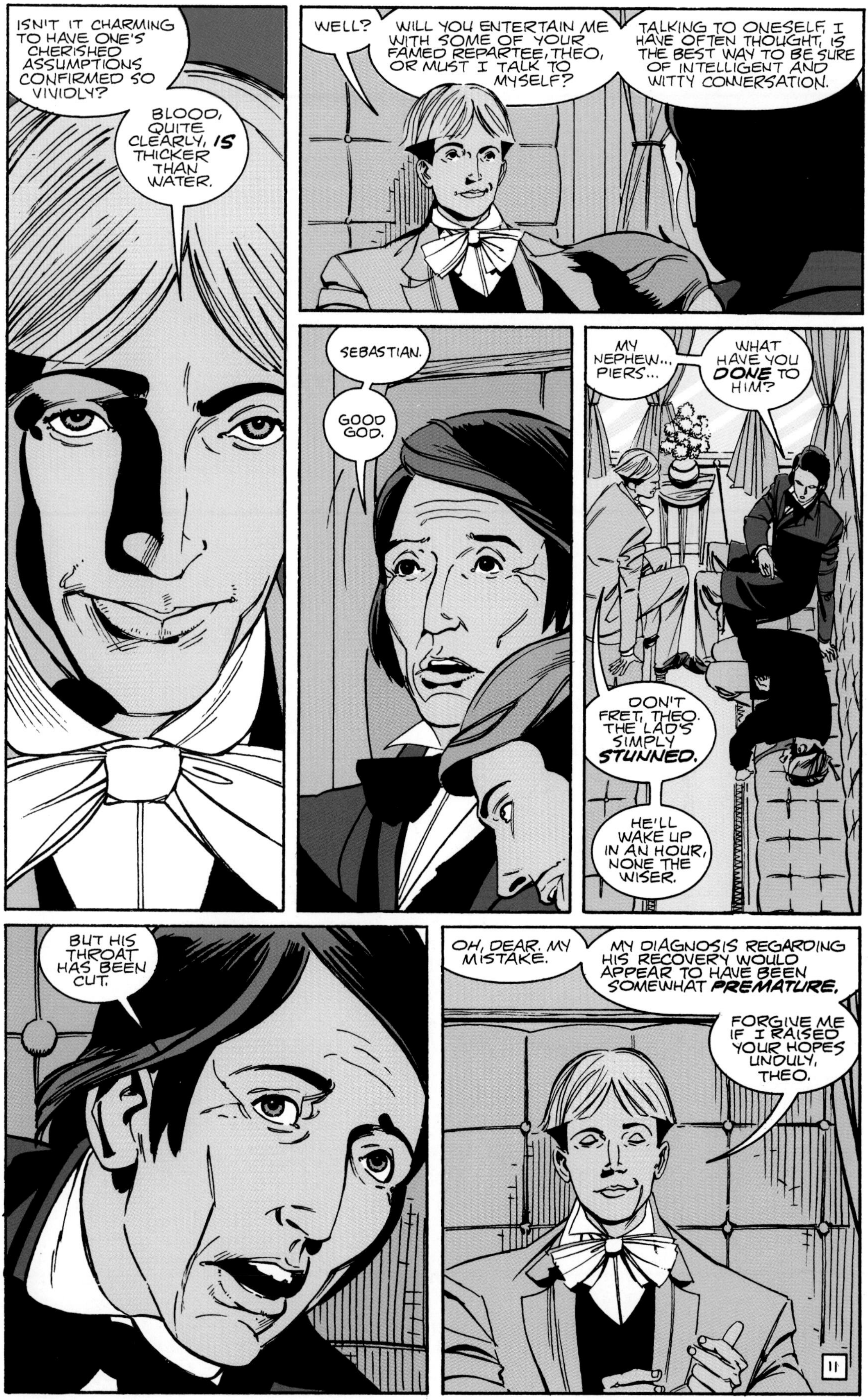

ISN'T IT CHARMING TO HAVE ONE'S CHERISHED ASSUMPTIONS CONFIRMED SO VIVIDLY?
BLOOD, QUITE CLEARLY, IS THICKER THAN WATER.
WELL?
WILL YOU ENTERTAIN ME WITH SOME OF YOUR FAMED REPARTEE, THEO, OR MUST I TALK TO MYSELF?
TALKING TO ONESELF, I HAVE OFTEN THOUGHT, IS THE BEST WAY TO BE SURE OF INTELLIGENT AND WITTY CONVERSATION.
SEBASTIAN.
GOOD GOD.
MY NEPHEW... PIERS...
WHAT HAVE YOU DONE TO HIM?
DON'T FRET, THEO. THE LAD'S SIMPLY STUNNED.
HE'LL WAKE UP IN AN HOUR, NONE THE WISER.
BUT HIS THROAT HAS BEEN CUT.
OH, DEAR. MY MISTAKE.
MY DIAGNOSIS REGARDING HIS RECOVERY WOULD APPEAR TO HAVE BEEN SOMEWHAT PREMATURE.
FORGIVE ME IF I RAISED YOUR HOPES UNDULY, THEO.
11

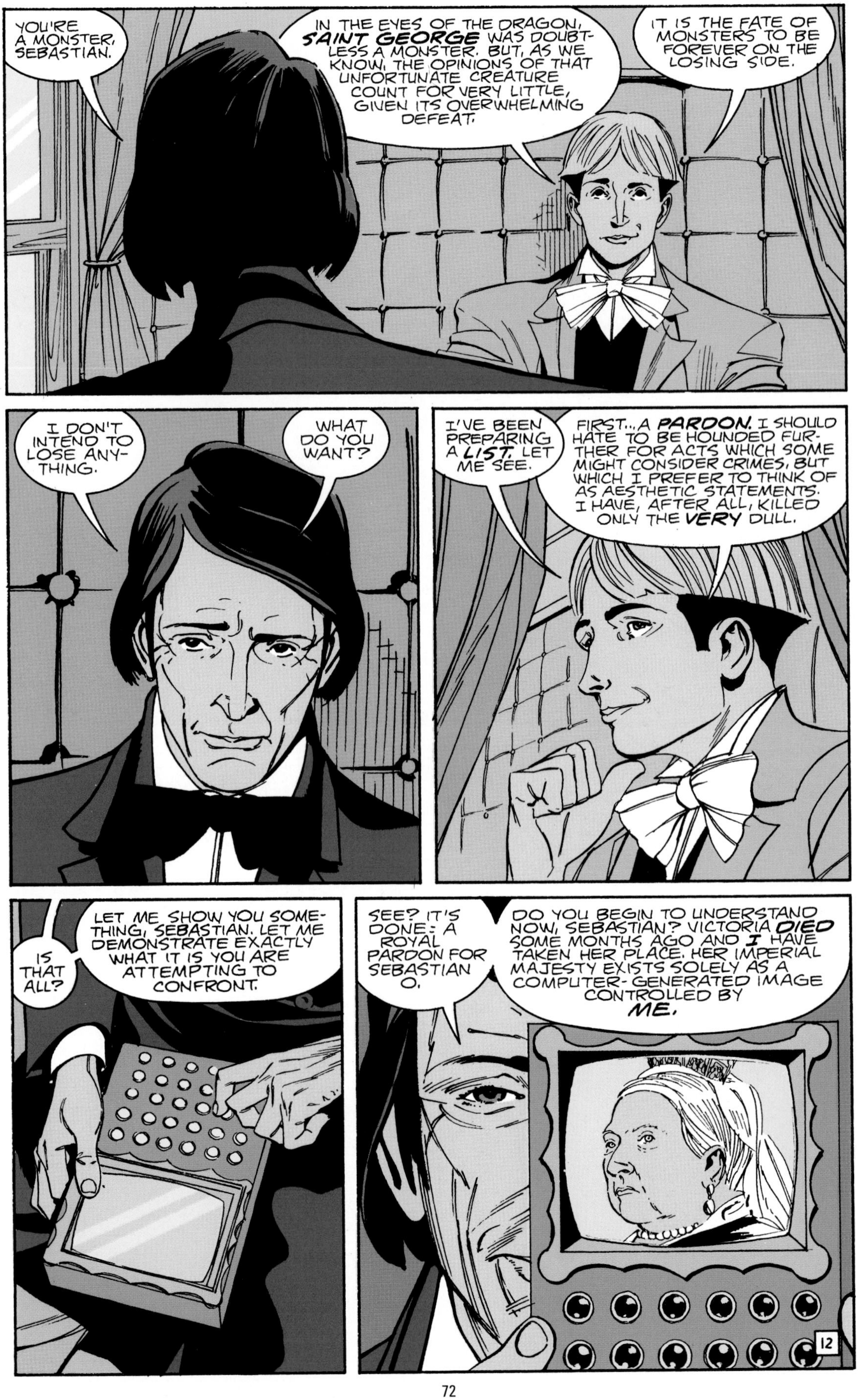
YOU'RE A MONSTER, SEBASTIAN.
IN THE EYES OF THE DRAGON, SAINT GEORGE WAS DOUBTLESS A MONSTER. BUT, AS WE KNOW, THE OPINIONS OF THAT UNFORTUNATE CREATURE COUNT FOR VERY LITTLE, GIVEN ITS OVERWHELMING DEFEAT.
IT IS THE FATE OF MONSTERS TO BE FOREVER ON THE LOSING SIDE.
I DON'T INTEND TO LOSE ANYTHING.
WHAT DO YOU WANT?
I'VE BEEN PREPARING A LIST. LET ME SEE.
FIRST... A PARDON. I SHOULD HATE TO BE HOUNDED FURTHER FOR ACTS WHICH SOME MIGHT CONSIDER CRIMES, BUT WHICH I PREFER TO THINK OF AS AESTHETIC STATEMENTS. I HAVE, AFTER ALL, KILLED ONLY THE VERY DULL.
IS THAT ALL?
LET ME SHOW YOU SOMETHING, SEBASTIAN. LET ME DEMONSTRATE EXACTLY WHAT IT IS YOU ARE ATTEMPTING TO CONFRONT.
SEE? IT'S DONE: A ROYAL PARDON FOR SEBASTIAN O.
DO YOU BEGIN TO UNDERSTAND NOW, SEBASTIAN? VICTORIA DIED SOME MONTHS AGO AND I HAVE TAKEN HER PLACE. HER IMPERIAL MAJESTY EXISTS SOLELY AS A COMPUTER-GENERATED IMAGE CONTROLLED BY ME.
12

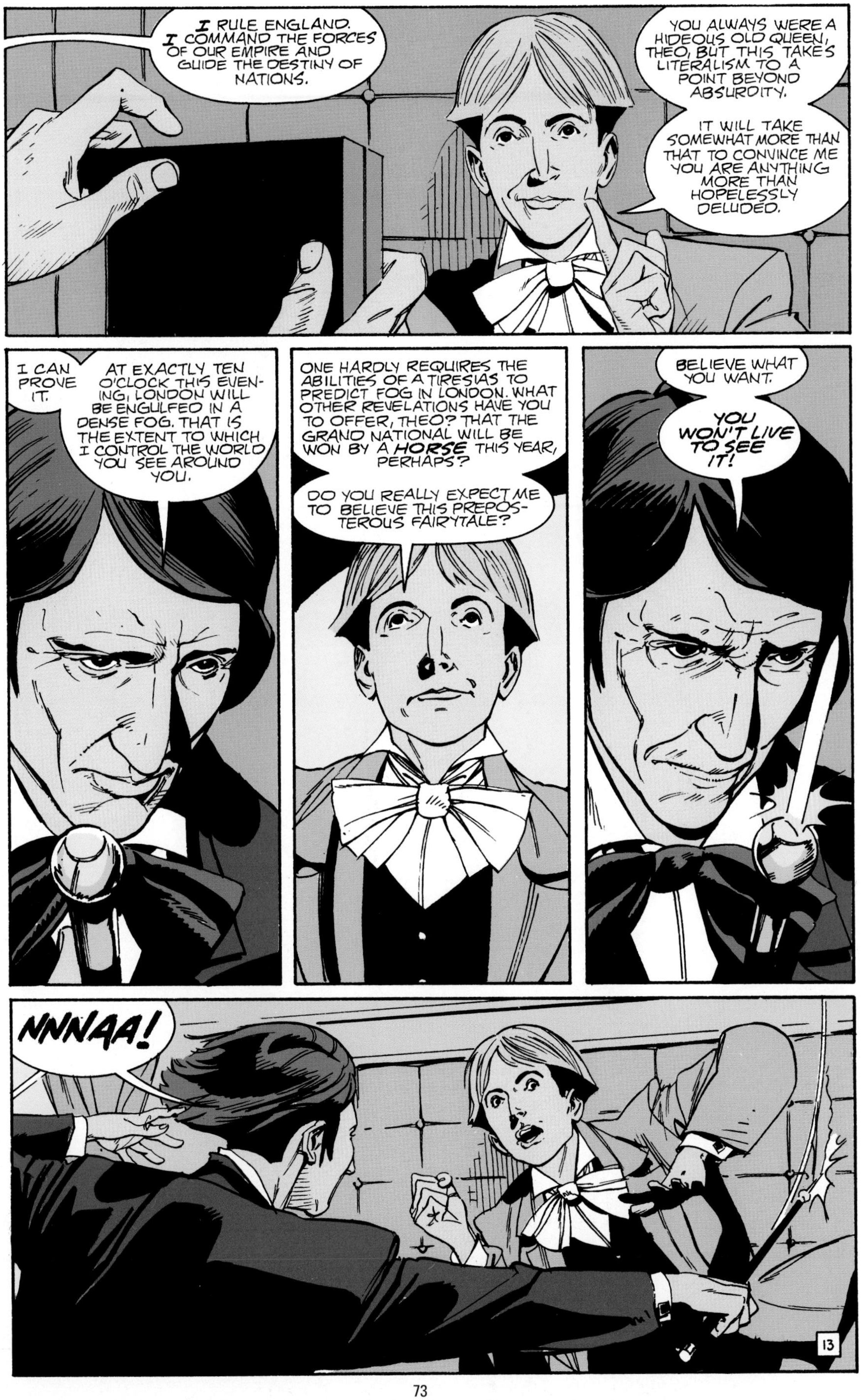
I RULE ENGLAND. I COMMAND THE FORCES OF OUR EMPIRE AND GUIDE THE DESTINY OF NATIONS.
YOU ALWAYS WERE A HIDEOUS OLD QUEEN, THEO, BUT THIS TAKES LITERALISM TO A POINT BEYOND ABSURDITY.
IT WILL TAKE SOMEWHAT MORE THAN THAT TO CONVINCE ME YOU ARE ANYTHING MORE THAN HOPELESSLY DELUDED.
I CAN PROVE IT.
AT EXACTLY TEN O'CLOCK THIS EVENING, LONDON WILL BE ENGULFED IN A DENSE FOG. THAT IS THE EXTENT TO WHICH I CONTROL THE WORLD YOU SEE AROUND YOU.
ONE HARDLY REQUIRES THE ABILITIES OF A TIRESIAS TO PREDICT FOG IN LONDON. WHAT OTHER REVELATIONS HAVE YOU TO OFFER, THEO? THAT THE GRAND NATIONAL WILL BE WON BY A HORSE THIS YEAR, PERHAPS?
DO YOU REALLY EXPECT ME TO BELIEVE THIS PREPOSTEROUS FAIRYTALE?
BELIEVE WHAT YOU WANT.
YOU WON'T LIVE TO SEE IT!
NNNAA!
13

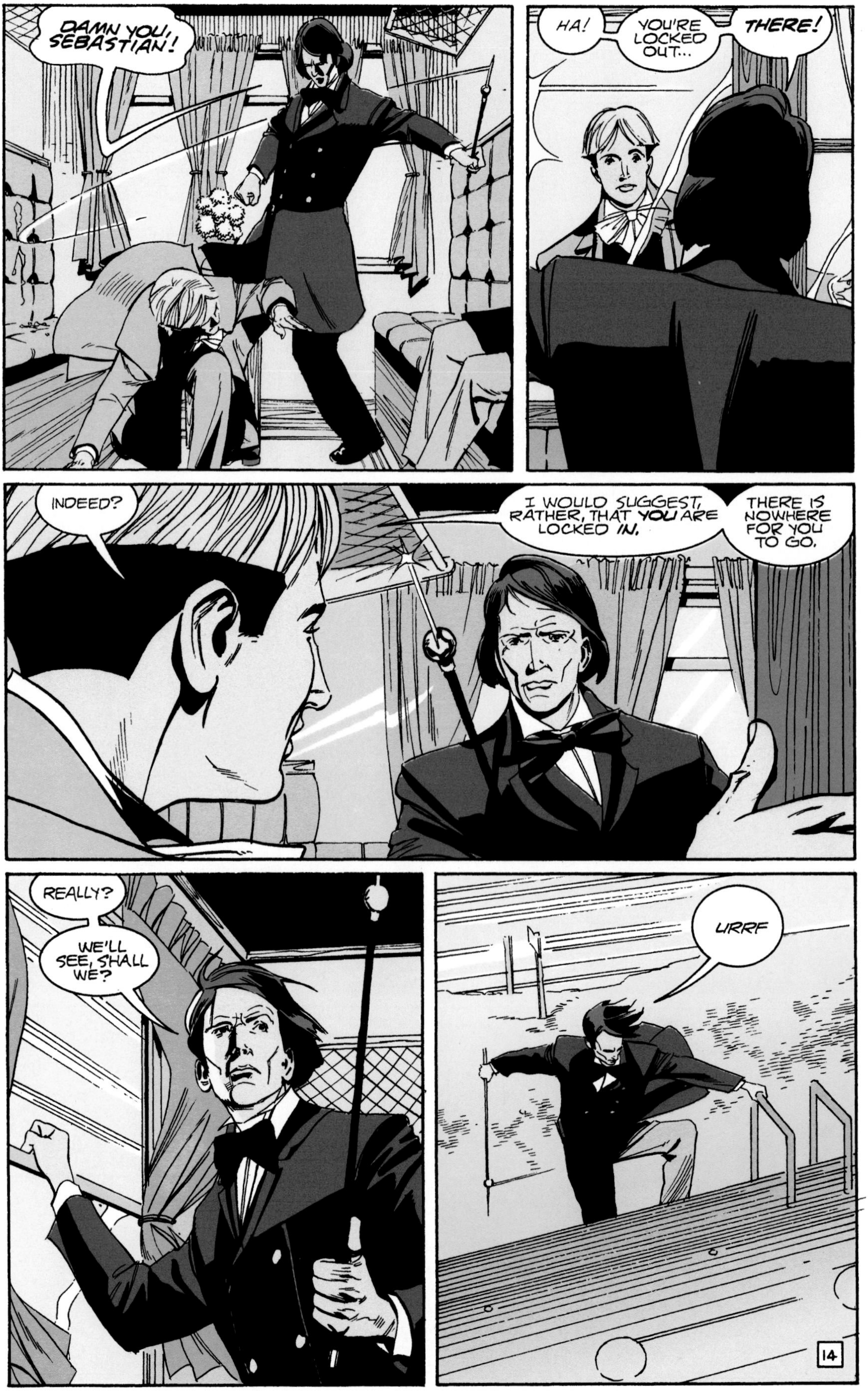
DAMN YOU, SEBASTIAN!
HA!
YOU'RE LOCKED OUT...
THERE!
INDEED?
I WOULD SUGGEST, RATHER, THAT YOU ARE LOCKED IN.
THERE IS NOWHERE FOR YOU TO GO.
REALLY?
WE'LL SEE, SHALL WE?
URRF
14

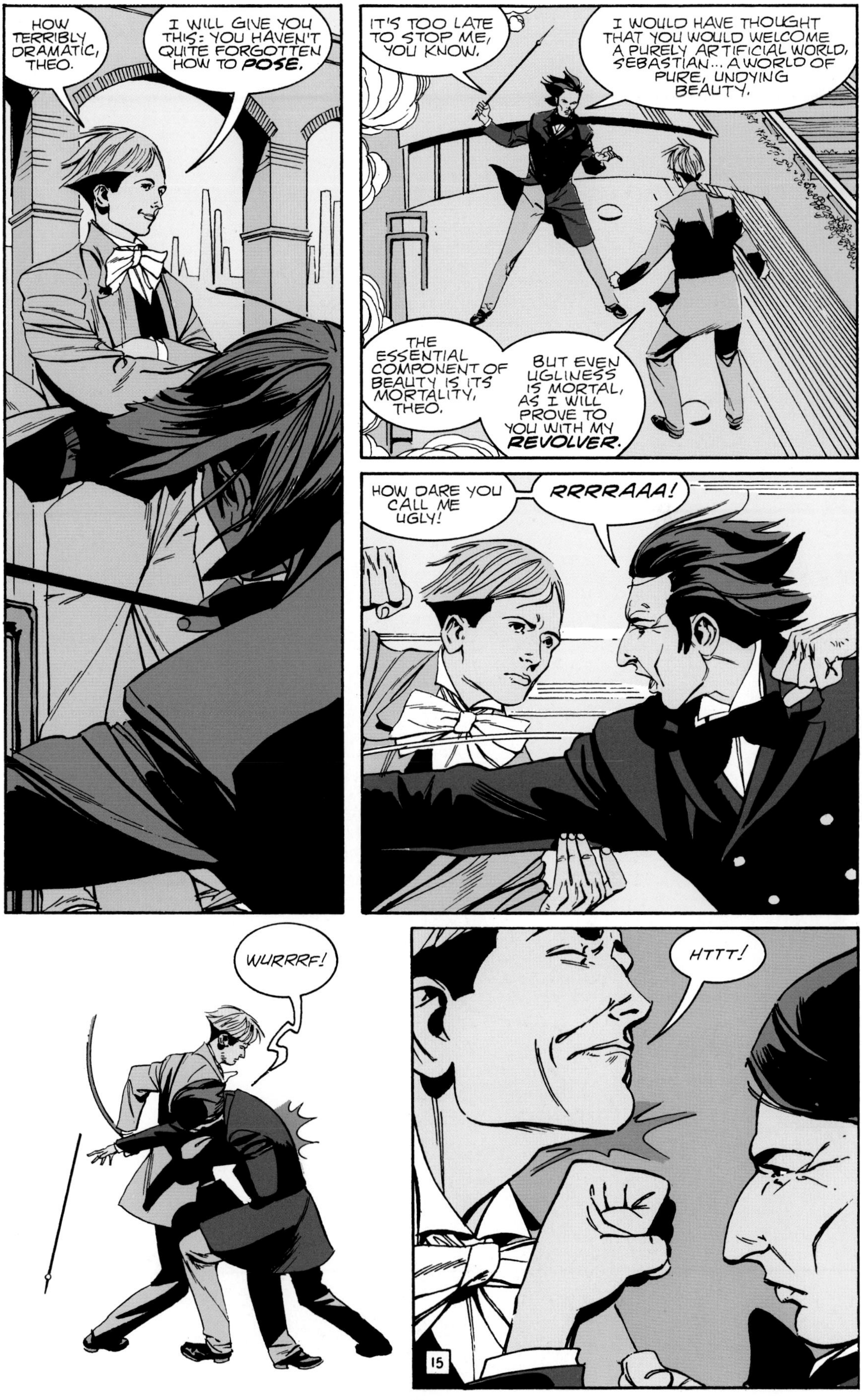
HOW TERRIBLY DRAMATIC, THEO.
I WILL GIVE YOU THIS: YOU HAVEN'T QUITE FORGOTTEN HOW TO POSE.
IT'S TOO LATE TO STOP ME, YOU KNOW.
I WOULD HAVE THOUGHT THAT YOU WOULD WELCOME A PURELY ARTIFICIAL WORLD, SEBASTIAN... A WORLD OF PURE, UNDYING BEAUTY.
THE ESSENTIAL COMPONENT OF BEAUTY IS ITS MORTALITY, THEO.
BUT EVEN UGLINESS IS MORTAL, AS I WILL PROVE TO YOU WITH MY REVOLVER.
HOW DARE YOU CALL ME UGLY!
RRRRAAA!
WURRRF!
HTTT!
15

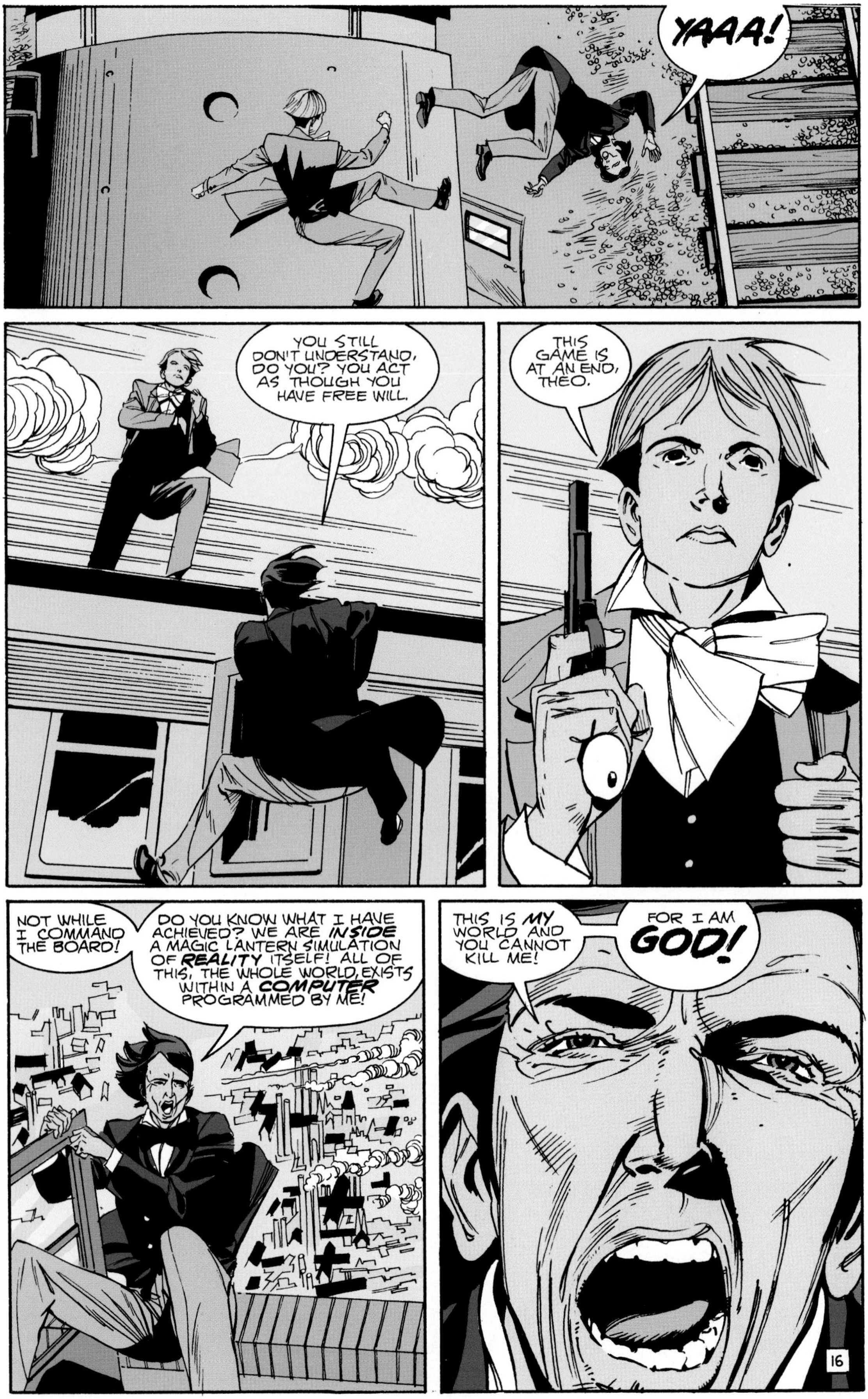
YAAA!
YOU STILL DON'T UNDERSTAND, DO YOU? YOU ACT AS THOUGH YOU HAVE FREE WILL.
THIS GAME IS AT AN END, THEO.
NOT WHILE I COMMAND THE BOARD!
DO YOU KNOW WHAT I HAVE ACHIEVED? WE ARE INSIDE A MAGIC LANTERN SIMULATION OF REALITY ITSELF! ALL OF THIS, THE WHOLE WORLD, EXISTS WITHIN A COMPUTER PROGRAMMED BY ME!
THIS IS MY WORLD AND YOU CANNOT KILL ME!
FOR I AM GOD!
16

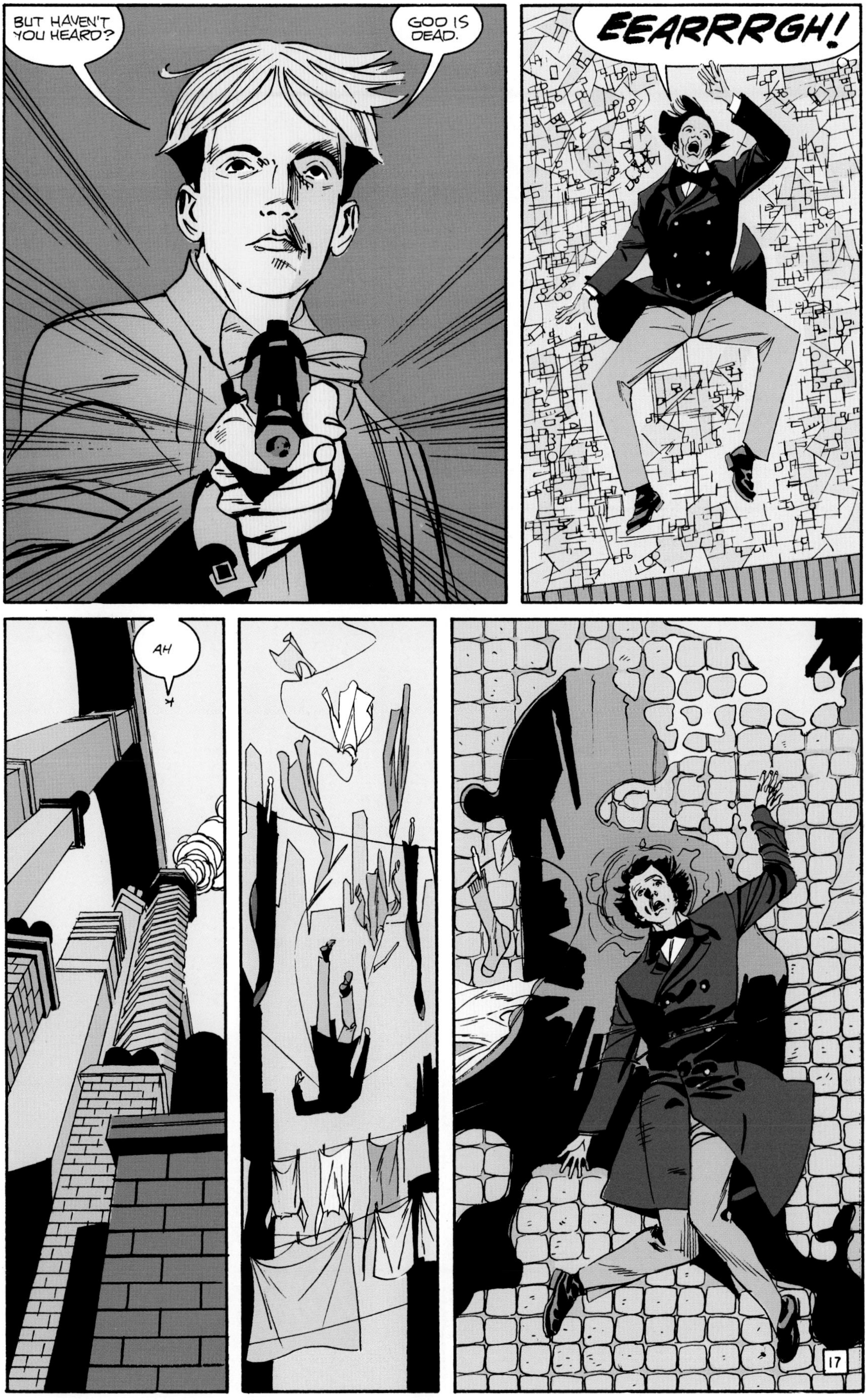

BUT HAVEN'T YOU HEARD?
GOD IS DEAD.
EEARRRGH!
AH
17

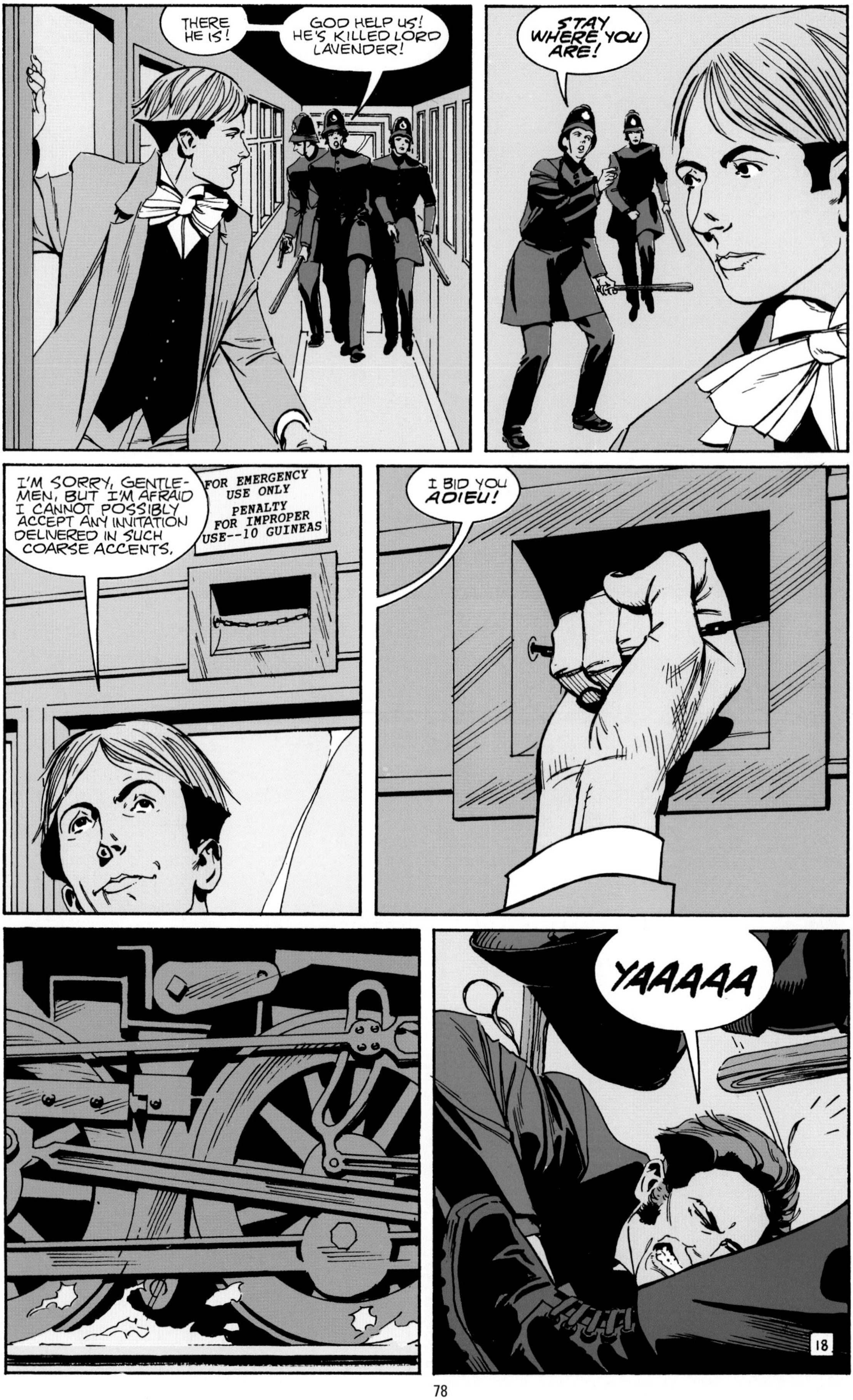
THERE HE IS!
GOD HELP US! HE'S KILLED LORD LAVENDER!
STAY WHERE YOU ARE!
I'M SORRY, GENTLEMEN, BUT I'M AFRAID I CANNOT POSSIBLY ACCEPT ANY INVITATION DELIVERED IN SUCH COARSE ACCENTS.
FOR EMERGENCY USE ONLY
PENALTY FOR IMPROPER USE--10 GUINEAS
I BID YOU ADIEU!
YAAAAA
18

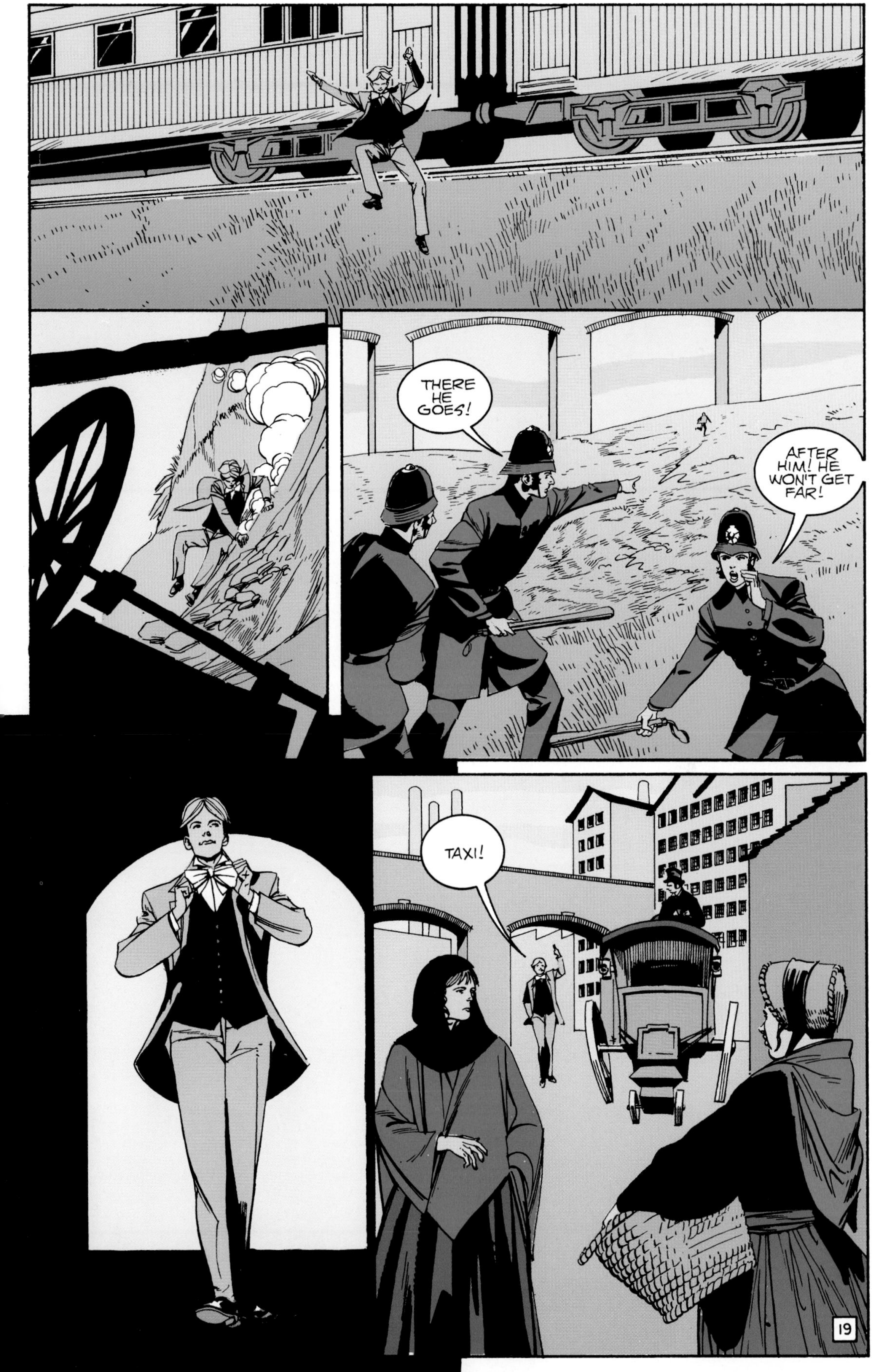
THERE HE GOES!
AFTER HIM! HE WON'T GET FAR!
TAXI!

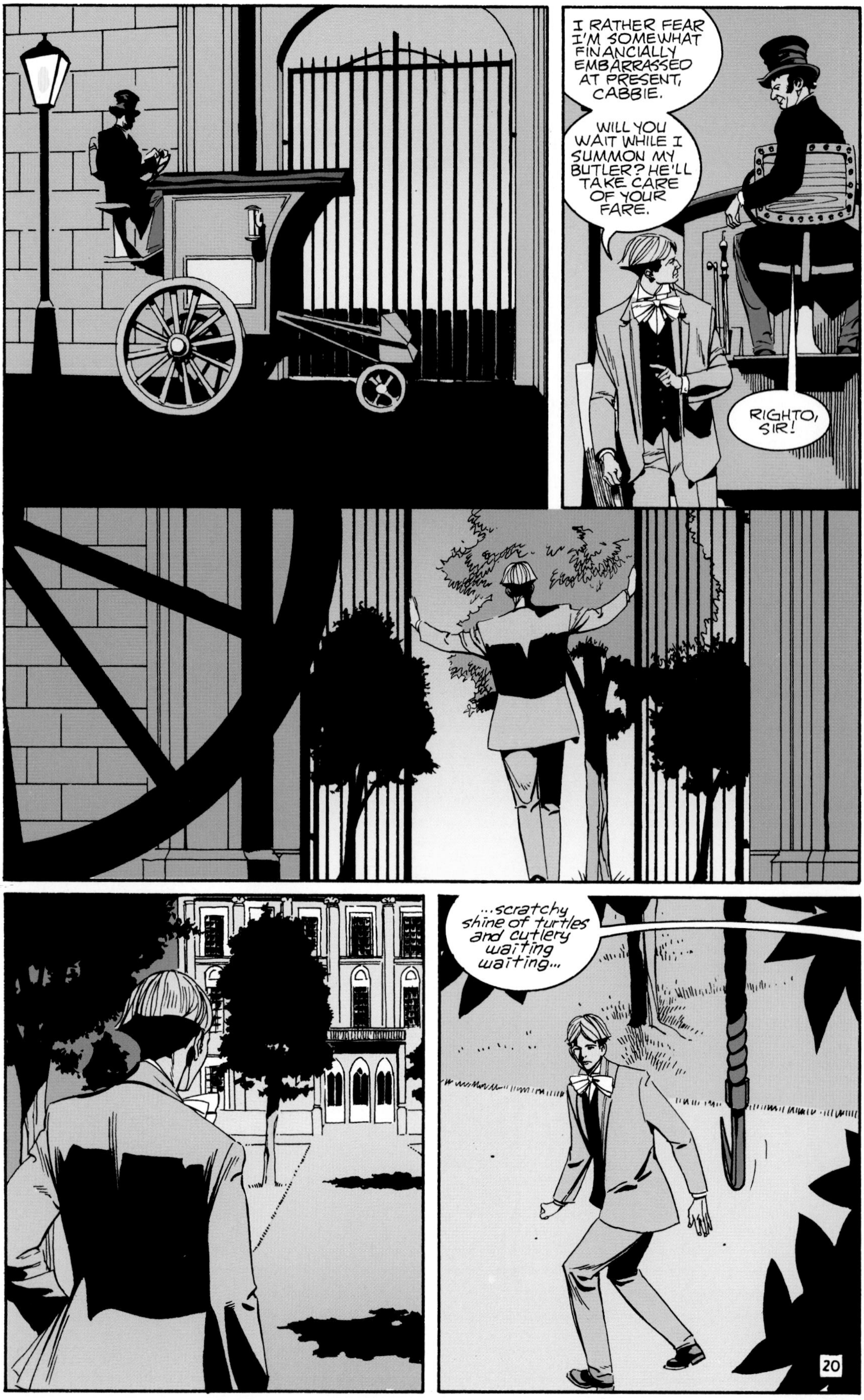
I RATHER FEAR I'M SOMEWHAT FINANCIALLY EMBARRASSED AT PRESENT, CABBIE.
WILL YOU WAIT WHILE I SUMMON MY BUTLER? HE'LL TAKE CARE OF YOUR FARE.
RIGHTO, SIR!
...scratchy shine of turtles and cutlery waiting waiting...
20

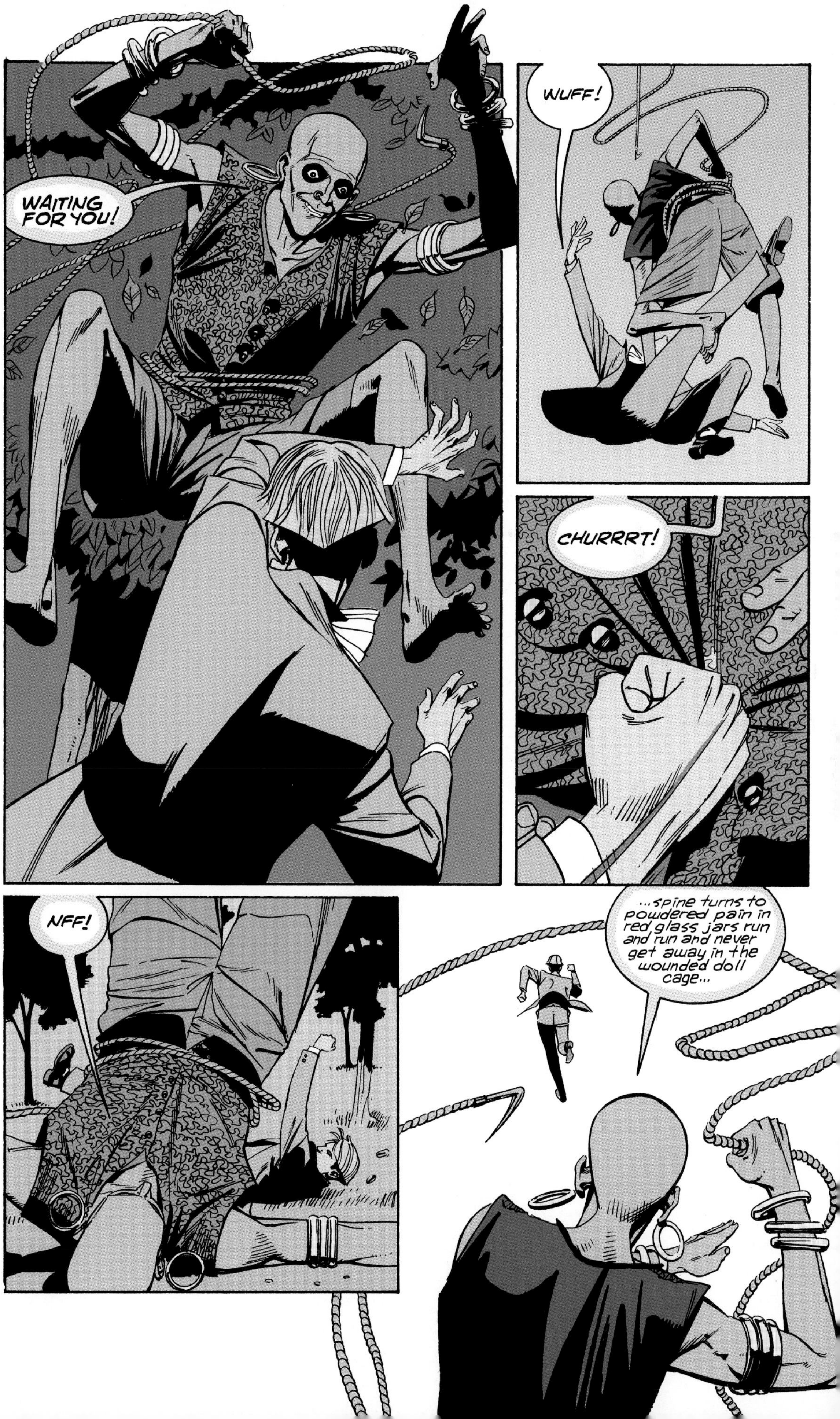
WAITING FOR YOU!
WUFF!
CHURRRT!
NFF!
...spine turns to powdered pain in red glass jars run and run and never get away in the wounded doll cage...

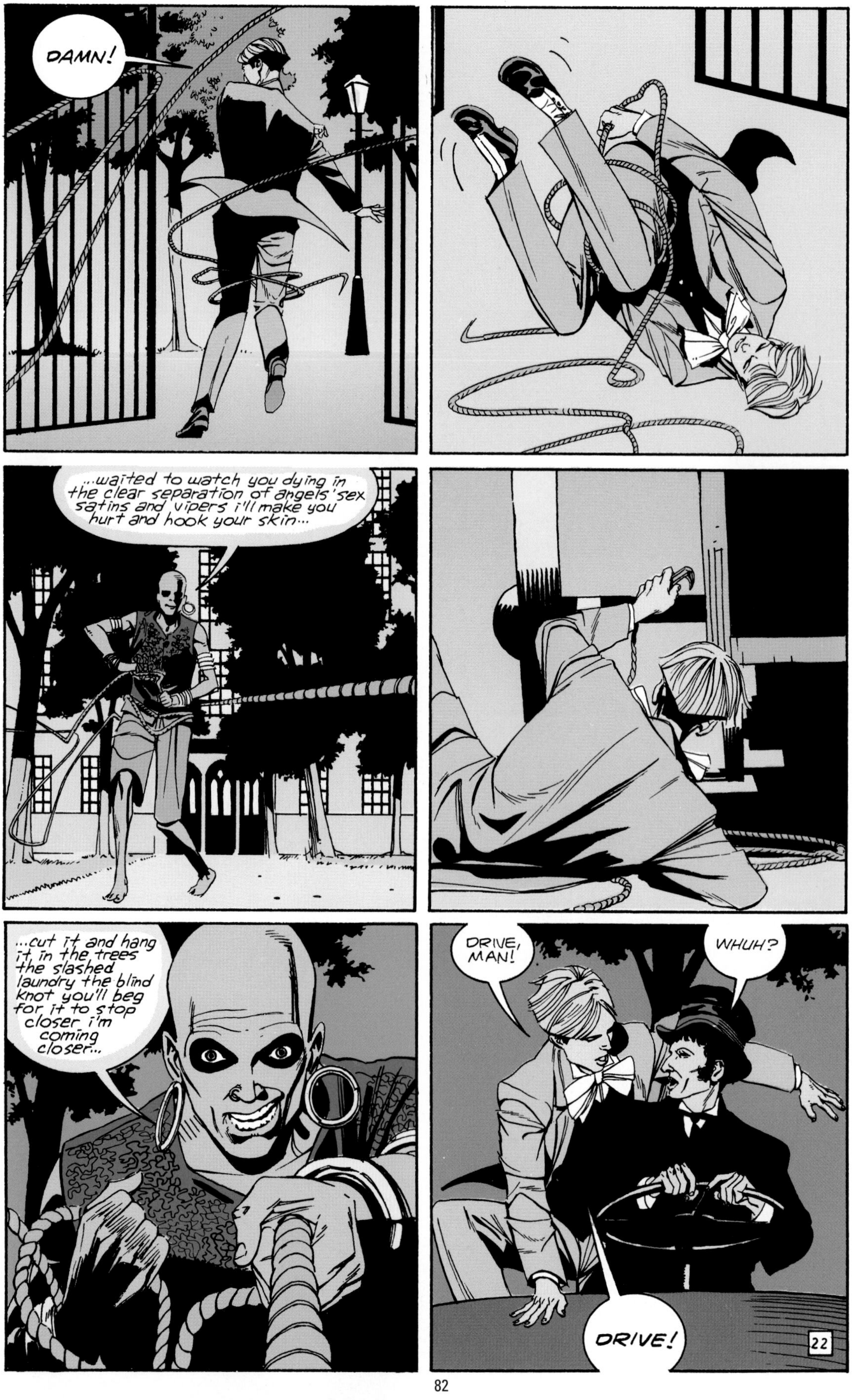
DAMN!
...waited to watch you dying in the clear separation of angels' sex satins and vipers i'll make you hurt and hook your skin...
...cut it and hang it in the trees the slashed laundry the blind knot you'll beg for it to stop closer i'm coming closer...
DRIVE, MAN!
WHUH?
DRIVE!
22

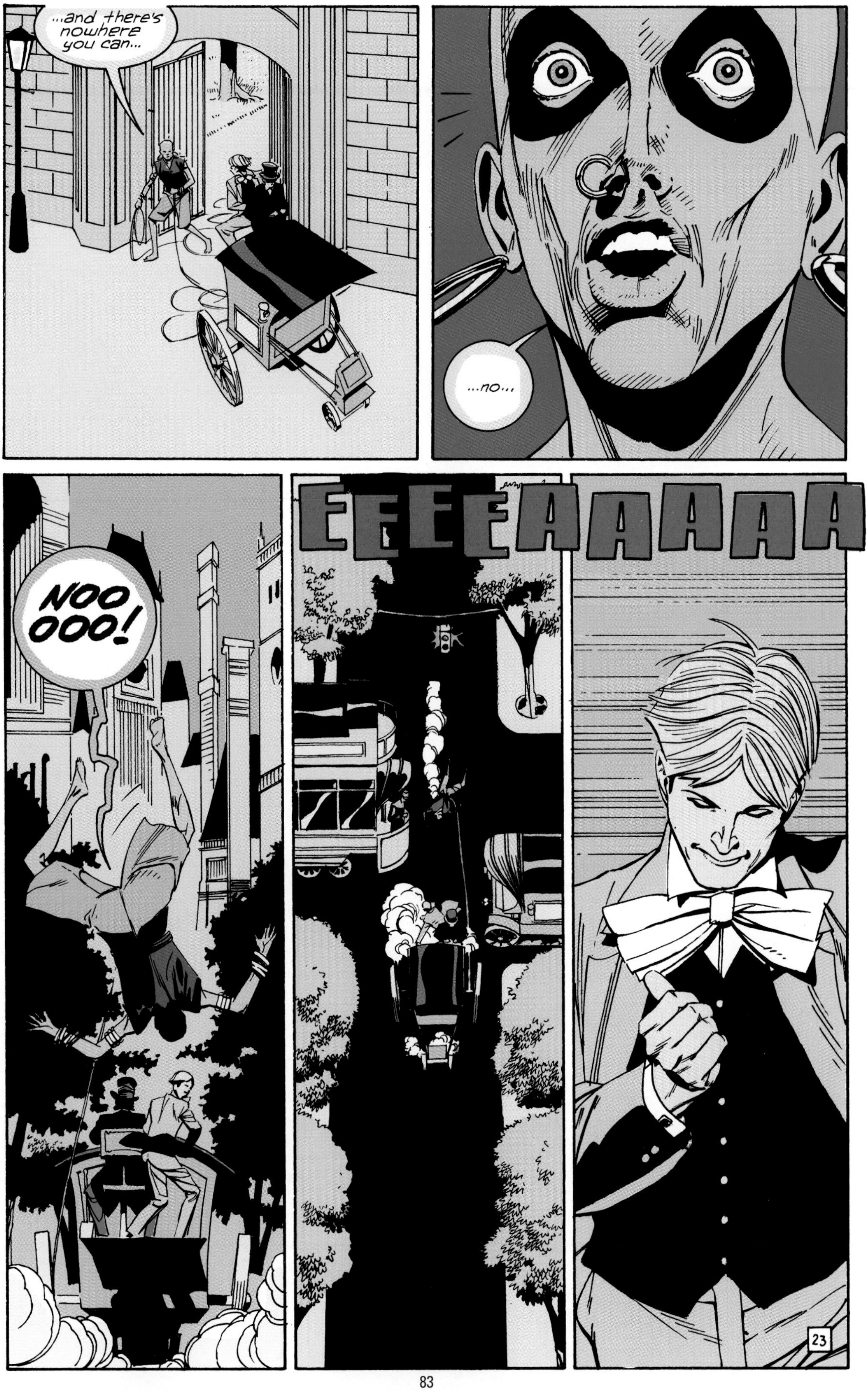
...and there's nowhere you can...
...no...
NOO OOO!
EEEAAAAAA
23

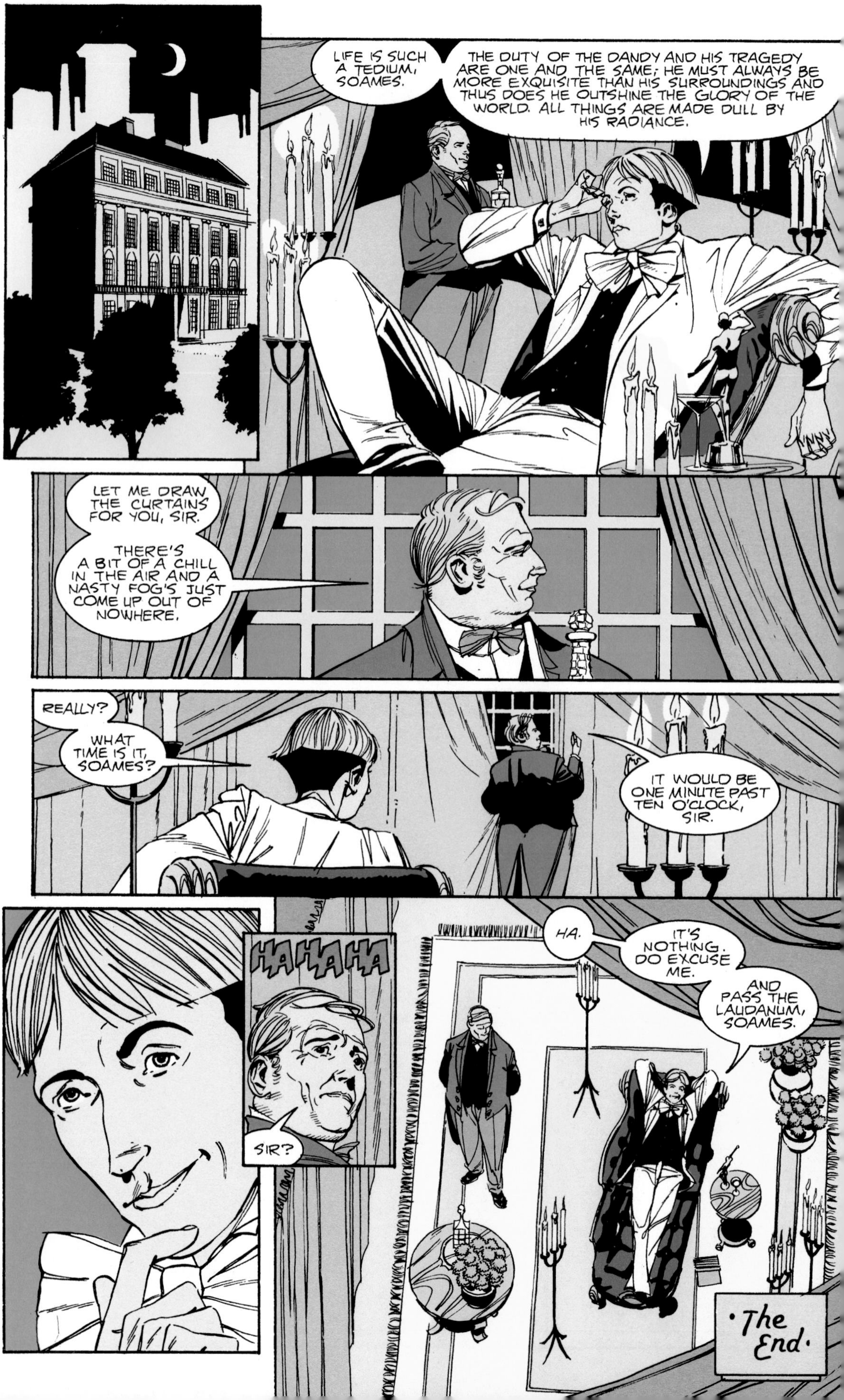
LIFE IS SUCH A TEDIUM, SOAMES.
THE DUTY OF THE DANDY AND HIS TRAGEDY ARE ONE AND THE SAME; HE MUST ALWAYS BE MORE EXQUISITE THAN HIS SURROUNDINGS AND THUS DOES HE OUTSHINE THE GLORY OF THE WORLD. ALL THINGS ARE MADE DULL BY HIS RADIANCE.
LET ME DRAW THE CURTAINS FOR YOU, SIR.
THERE'S A BIT OF A CHILL IN THE AIR AND A NASTY FOG'S JUST COME UP OUT OF NOWHERE.
REALLY?
WHAT TIME IS IT, SOAMES?
IT WOULD BE ONE MINUTE PAST TEN O'CLOCK, SIR.
HAHAHA
SIR?
HA.
IT'S NOTHING. DO EXCUSE ME.
AND PASS THE LAUDANUM, SOAMES.
·The End·

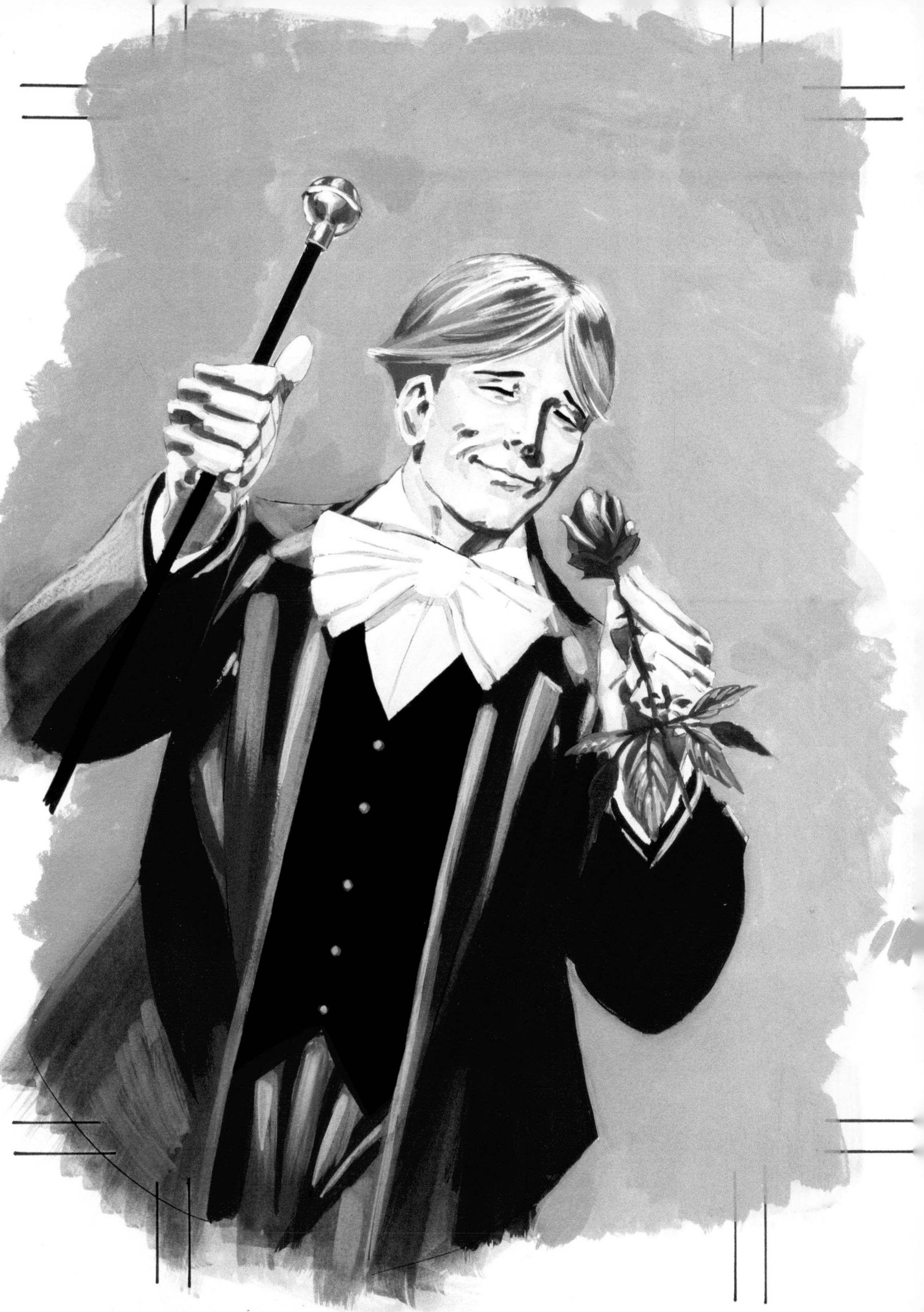

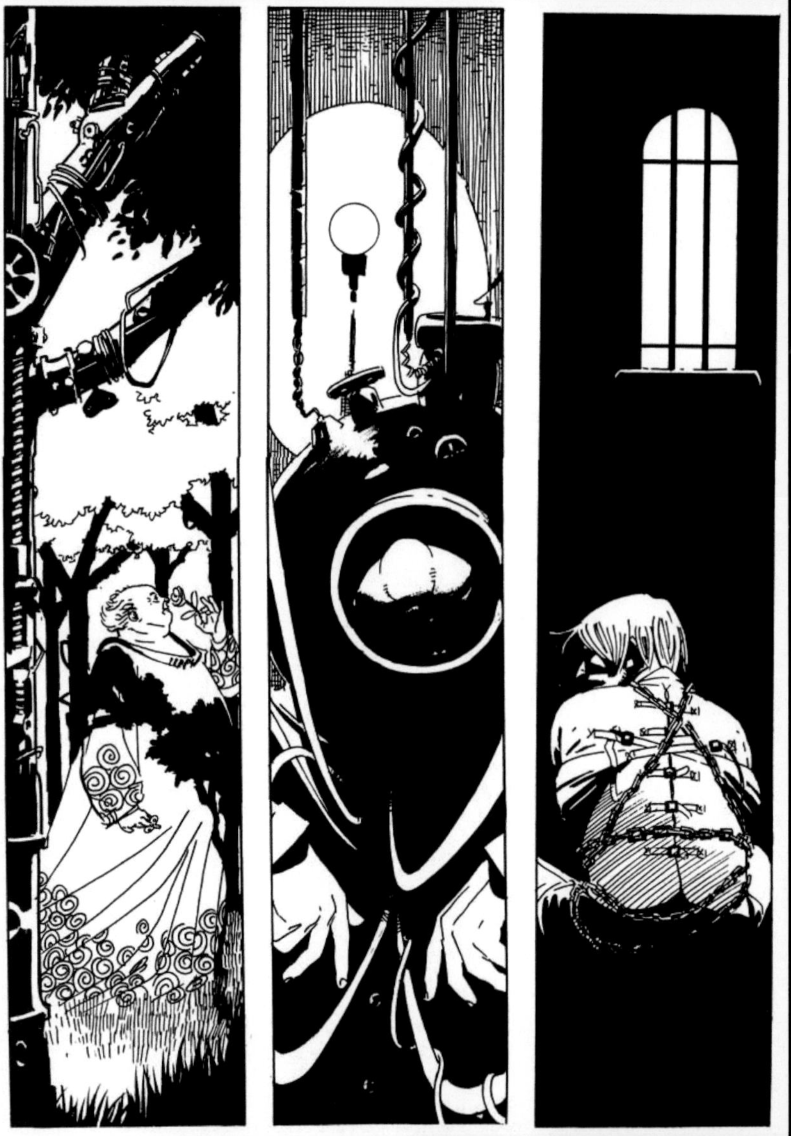

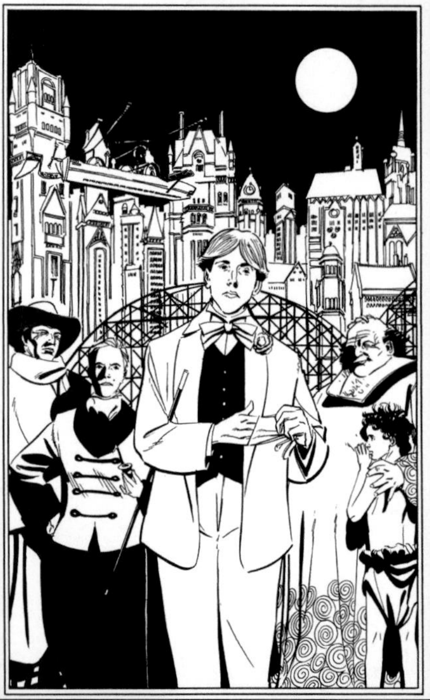

Promotional art for the series by Steve Ye

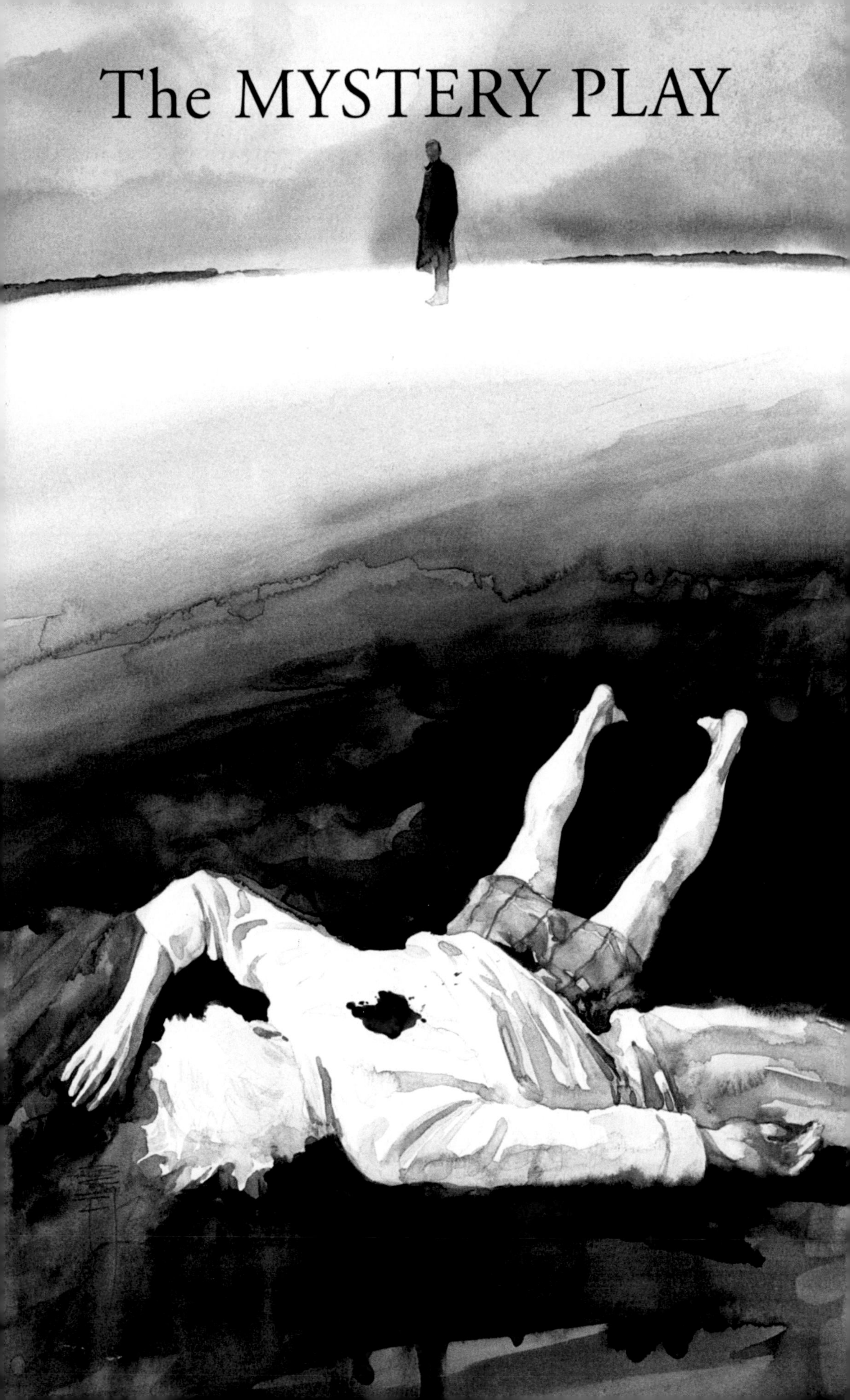
The MYSTERY PLAY

THE MYSTERY PLAY

A Graphic Novel

Written by
GRANT MORRISON

Illustrated by
JON J MUTH

Lettered by
TODD KLEIN

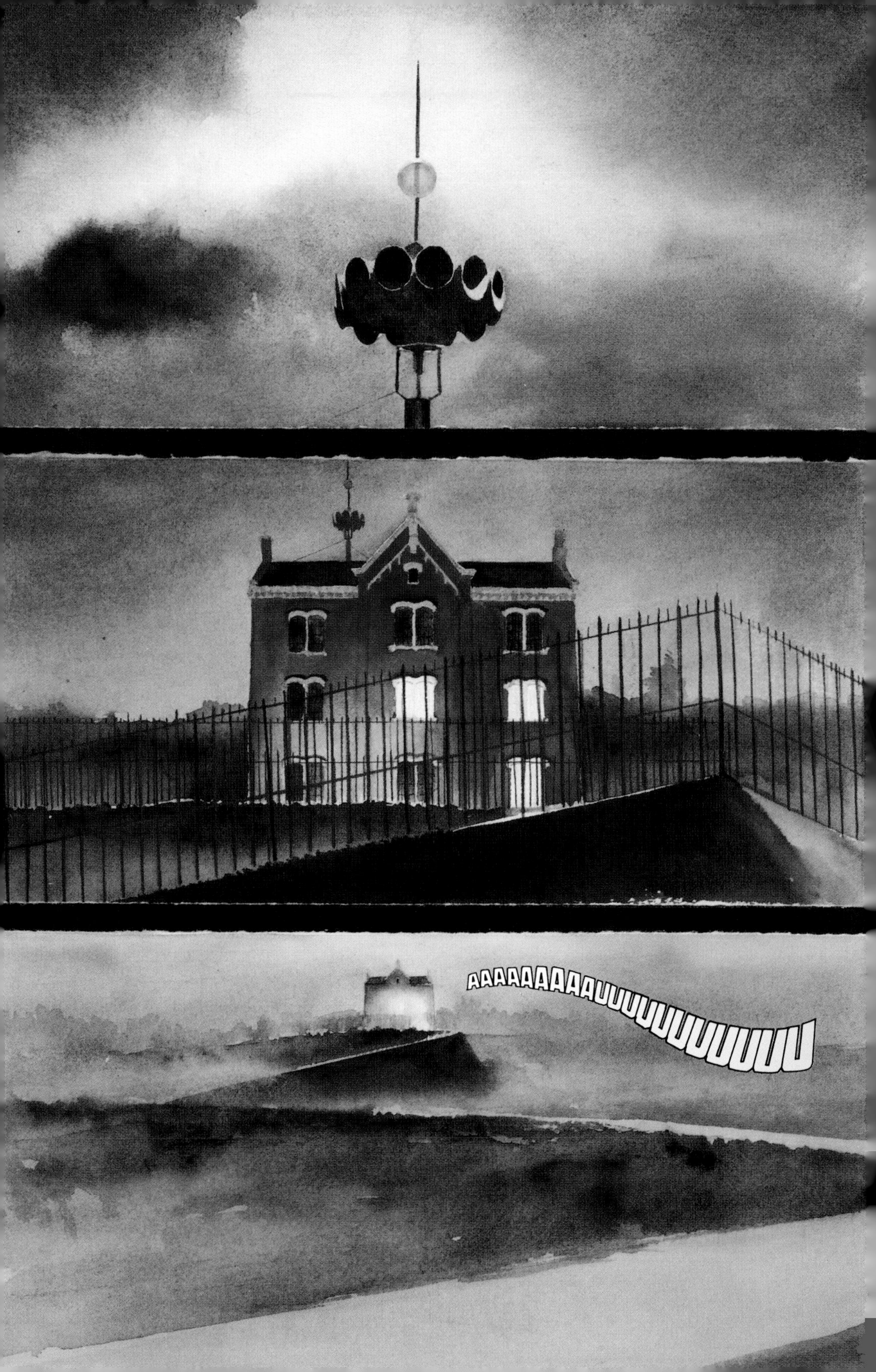
AAAAAAAAAUUUUUUUUUUU

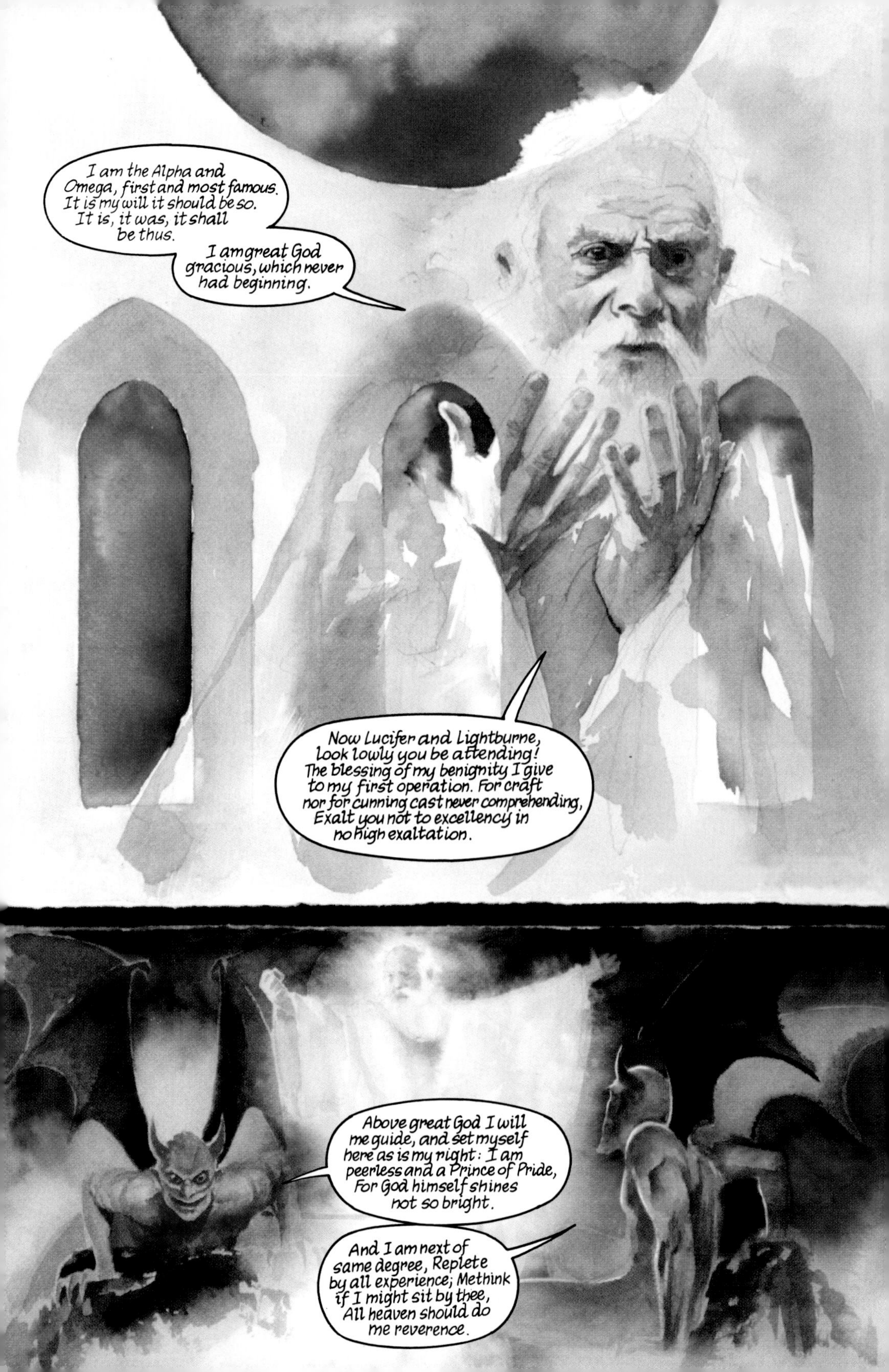

I am the Alpha and Omega, first and most famous. It is my will it should be so. It is, it was, it shall be thus.
I am great God gracious, which never had beginning.
Now Lucifer and Lightburne, look lowly you be attending! The blessing of my benignity I give to my first operation. For craft nor for cunning cast never comprehending, Exalt you not to excellency in no high exaltation.
Above great God I will me guide, and set myself here as is my right: I am peerless and a Prince of Pride, For God himself shines not so bright.
And I am next of same degree, Replete by all experience; Methink if I might sit by thee, All heaven should do me reverence.

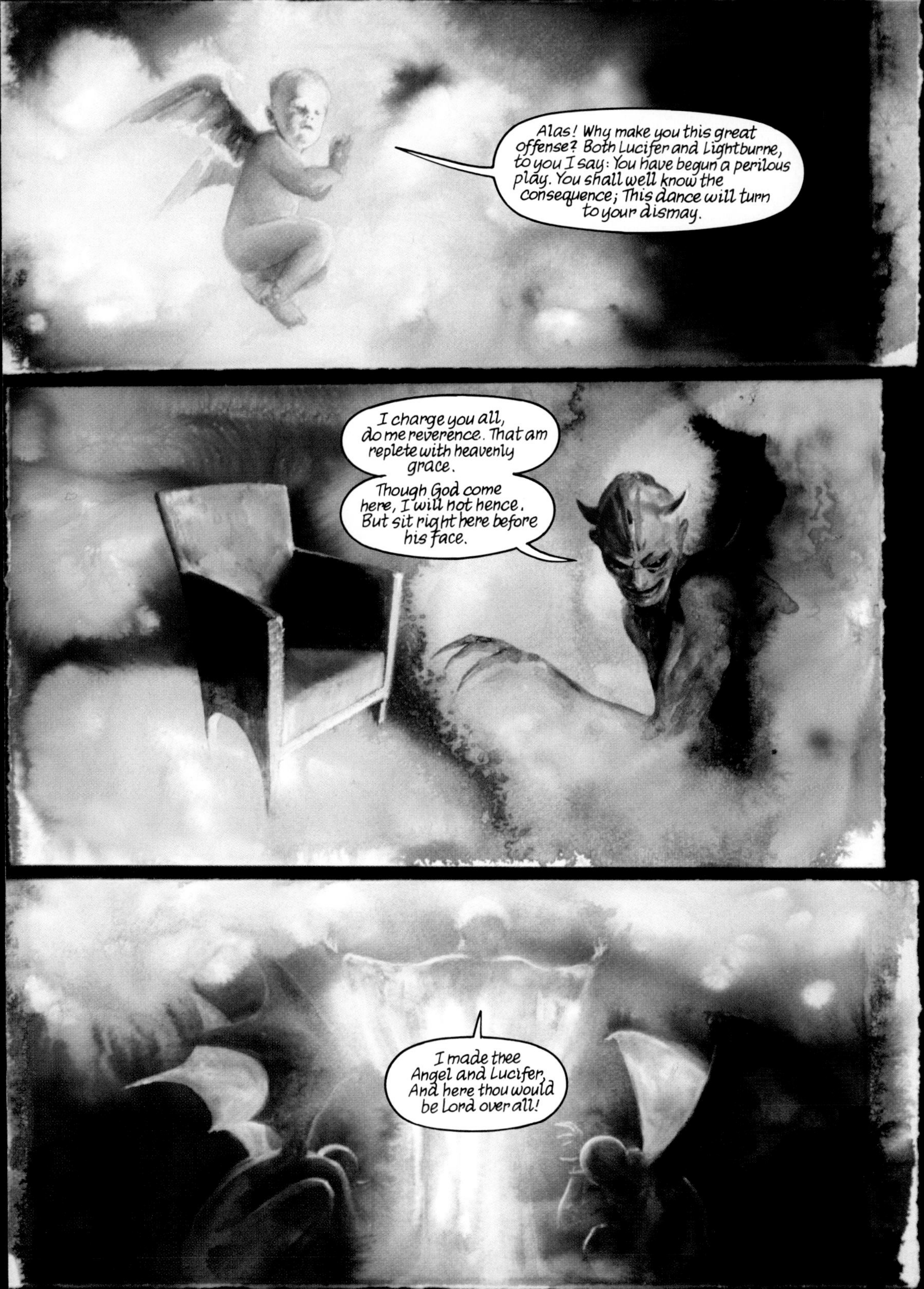

Alas! Why make you this great offense? Both Lucifer and Lightburne, to you I say: You have begun a perilous play. You shall well know the consequence; This dance will turn to your dismay.
I charge you all, do me reverence. That am replete with heavenly grace.
Though God come here, I will not hence. But sit right here before his face.
I made thee Angel and Lucifer, And here thou would be Lord over all!

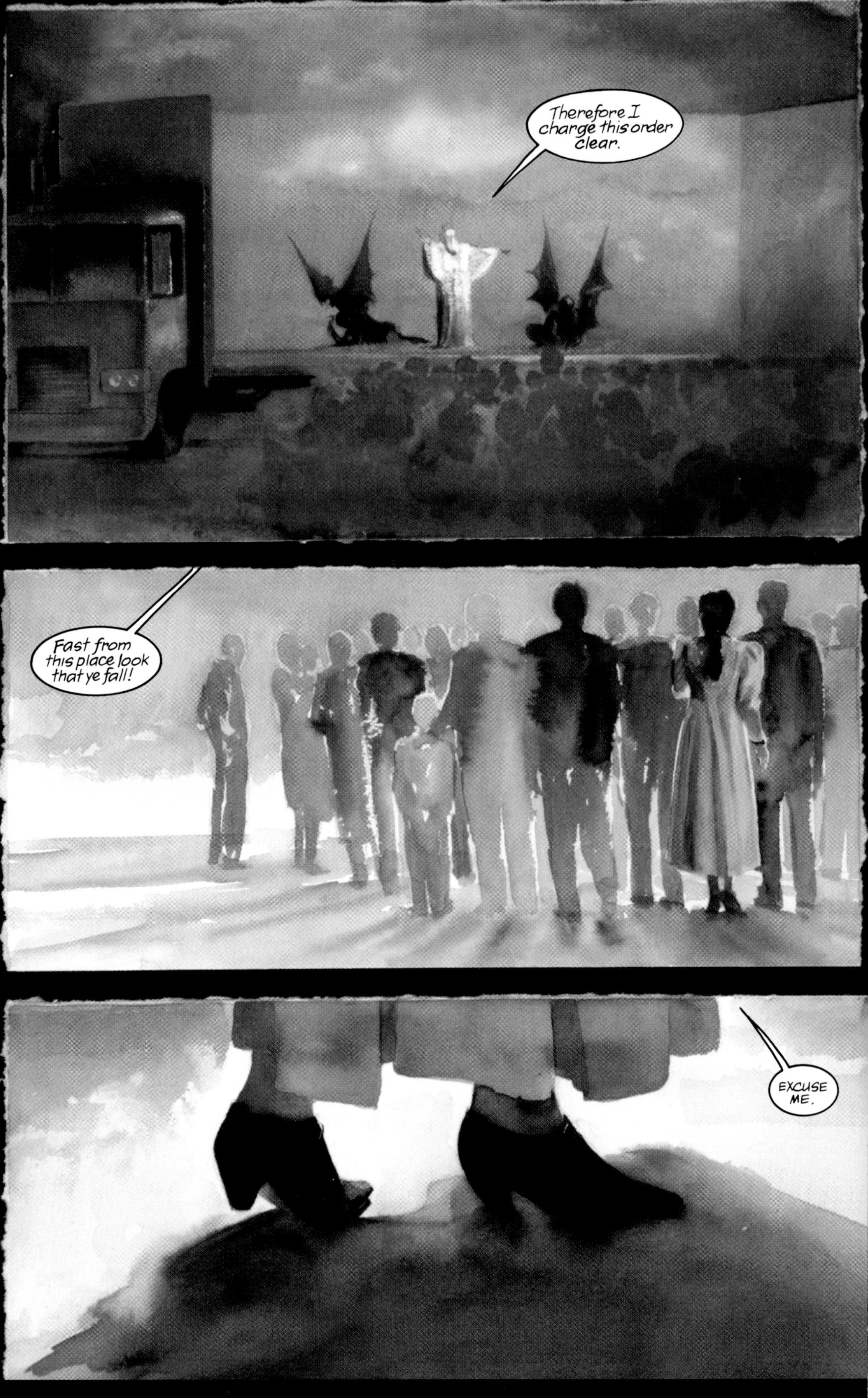
Therefore I charge this order clear.
Fast from this place look that ye fall!
EXCUSE ME.

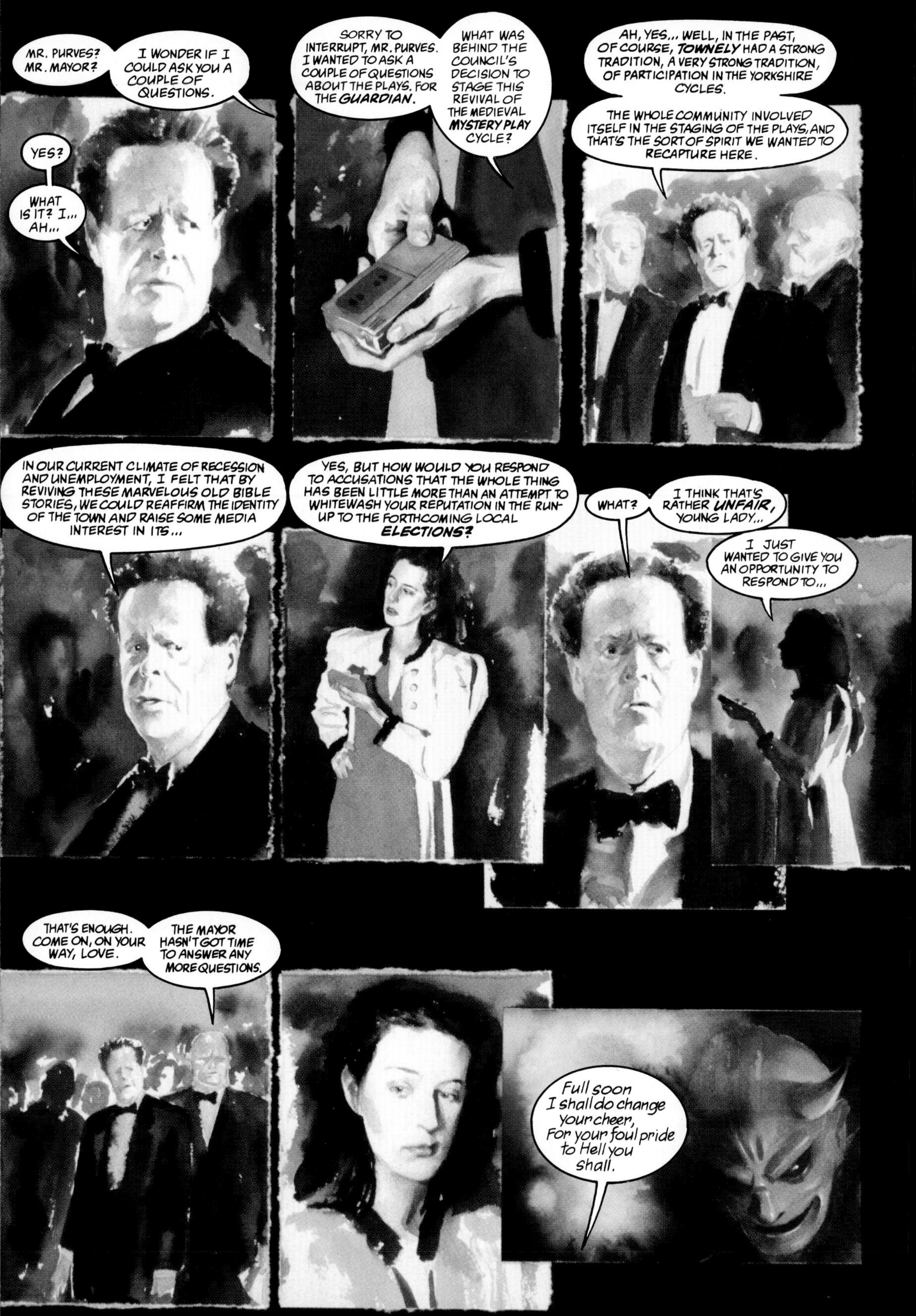
MR. PURVES? MR. MAYOR?
I WONDER IF I COULD ASK YOU A COUPLE OF QUESTIONS.
YES?
WHAT IS IT? I... AH...
SORRY TO INTERRUPT, MR. PURVES. I WANTED TO ASK A COUPLE OF QUESTIONS ABOUT THE PLAYS. FOR THE GUARDIAN.
WHAT WAS BEHIND THE COUNCIL'S DECISION TO STAGE THIS REVIVAL OF THE MEDIEVAL MYSTERY PLAY CYCLE?
AH, YES... WELL, IN THE PAST, OF COURSE, TOWNELY HAD A STRONG TRADITION, A VERY STRONG TRADITION, OF PARTICIPATION IN THE YORKSHIRE CYCLES.
THE WHOLE COMMUNITY INVOLVED ITSELF IN THE STAGING OF THE PLAYS, AND THAT'S THE SORT OF SPIRIT WE WANTED TO RECAPTURE HERE.
IN OUR CURRENT CLIMATE OF RECESSION AND UNEMPLOYMENT, I FELT THAT BY REVIVING THESE MARVELOUS OLD BIBLE STORIES, WE COULD REAFFIRM THE IDENTITY OF THE TOWN AND RAISE SOME MEDIA INTEREST IN ITS...
YES, BUT HOW WOULD YOU RESPOND TO ACCUSATIONS THAT THE WHOLE THING HAS BEEN LITTLE MORE THAN AN ATTEMPT TO WHITEWASH YOUR REPUTATION IN THE RUN-UP TO THE FORTHCOMING LOCAL ELECTIONS?
WHAT?
I THINK THAT'S RATHER UNFAIR, YOUNG LADY...
I JUST WANTED TO GIVE YOU AN OPPORTUNITY TO RESPOND TO...
THAT'S ENOUGH. COME ON, ON YOUR WAY, LOVE.
THE MAYOR HASN'T GOT TIME TO ANSWER ANY MORE QUESTIONS.
Full soon I shall do change your cheer, For your foul pride to Hell you shall.

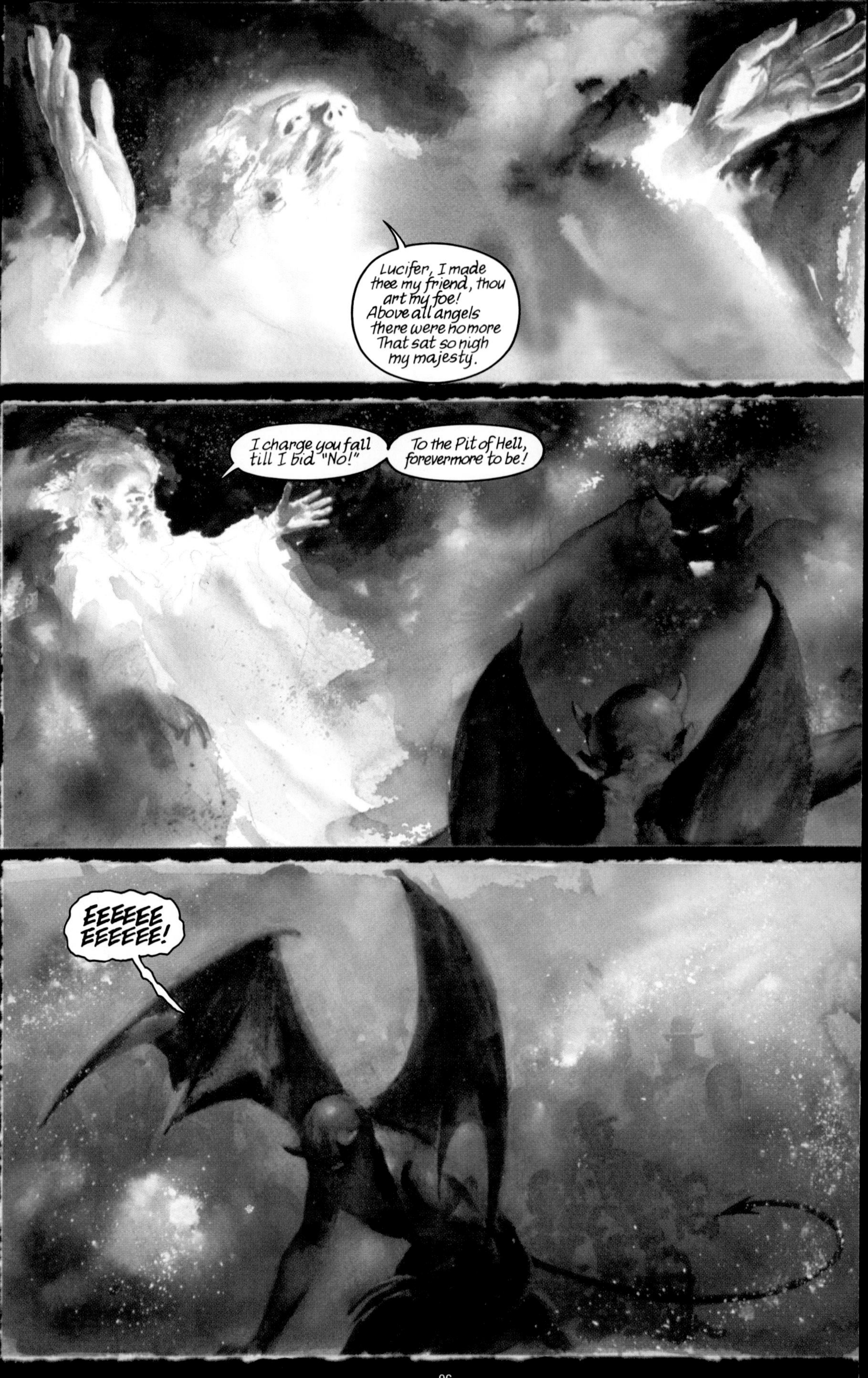
Lucifer, I made thee my friend, thou art my foe! Above all angels there were no more That sat so nigh my majesty.
I charge you fall till I bid "No!"
To the Pit of Hell, forevermore to be!
EEEEEE EEEEEE!

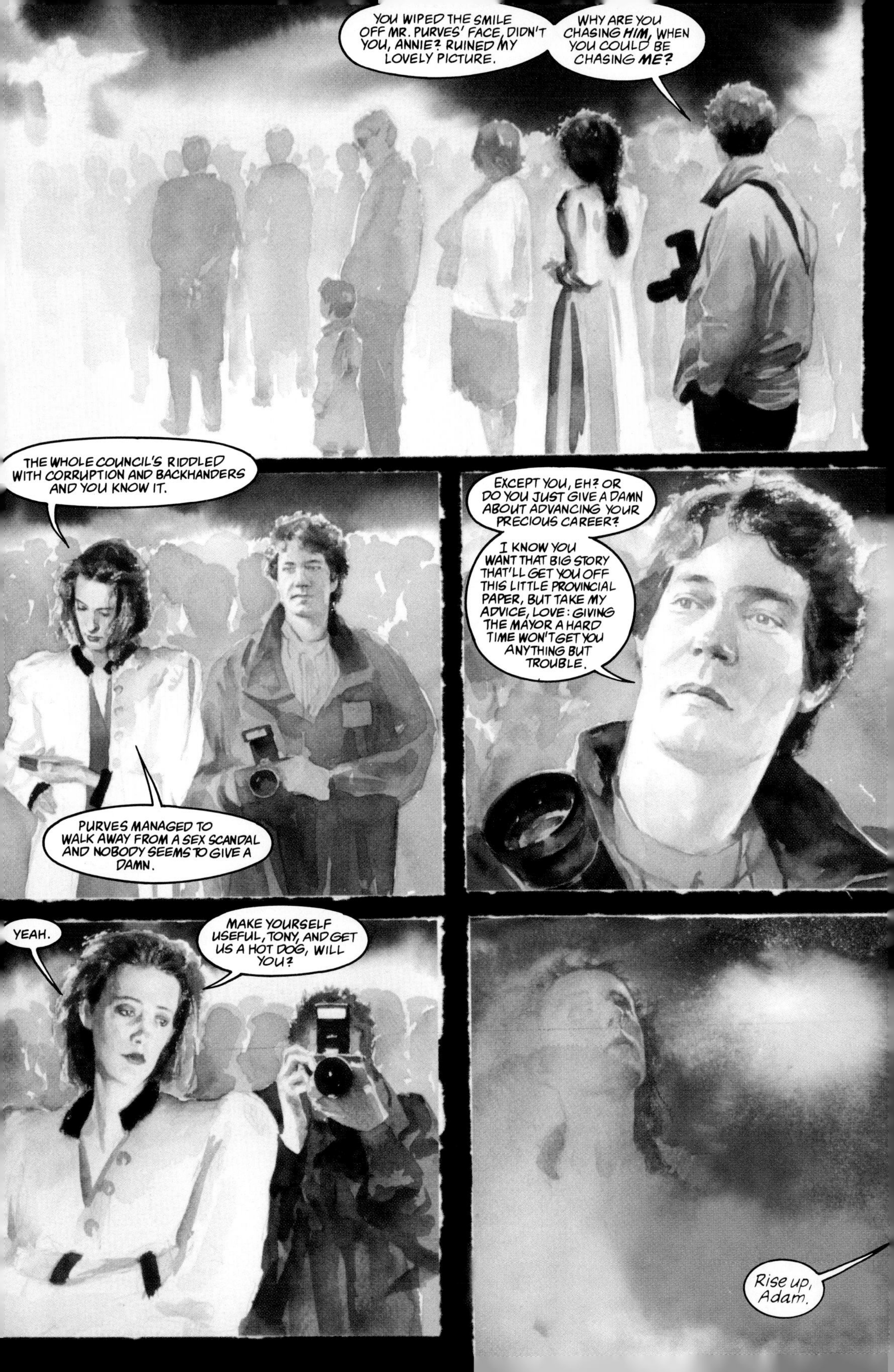
YOU WIPED THE SMILE OFF MR. PURVES' FACE, DIDN'T YOU, ANNIE? RUINED MY LOVELY PICTURE.
WHY ARE YOU CHASING HIM, WHEN YOU COULD BE CHASING ME?
THE WHOLE COUNCIL'S RIDDLED WITH CORRUPTION AND BACKHANDERS AND YOU KNOW IT.
PURVES MANAGED TO WALK AWAY FROM A SEX SCANDAL AND NOBODY SEEMS TO GIVE A DAMN.
EXCEPT YOU, EH? OR DO YOU JUST GIVE A DAMN ABOUT ADVANCING YOUR PRECIOUS CAREER?
I KNOW YOU WANT THAT BIG STORY THAT'LL GET YOU OFF THIS LITTLE PROVINCIAL PAPER, BUT TAKE MY ADVICE, LOVE: GIVING THE MAYOR A HARD TIME WON'T GET YOU ANYTHING BUT TROUBLE.
YEAH.
MAKE YOURSELF USEFUL, TONY, AND GET US A HOT DOG, WILL YOU?
Rise up, Adam.

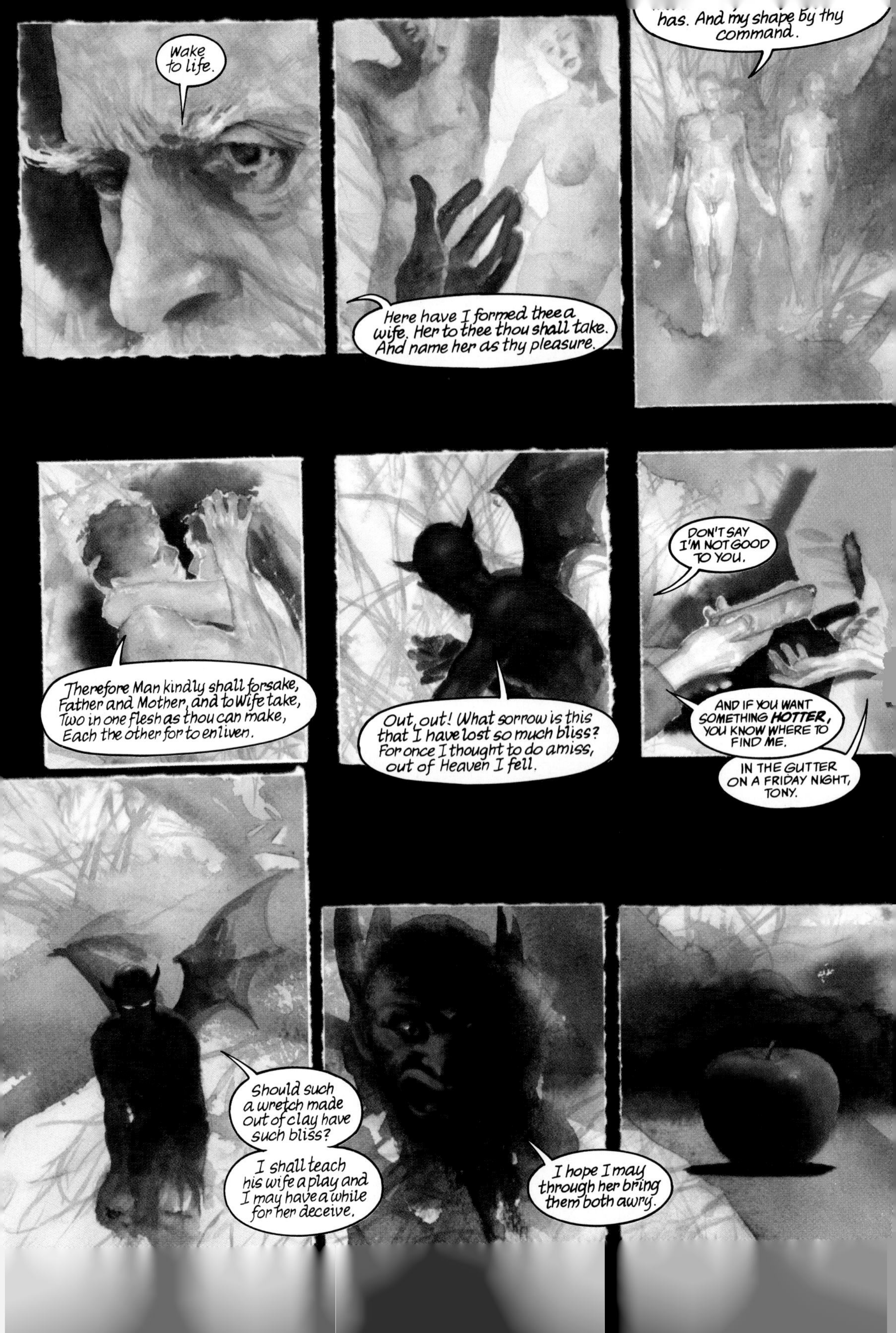

Wake to life.
Here have I formed thee a wife. Her to thee thou shall take. And name her as thy pleasure.
has. And my shape by thy command.
Therefore Man kindly shall forsake, Father and Mother, and to Wife take, Two in one flesh as thou can make, Each the other for to enliven.
Out, out! What sorrow is this that I have lost so much bliss? For once I thought to do amiss, out of Heaven I fell.
DON'T SAY I'M NOT GOOD TO YOU.
AND IF YOU WANT SOMETHING HOTTER, YOU KNOW WHERE TO FIND ME.
IN THE GUTTER ON A FRIDAY NIGHT, TONY.
Should such a wretch made out of clay have such bliss?
I shall teach his wife a play and I may have a while for her deceive.
I hope I may through her bring them both awry.

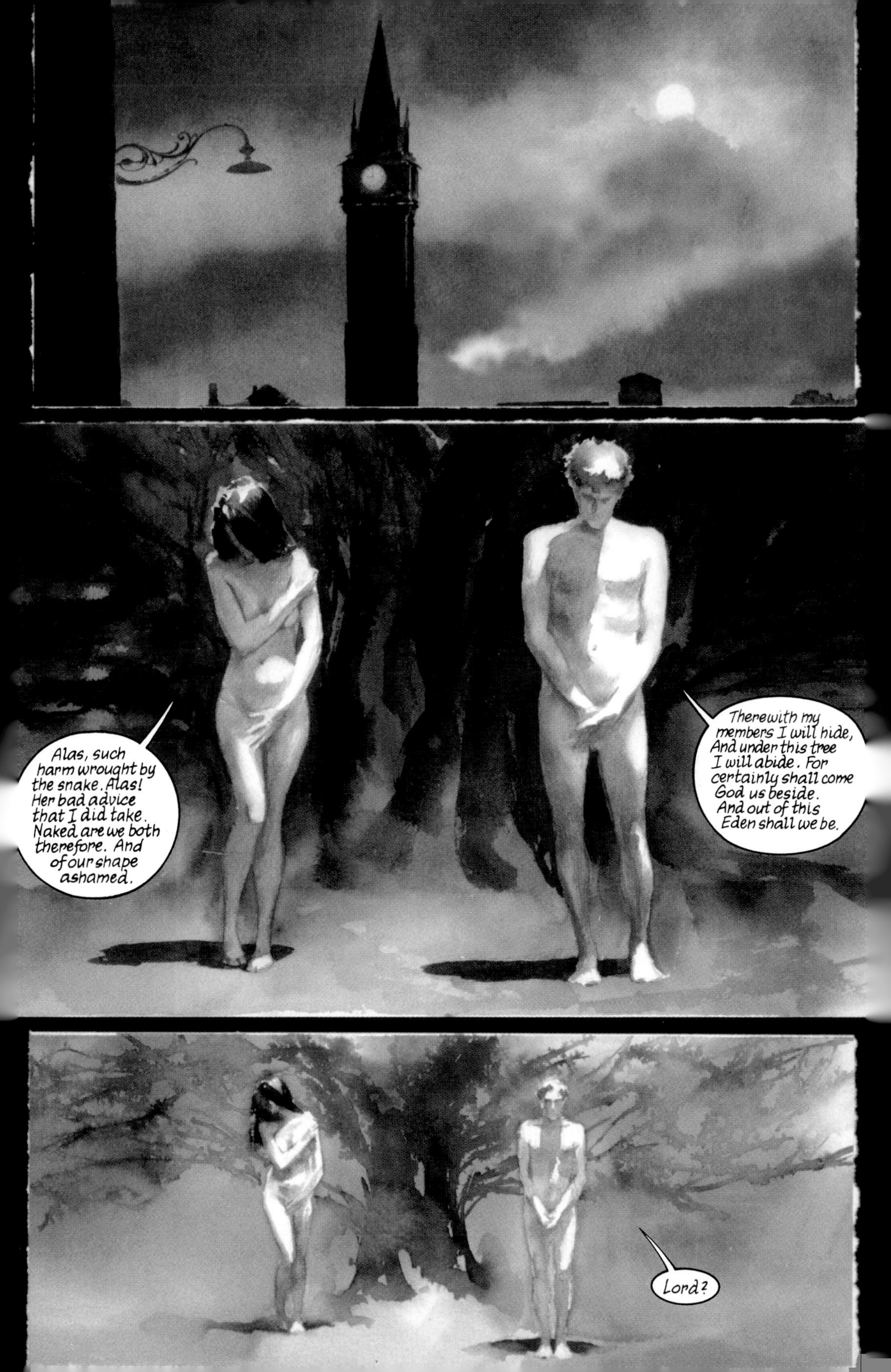
Alas, such harm wrought by the snake. Alas! Her bad advice that I did take. Naked are we both therefore. And of our shape ashamed.
Therewith my members I will hide, And under this tree I will abide. For certainly shall come God us beside. And out of this Eden shall we be.
Lord?

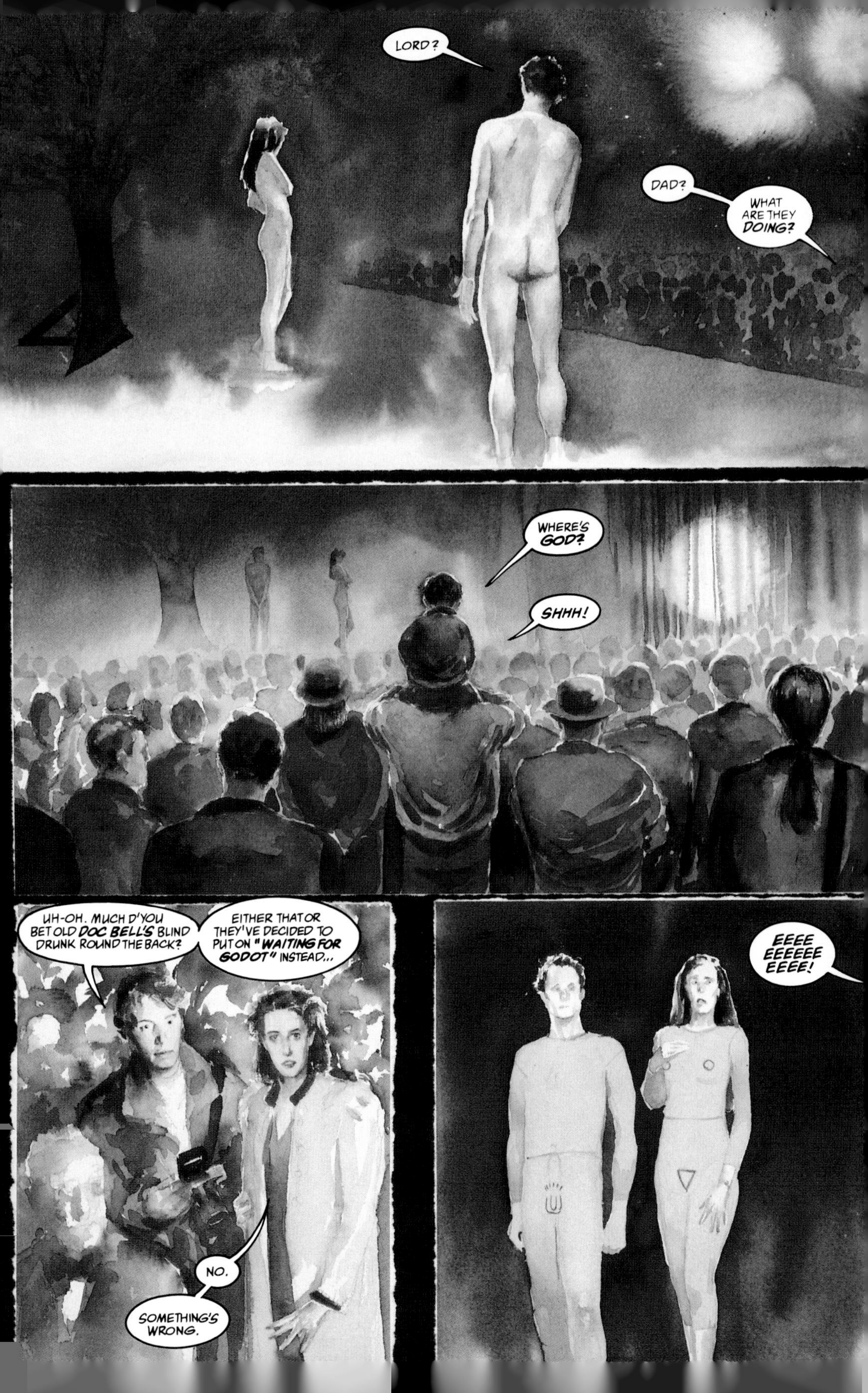
LORD?
DAD?
WHAT ARE THEY DOING?
WHERE'S GOD?
SHHH!
UH-OH. MUCH D'YOU BET OLD DOC BELL'S BLIND DRUNK ROUND THE BACK?
EITHER THAT OR THEY'VE DECIDED TO PUT ON "WAITING FOR GODOT" INSTEAD...
NO.
SOMETHING'S WRONG.
EEEE EEEEEE EEEE!

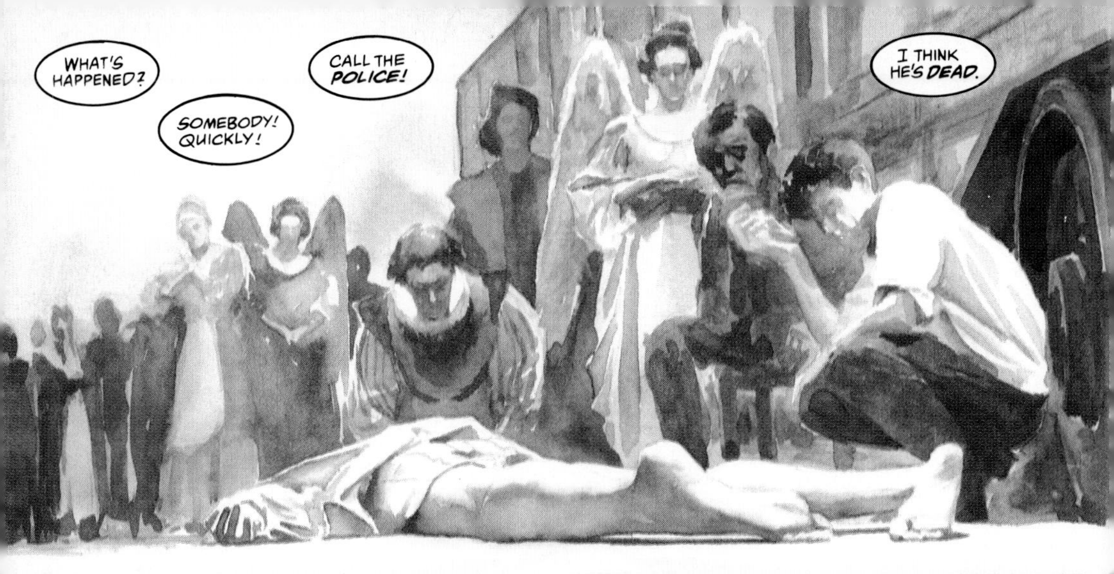
WHAT'S HAPPENED?
SOMEBODY! QUICKLY!
CALL THE POLICE!
I THINK HE'S DEAD.

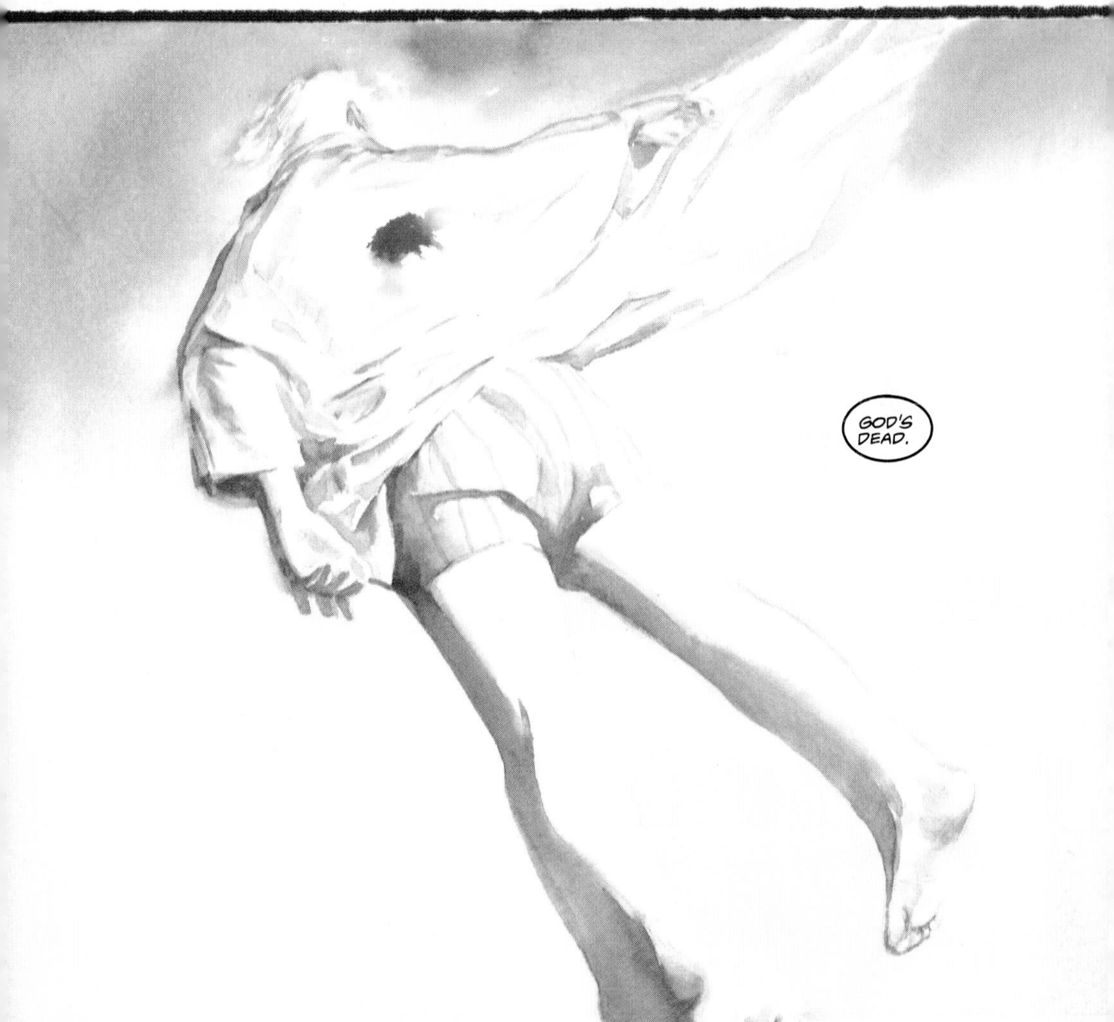
GOD'S DEAD.

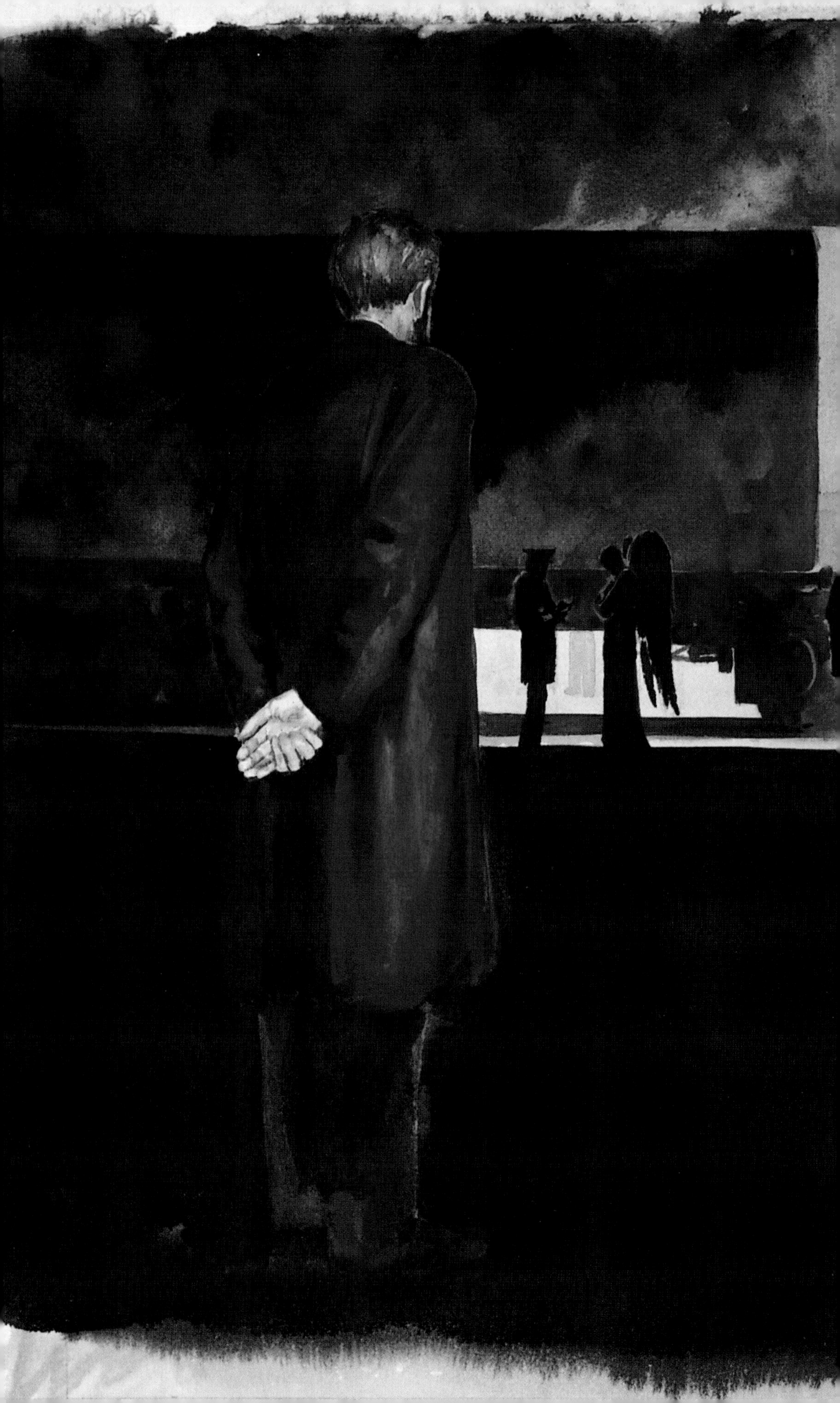

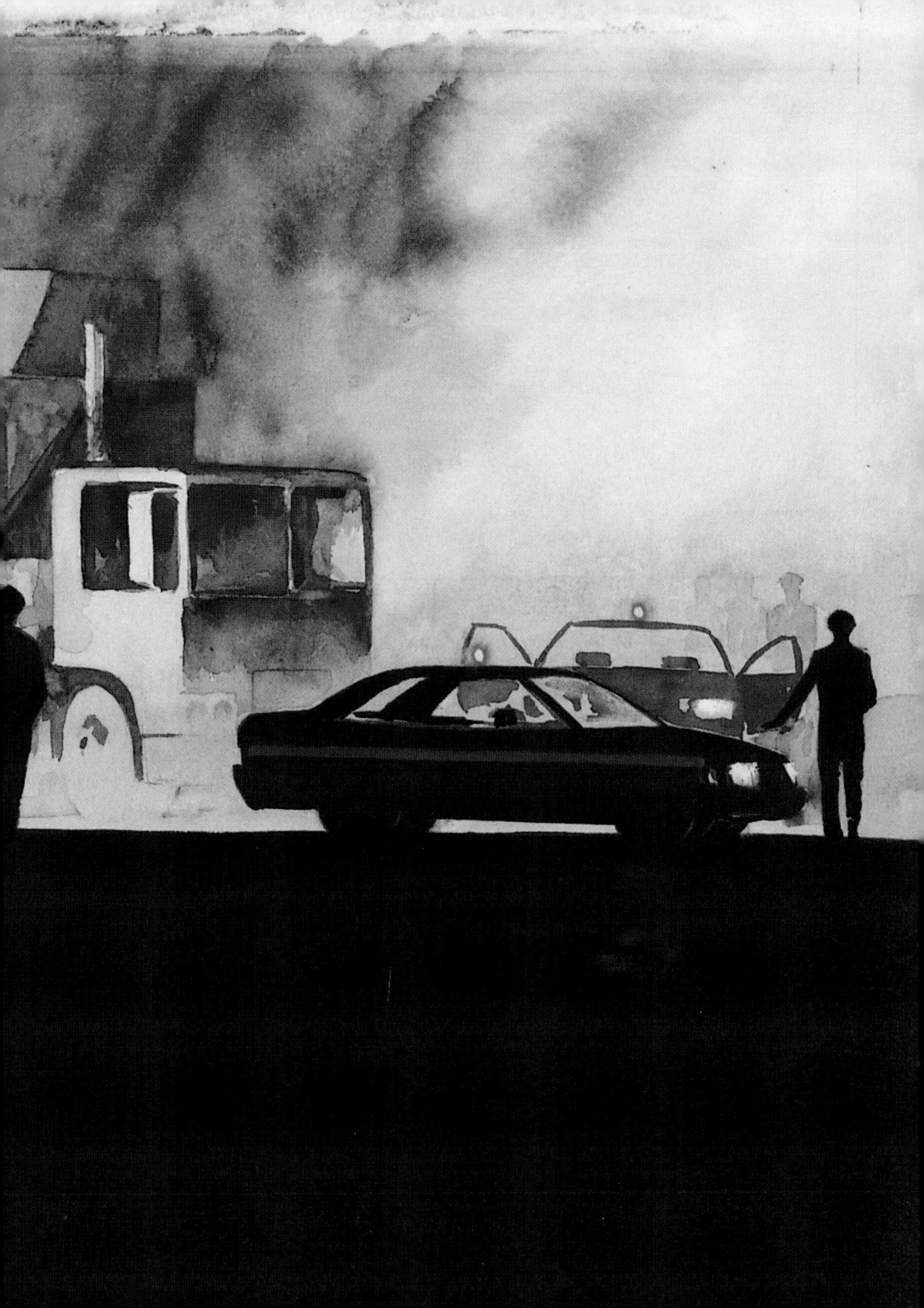

The MYSTERY PLAY

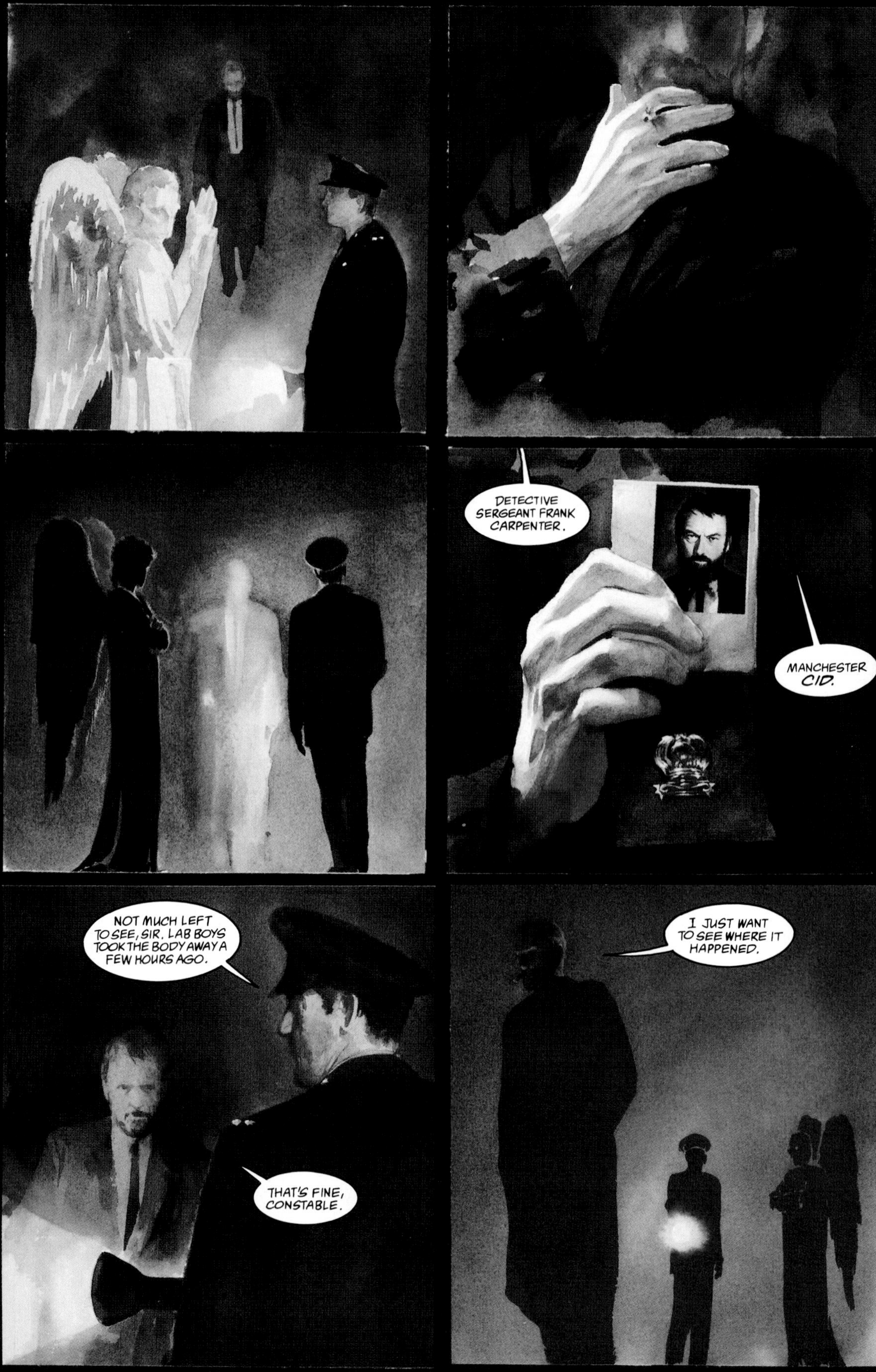
DETECTIVE SERGEANT FRANK CARPENTER.
MANCHESTER CID.
NOT MUCH LEFT TO SEE, SIR. LAB BOYS TOOK THE BODY AWAY A FEW HOURS AGO.
THAT'S FINE, CONSTABLE.
I JUST WANT TO SEE WHERE IT HAPPENED.

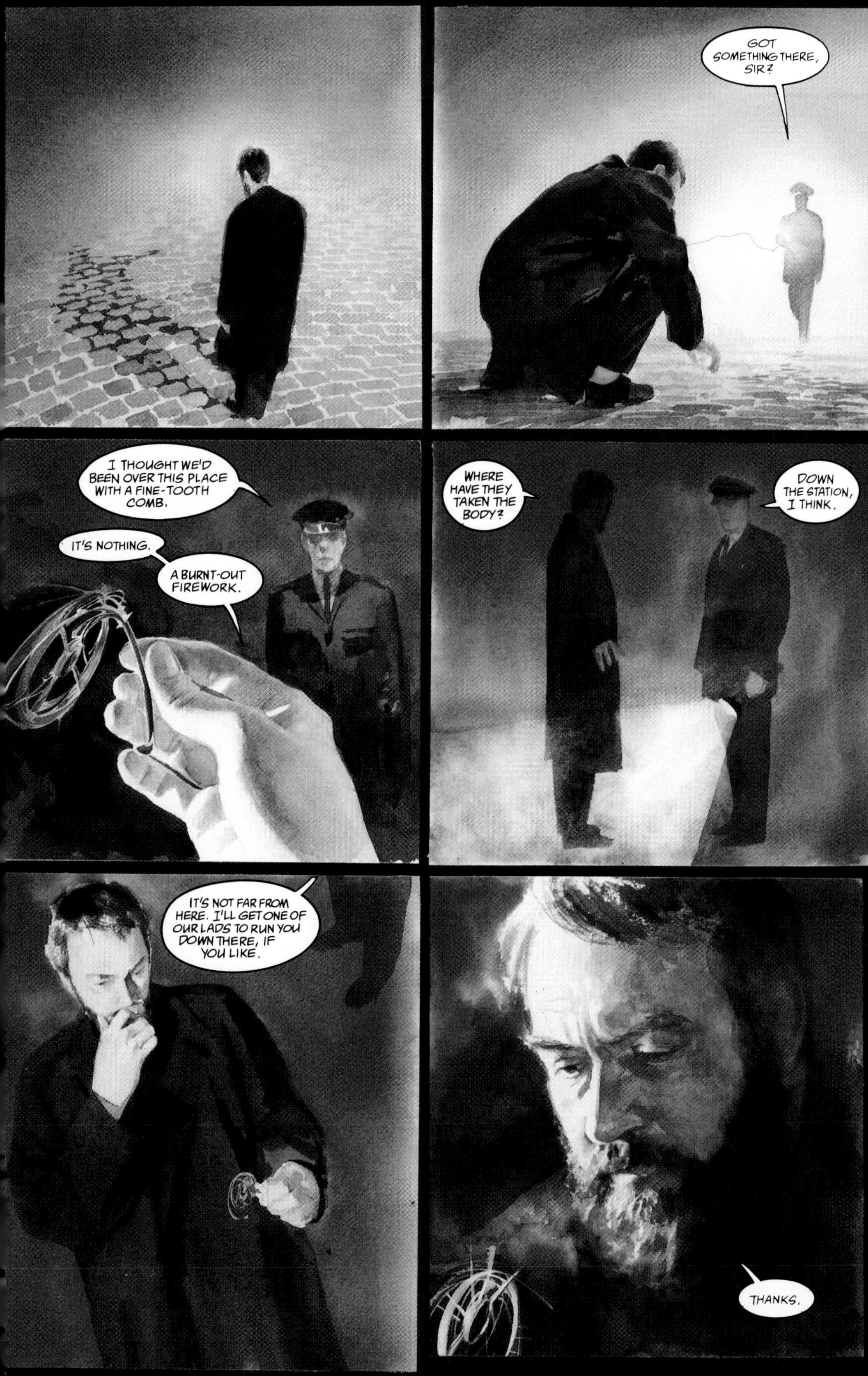
GOT SOMETHING THERE, SIR?
I THOUGHT WE'D BEEN OVER THIS PLACE WITH A FINE-TOOTH COMB.
IT'S NOTHING.
A BURNT-OUT FIREWORK.
WHERE HAVE THEY TAKEN THE BODY?
DOWN THE STATION, I THINK.
IT'S NOT FAR FROM HERE. I'LL GET ONE OF OUR LADS TO RUN YOU DOWN THERE, IF YOU LIKE.
THANKS.

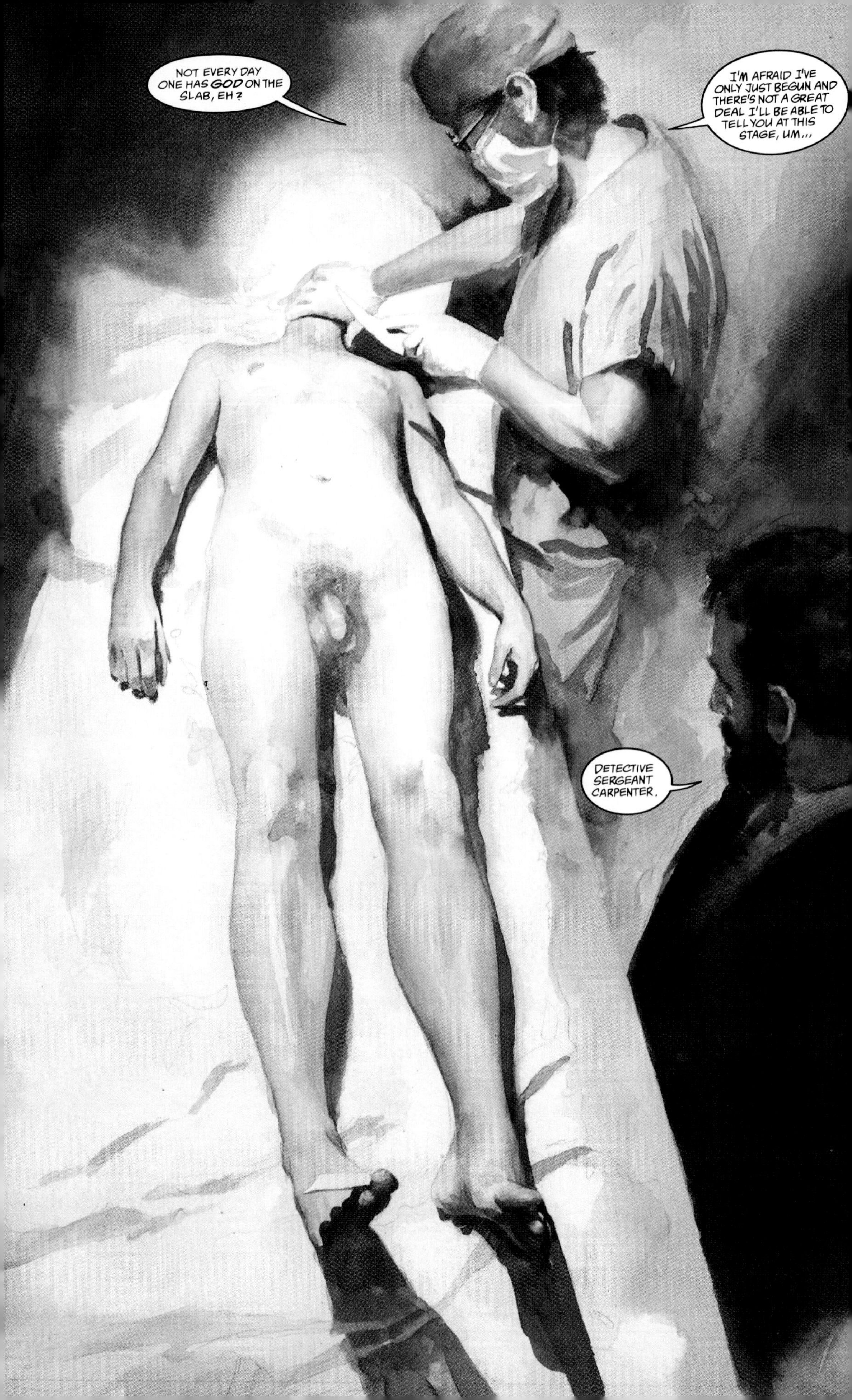
NOT EVERY DAY ONE HAS GOD ON THE SLAB, EH?
I'M AFRAID I'VE ONLY JUST BEGUN AND THERE'S NOT A GREAT DEAL I'LL BE ABLE TO TELL YOU AT THIS STAGE, UM...
DETECTIVE SERGEANT CARPENTER.

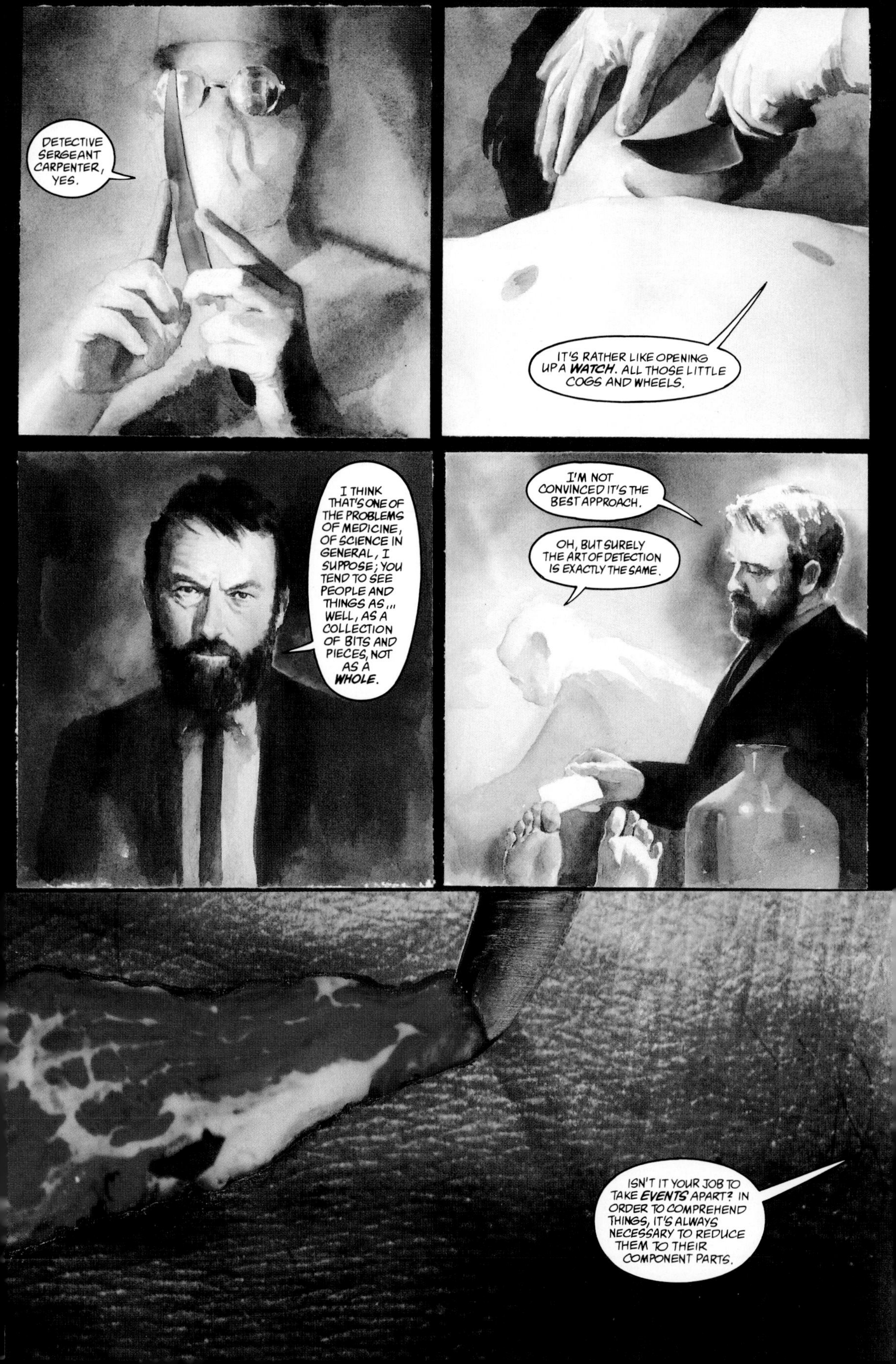
DETECTIVE SERGEANT CARPENTER, YES.
IT'S RATHER LIKE OPENING UP A WATCH. ALL THOSE LITTLE COGS AND WHEELS.
I THINK THAT'S ONE OF THE PROBLEMS OF MEDICINE, OF SCIENCE IN GENERAL, I SUPPOSE; YOU TEND TO SEE PEOPLE AND THINGS AS... WELL, AS A COLLECTION OF BITS AND PIECES, NOT AS A WHOLE.
I'M NOT CONVINCED IT'S THE BEST APPROACH.
OH, BUT SURELY THE ART OF DETECTION IS EXACTLY THE SAME.
ISN'T IT YOUR JOB TO TAKE EVENTS APART? IN ORDER TO COMPREHEND THINGS, IT'S ALWAYS NECESSARY TO REDUCE THEM TO THEIR COMPONENT PARTS.

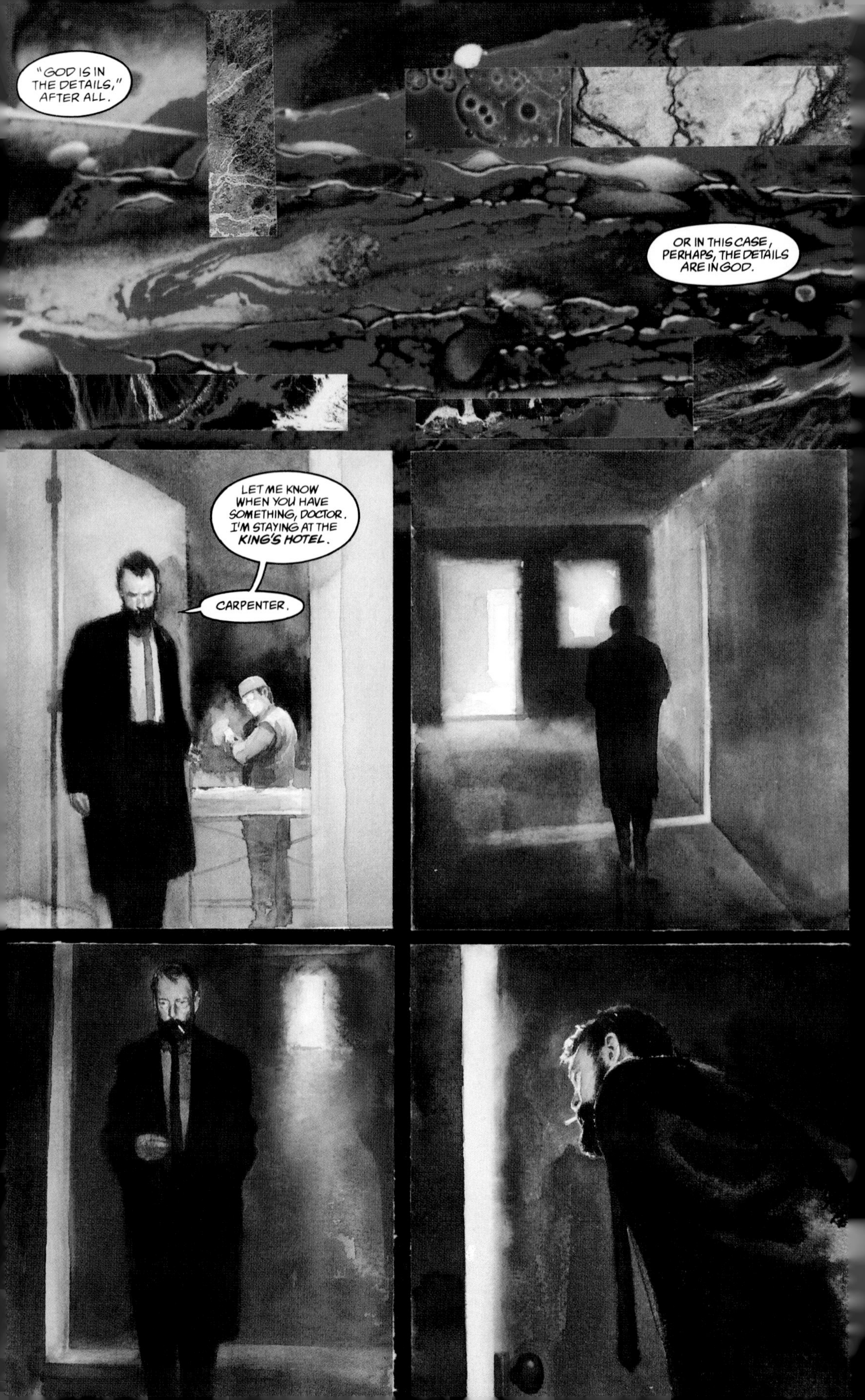
"GOD IS IN THE DETAILS," AFTER ALL.
OR IN THIS CASE, PERHAPS, THE DETAILS ARE IN GOD.
LET ME KNOW WHEN YOU HAVE SOMETHING, DOCTOR. I'M STAYING AT THE KING'S HOTEL.
CARPENTER.

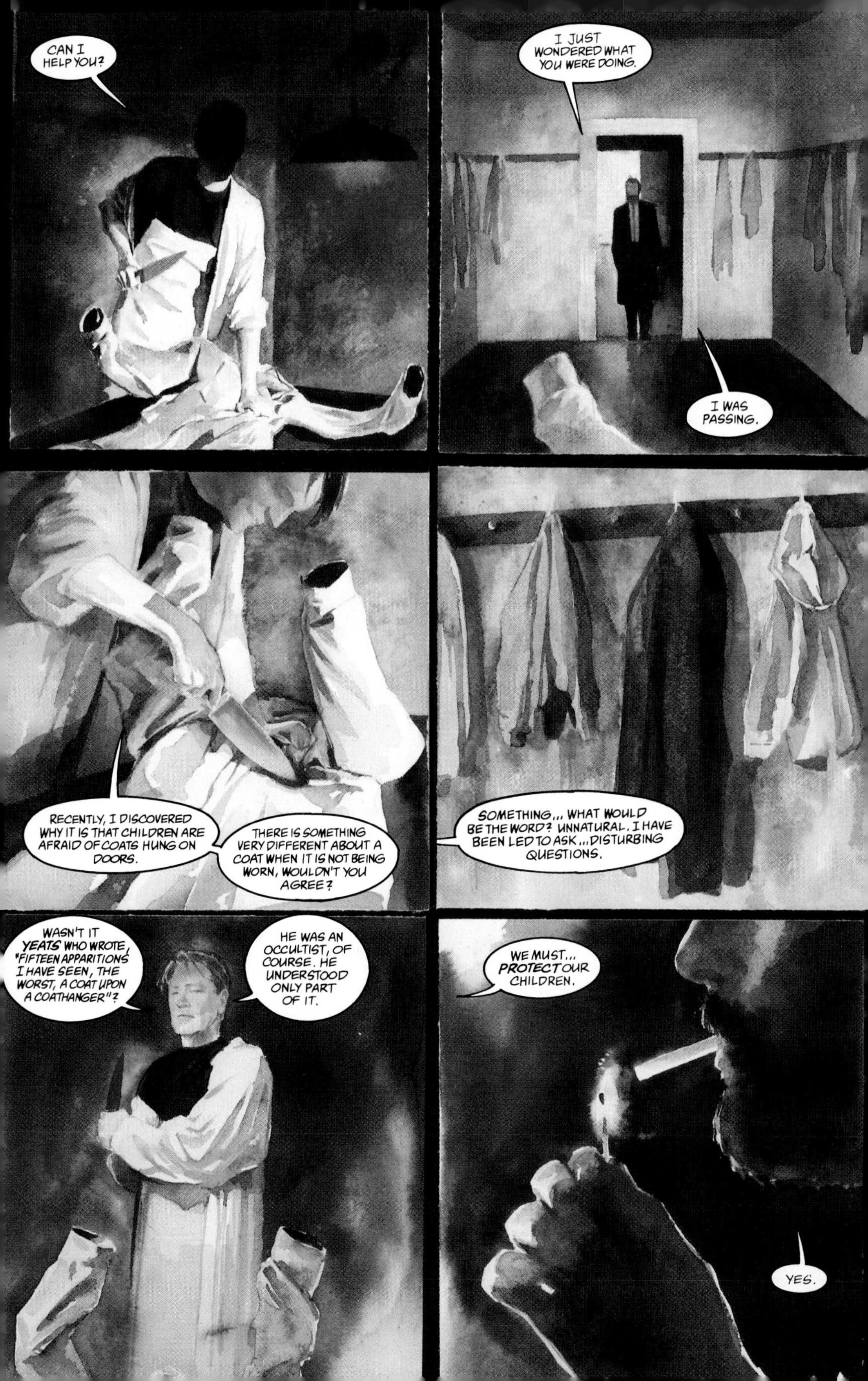
CAN I HELP YOU?
I JUST WONDERED WHAT YOU WERE DOING.
I WAS PASSING.
RECENTLY, I DISCOVERED WHY IT IS THAT CHILDREN ARE AFRAID OF COATS HUNG ON DOORS.
THERE IS SOMETHING VERY DIFFERENT ABOUT A COAT WHEN IT IS NOT BEING WORN, WOULDN'T YOU AGREE?
SOMETHING... WHAT WOULD BE THE WORD? UNNATURAL. I HAVE BEEN LED TO ASK... DISTURBING QUESTIONS.
WASN'T IT YEATS WHO WROTE, "FIFTEEN APPARITIONS I HAVE SEEN, THE WORST, A COAT UPON A COATHANGER"?
HE WAS AN OCCULTIST, OF COURSE. HE UNDERSTOOD ONLY PART OF IT.
WE MUST... PROTECT OUR CHILDREN.
YES.

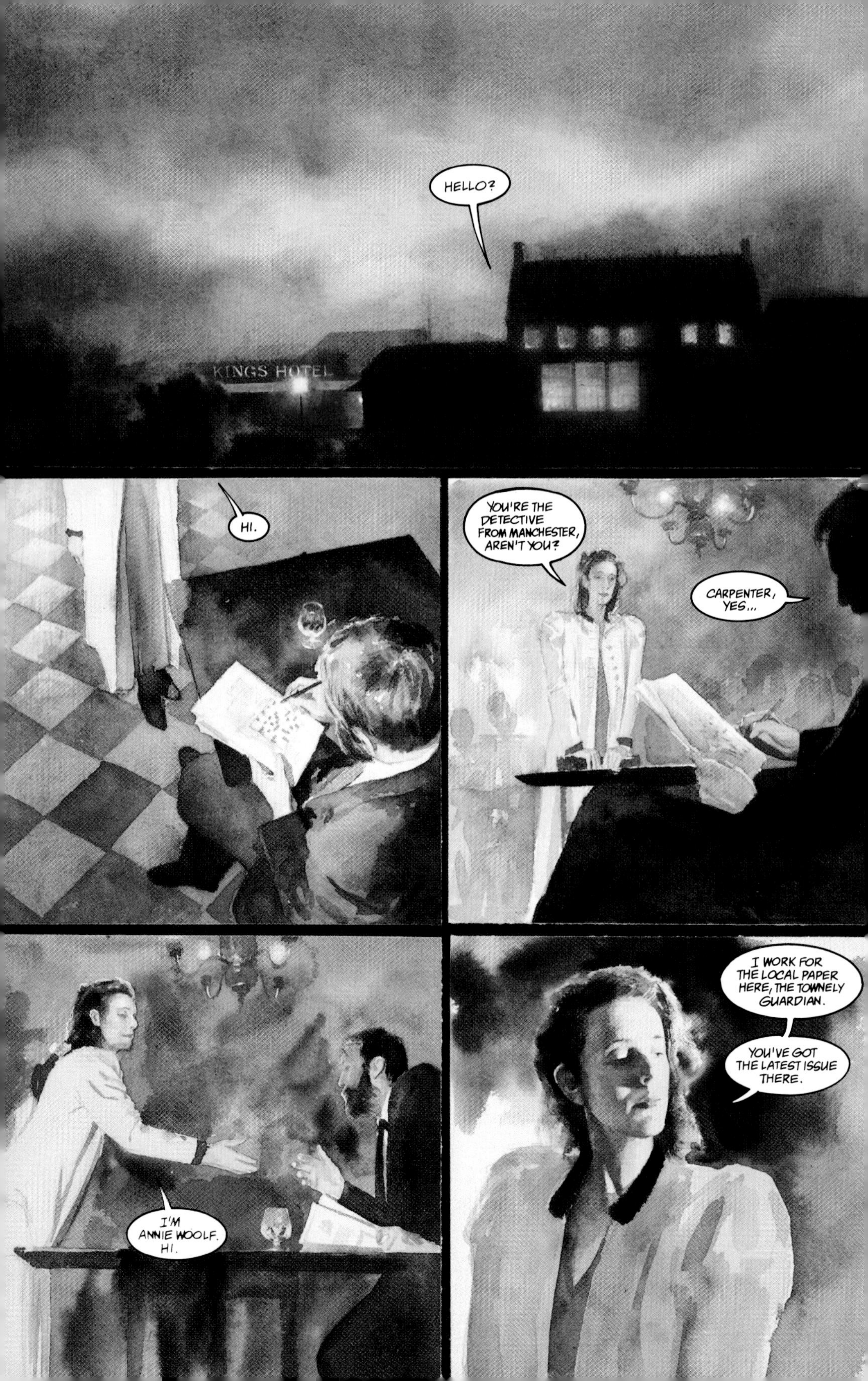
KINGS HOTEL
HELLO?
HI.
YOU'RE THE DETECTIVE FROM MANCHESTER, AREN'T YOU?
CARPENTER, YES...
I'M ANNIE WOOLF. HI.
I WORK FOR THE LOCAL PAPER HERE, THE TOWNELY GUARDIAN.
YOU'VE GOT THE LATEST ISSUE THERE.

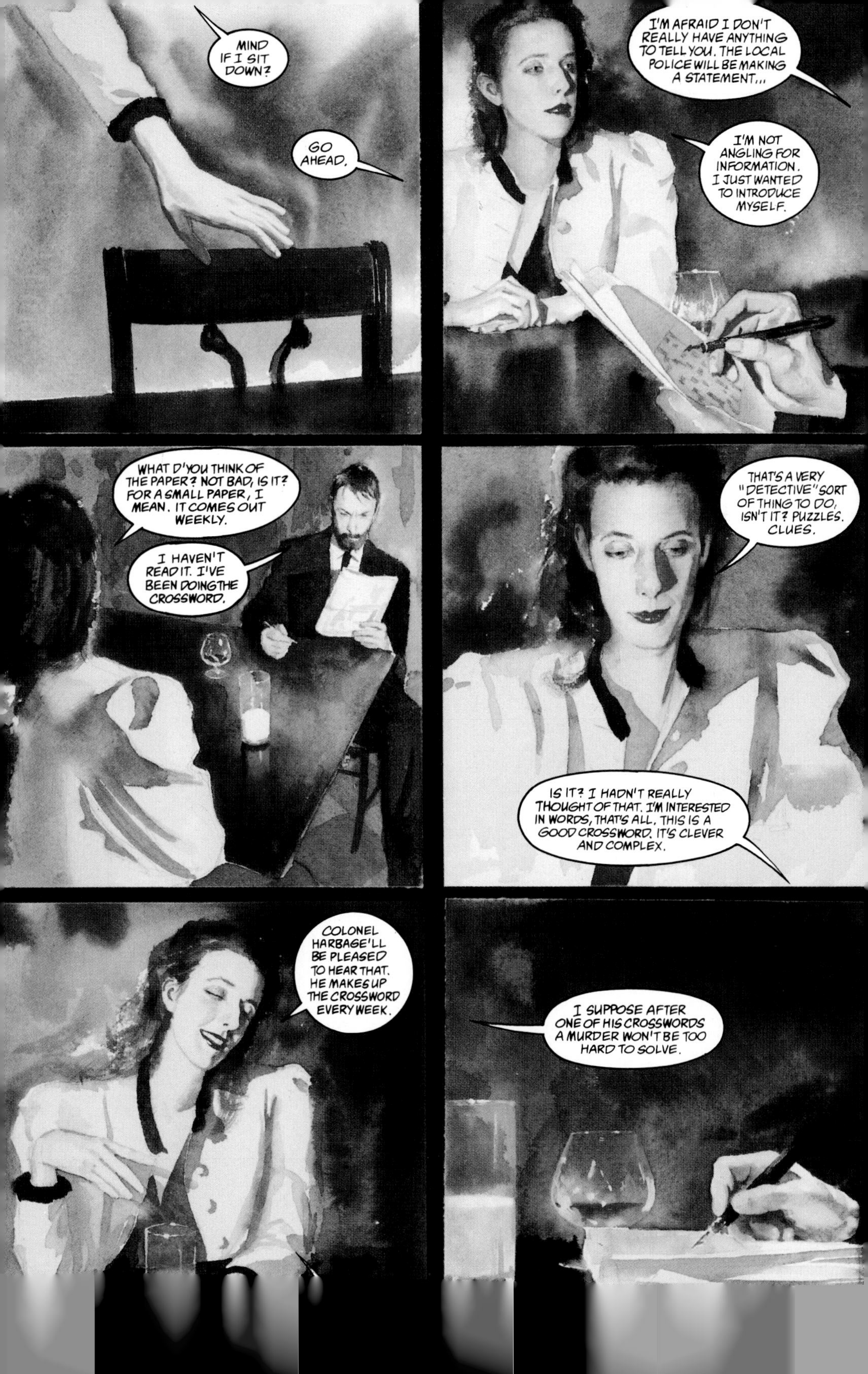
MIND IF I SIT DOWN?
GO AHEAD.
I'M AFRAID I DON'T REALLY HAVE ANYTHING TO TELL YOU. THE LOCAL POLICE WILL BE MAKING A STATEMENT...
I'M NOT ANGLING FOR INFORMATION. I JUST WANTED TO INTRODUCE MYSELF.
WHAT D'YOU THINK OF THE PAPER? NOT BAD, IS IT? FOR A SMALL PAPER, I MEAN. IT COMES OUT WEEKLY.
I HAVEN'T READ IT. I'VE BEEN DOING THE CROSSWORD.
THAT'S A VERY "DETECTIVE" SORT OF THING TO DO, ISN'T IT? PUZZLES. CLUES.
IS IT? I HADN'T REALLY THOUGHT OF THAT. I'M INTERESTED IN WORDS, THAT'S ALL. THIS IS A GOOD CROSSWORD. IT'S CLEVER AND COMPLEX.
COLONEL HARBAGE'LL BE PLEASED TO HEAR THAT. HE MAKES UP THE CROSSWORD EVERY WEEK.
I SUPPOSE AFTER ONE OF HIS CROSSWORDS A MURDER WON'T BE TOO HARD TO SOLVE.

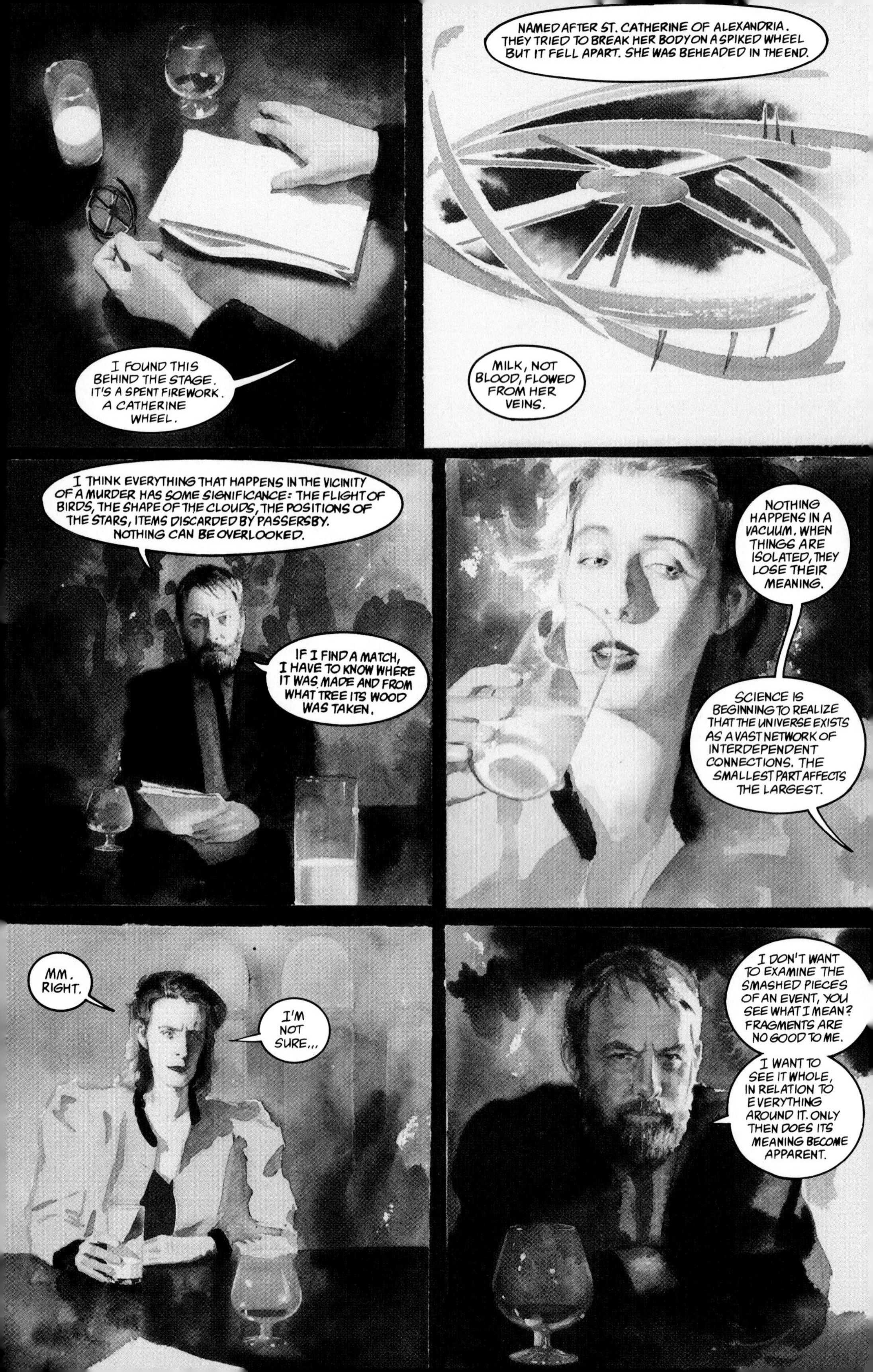
I FOUND THIS BEHIND THE STAGE. IT'S A SPENT FIREWORK. A CATHERINE WHEEL.
NAMED AFTER ST. CATHERINE OF ALEXANDRIA. THEY TRIED TO BREAK HER BODY ON A SPIKED WHEEL BUT IT FELL APART. SHE WAS BEHEADED IN THE END.
MILK, NOT BLOOD, FLOWED FROM HER VEINS.
I THINK EVERYTHING THAT HAPPENS IN THE VICINITY OF A MURDER HAS SOME SIGNIFICANCE: THE FLIGHT OF BIRDS, THE SHAPE OF THE CLOUDS, THE POSITIONS OF THE STARS, ITEMS DISCARDED BY PASSERSBY. NOTHING CAN BE OVERLOOKED.
IF I FIND A MATCH, I HAVE TO KNOW WHERE IT WAS MADE AND FROM WHAT TREE ITS WOOD WAS TAKEN.
NOTHING HAPPENS IN A VACUUM. WHEN THINGS ARE ISOLATED, THEY LOSE THEIR MEANING.
SCIENCE IS BEGINNING TO REALIZE THAT THE UNIVERSE EXISTS AS A VAST NETWORK OF INTERDEPENDENT CONNECTIONS. THE SMALLEST PART AFFECTS THE LARGEST.
MM. RIGHT.
I'M NOT SURE...
I DON'T WANT TO EXAMINE THE SMASHED PIECES OF AN EVENT, YOU SEE WHAT I MEAN? FRAGMENTS ARE NO GOOD TO ME.
I WANT TO SEE IT WHOLE, IN RELATION TO EVERYTHING AROUND IT. ONLY THEN DOES ITS MEANING BECOME APPARENT.

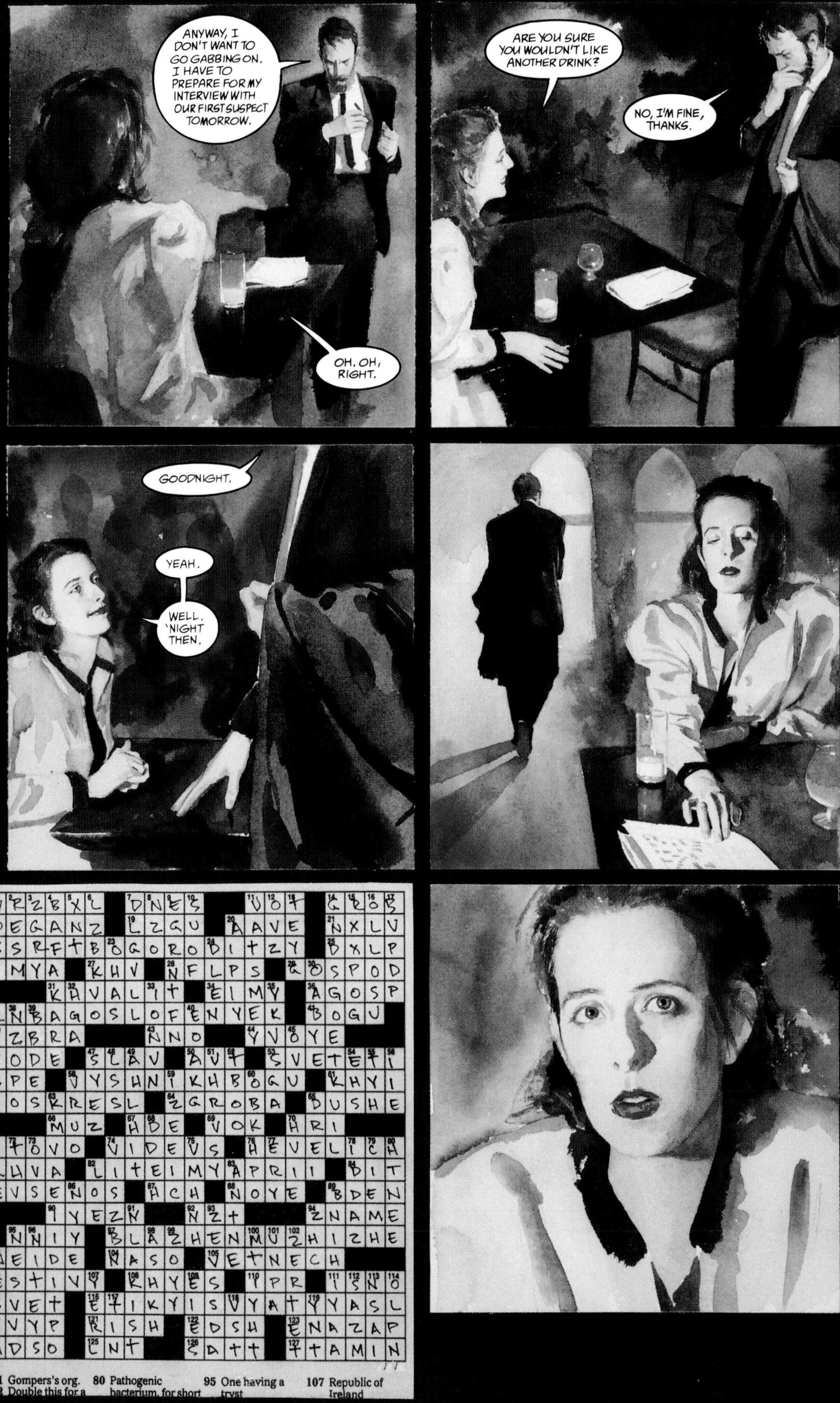
ANYWAY, I DON'T WANT TO GO GABBING ON. I HAVE TO PREPARE FOR MY INTERVIEW WITH OUR FIRST SUSPECT TOMORROW.
OH. OH, RIGHT.
ARE YOU SURE YOU WOULDN'T LIKE ANOTHER DRINK?
NO, I'M FINE, THANKS.
GOODNIGHT.
YEAH.
WELL. 'NIGHT THEN.
1 Gompers's org.
2 Double this for a
80 Pathogenic bacterium, for short
95 One having a tryst
107 Republic of Ireland

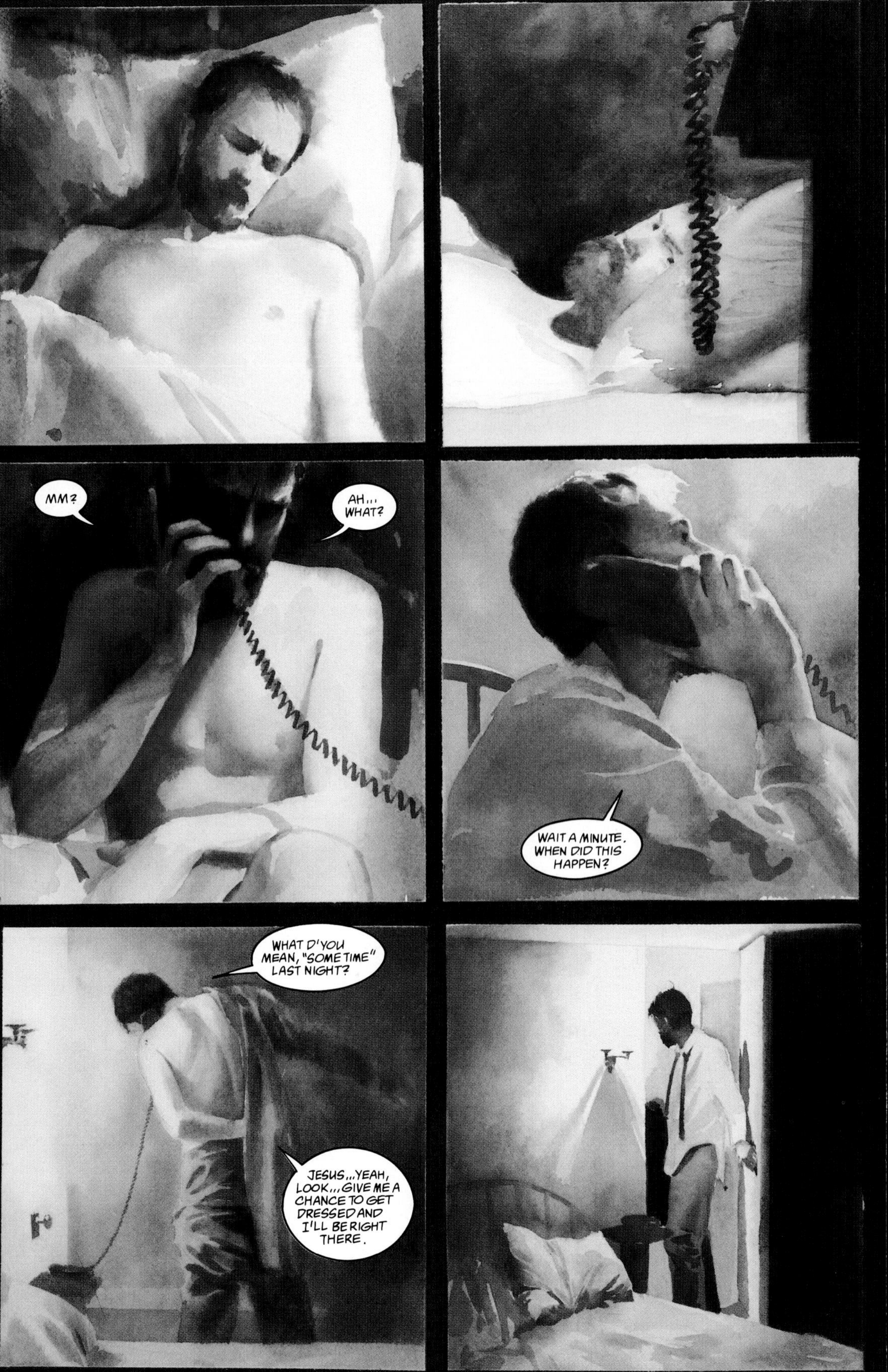
MM?
AH... WHAT?
WAIT A MINUTE. WHEN DID THIS HAPPEN?
WHAT D'YOU MEAN, "SOME TIME" LAST NIGHT?
JESUS...YEAH, LOOK...GIVE ME A CHANCE TO GET DRESSED AND I'LL BE RIGHT THERE.

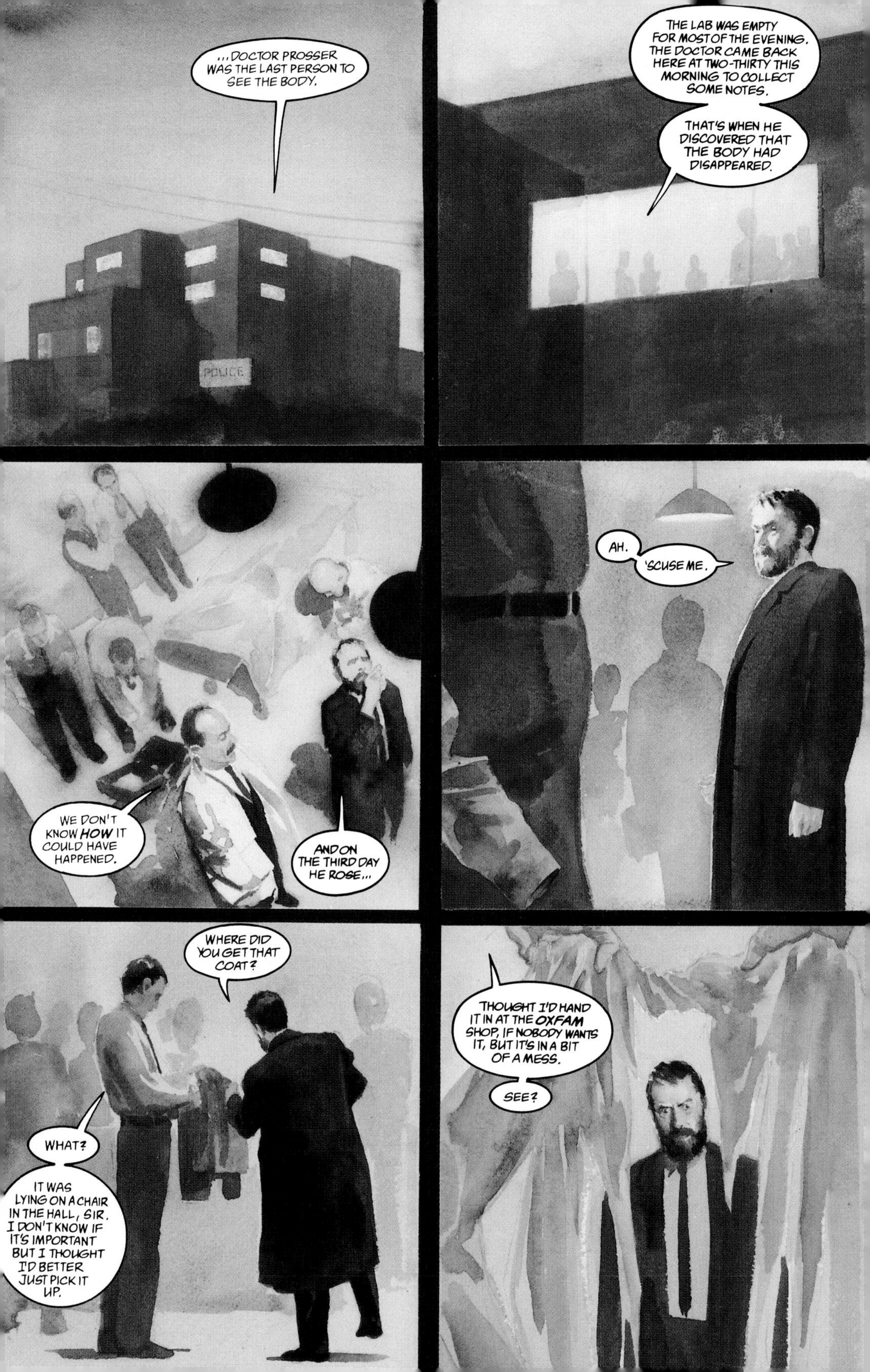
...DOCTOR PROSSER WAS THE LAST PERSON TO SEE THE BODY.
POLICE
THE LAB WAS EMPTY FOR MOST OF THE EVENING. THE DOCTOR CAME BACK HERE AT TWO-THIRTY THIS MORNING TO COLLECT SOME NOTES.
THAT'S WHEN HE DISCOVERED THAT THE BODY HAD DISAPPEARED.
WE DON'T KNOW HOW IT COULD HAVE HAPPENED.
AND ON THE THIRD DAY HE ROSE...
AH.
'SCUSE ME.
WHERE DID YOU GET THAT COAT?
WHAT?
IT WAS LYING ON A CHAIR IN THE HALL, SIR. I DON'T KNOW IF IT'S IMPORTANT BUT I THOUGHT I'D BETTER JUST PICK IT UP.
THOUGHT I'D HAND IT IN AT THE OXFAM SHOP, IF NOBODY WANTS IT, BUT IT'S IN A BIT OF A MESS.
SEE?

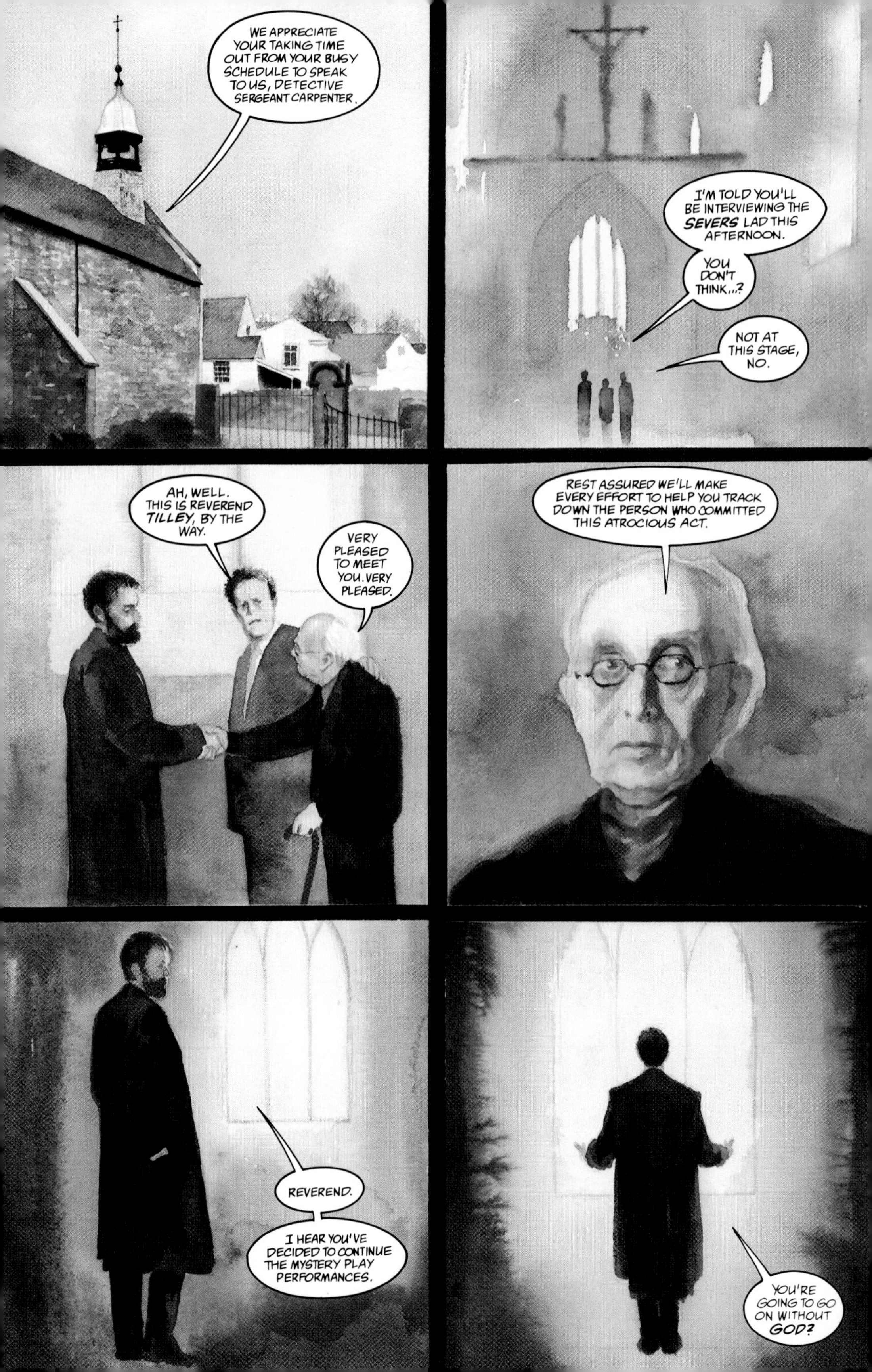
WE APPRECIATE YOUR TAKING TIME OUT FROM YOUR BUSY SCHEDULE TO SPEAK TO US, DETECTIVE SERGEANT CARPENTER.
I'M TOLD YOU'LL BE INTERVIEWING THE SEVERS LAD THIS AFTERNOON.
YOU DON'T THINK...?
NOT AT THIS STAGE, NO.
AH, WELL. THIS IS REVEREND TILLEY, BY THE WAY.
VERY PLEASED TO MEET YOU. VERY PLEASED.
REST ASSURED WE'LL MAKE EVERY EFFORT TO HELP YOU TRACK DOWN THE PERSON WHO COMMITTED THIS ATROCIOUS ACT.
REVEREND.
I HEAR YOU'VE DECIDED TO CONTINUE THE MYSTERY PLAY PERFORMANCES.
YOU'RE GOING TO GO ON WITHOUT GOD?

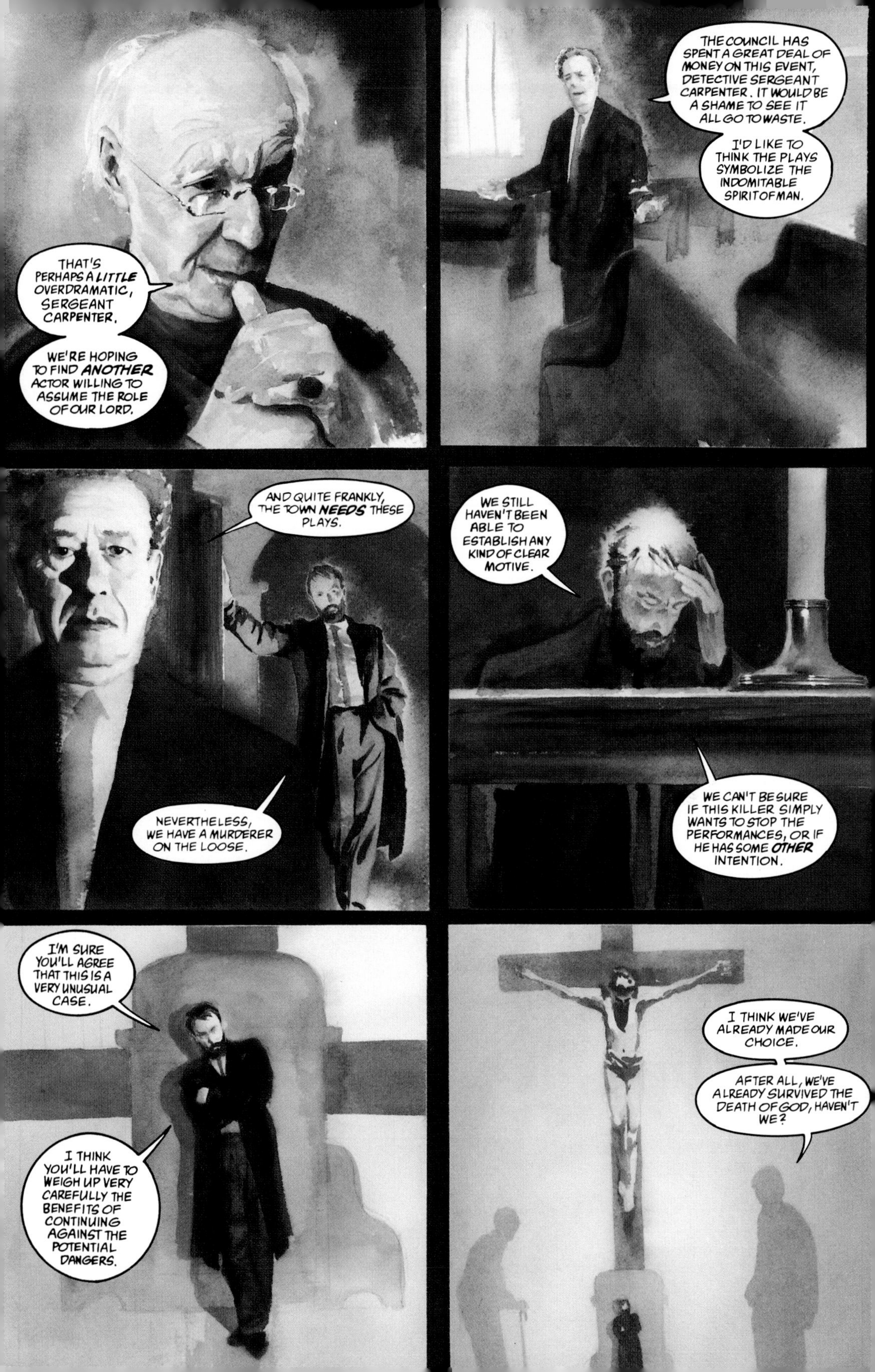
THAT'S PERHAPS A LITTLE OVERDRAMATIC, SERGEANT CARPENTER.
WE'RE HOPING TO FIND ANOTHER ACTOR WILLING TO ASSUME THE ROLE OF OUR LORD.
THE COUNCIL HAS SPENT A GREAT DEAL OF MONEY ON THIS EVENT, DETECTIVE SERGEANT CARPENTER. IT WOULD BE A SHAME TO SEE IT ALL GO TO WASTE.
I'D LIKE TO THINK THE PLAYS SYMBOLIZE THE INDOMITABLE SPIRIT OF MAN.
AND QUITE FRANKLY, THE TOWN NEEDS THESE PLAYS.
NEVERTHELESS, WE HAVE A MURDERER ON THE LOOSE.
WE STILL HAVEN'T BEEN ABLE TO ESTABLISH ANY KIND OF CLEAR MOTIVE.
WE CAN'T BE SURE IF THIS KILLER SIMPLY WANTS TO STOP THE PERFORMANCES, OR IF HE HAS SOME OTHER INTENTION.
I'M SURE YOU'LL AGREE THAT THIS IS A VERY UNUSUAL CASE.
I THINK YOU'LL HAVE TO WEIGH UP VERY CAREFULLY THE BENEFITS OF CONTINUING AGAINST THE POTENTIAL DANGERS.
I THINK WE'VE ALREADY MADE OUR CHOICE.
AFTER ALL, WE'VE ALREADY SURVIVED THE DEATH OF GOD, HAVEN'T WE?

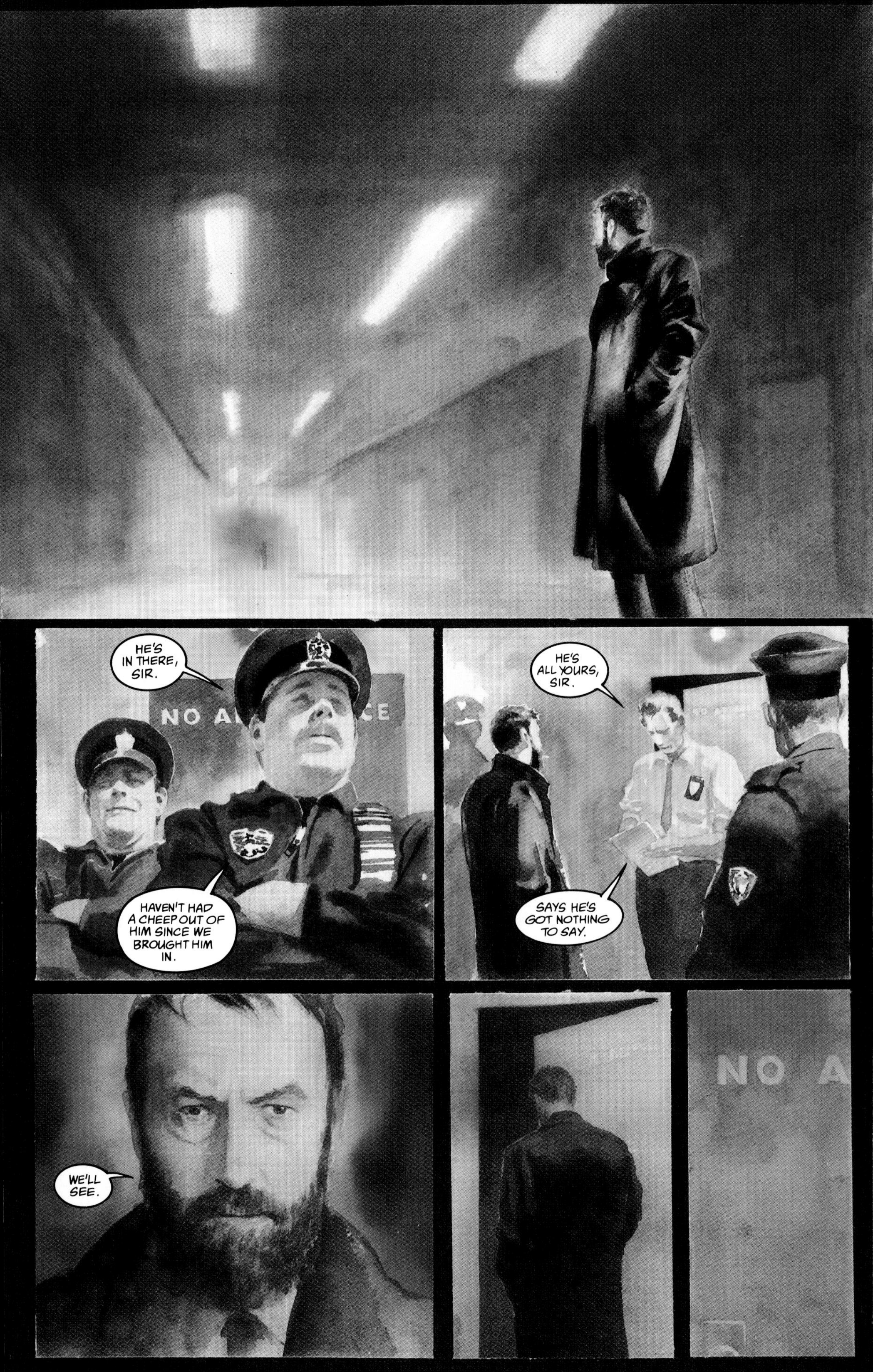
HE'S IN THERE, SIR.
NO A CE
HAVEN'T HAD A CHEEP OUT OF HIM SINCE WE BROUGHT HIM IN.
HE'S ALL YOURS, SIR.
SAYS HE'S GOT NOTHING TO SAY.
WE'LL SEE.
NO A

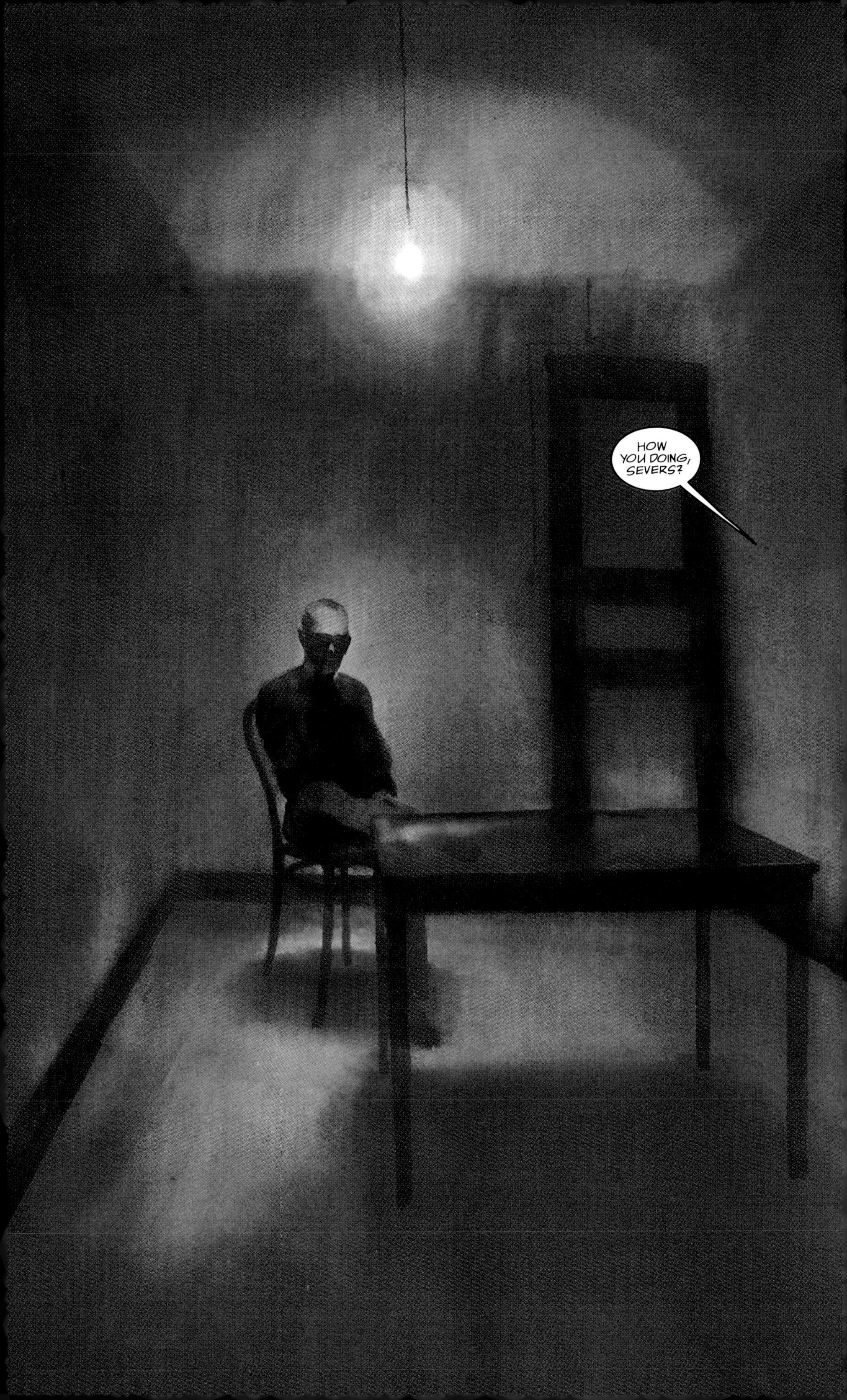
HOW YOU DOING, SEVERS?

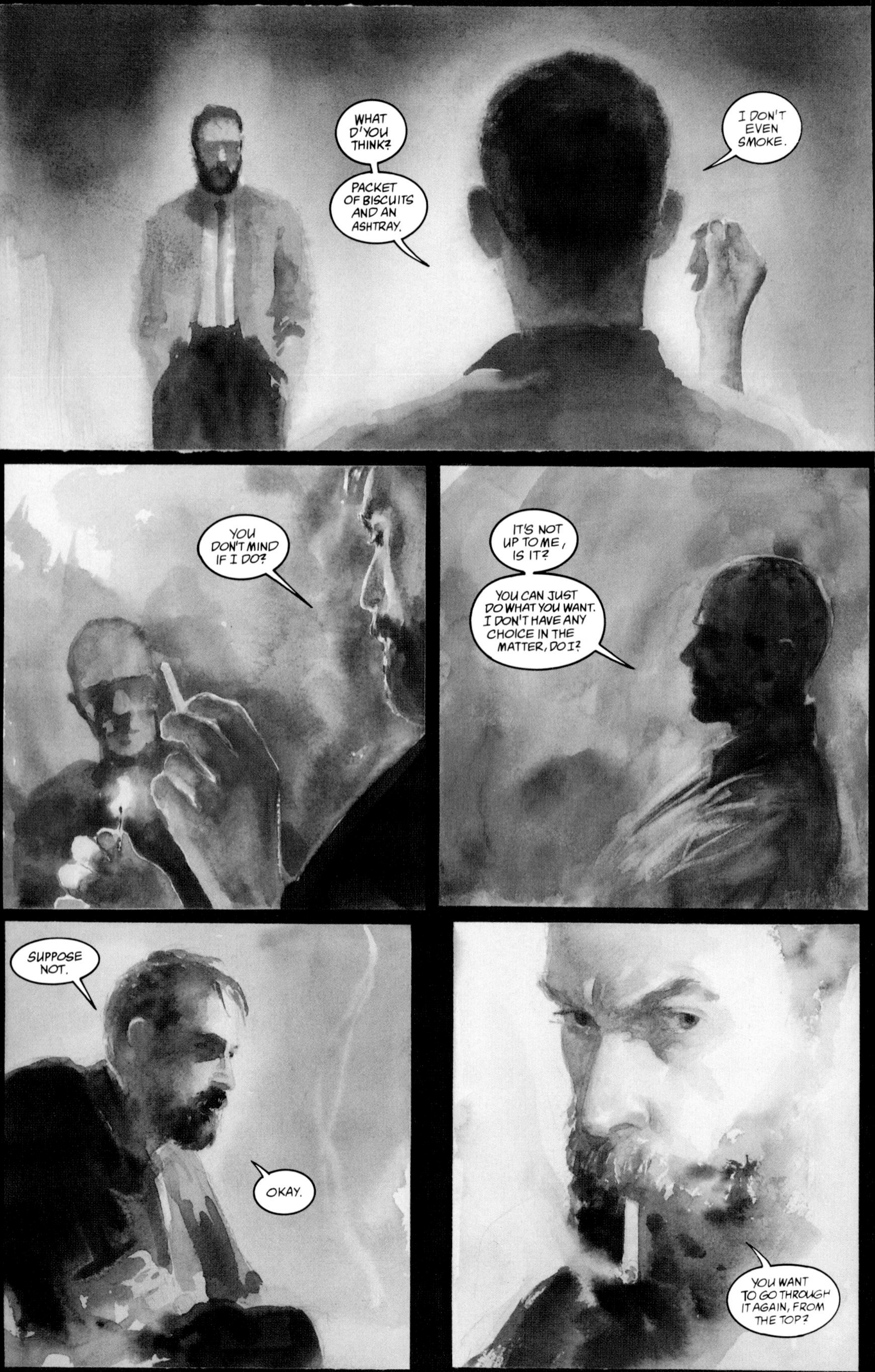
WHAT D'YOU THINK?
PACKET OF BISCUITS AND AN ASHTRAY.
I DON'T EVEN SMOKE.
YOU DON'T MIND IF I DO?
IT'S NOT UP TO ME, IS IT?
YOU CAN JUST DO WHAT YOU WANT. I DON'T HAVE ANY CHOICE IN THE MATTER, DO I?
SUPPOSE NOT.
OKAY.
YOU WANT TO GO THROUGH IT AGAIN, FROM THE TOP?

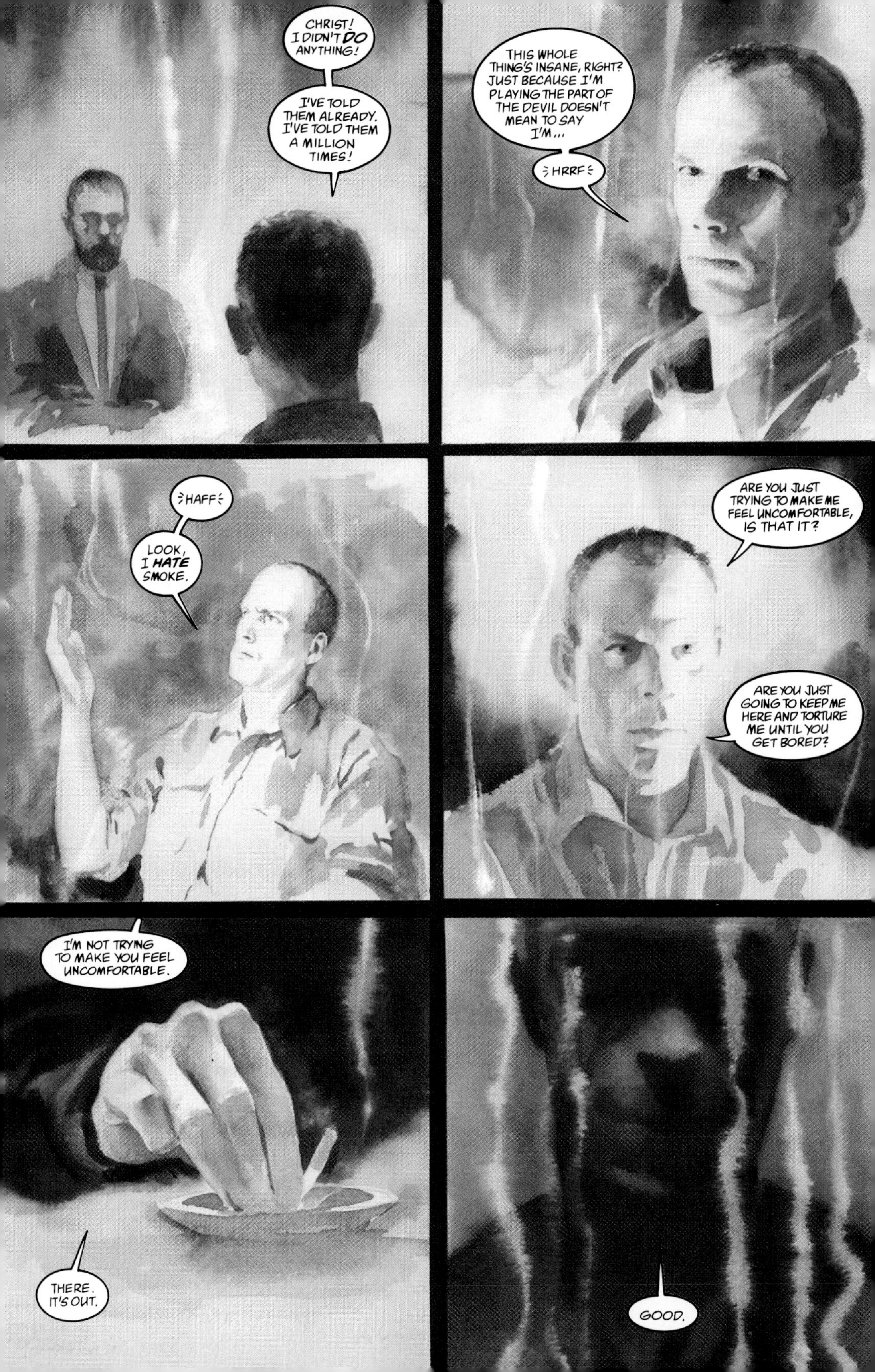
CHRIST! I DIDN'T DO ANYTHING!
I'VE TOLD THEM ALREADY. I'VE TOLD THEM A MILLION TIMES!
THIS WHOLE THING'S INSANE, RIGHT? JUST BECAUSE I'M PLAYING THE PART OF THE DEVIL DOESN'T MEAN TO SAY I'M...
HRRF
HAFF
LOOK, I HATE SMOKE.
ARE YOU JUST TRYING TO MAKE ME FEEL UNCOMFORTABLE, IS THAT IT?
ARE YOU JUST GOING TO KEEP ME HERE AND TORTURE ME UNTIL YOU GET BORED?
I'M NOT TRYING TO MAKE YOU FEEL UNCOMFORTABLE.
THERE. IT'S OUT.
GOOD.

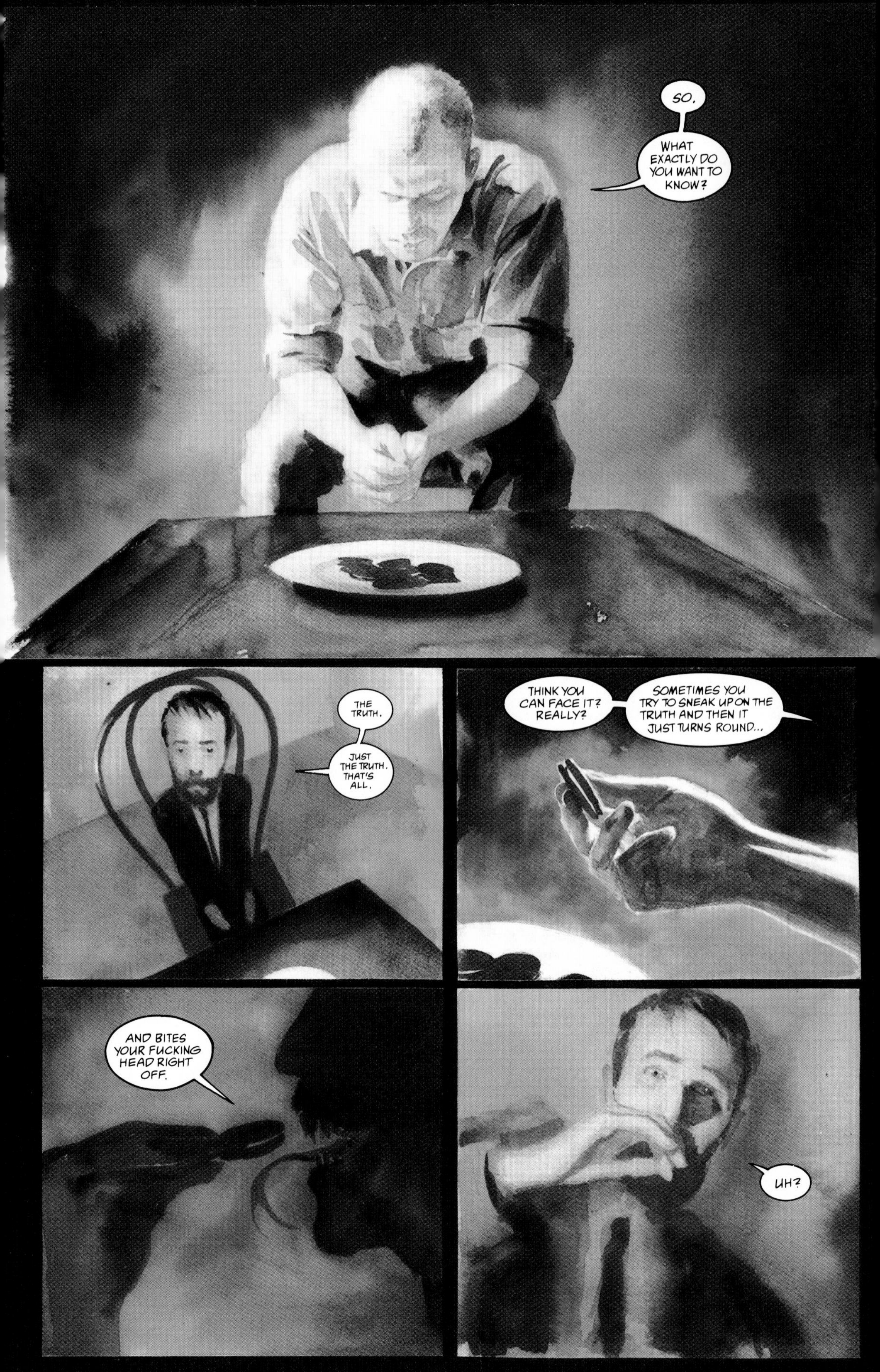
SO,
WHAT EXACTLY DO YOU WANT TO KNOW?
THE TRUTH.
JUST THE TRUTH. THAT'S ALL.
THINK YOU CAN FACE IT? REALLY?
SOMETIMES YOU TRY TO SNEAK UP ON THE TRUTH AND THEN IT JUST TURNS ROUND...
AND BITES YOUR FUCKING HEAD RIGHT OFF.
UH?

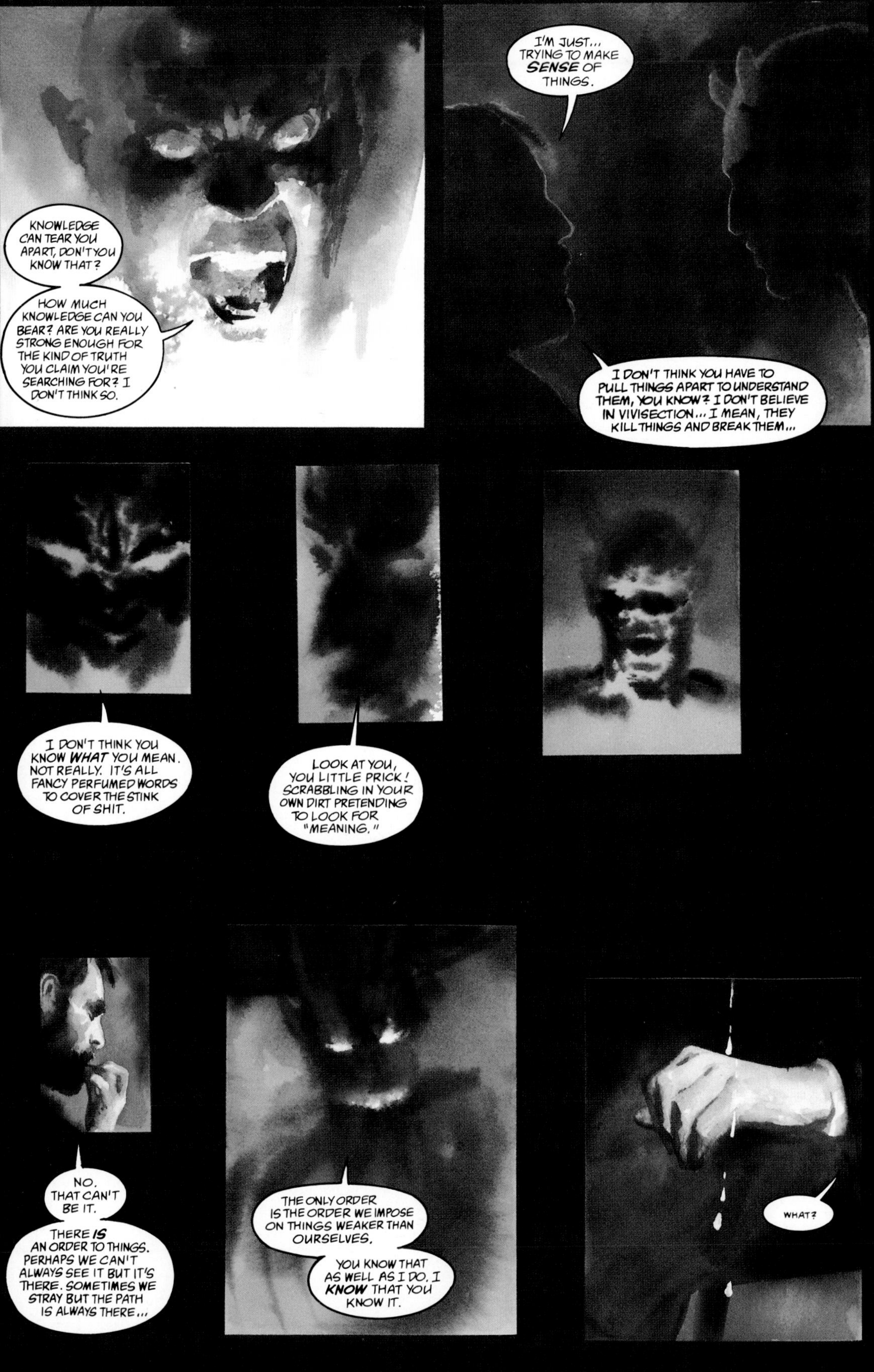
KNOWLEDGE CAN TEAR YOU APART, DON'T YOU KNOW THAT?
HOW MUCH KNOWLEDGE CAN YOU BEAR? ARE YOU REALLY STRONG ENOUGH FOR THE KIND OF TRUTH YOU CLAIM YOU'RE SEARCHING FOR? I DON'T THINK SO.
I'M JUST... TRYING TO MAKE **SENSE** OF THINGS.
I DON'T THINK YOU HAVE TO PULL THINGS APART TO UNDERSTAND THEM, YOU KNOW? I DON'T BELIEVE IN VIVISECTION... I MEAN, THEY KILL THINGS AND BREAK THEM...
I DON'T THINK YOU KNOW **WHAT** YOU MEAN. NOT REALLY. IT'S ALL FANCY PERFUMED WORDS TO COVER THE STINK OF SHIT.
LOOK AT YOU, YOU LITTLE PRICK! SCRABBLING IN YOUR OWN DIRT PRETENDING TO LOOK FOR "MEANING."
NO. THAT CAN'T BE IT.
THERE **IS** AN ORDER TO THINGS. PERHAPS WE CAN'T ALWAYS SEE IT BUT IT'S THERE. SOMETIMES WE STRAY BUT THE PATH IS ALWAYS THERE...
THE ONLY ORDER IS THE ORDER WE IMPOSE ON THINGS WEAKER THAN OURSELVES.
YOU KNOW THAT AS WELL AS I DO. I **KNOW** THAT YOU KNOW IT.
WHAT?

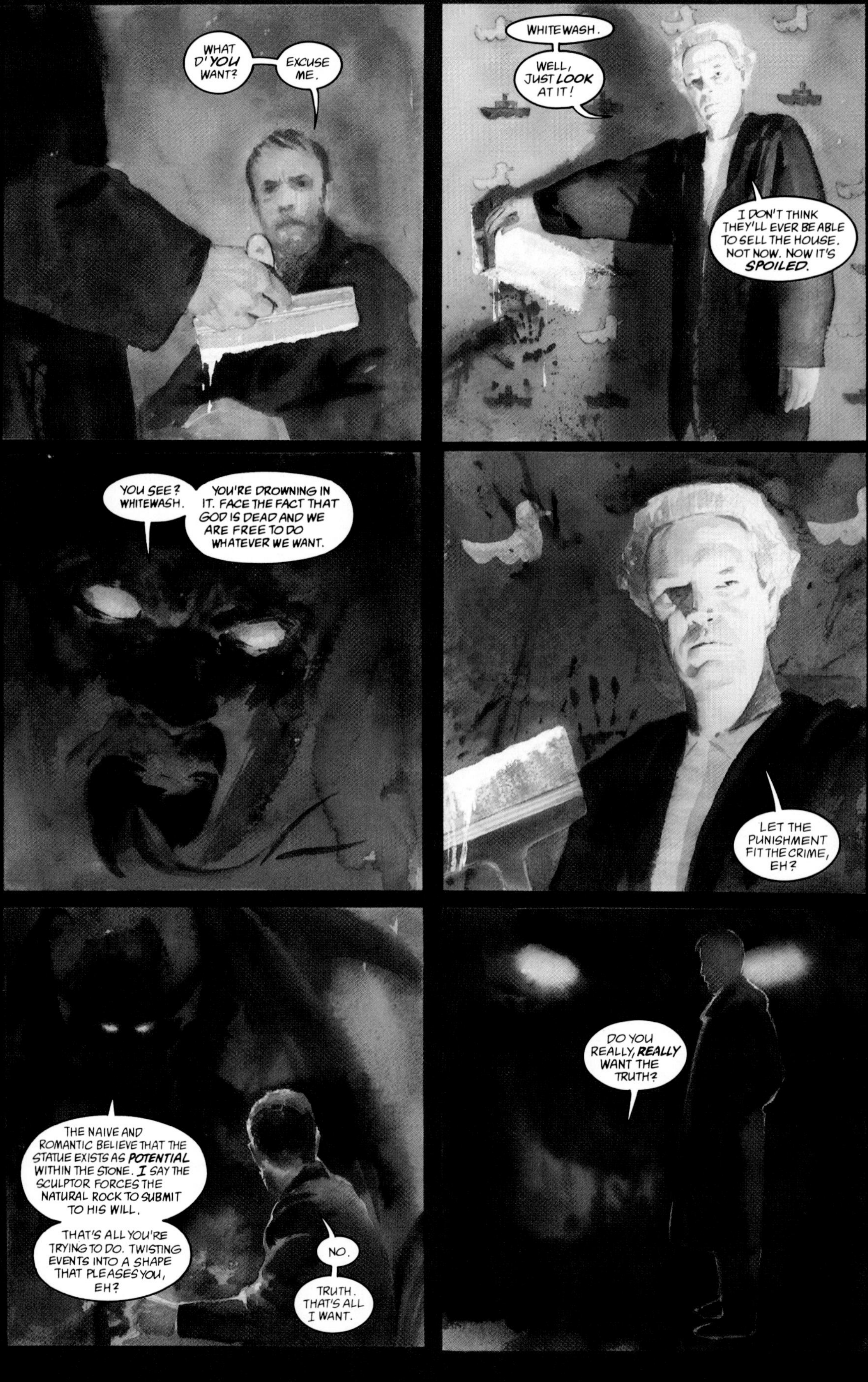

WHAT D'YOU WANT?
EXCUSE ME.
WHITEWASH.
WELL, JUST LOOK AT IT!
I DON'T THINK THEY'LL EVER BE ABLE TO SELL THE HOUSE. NOT NOW. NOW IT'S SPOILED.
YOU SEE? WHITEWASH.
YOU'RE DROWNING IN IT. FACE THE FACT THAT GOD IS DEAD AND WE ARE FREE TO DO WHATEVER WE WANT.
LET THE PUNISHMENT FIT THE CRIME, EH?
THE NAIVE AND ROMANTIC BELIEVE THAT THE STATUE EXISTS AS POTENTIAL WITHIN THE STONE. I SAY THE SCULPTOR FORCES THE NATURAL ROCK TO SUBMIT TO HIS WILL.
THAT'S ALL YOU'RE TRYING TO DO. TWISTING EVENTS INTO A SHAPE THAT PLEASES YOU, EH?
NO.
TRUTH. THAT'S ALL I WANT.
DO YOU REALLY, REALLY WANT THE TRUTH?

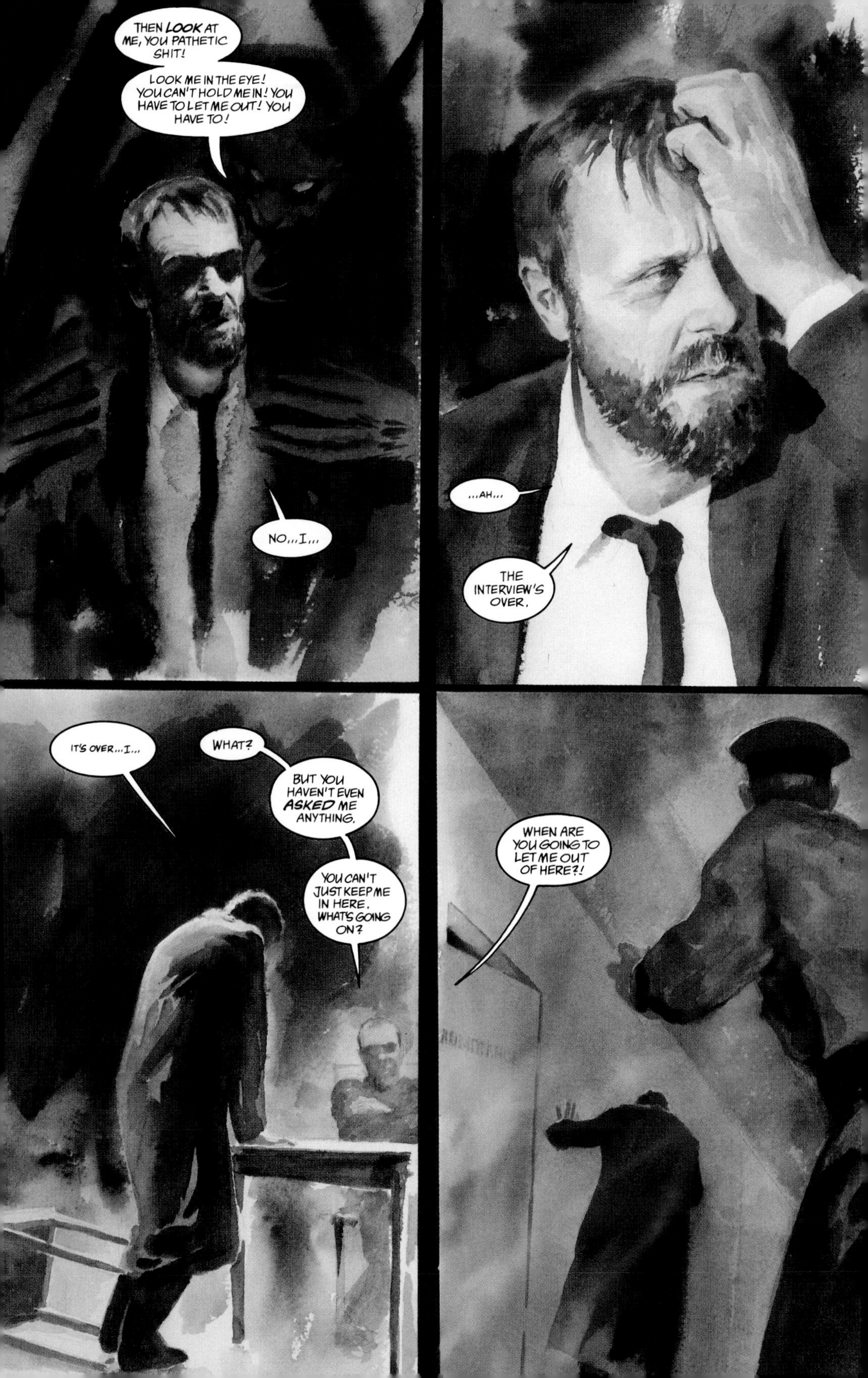
THEN LOOK AT ME, YOU PATHETIC SHIT!
LOOK ME IN THE EYE! YOU CAN'T HOLD ME IN! YOU HAVE TO LET ME OUT! YOU HAVE TO!
NO... I...
...AH...
THE INTERVIEW'S OVER.
IT'S OVER... I...
WHAT?
BUT YOU HAVEN'T EVEN ASKED ME ANYTHING.
YOU CAN'T JUST KEEP ME IN HERE. WHAT'S GOING ON?
WHEN ARE YOU GOING TO LET ME OUT OF HERE?!

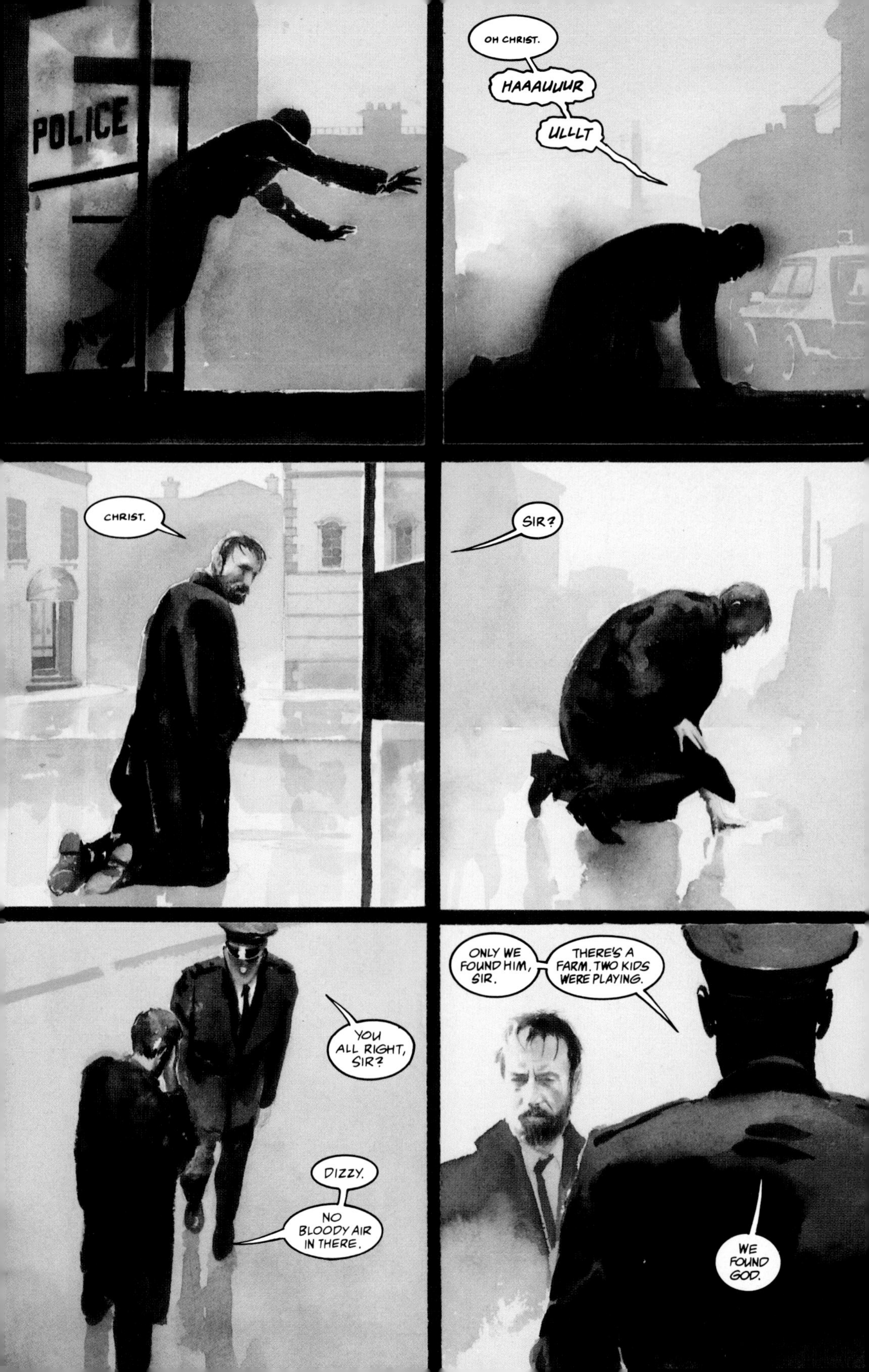
POLICE
OH CHRIST.
HAAAUUUR
ULLLT
CHRIST.
SIR?
YOU ALL RIGHT, SIR?
DIZZY.
NO BLOODY AIR IN THERE.
ONLY WE FOUND HIM, SIR.
THERE'S A FARM. TWO KIDS WERE PLAYING.
WE FOUND GOD.

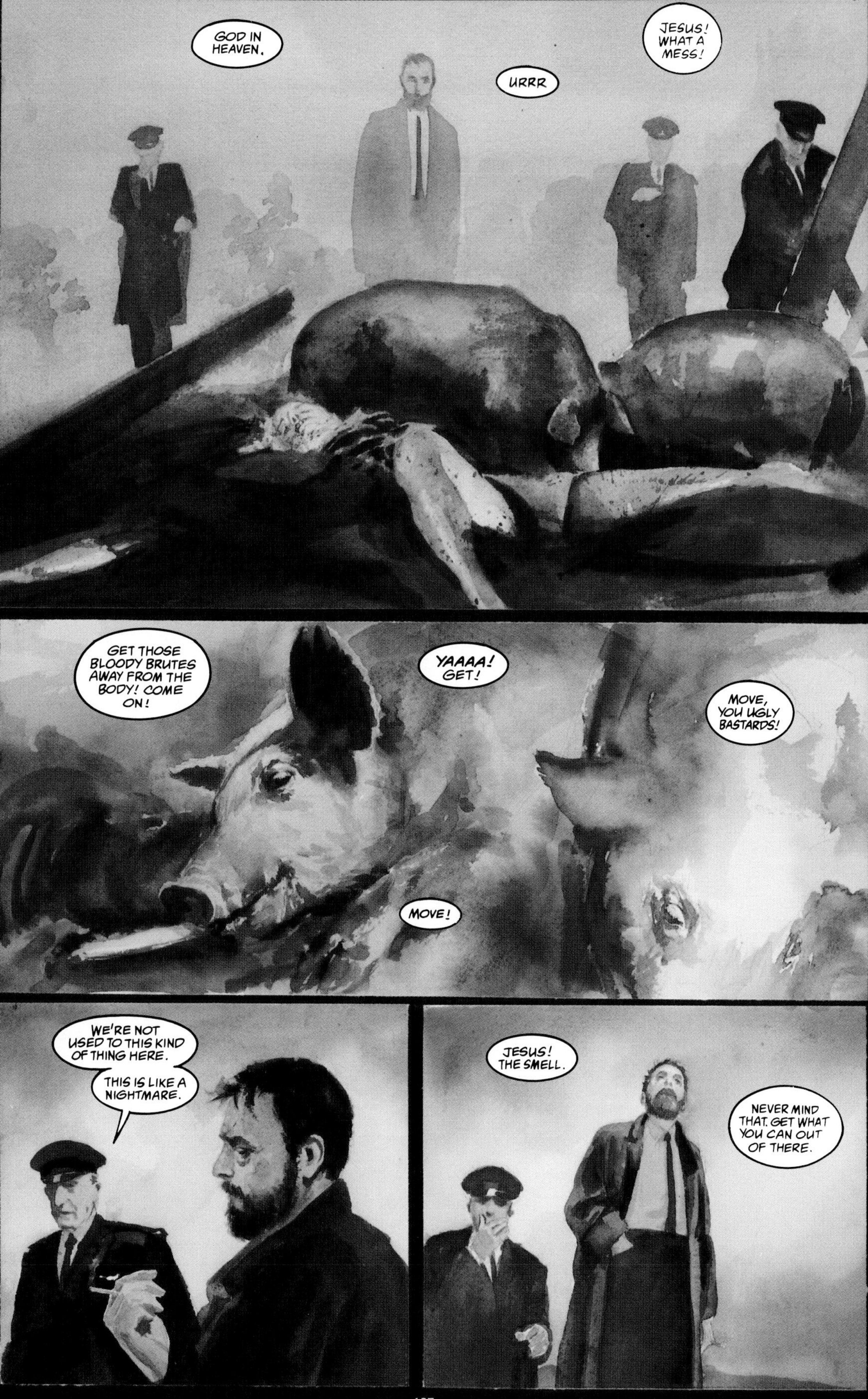
GOD IN HEAVEN.
URRR
JESUS! WHAT A MESS!
GET THOSE BLOODY BRUTES AWAY FROM THE BODY! COME ON!
YAAAA! GET!
MOVE, YOU UGLY BASTARDS!
MOVE!
WE'RE NOT USED TO THIS KIND OF THING HERE.
THIS IS LIKE A NIGHTMARE.
JESUS! THE SMELL.
NEVER MIND THAT. GET WHAT YOU CAN OUT OF THERE.

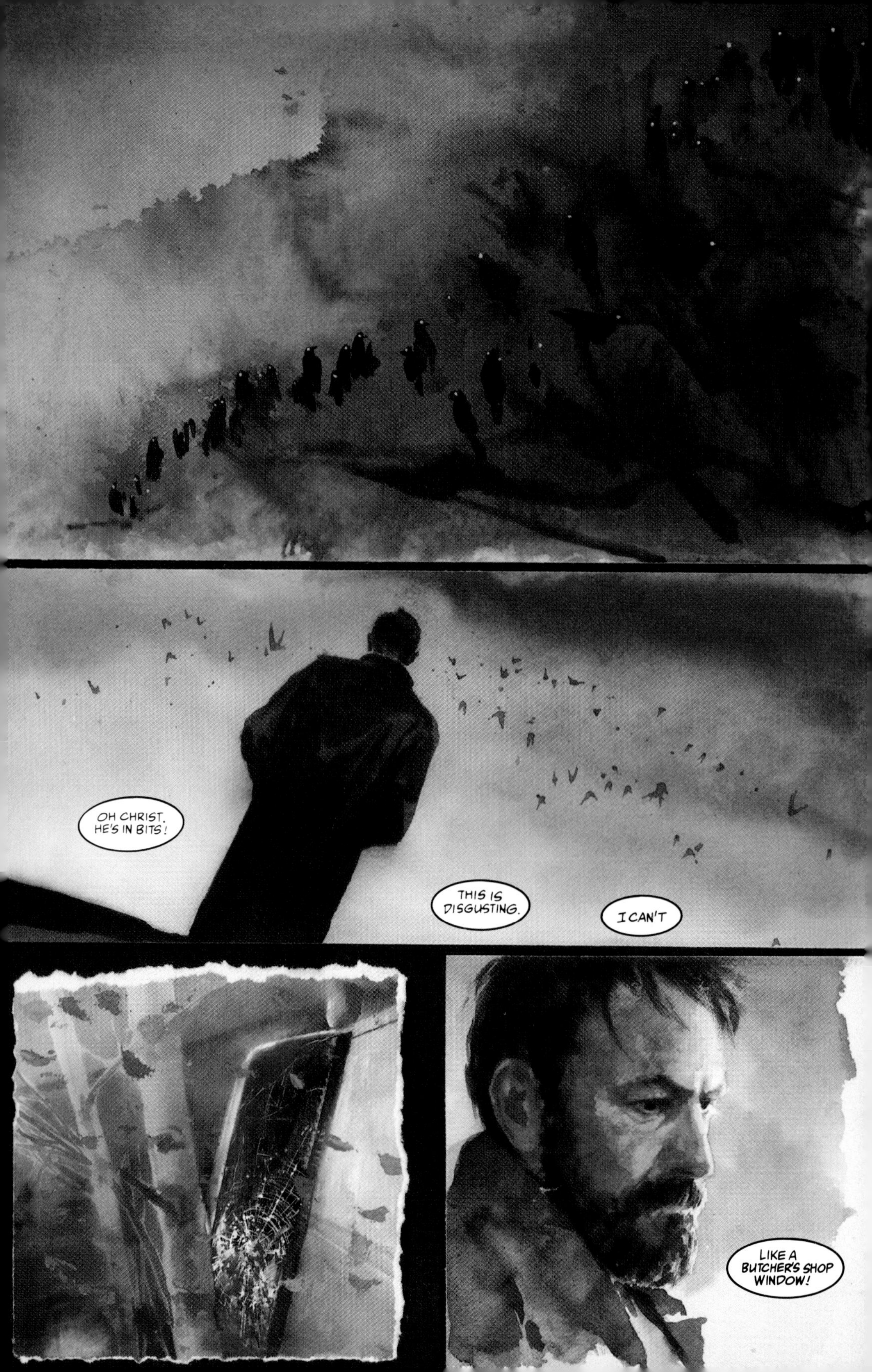
OH CHRIST. HE'S IN BITS!
THIS IS DISGUSTING.
I CAN'T
LIKE A BUTCHER'S SHOP WINDOW!

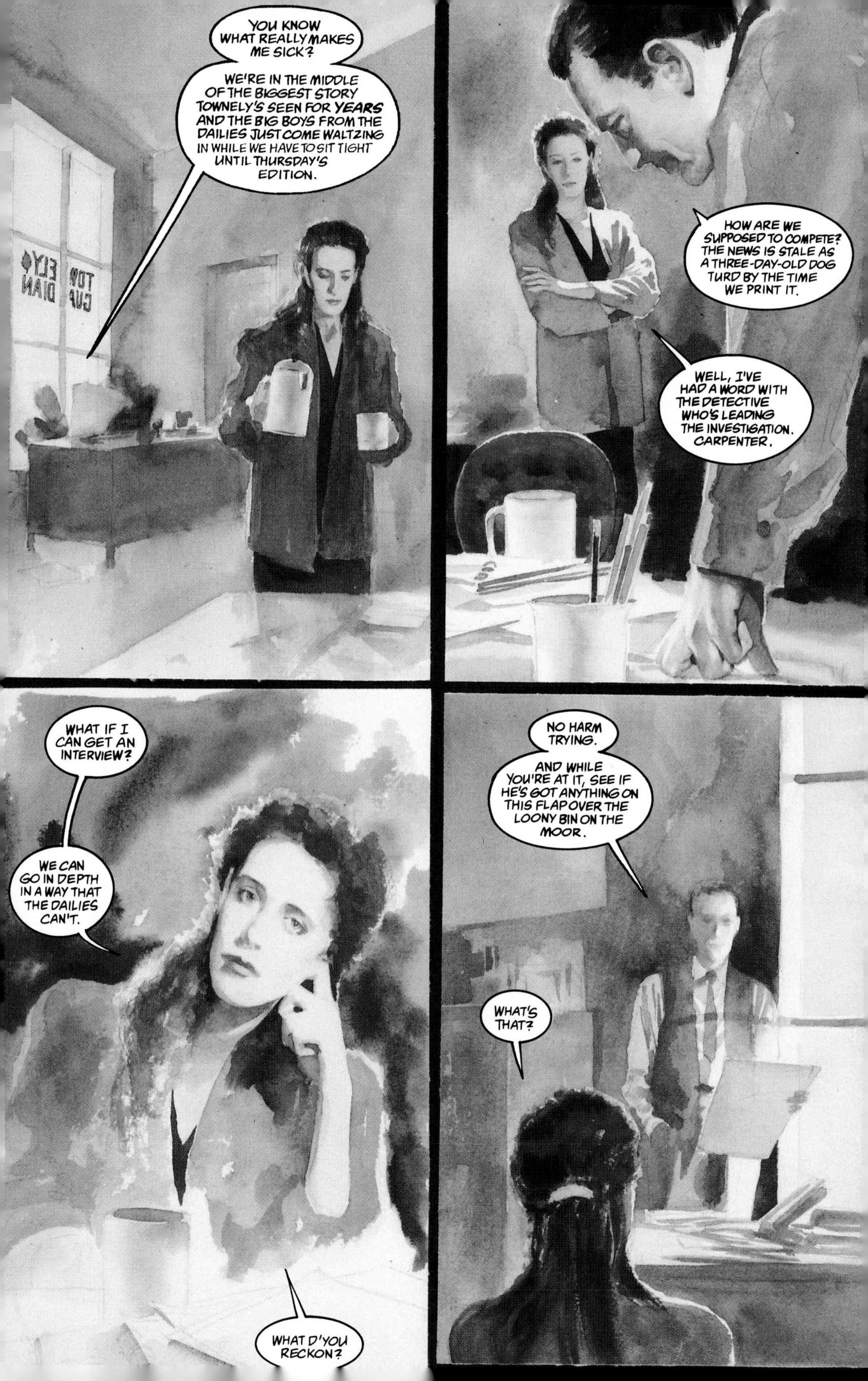
YOU KNOW WHAT REALLY MAKES ME SICK?
WE'RE IN THE MIDDLE OF THE BIGGEST STORY TOWNELY'S SEEN FOR YEARS AND THE BIG BOYS FROM THE DAILIES JUST COME WALTZING IN WHILE WE HAVE TO SIT TIGHT UNTIL THURSDAY'S EDITION.
HOW ARE WE SUPPOSED TO COMPETE? THE NEWS IS STALE AS A THREE-DAY-OLD DOG TURD BY THE TIME WE PRINT IT.
WELL, I'VE HAD A WORD WITH THE DETECTIVE WHO'S LEADING THE INVESTIGATION. CARPENTER.
WHAT IF I CAN GET AN INTERVIEW?
WE CAN GO IN DEPTH IN A WAY THAT THE DAILIES CAN'T.
WHAT D'YOU RECKON?
NO HARM TRYING.
AND WHILE YOU'RE AT IT, SEE IF HE'S GOT ANYTHING ON THIS FLAP OVER THE LOONY BIN ON THE MOOR.
WHAT'S THAT?

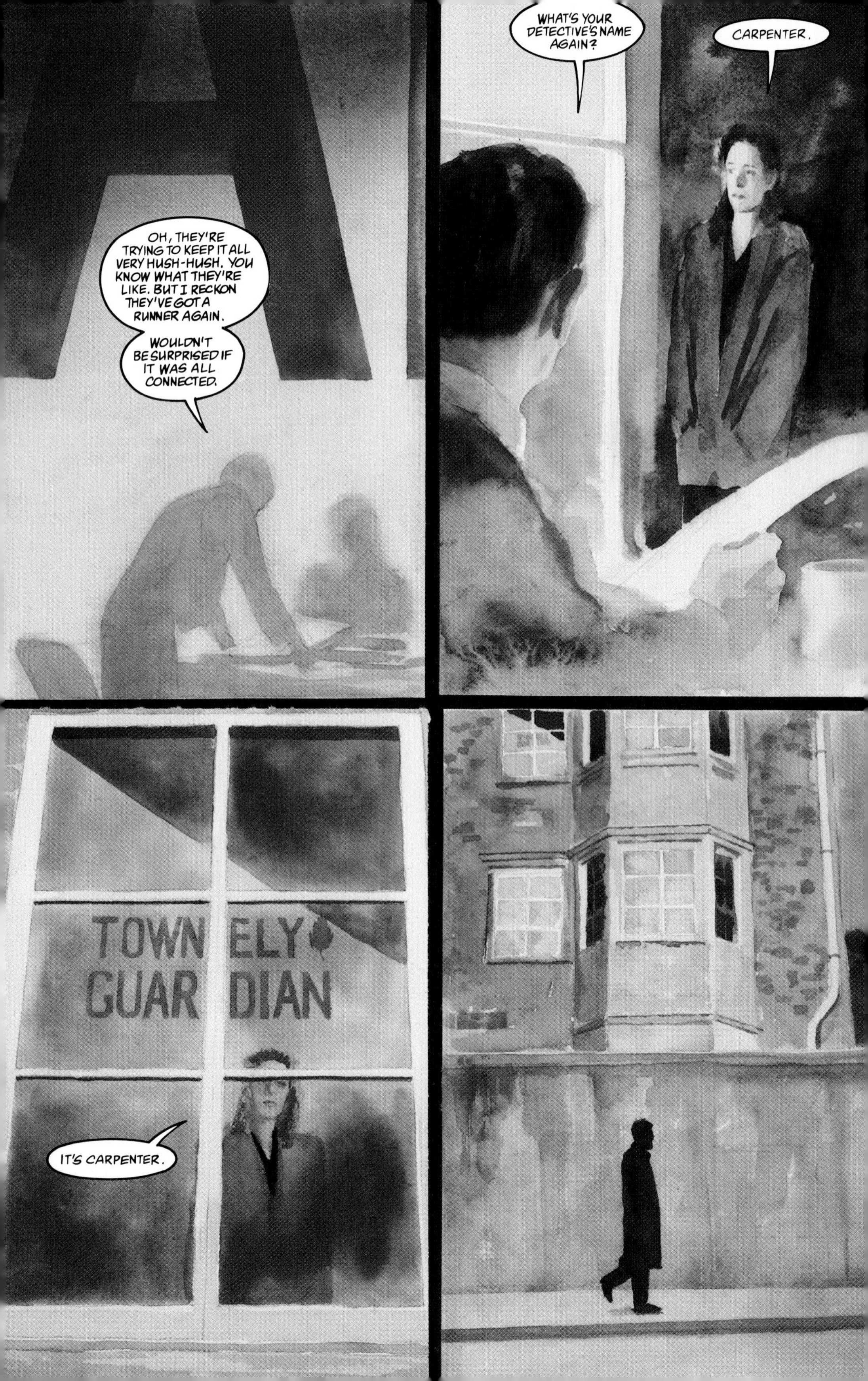

OH, THEY'RE TRYING TO KEEP IT ALL VERY HUSH-HUSH. YOU KNOW WHAT THEY'RE LIKE. BUT I RECKON THEY'VE GOT A RUNNER AGAIN.
WOULDN'T BE SURPRISED IF IT WAS ALL CONNECTED.
WHAT'S YOUR DETECTIVE'S NAME AGAIN?
CARPENTER.
TOWN ELY GUAR DIAN
IT'S CARPENTER.

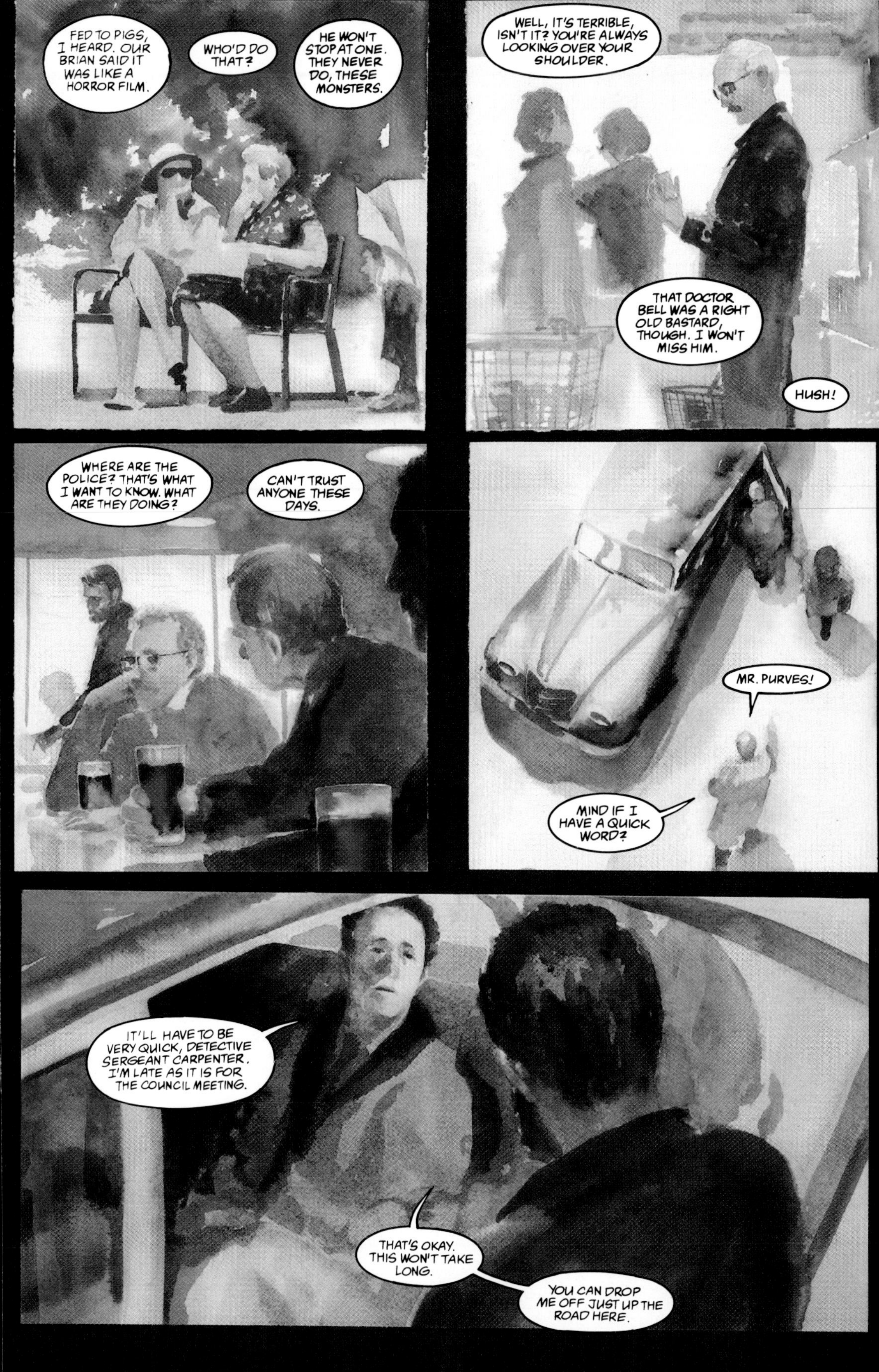
FED TO PIGS, I HEARD. OUR BRIAN SAID IT WAS LIKE A HORROR FILM.
WHO'D DO THAT?
HE WON'T STOP AT ONE. THEY NEVER DO, THESE MONSTERS.
WELL, IT'S TERRIBLE, ISN'T IT? YOU'RE ALWAYS LOOKING OVER YOUR SHOULDER.
THAT DOCTOR BELL WAS A RIGHT OLD BASTARD, THOUGH. I WON'T MISS HIM.
HUSH!
WHERE ARE THE POLICE? THAT'S WHAT I WANT TO KNOW. WHAT ARE THEY DOING?
CAN'T TRUST ANYONE THESE DAYS.
MR. PURVES!
MIND IF I HAVE A QUICK WORD?
IT'LL HAVE TO BE VERY QUICK, DETECTIVE SERGEANT CARPENTER. I'M LATE AS IT IS FOR THE COUNCIL MEETING.
THAT'S OKAY. THIS WON'T TAKE LONG.
YOU CAN DROP ME OFF JUST UP THE ROAD HERE.

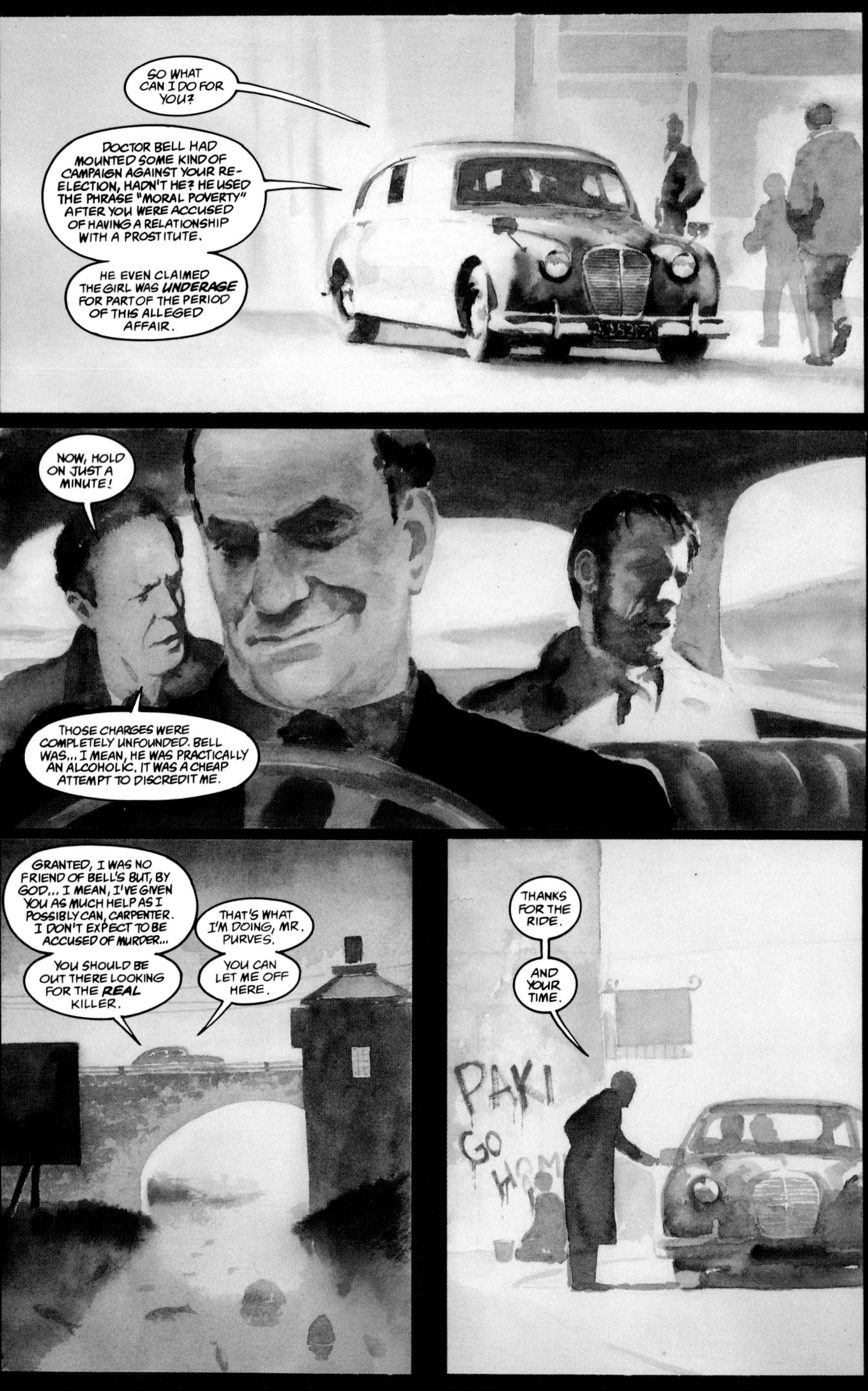
SO WHAT CAN I DO FOR YOU?
DOCTOR BELL HAD MOUNTED SOME KIND OF CAMPAIGN AGAINST YOUR RE-ELECTION, HADN'T HE? HE USED THE PHRASE "MORAL POVERTY" AFTER YOU WERE ACCUSED OF HAVING A RELATIONSHIP WITH A PROSTITUTE.
HE EVEN CLAIMED THE GIRL WAS UNDERAGE FOR PART OF THE PERIOD OF THIS ALLEGED AFFAIR.
NOW, HOLD ON JUST A MINUTE!
THOSE CHARGES WERE COMPLETELY UNFOUNDED. BELL WAS... I MEAN, HE WAS PRACTICALLY AN ALCOHOLIC. IT WAS A CHEAP ATTEMPT TO DISCREDIT ME.
GRANTED, I WAS NO FRIEND OF BELL'S BUT, BY GOD... I MEAN, I'VE GIVEN YOU AS MUCH HELP AS I POSSIBLY CAN, CARPENTER. I DON'T EXPECT TO BE ACCUSED OF MURDER...
YOU SHOULD BE OUT THERE LOOKING FOR THE REAL KILLER.
THAT'S WHAT I'M DOING, MR. PURVES.
YOU CAN LET ME OFF HERE.
THANKS FOR THE RIDE.
AND YOUR TIME.
PAKI GO HOM

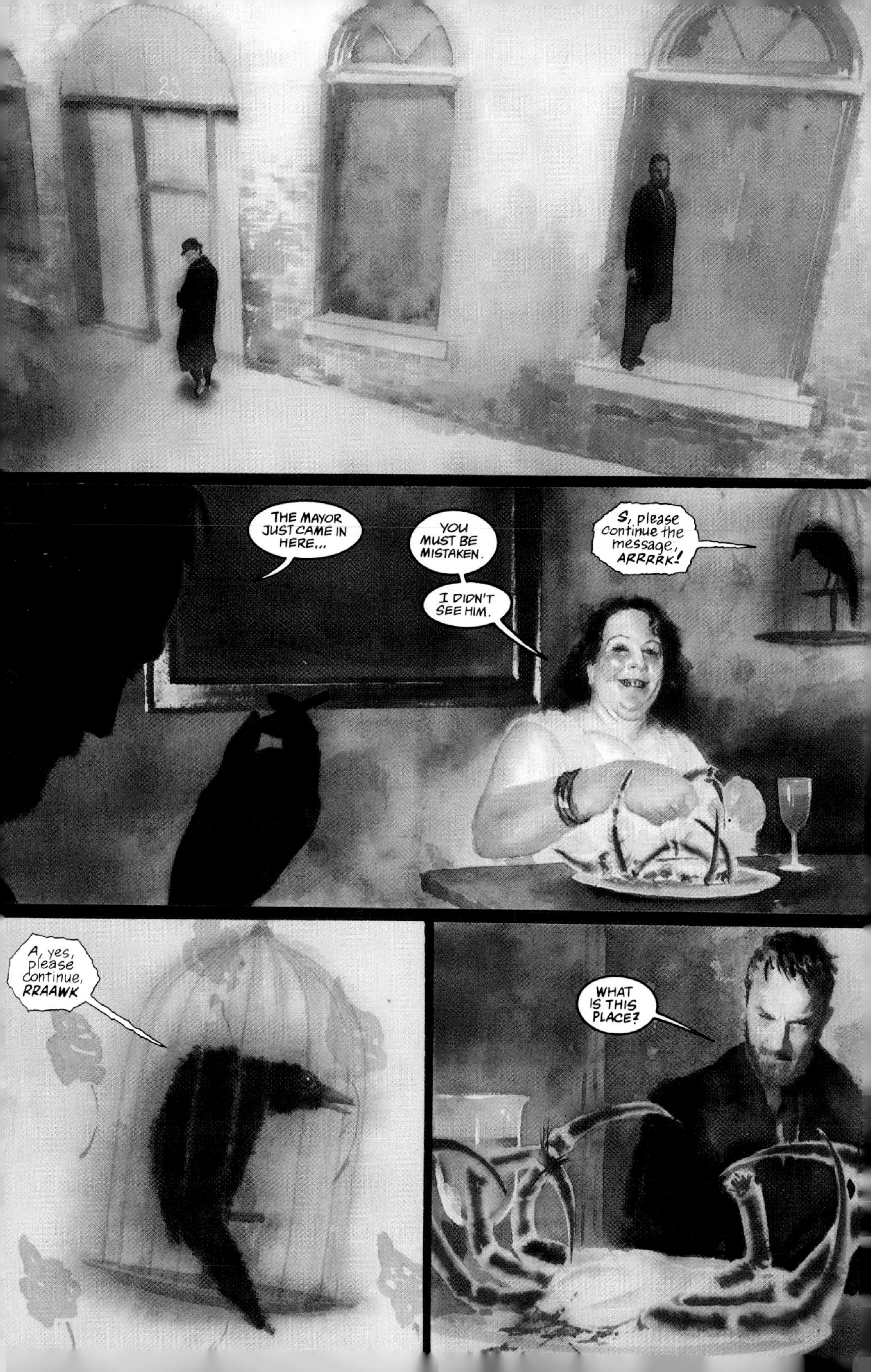
THE MAYOR JUST CAME IN HERE...
YOU MUST BE MISTAKEN.
I DIDN'T SEE HIM.
S, please continue the message, ARRRRK!
A, yes, please continue, RRAAWK
WHAT IS THIS PLACE?

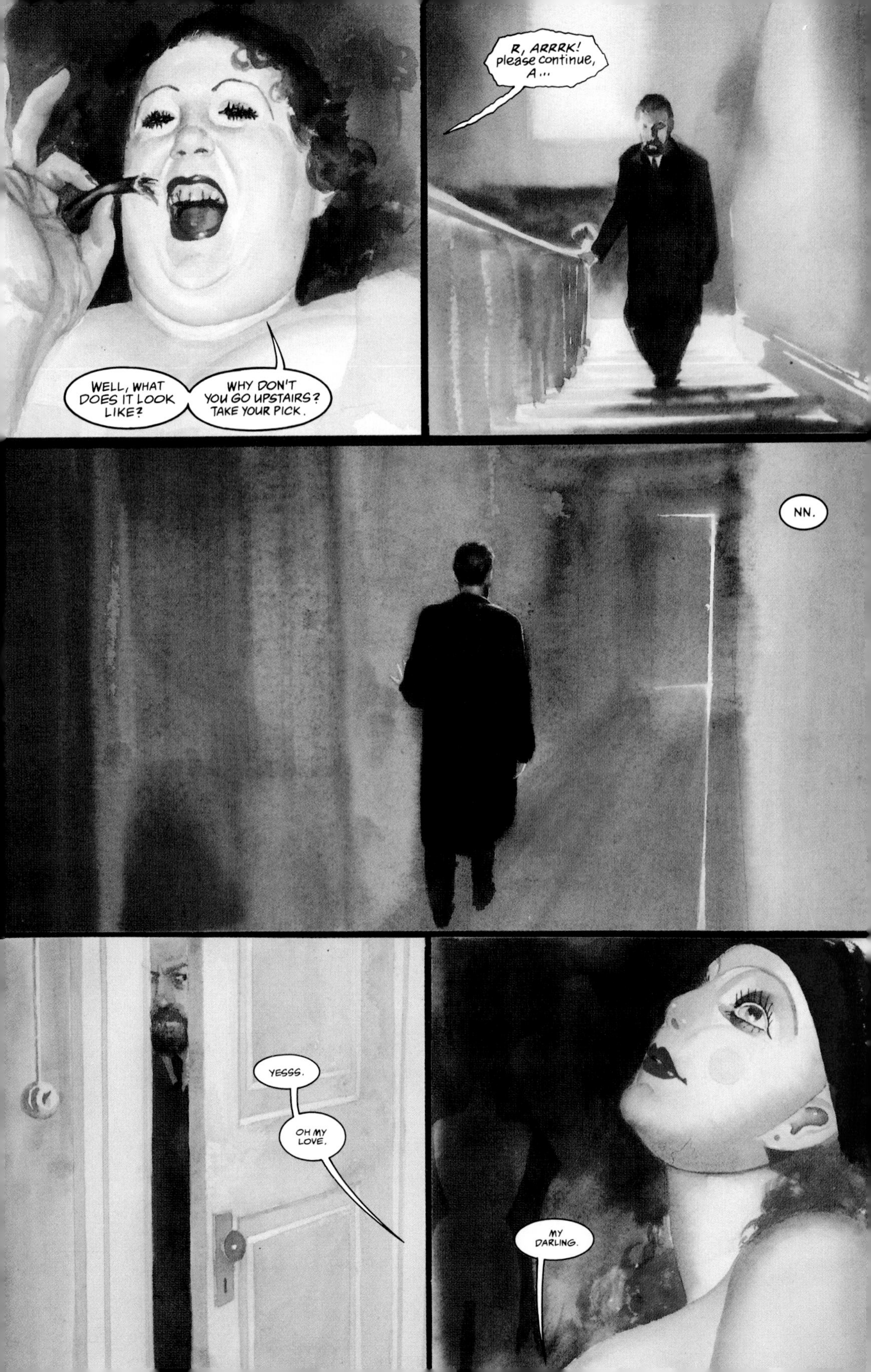
WELL, WHAT DOES IT LOOK LIKE?
WHY DON'T YOU GO UPSTAIRS? TAKE YOUR PICK.
R, ARRRK! please continue, A...
NN.
YESSS.
OH MY LOVE.
MY DARLING.

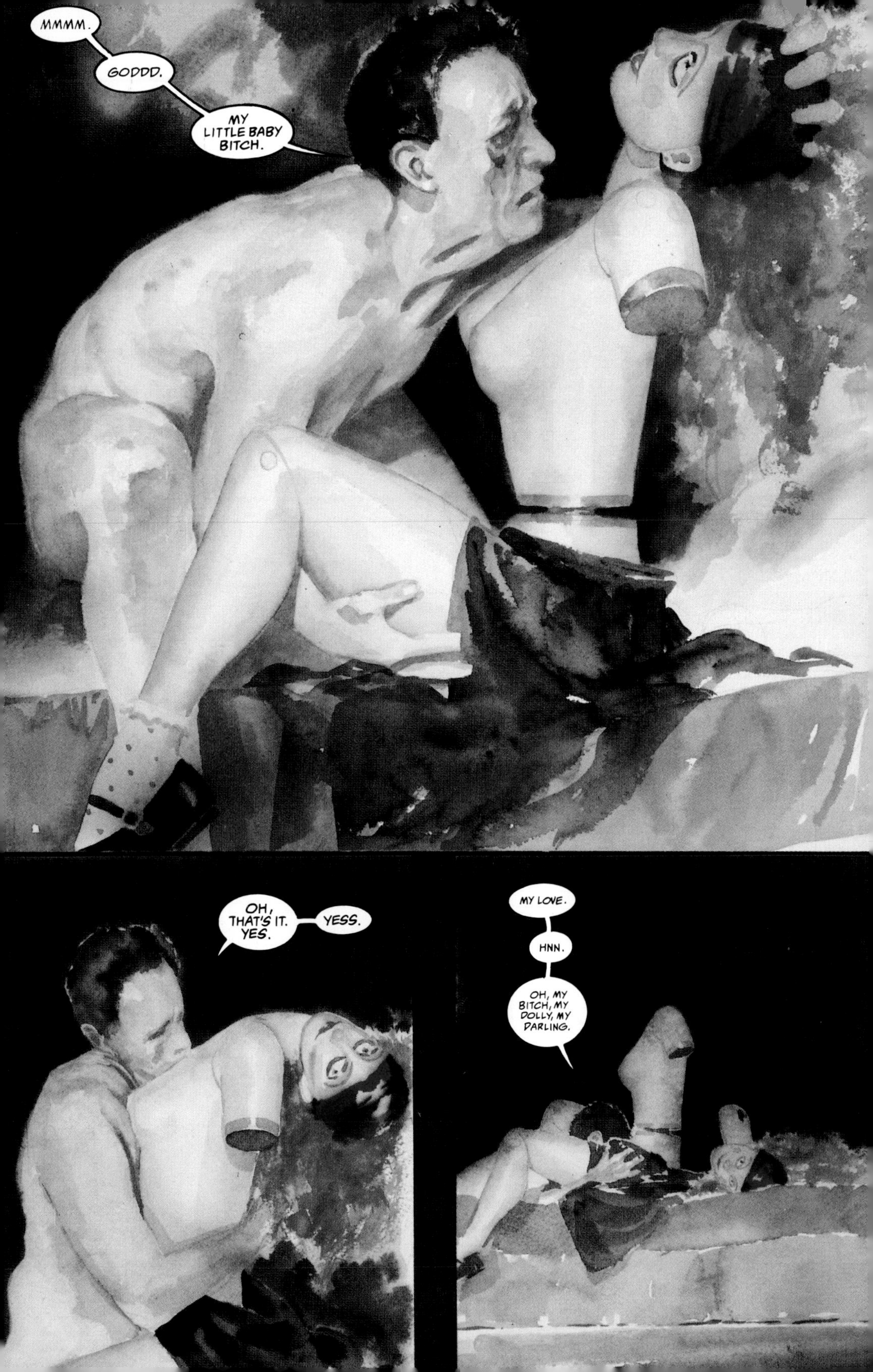
MMMM.
GODDD.
MY LITTLE BABY BITCH.
OH, THAT'S IT. YES.
YESS.
MY LOVE.
HNN.
OH, MY BITCH, MY DOLLY, MY DARLING.

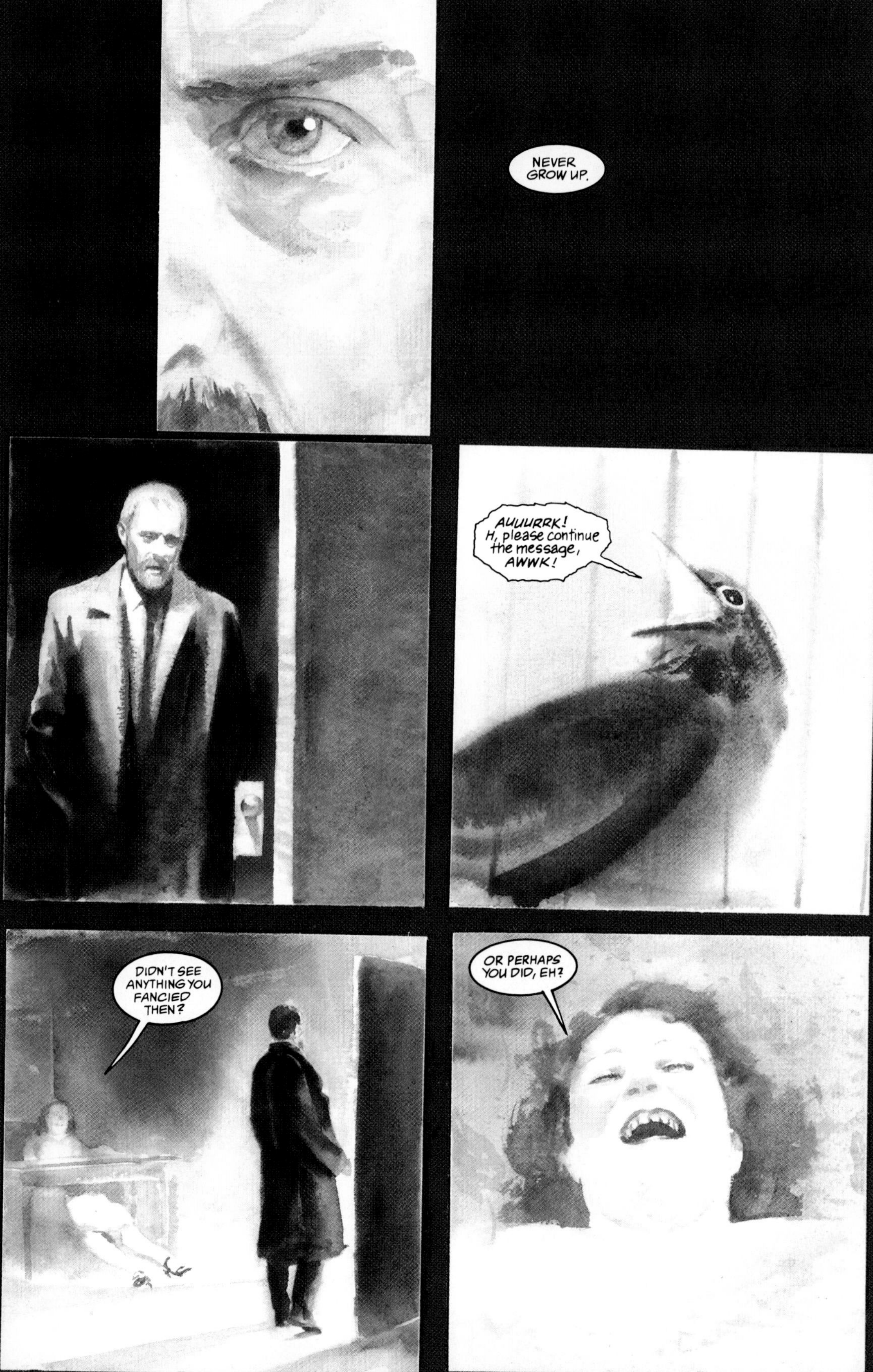
NEVER GROW UP.
AUUURRK! H, please continue the message, AWWK!
DIDN'T SEE ANYTHING YOU FANCIED THEN?
OR PERHAPS YOU DID, EH?

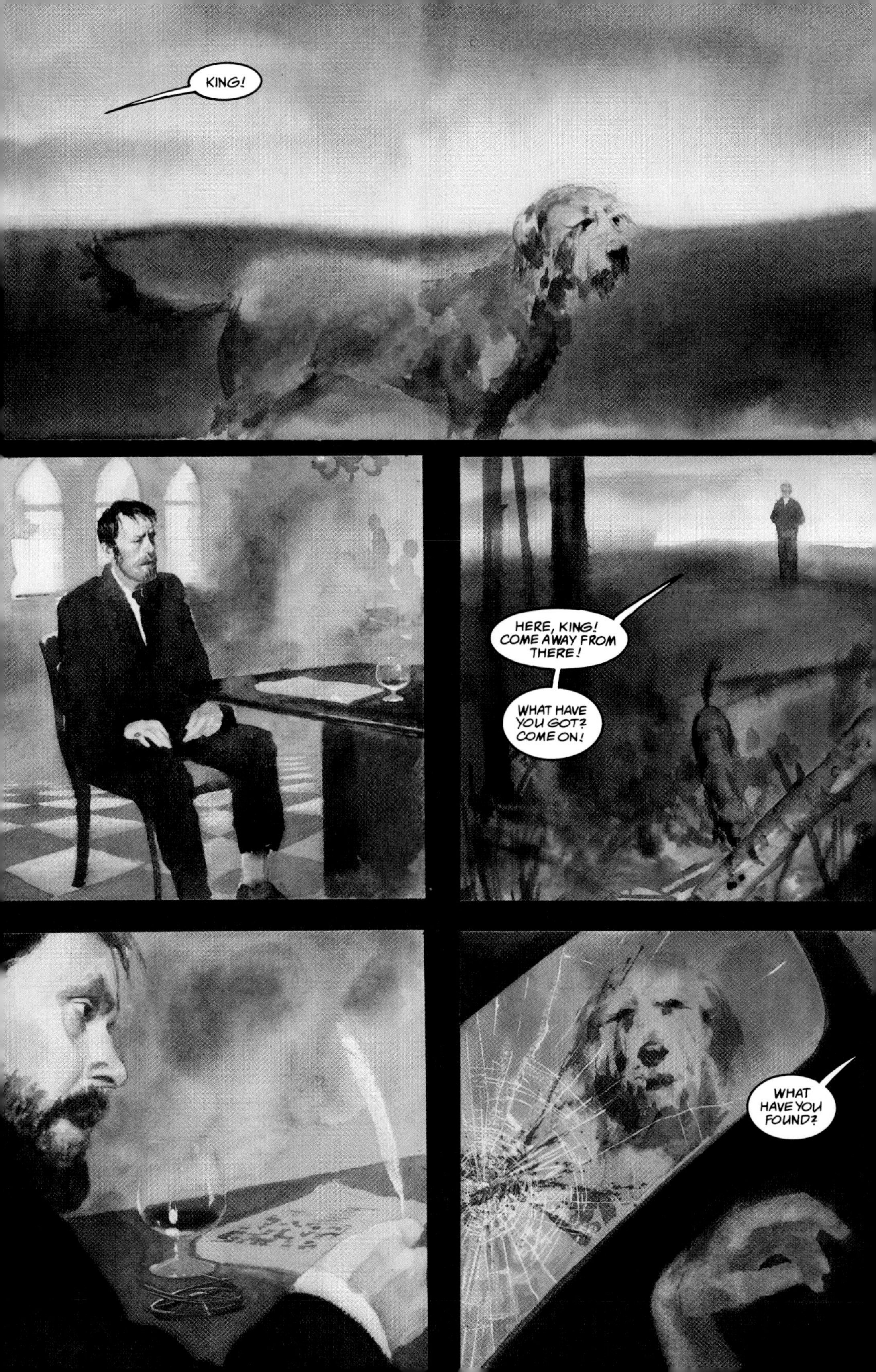
KING!
HERE, KING! COME AWAY FROM THERE!
WHAT HAVE YOU GOT? COME ON!
WHAT HAVE YOU FOUND?

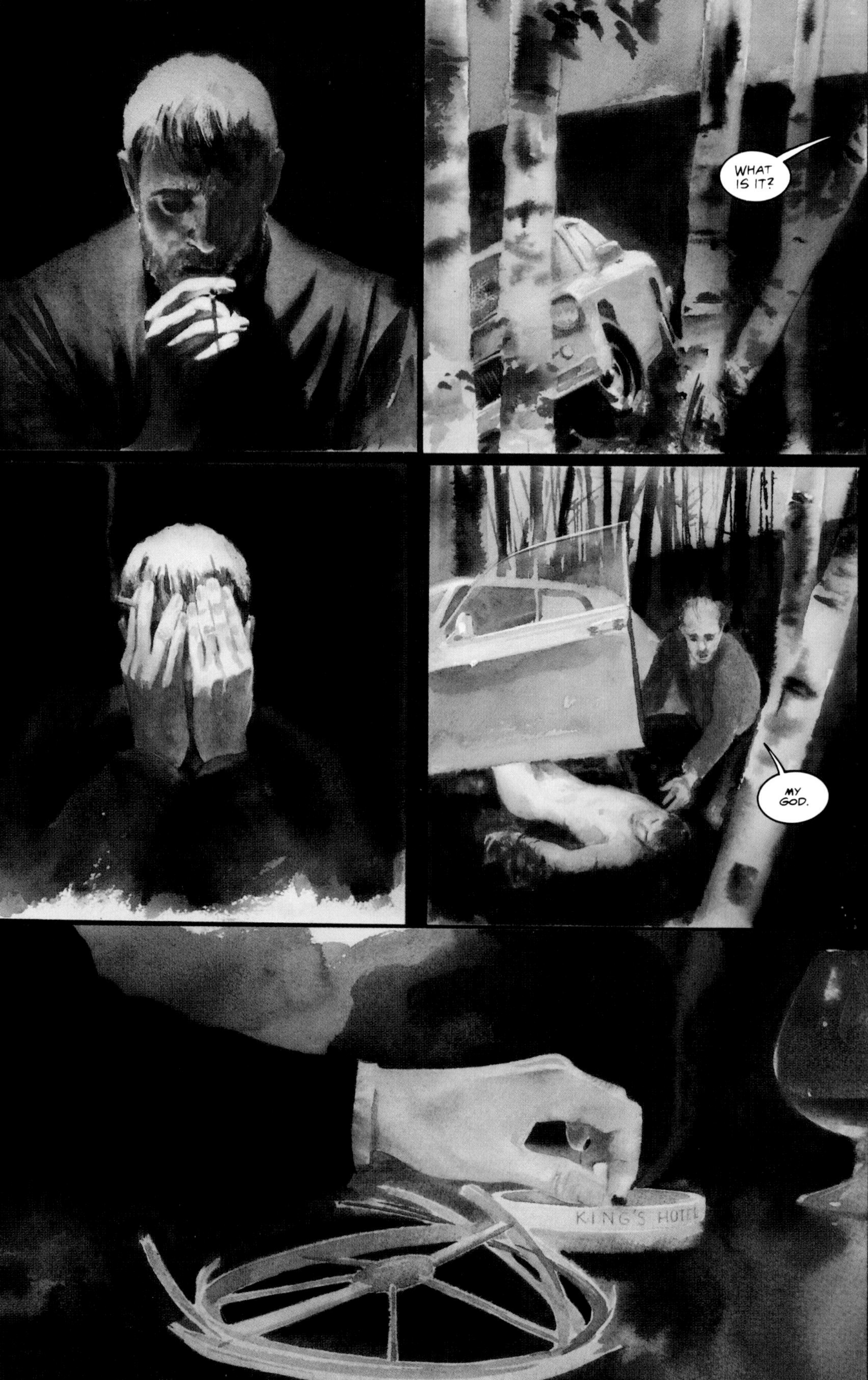
WHAT IS IT?
MY GOD.
KING'S HOTEL

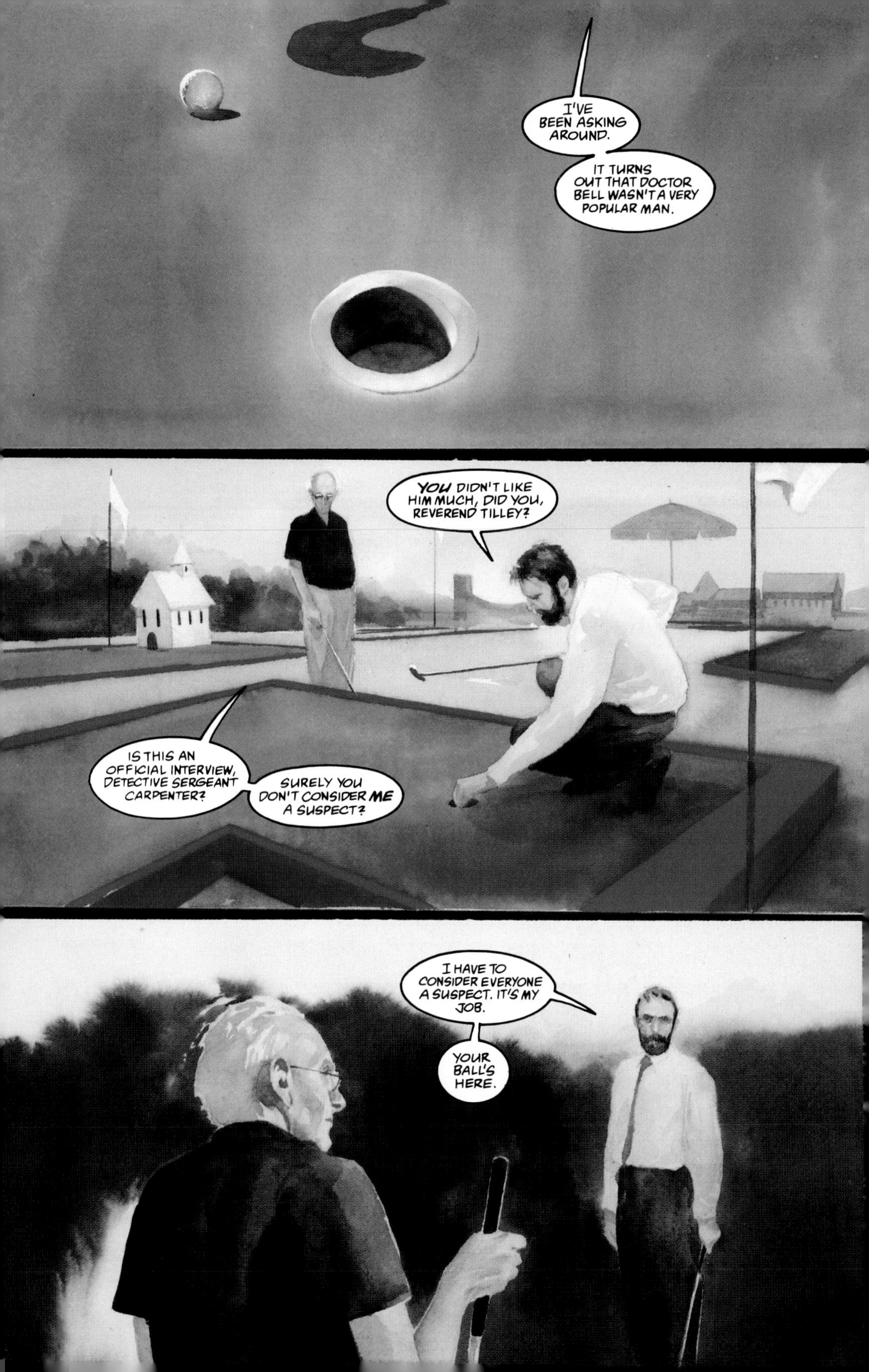
I'VE BEEN ASKING AROUND.
IT TURNS OUT THAT DOCTOR BELL WASN'T A VERY POPULAR MAN.
YOU DIDN'T LIKE HIM MUCH, DID YOU, REVEREND TILLEY?
IS THIS AN OFFICIAL INTERVIEW, DETECTIVE SERGEANT CARPENTER?
SURELY YOU DON'T CONSIDER ME A SUSPECT?
I HAVE TO CONSIDER EVERYONE A SUSPECT. IT'S MY JOB.
YOUR BALL'S HERE.

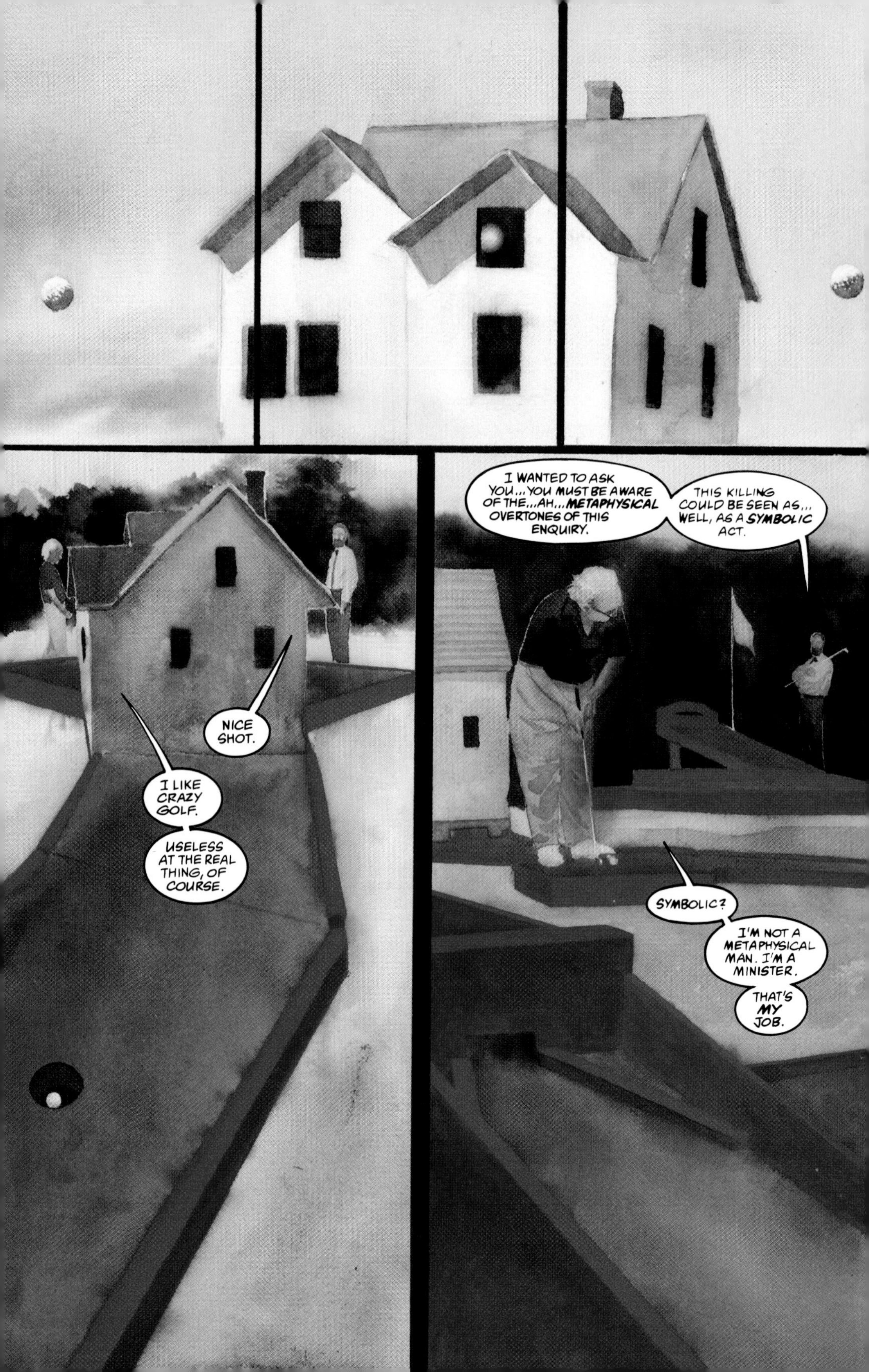
NICE SHOT.
I LIKE CRAZY GOLF.
USELESS AT THE REAL THING, OF COURSE.
I WANTED TO ASK YOU... YOU MUST BE AWARE OF THE... AH... METAPHYSICAL OVERTONES OF THIS ENQUIRY.
THIS KILLING COULD BE SEEN AS... WELL, AS A SYMBOLIC ACT.
SYMBOLIC?
I'M NOT A METAPHYSICAL MAN. I'M A MINISTER.
THAT'S MY JOB.

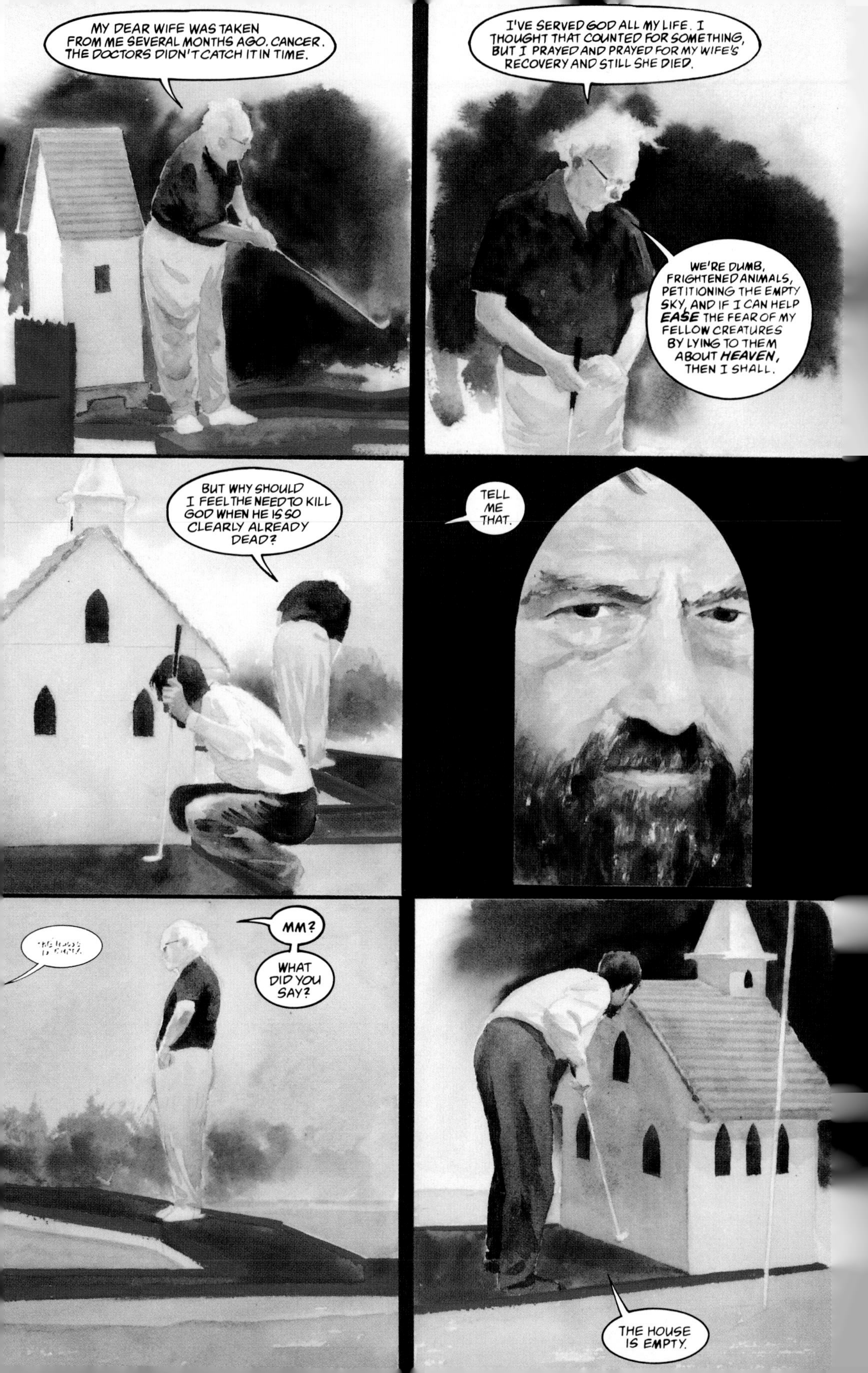
MY DEAR WIFE WAS TAKEN FROM ME SEVERAL MONTHS AGO. CANCER. THE DOCTORS DIDN'T CATCH IT IN TIME.
I'VE SERVED GOD ALL MY LIFE. I THOUGHT THAT COUNTED FOR SOMETHING, BUT I PRAYED AND PRAYED FOR MY WIFE'S RECOVERY AND STILL SHE DIED.
WE'RE DUMB, FRIGHTENED ANIMALS, PETITIONING THE EMPTY SKY, AND IF I CAN HELP EASE THE FEAR OF MY FELLOW CREATURES BY LYING TO THEM ABOUT HEAVEN, THEN I SHALL.
BUT WHY SHOULD I FEEL THE NEED TO KILL GOD WHEN HE IS SO CLEARLY ALREADY DEAD?
TELL ME THAT.
MM?
WHAT DID YOU SAY?
THE HOUSE IS EMPTY.

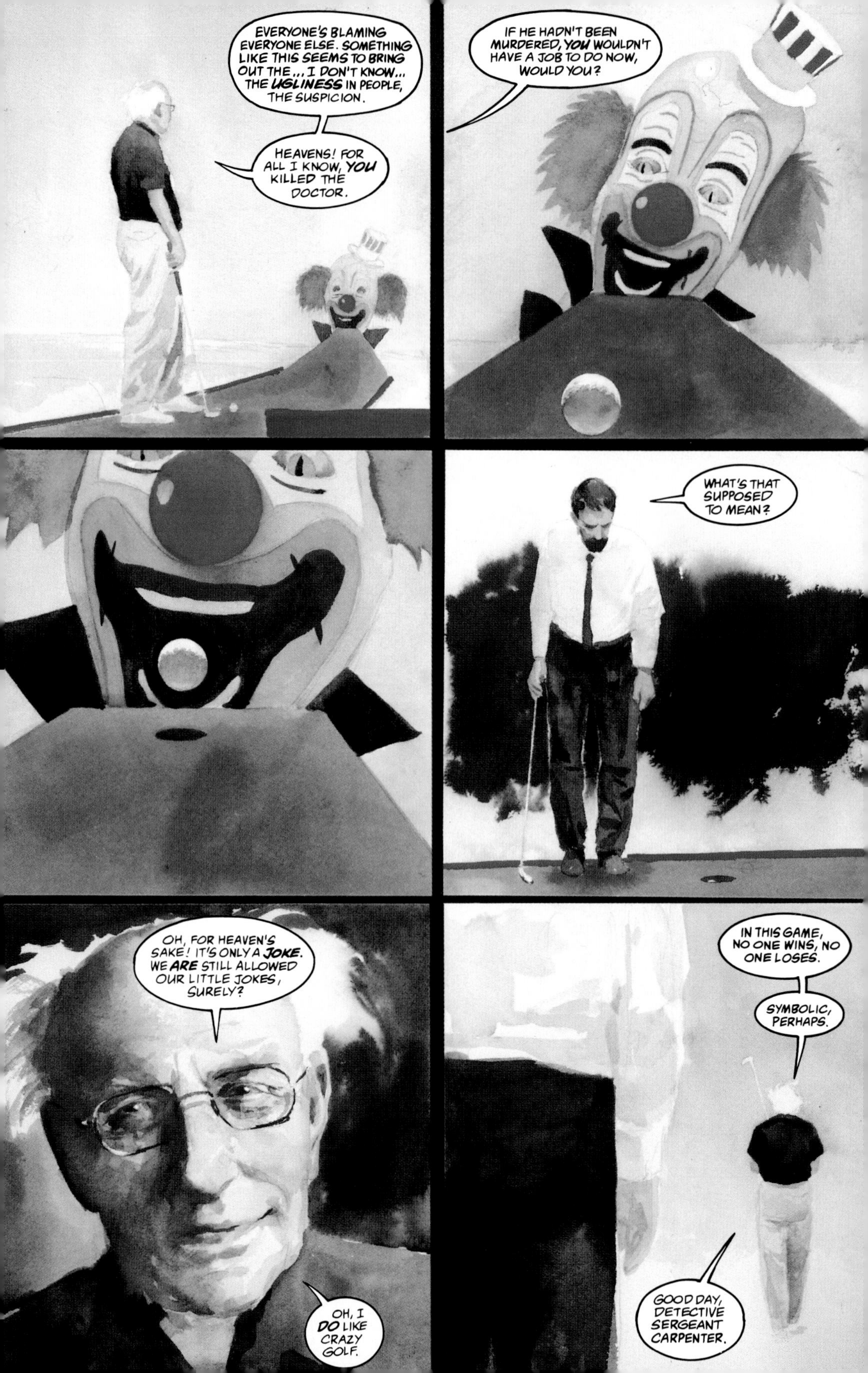
EVERYONE'S BLAMING EVERYONE ELSE. SOMETHING LIKE THIS SEEMS TO BRING OUT THE... I DON'T KNOW... THE UGLINESS IN PEOPLE, THE SUSPICION.
HEAVENS! FOR ALL I KNOW, YOU KILLED THE DOCTOR.
IF HE HADN'T BEEN MURDERED, YOU WOULDN'T HAVE A JOB TO DO NOW, WOULD YOU?
WHAT'S THAT SUPPOSED TO MEAN?
OH, FOR HEAVEN'S SAKE! IT'S ONLY A JOKE. WE ARE STILL ALLOWED OUR LITTLE JOKES, SURELY?
OH, I DO LIKE CRAZY GOLF.
IN THIS GAME, NO ONE WINS, NO ONE LOSES.
SYMBOLIC, PERHAPS.
GOOD DAY, DETECTIVE SERGEANT CARPENTER.

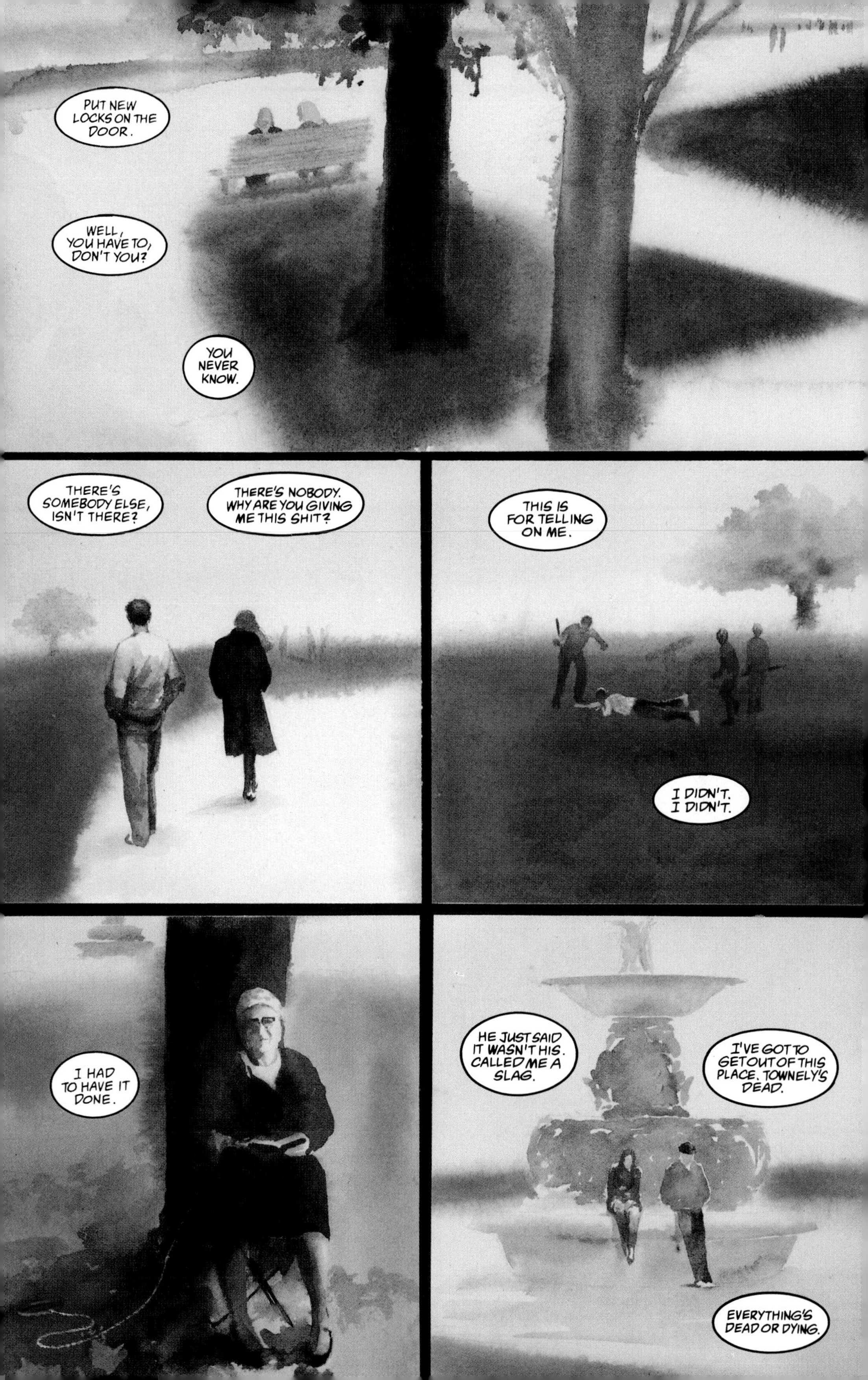
PUT NEW LOCKS ON THE DOOR.
WELL, YOU HAVE TO, DON'T YOU?
YOU NEVER KNOW.
THERE'S SOMEBODY ELSE, ISN'T THERE?
THERE'S NOBODY. WHY ARE YOU GIVING ME THIS SHIT?
THIS IS FOR TELLING ON ME.
I DIDN'T. I DIDN'T.
I HAD TO HAVE IT DONE.
HE JUST SAID IT WASN'T THIS. CALLED ME A SLAG.
I'VE GOT TO GET OUT OF THIS PLACE. TOWNELY'S DEAD.
EVERYTHING'S DEAD OR DYING.

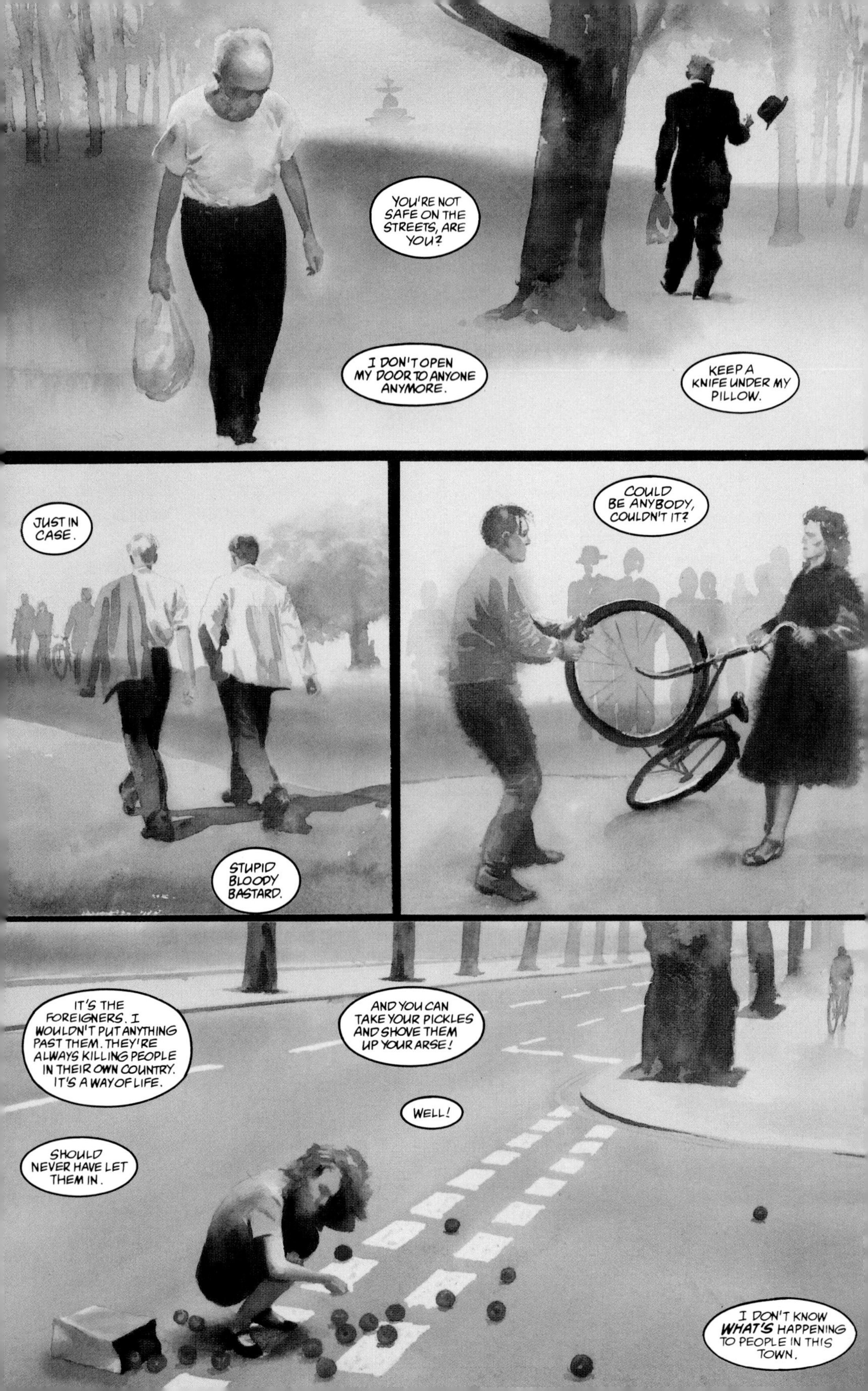
YOU'RE NOT SAFE ON THE STREETS, ARE YOU?
I DON'T OPEN MY DOOR TO ANYONE ANYMORE.
KEEP A KNIFE UNDER MY PILLOW.
JUST IN CASE.
STUPID BLOODY BASTARD.
COULD BE ANYBODY, COULDN'T IT?
IT'S THE FOREIGNERS. I WOULDN'T PUT ANYTHING PAST THEM. THEY'RE ALWAYS KILLING PEOPLE IN THEIR OWN COUNTRY. IT'S A WAY OF LIFE.
SHOULD NEVER HAVE LET THEM IN.
AND YOU CAN TAKE YOUR PICKLES AND SHOVE THEM UP YOUR ARSE!
WELL!
I DON'T KNOW WHAT'S HAPPENING TO PEOPLE IN THIS TOWN.

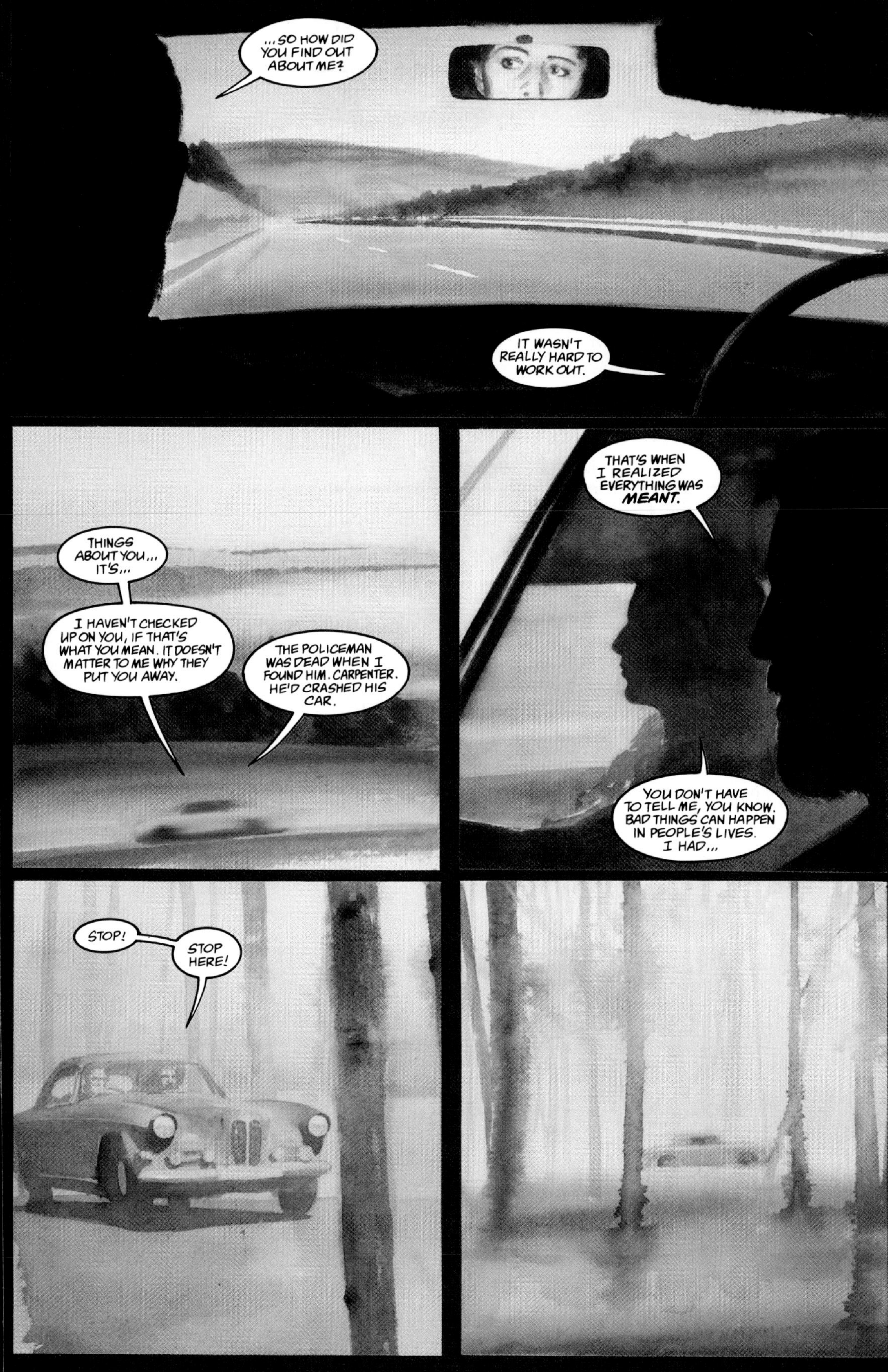

...SO HOW DID YOU FIND OUT ABOUT ME?
IT WASN'T REALLY HARD TO WORK OUT.
THINGS ABOUT YOU... IT'S...
I HAVEN'T CHECKED UP ON YOU, IF THAT'S WHAT YOU MEAN. IT DOESN'T MATTER TO ME WHY THEY PUT YOU AWAY.
THE POLICEMAN WAS DEAD WHEN I FOUND HIM. CARPENTER. HE'D CRASHED HIS CAR.
THAT'S WHEN I REALIZED EVERYTHING WAS **MEANT**.
YOU DON'T HAVE TO TELL ME, YOU KNOW. BAD THINGS CAN HAPPEN IN PEOPLE'S LIVES. I HAD...
STOP!
STOP HERE!

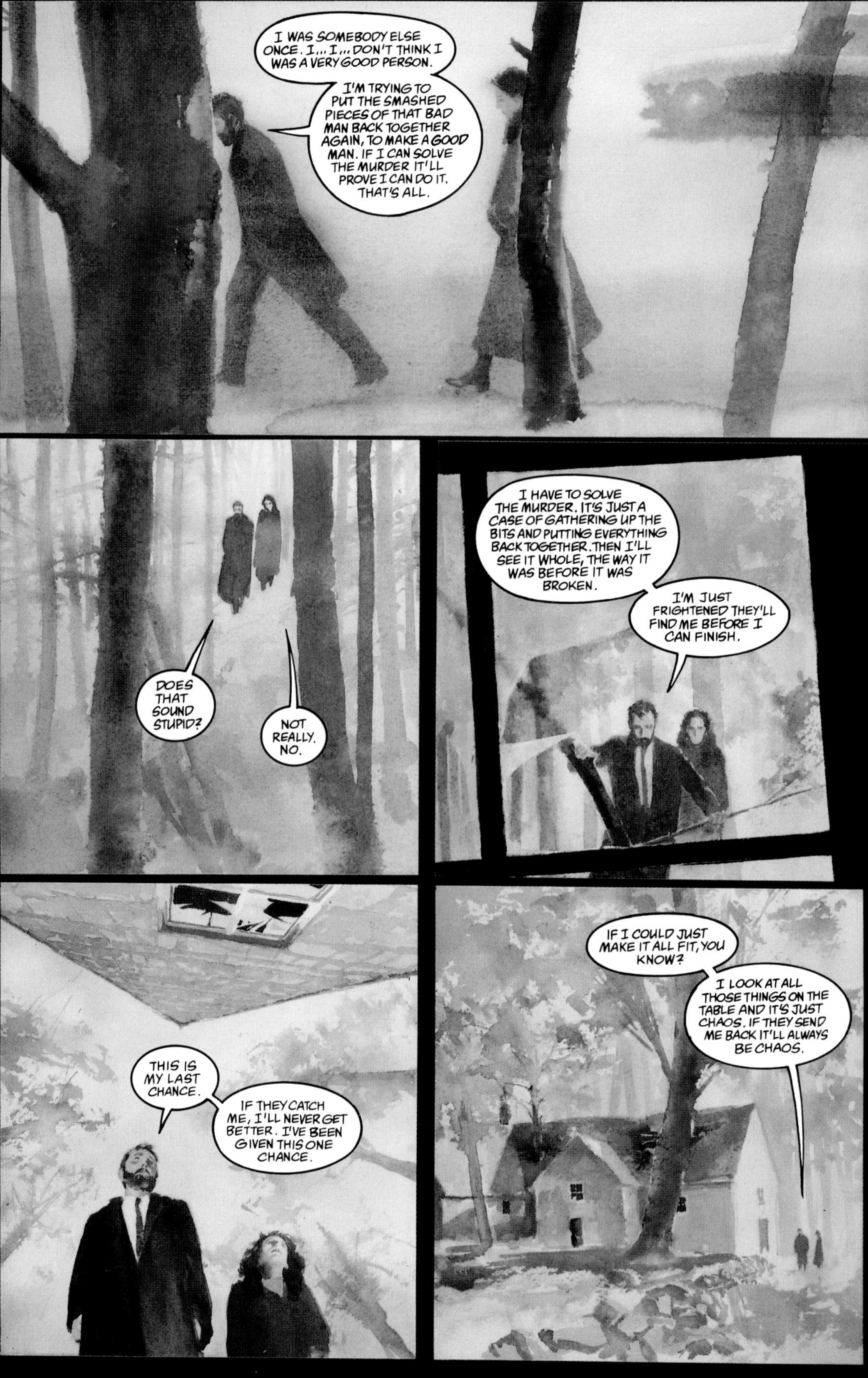
I WAS SOMEBODY ELSE ONCE. I... I... DON'T THINK I WAS A VERY GOOD PERSON.
I'M TRYING TO PUT THE SMASHED PIECES OF THAT BAD MAN BACK TOGETHER AGAIN, TO MAKE A GOOD MAN. IF I CAN SOLVE THE MURDER IT'LL PROVE I CAN DO IT. THAT'S ALL.
DOES THAT SOUND STUPID?
NOT REALLY. NO.
I HAVE TO SOLVE THE MURDER. IT'S JUST A CASE OF GATHERING UP THE BITS AND PUTTING EVERYTHING BACK TOGETHER. THEN I'LL SEE IT WHOLE, THE WAY IT WAS BEFORE IT WAS BROKEN.
I'M JUST FRIGHTENED THEY'LL FIND ME BEFORE I CAN FINISH.
THIS IS MY LAST CHANCE.
IF THEY CATCH ME, I'LL NEVER GET BETTER. I'VE BEEN GIVEN THIS ONE CHANCE.
IF I COULD JUST MAKE IT ALL FIT, YOU KNOW?
I LOOK AT ALL THOSE THINGS ON THE TABLE AND IT'S JUST CHAOS. IF THEY SEND ME BACK IT'LL ALWAYS BE CHAOS.

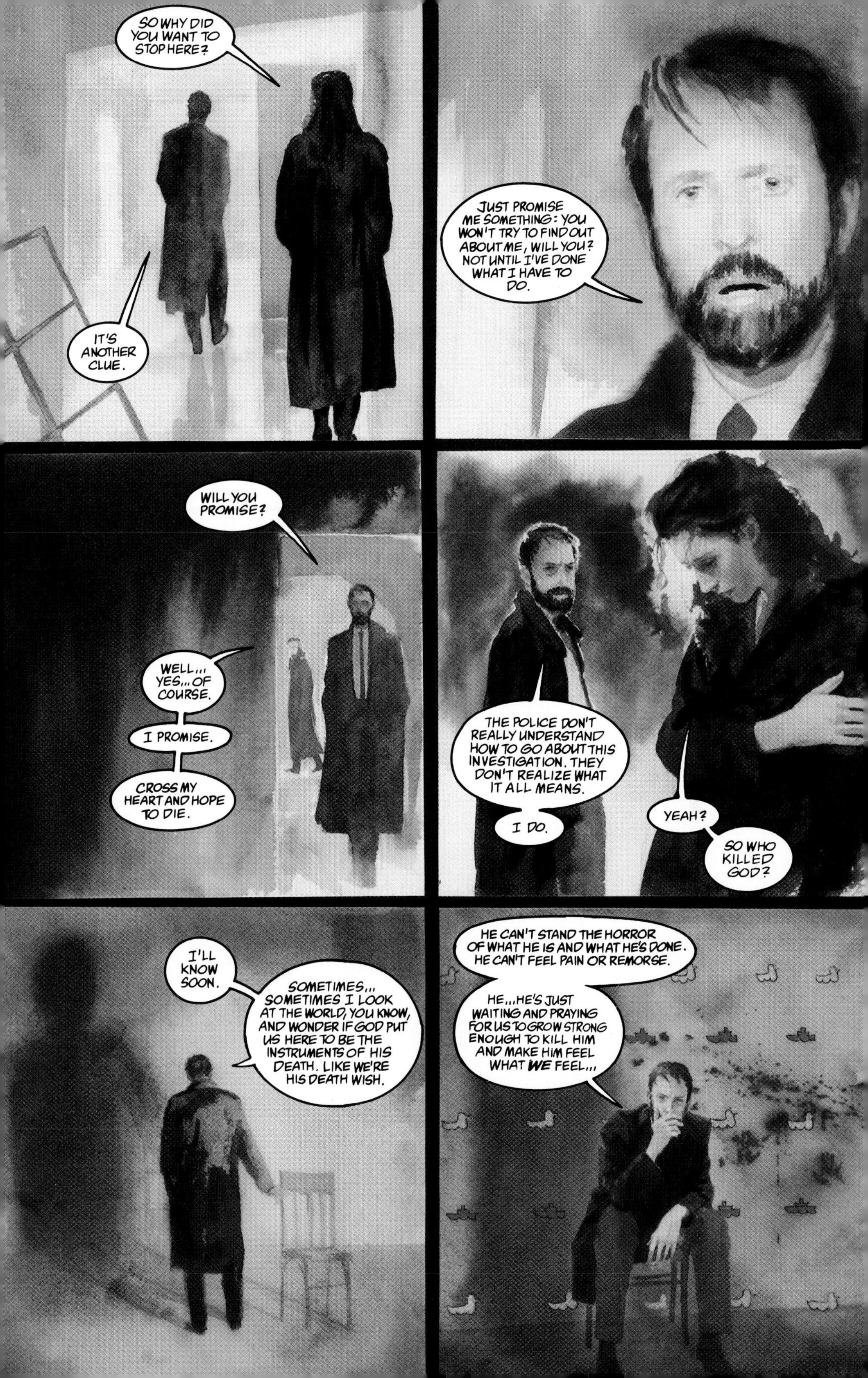
SO WHY DID YOU WANT TO STOP HERE?
IT'S ANOTHER CLUE.
JUST PROMISE ME SOMETHING: YOU WON'T TRY TO FIND OUT ABOUT ME, WILL YOU? NOT UNTIL I'VE DONE WHAT I HAVE TO DO.
WILL YOU PROMISE?
WELL... YES... OF COURSE.
I PROMISE.
CROSS MY HEART AND HOPE TO DIE.
THE POLICE DON'T REALLY UNDERSTAND HOW TO GO ABOUT THIS INVESTIGATION. THEY DON'T REALIZE WHAT IT ALL MEANS.
I DO.
YEAH?
SO WHO KILLED GOD?
I'LL KNOW SOON.
SOMETIMES... SOMETIMES I LOOK AT THE WORLD, YOU KNOW, AND WONDER IF GOD PUT US HERE TO BE THE INSTRUMENTS OF HIS DEATH. LIKE WE'RE HIS DEATH WISH.
HE CAN'T STAND THE HORROR OF WHAT HE IS AND WHAT HE'S DONE. HE CAN'T FEEL PAIN OR REMORSE.
HE... HE'S JUST WAITING AND PRAYING FOR US TO GROW STRONG ENOUGH TO KILL HIM AND MAKE HIM FEEL WHAT WE FEEL...

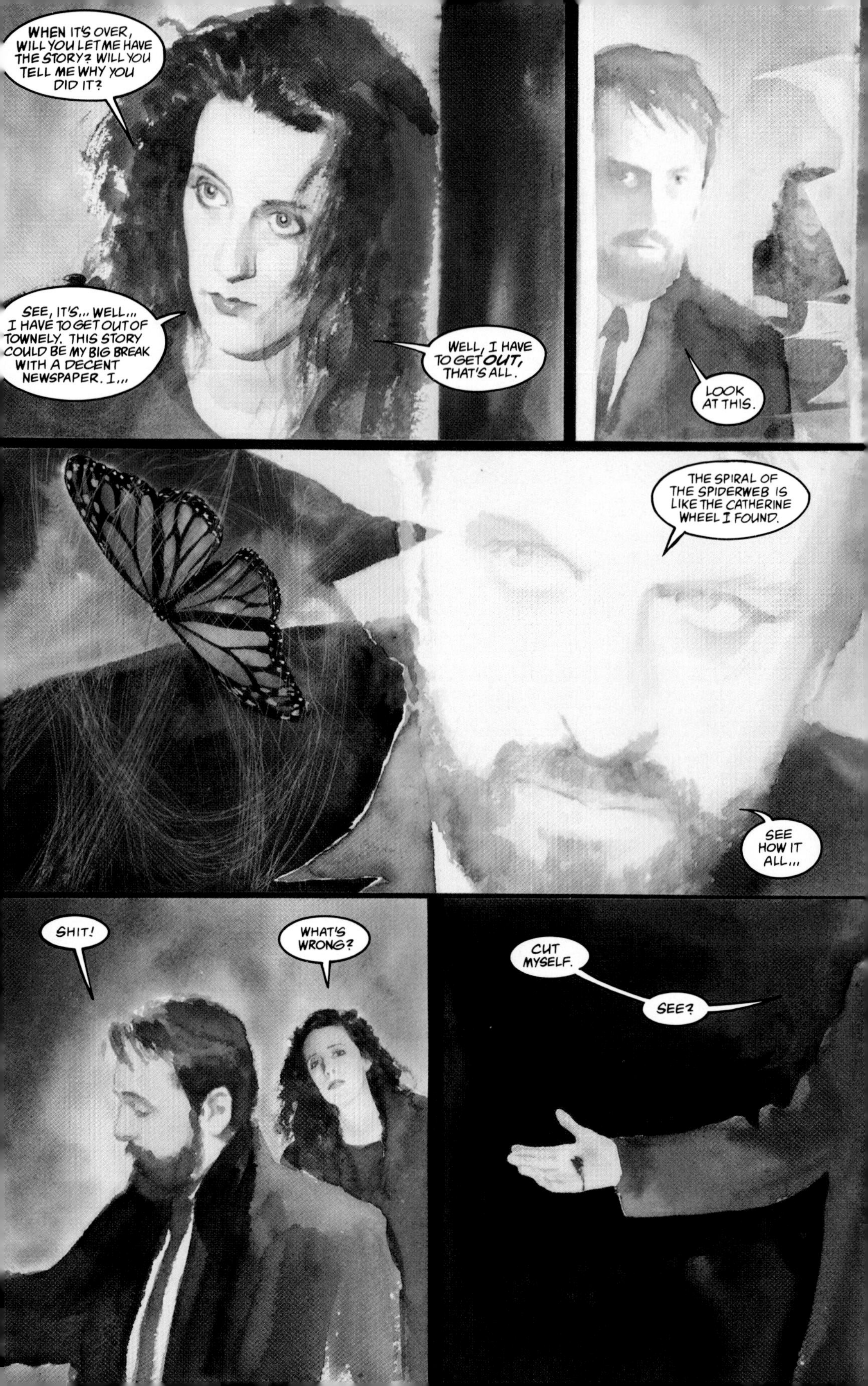
WHEN IT'S OVER, WILL YOU LET ME HAVE THE STORY? WILL YOU TELL ME WHY YOU DID IT?
SEE, IT'S... WELL... I HAVE TO GET OUT OF TOWNELY. THIS STORY COULD BE MY BIG BREAK WITH A DECENT NEWSPAPER. I...
WELL, I HAVE TO GET *OUT,* THAT'S ALL.
LOOK AT THIS.
THE SPIRAL OF THE SPIDERWEB IS LIKE THE CATHERINE WHEEL I FOUND.
SEE HOW IT ALL...
SHIT!
WHAT'S WRONG?
CUT MYSELF.
SEE?

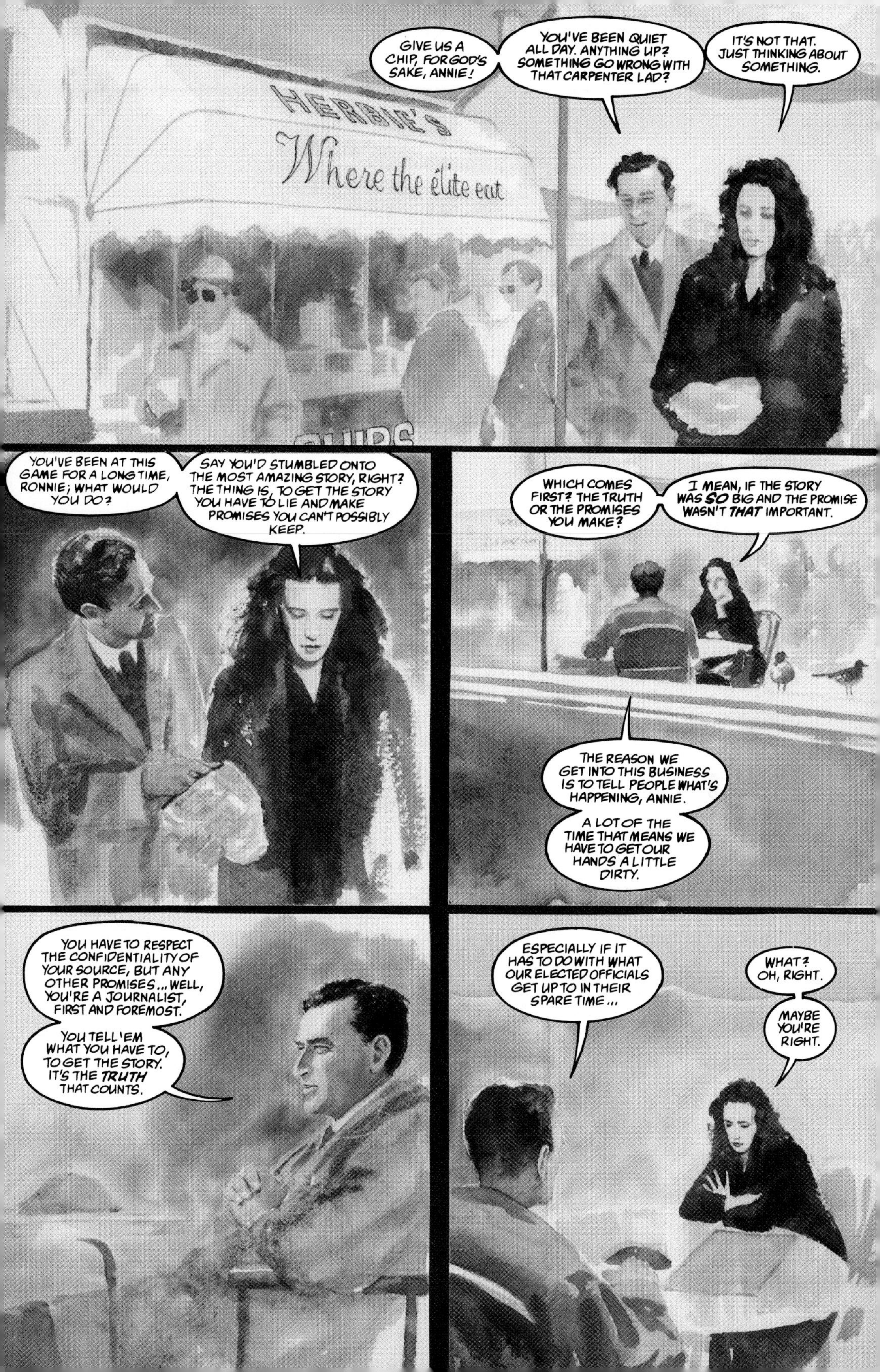
HERBIE'S
Where the élite eat
GIVE US A CHIP, FOR GOD'S SAKE, ANNIE!
YOU'VE BEEN QUIET ALL DAY. ANYTHING UP? SOMETHING GO WRONG WITH THAT CARPENTER LAD?
IT'S NOT THAT. JUST THINKING ABOUT SOMETHING.
YOU'VE BEEN AT THIS GAME FOR A LONG TIME, RONNIE; WHAT WOULD YOU DO?
SAY YOU'D STUMBLED ONTO THE MOST AMAZING STORY, RIGHT? THE THING IS, TO GET THE STORY YOU HAVE TO LIE AND MAKE PROMISES YOU CAN'T POSSIBLY KEEP.
WHICH COMES FIRST? THE TRUTH OR THE PROMISES YOU MAKE?
I MEAN, IF THE STORY WAS SO BIG AND THE PROMISE WASN'T THAT IMPORTANT.
THE REASON WE GET INTO THIS BUSINESS IS TO TELL PEOPLE WHAT'S HAPPENING, ANNIE.
A LOT OF THE TIME THAT MEANS WE HAVE TO GET OUR HANDS A LITTLE DIRTY.
YOU HAVE TO RESPECT THE CONFIDENTIALITY OF YOUR SOURCE, BUT ANY OTHER PROMISES... WELL, YOU'RE A JOURNALIST, FIRST AND FOREMOST.
YOU TELL 'EM WHAT YOU HAVE TO, TO GET THE STORY. IT'S THE TRUTH THAT COUNTS.
ESPECIALLY IF IT HAS TO DO WITH WHAT OUR ELECTED OFFICIALS GET UP TO IN THEIR SPARE TIME...
WHAT? OH, RIGHT.
MAYBE YOU'RE RIGHT.

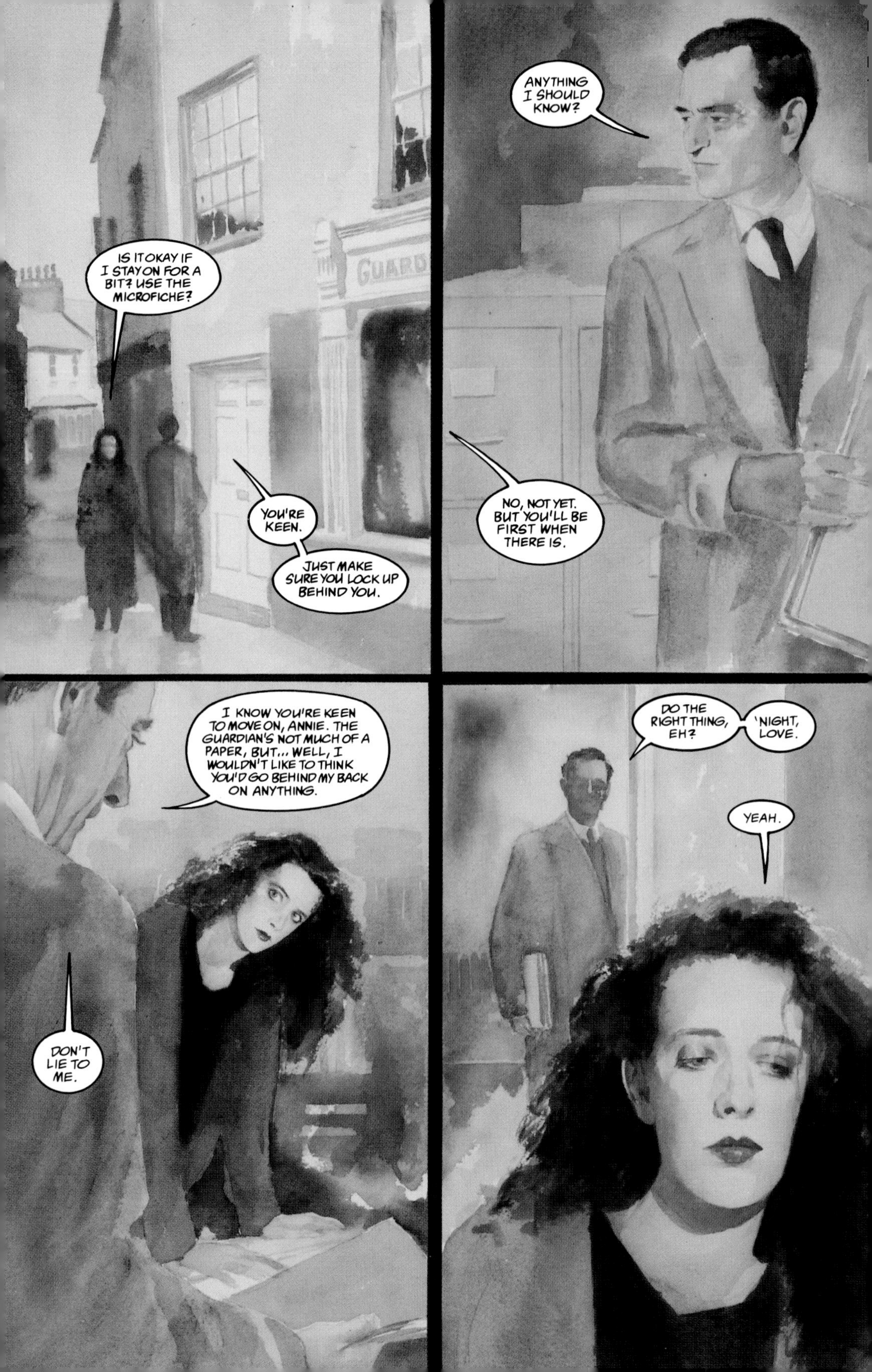
IS IT OKAY IF I STAY ON FOR A BIT? USE THE MICROFICHE?
GUARD
YOU'RE KEEN.
JUST MAKE SURE YOU LOCK UP BEHIND YOU.
ANYTHING I SHOULD KNOW?
NO, NOT YET. BUT YOU'LL BE FIRST WHEN THERE IS.
I KNOW YOU'RE KEEN TO MOVE ON, ANNIE. THE GUARDIAN'S NOT MUCH OF A PAPER, BUT... WELL, I WOULDN'T LIKE TO THINK YOU'D GO BEHIND MY BACK ON ANYTHING.
DON'T LIE TO ME.
DO THE RIGHT THING, EH?
'NIGHT, LOVE.
YEAH.

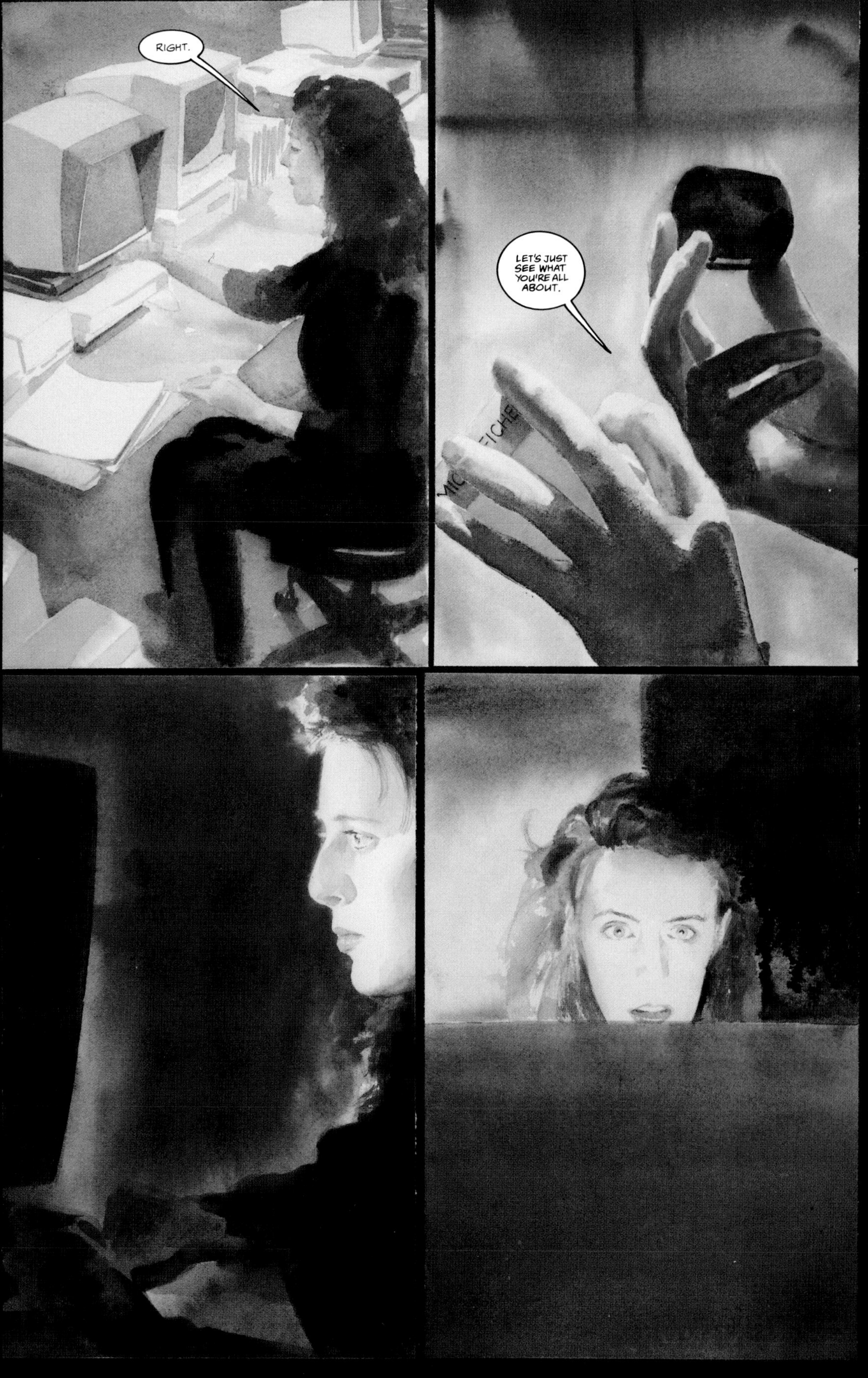
RIGHT.
LET'S JUST SEE WHAT YOU'RE ALL ABOUT.
MICROFICHE

Man Charged With Brutal Rape and Murder of Little Sa

"Raincoat Man" is forme Psychiatric Patient

rder of Little Sarah stuns Townely

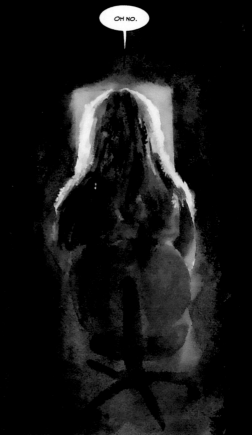

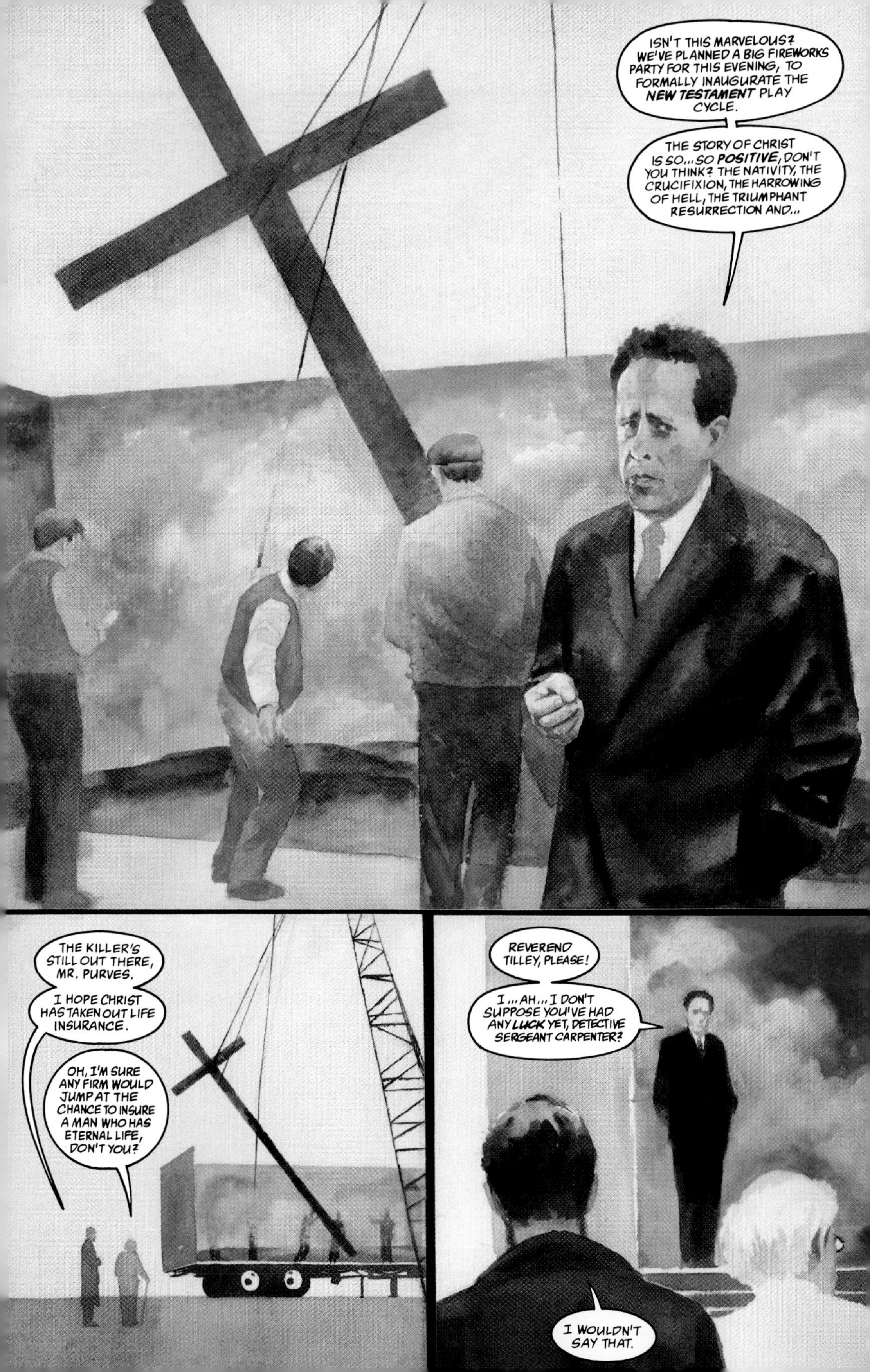
ISN'T THIS MARVELOUS? WE'VE PLANNED A BIG FIREWORKS PARTY FOR THIS EVENING, TO FORMALLY INAUGURATE THE NEW TESTAMENT PLAY CYCLE.
THE STORY OF CHRIST IS SO... SO POSITIVE, DON'T YOU THINK? THE NATIVITY, THE CRUCIFIXION, THE HARROWING OF HELL, THE TRIUMPHANT RESURRECTION AND...
THE KILLER'S STILL OUT THERE, MR. PURVES.
I HOPE CHRIST HAS TAKEN OUT LIFE INSURANCE.
OH, I'M SURE ANY FIRM WOULD JUMP AT THE CHANCE TO INSURE A MAN WHO HAS ETERNAL LIFE, DON'T YOU?
REVEREND TILLEY, PLEASE!
I... AH... I DON'T SUPPOSE YOU'VE HAD ANY LUCK YET, DETECTIVE SERGEANT CARPENTER?
I WOULDN'T SAY THAT.

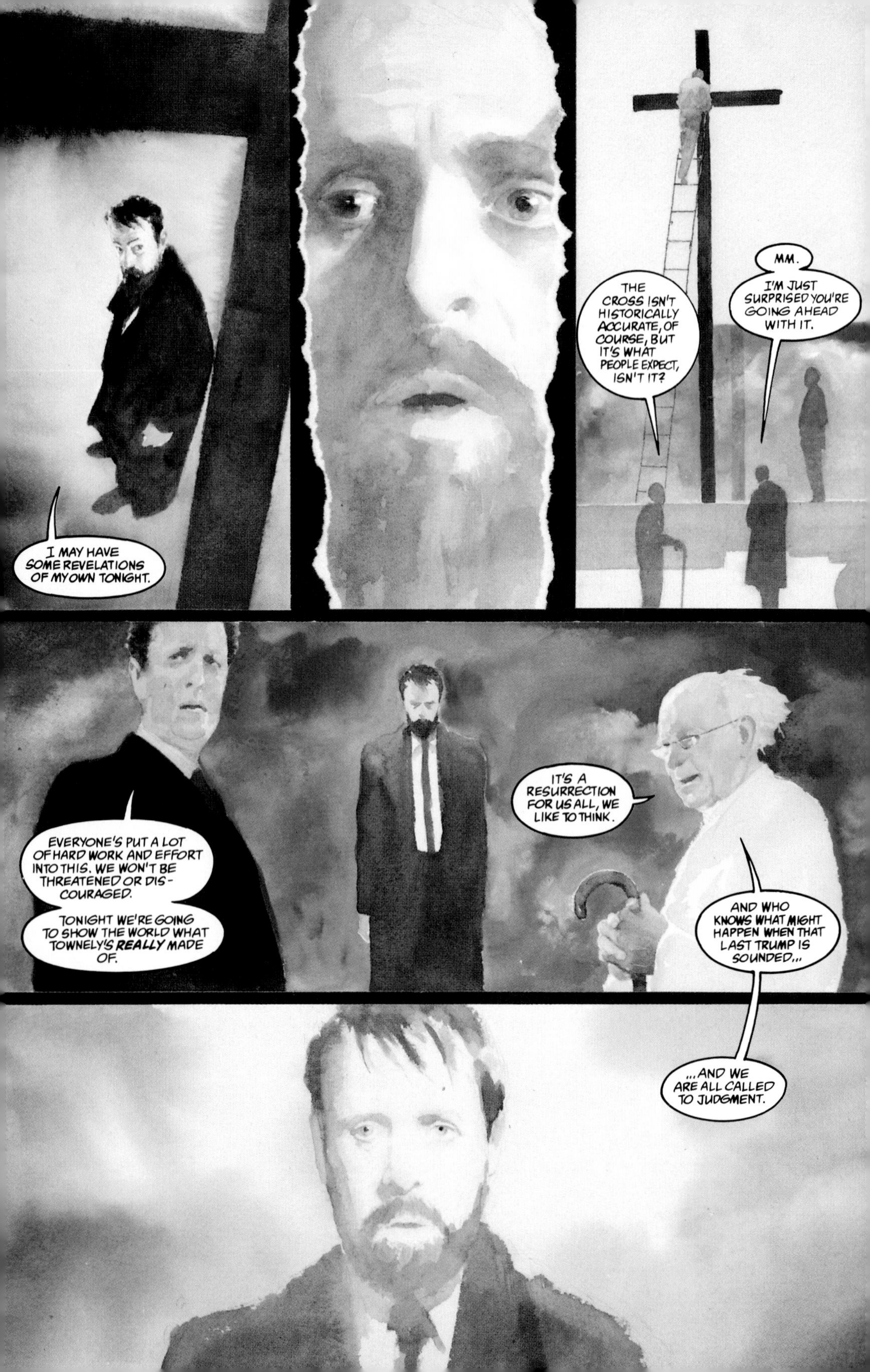
I MAY HAVE SOME REVELATIONS OF MY OWN TONIGHT.
THE CROSS ISN'T HISTORICALLY ACCURATE, OF COURSE, BUT IT'S WHAT PEOPLE EXPECT, ISN'T IT?
MM.
I'M JUST SURPRISED YOU'RE GOING AHEAD WITH IT.
EVERYONE'S PUT A LOT OF HARD WORK AND EFFORT INTO THIS. WE WON'T BE THREATENED OR DIS-COURAGED.
TONIGHT WE'RE GOING TO SHOW THE WORLD WHAT TOWNELY'S REALLY MADE OF.
IT'S A RESURRECTION FOR US ALL, WE LIKE TO THINK.
AND WHO KNOWS WHAT MIGHT HAPPEN WHEN THAT LAST TRUMP IS SOUNDED...
...AND WE ARE ALL CALLED TO JUDGMENT.

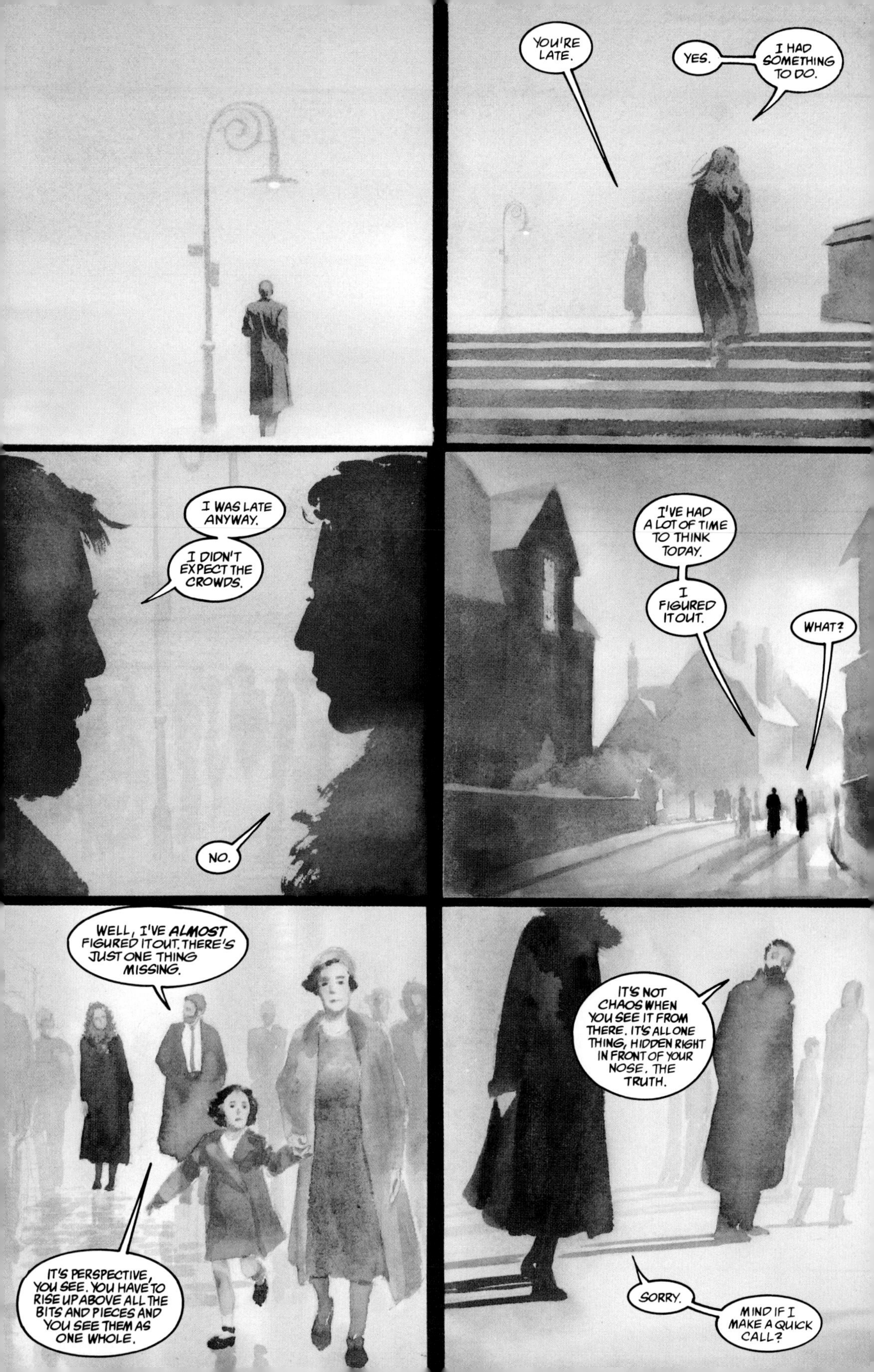
YOU'RE LATE.
YES.
I HAD SOMETHING TO DO.
I WAS LATE ANYWAY.
I DIDN'T EXPECT THE CROWDS.
NO.
I'VE HAD A LOT OF TIME TO THINK TODAY.
I FIGURED IT OUT.
WHAT?
WELL, I'VE ALMOST FIGURED IT OUT. THERE'S JUST ONE THING MISSING.
IT'S PERSPECTIVE, YOU SEE. YOU HAVE TO RISE UP ABOVE ALL THE BITS AND PIECES AND YOU SEE THEM AS ONE WHOLE.
IT'S NOT CHAOS WHEN YOU SEE IT FROM THERE. IT'S ALL ONE THING, HIDDEN RIGHT IN FRONT OF YOUR NOSE. THE TRUTH.
SORRY.
MIND IF I MAKE A QUICK CALL?

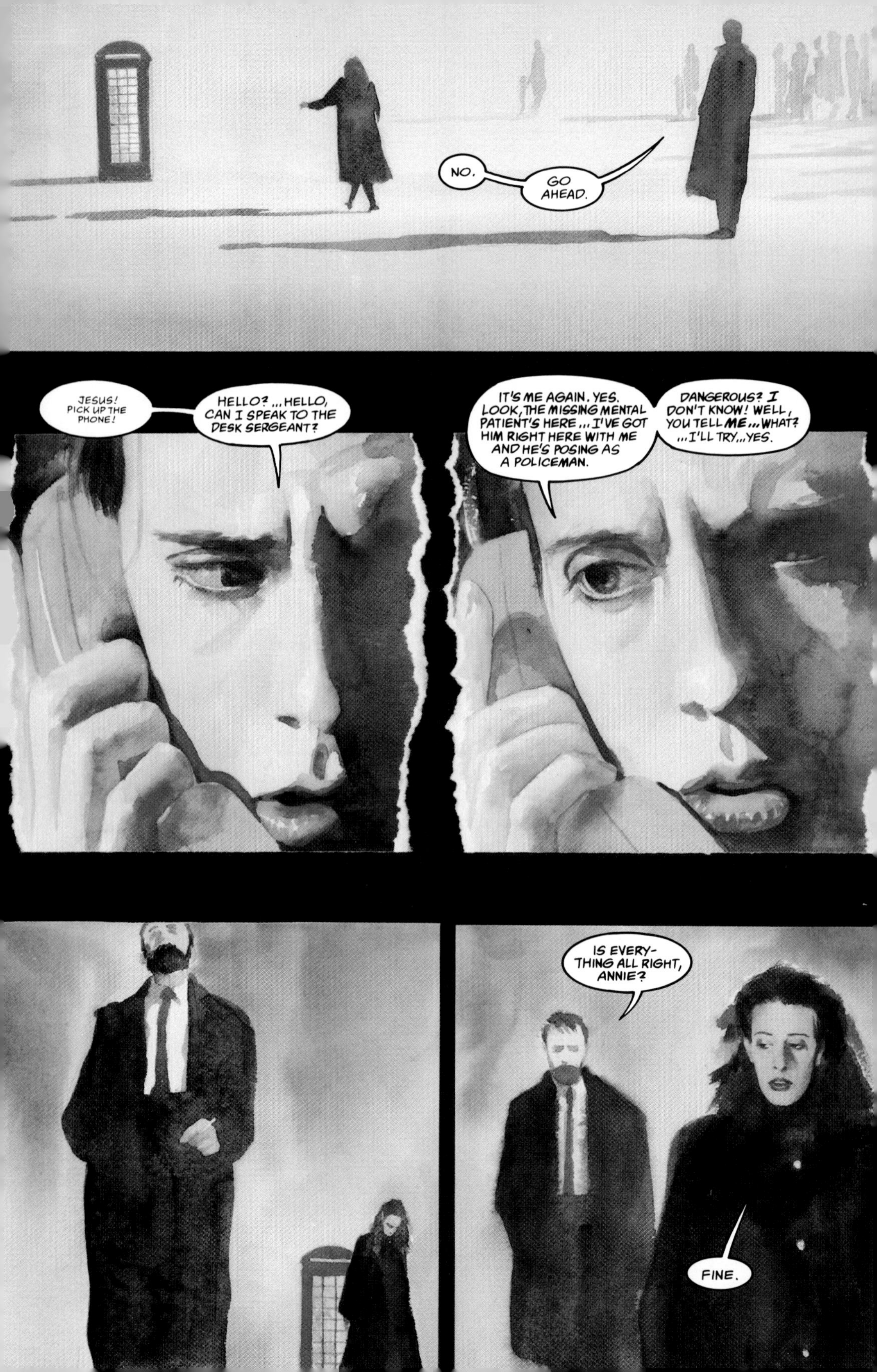
NO.
GO AHEAD.
JESUS! PICK UP THE PHONE!
HELLO? ... HELLO, CAN I SPEAK TO THE DESK SERGEANT?
IT'S ME AGAIN. YES. LOOK, THE MISSING MENTAL PATIENT'S HERE ... I'VE GOT HIM RIGHT HERE WITH ME AND HE'S POSING AS A POLICEMAN.
DANGEROUS? I DON'T KNOW! WELL, YOU TELL ME ... WHAT? ... I'LL TRY ... YES.
IS EVERY-THING ALL RIGHT, ANNIE?
FINE.

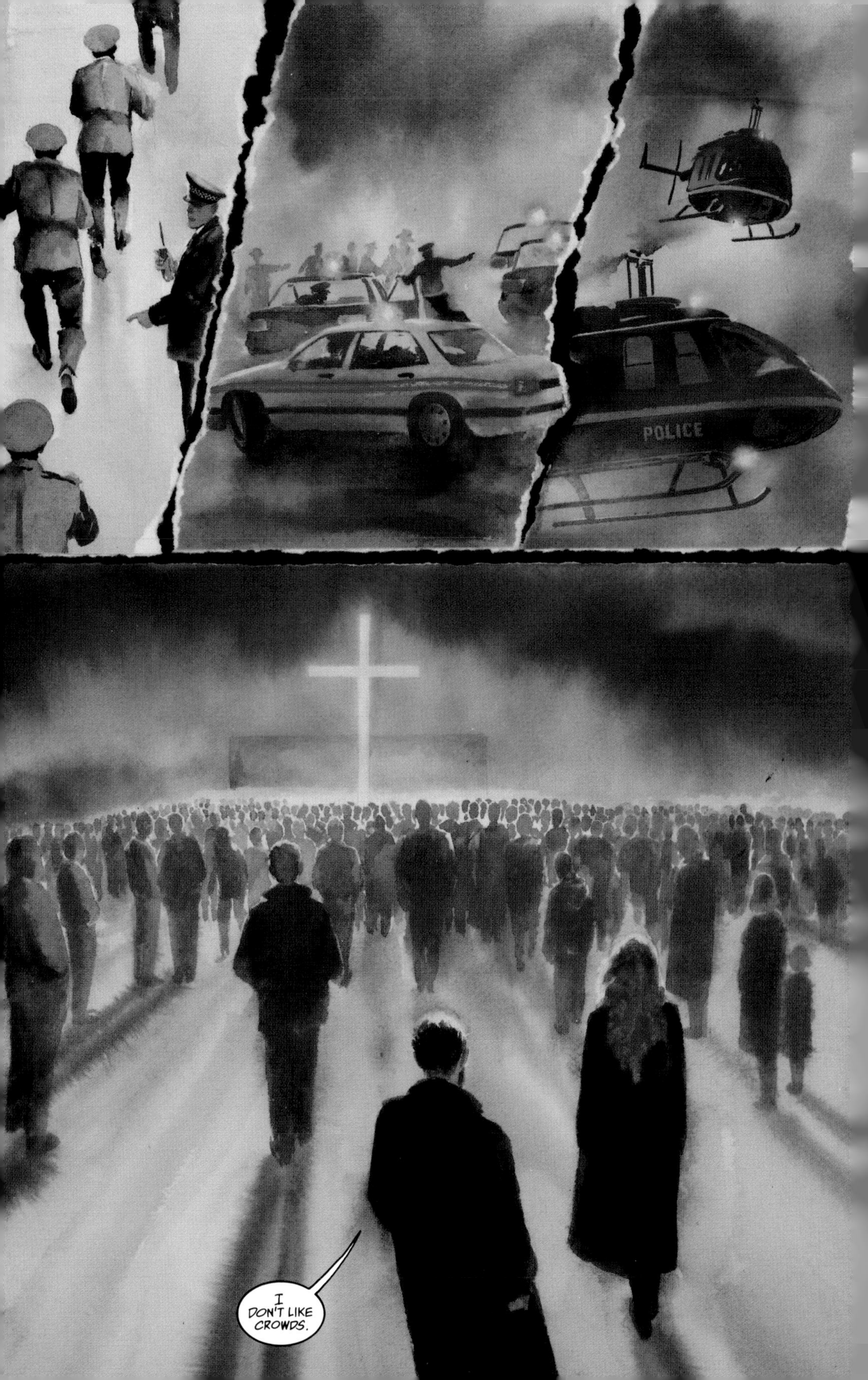
POLICE
I DON'T LIKE CROWDS.

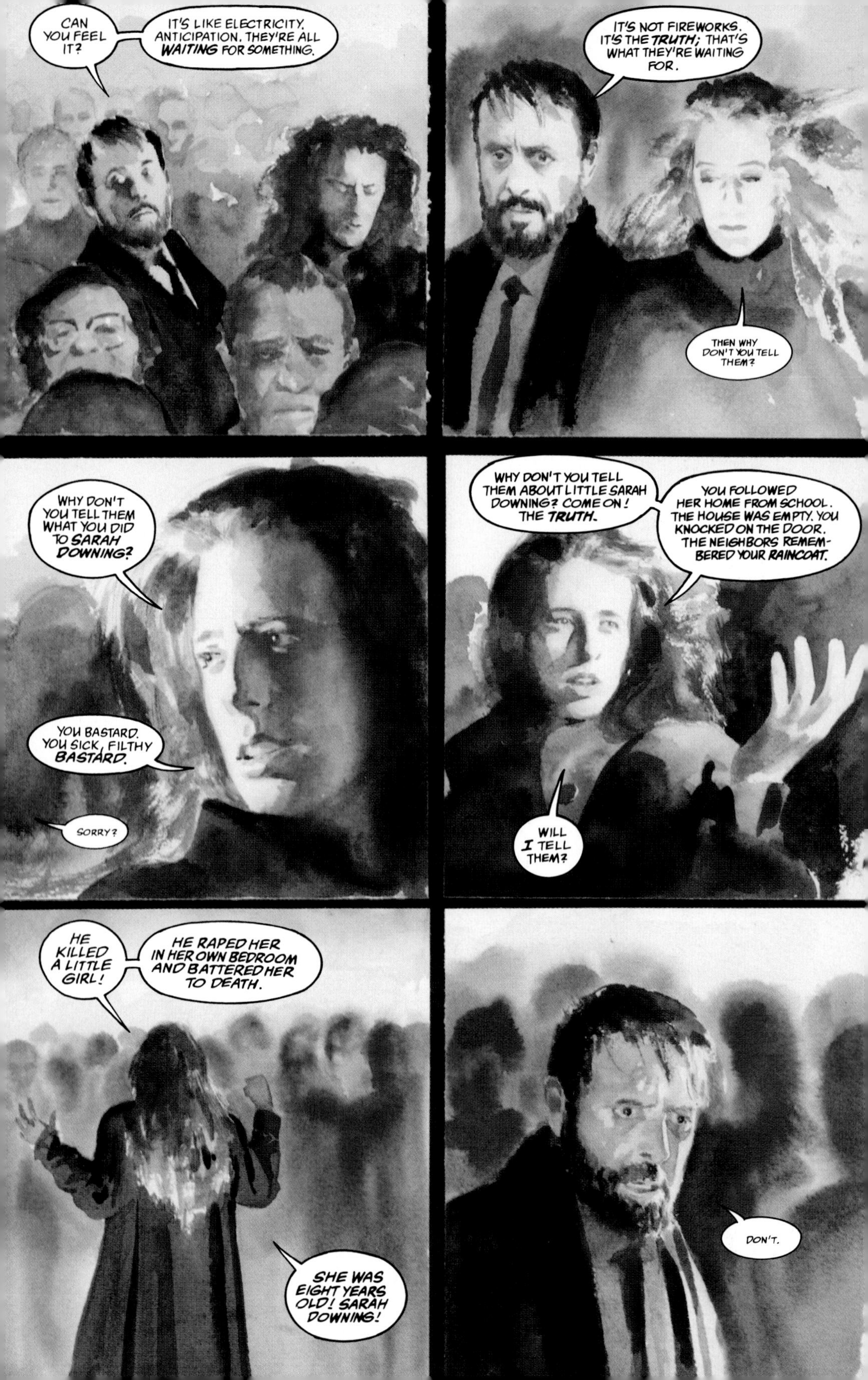
CAN YOU FEEL IT?
IT'S LIKE ELECTRICITY, ANTICIPATION. THEY'RE ALL WAITING FOR SOMETHING.
IT'S NOT FIREWORKS. IT'S THE TRUTH; THAT'S WHAT THEY'RE WAITING FOR.
THEN WHY DON'T YOU TELL THEM?
WHY DON'T YOU TELL THEM WHAT YOU DID TO SARAH DOWNING?
YOU BASTARD. YOU SICK, FILTHY BASTARD.
SORRY?
WHY DON'T YOU TELL THEM ABOUT LITTLE SARAH DOWNING? COME ON! THE TRUTH.
YOU FOLLOWED HER HOME FROM SCHOOL. THE HOUSE WAS EMPTY. YOU KNOCKED ON THE DOOR. THE NEIGHBORS REMEMBERED YOUR RAINCOAT.
WILL I TELL THEM?
HE KILLED A LITTLE GIRL!
HE RAPED HER IN HER OWN BEDROOM AND BATTERED HER TO DEATH.
SHE WAS EIGHT YEARS OLD! SARAH DOWNING!
DON'T.

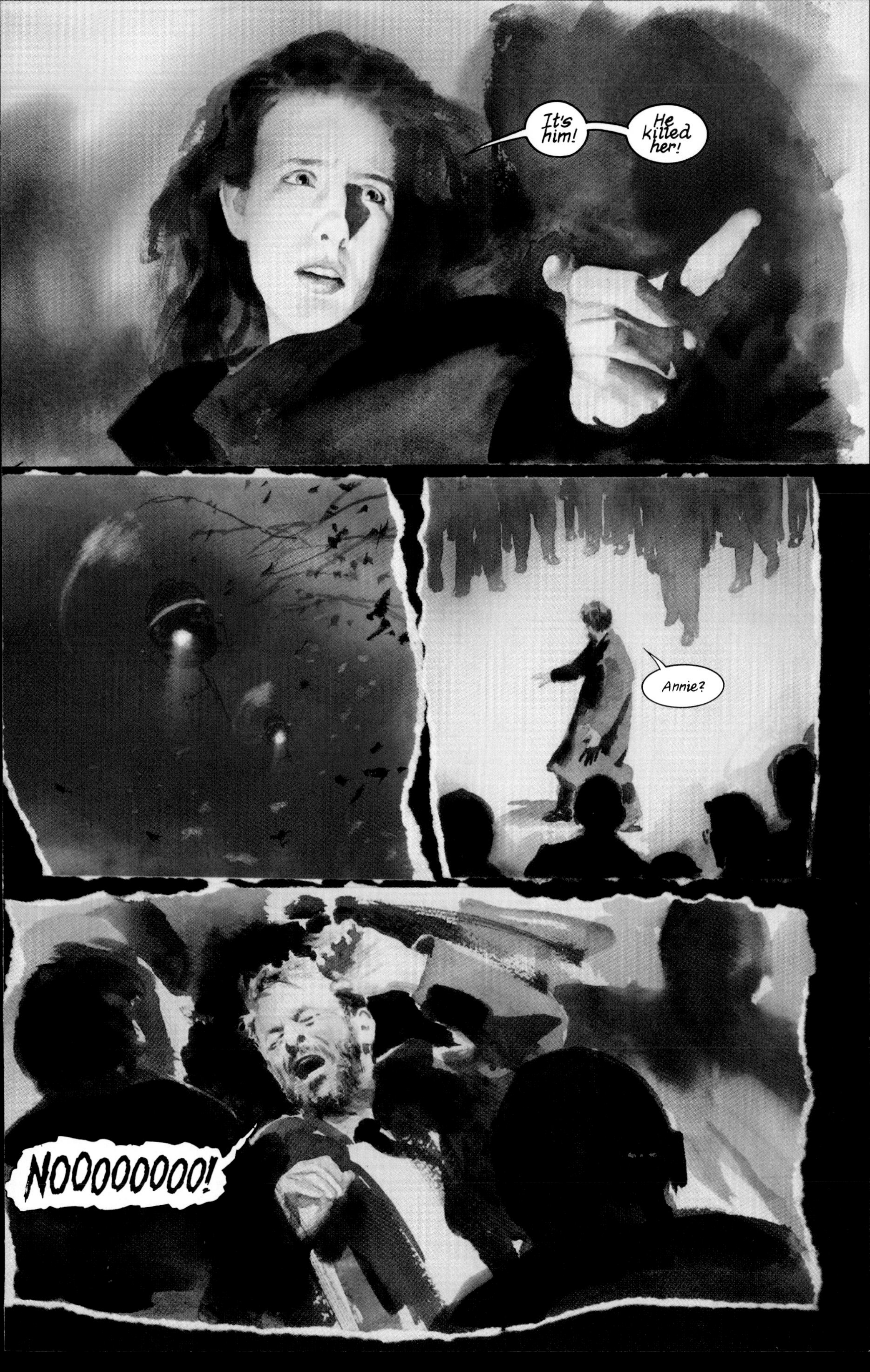
It's him!
He killed her!
Annie?
NOOOOOOOO!

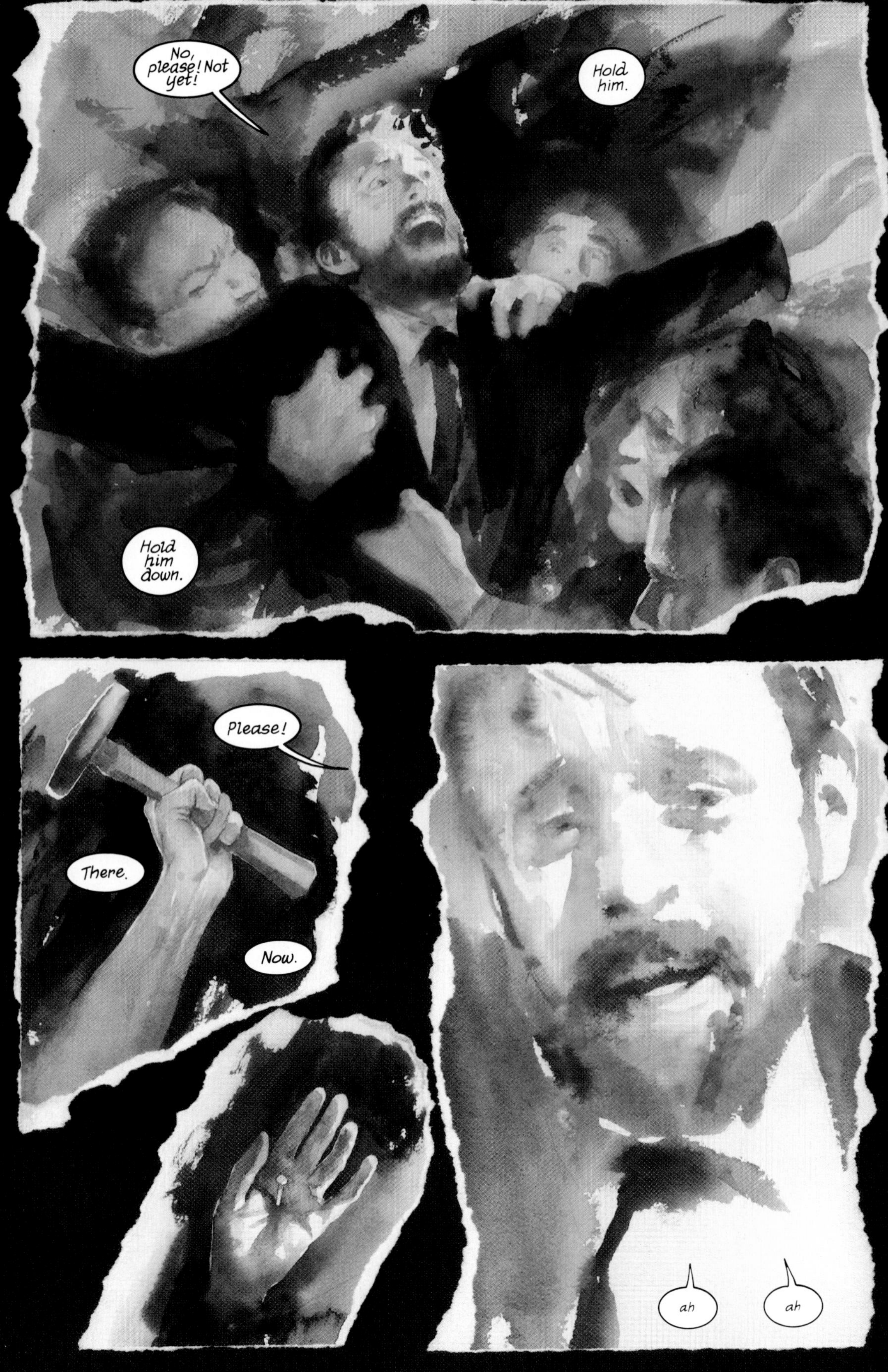
No, please! Not yet!
Hold him.
Hold him down.
Please!
There.
Now.
ah
ah

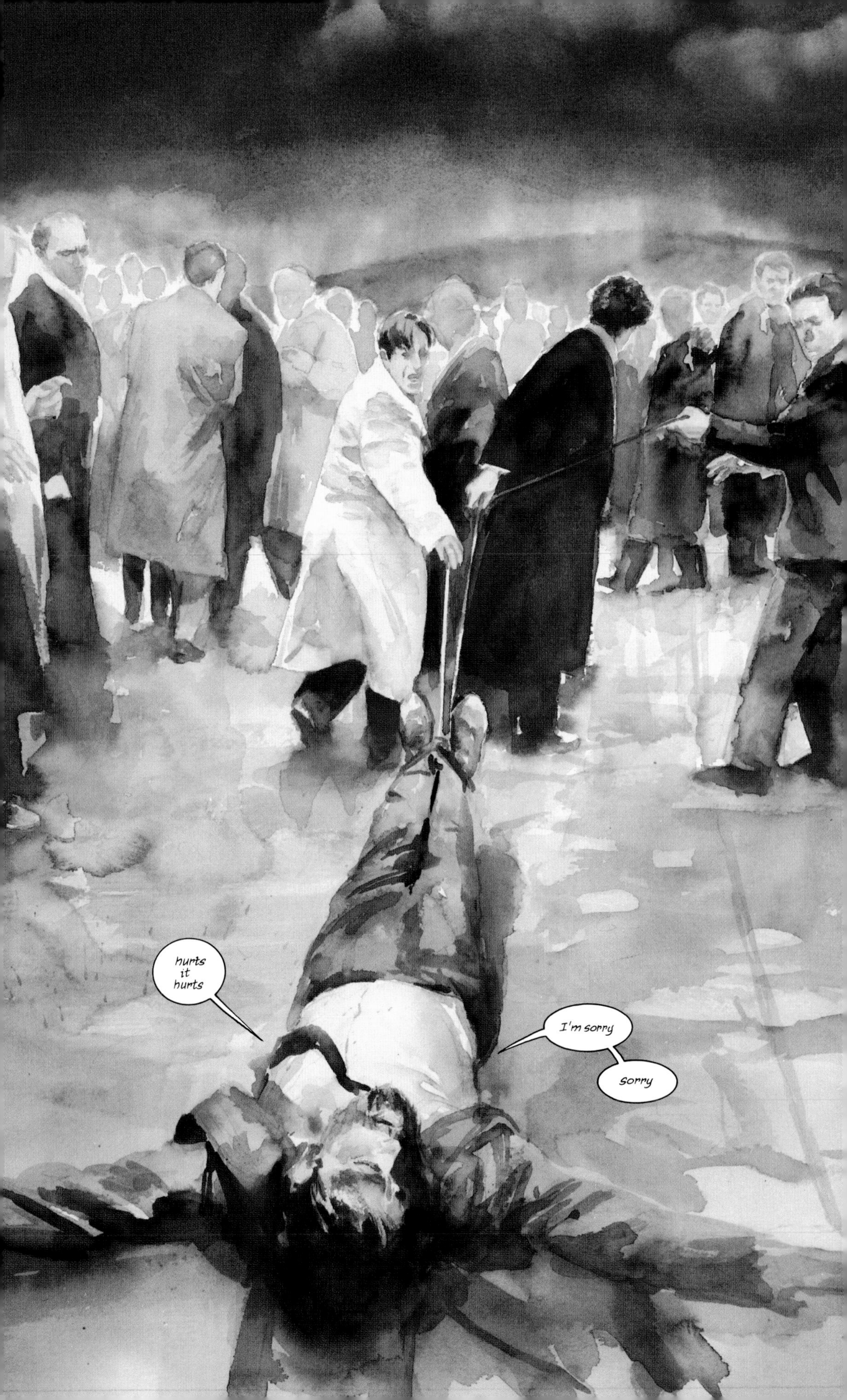
hurts it hurts
I'm sorry
sorry

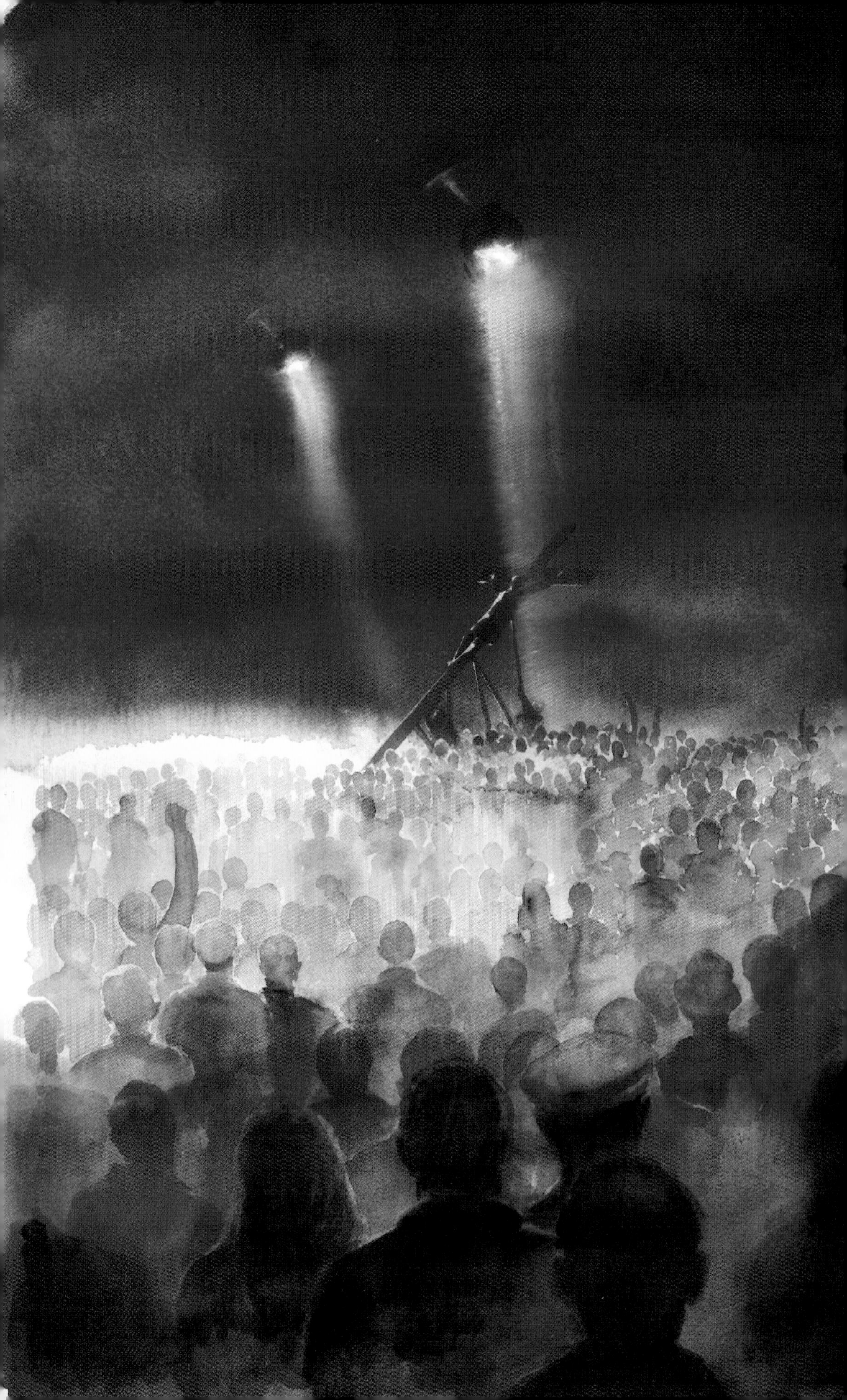

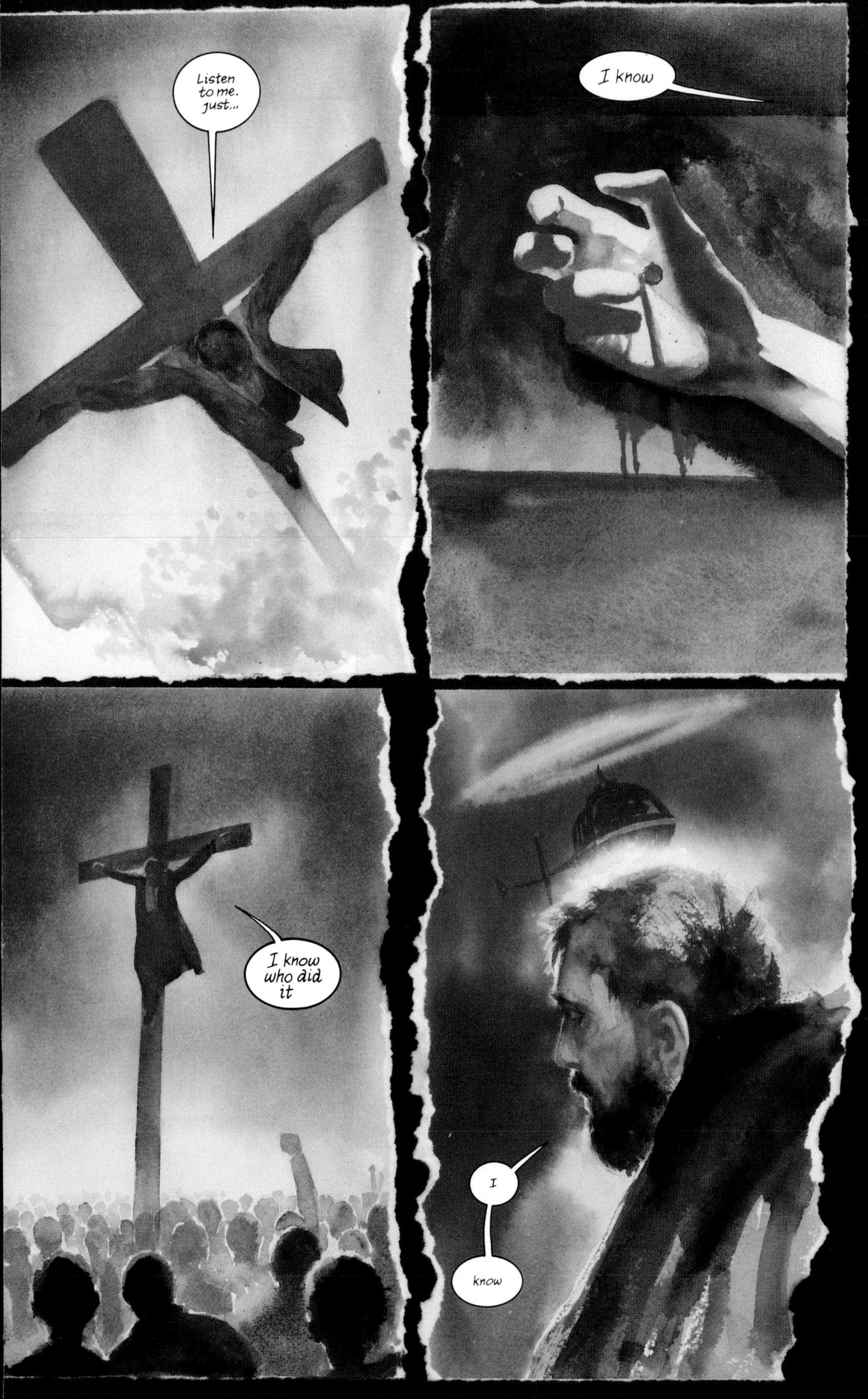
Listen to me. just...
I know
I know who did it
I
know

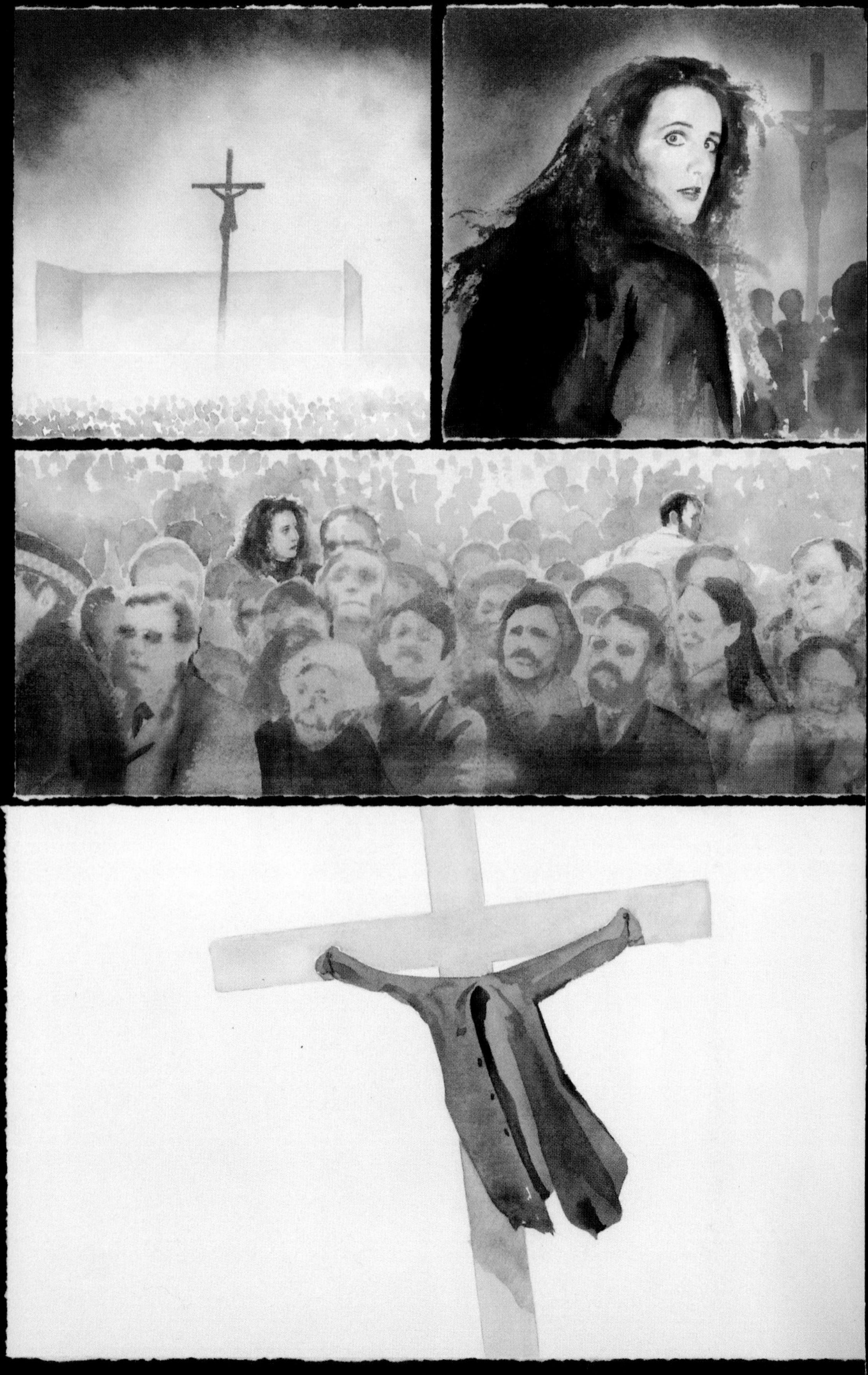

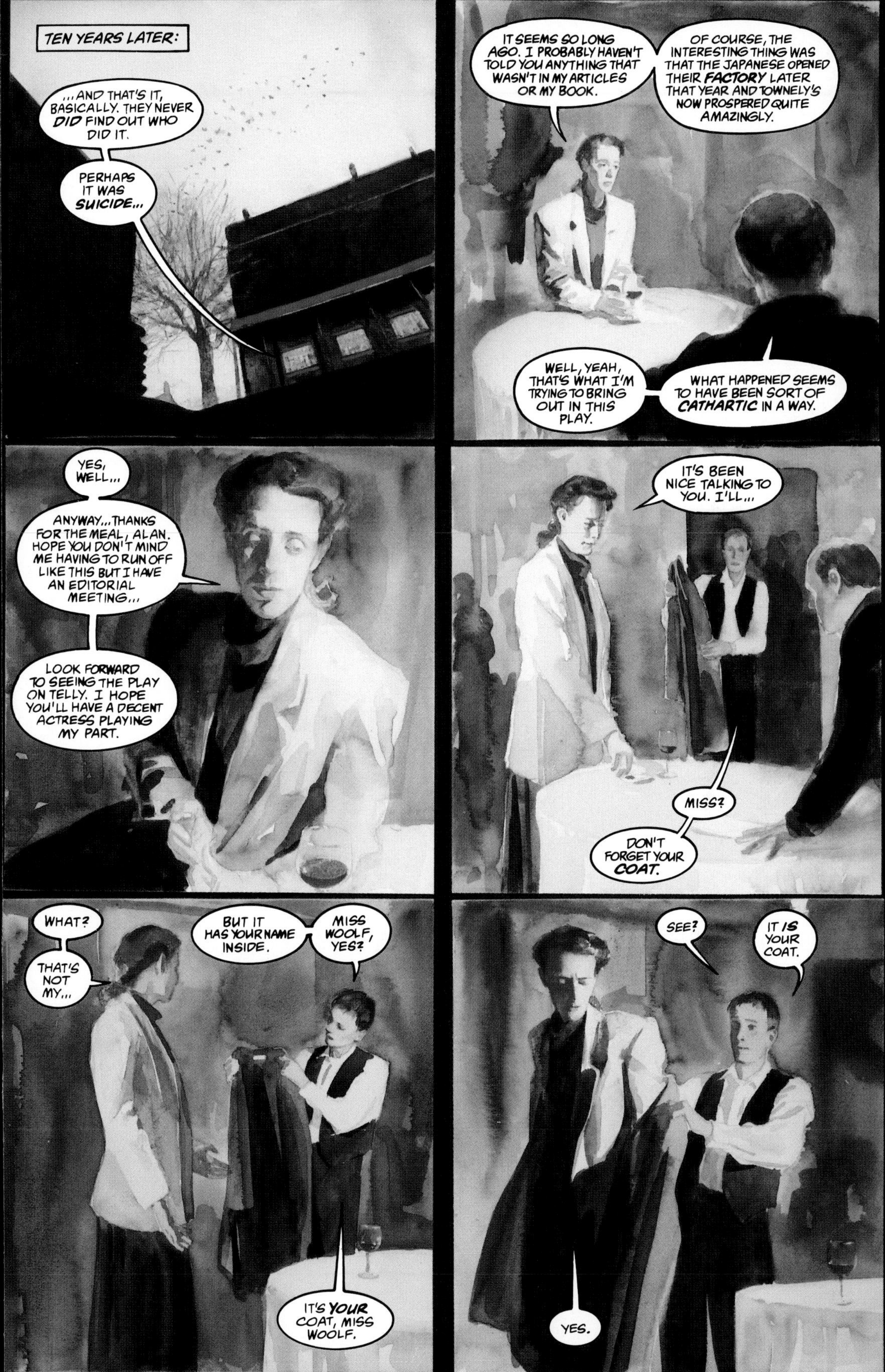
TEN YEARS LATER:
...AND THAT'S IT, BASICALLY. THEY NEVER DID FIND OUT WHO DID IT.
PERHAPS IT WAS SUICIDE...
IT SEEMS SO LONG AGO. I PROBABLY HAVEN'T TOLD YOU ANYTHING THAT WASN'T IN MY ARTICLES OR MY BOOK.
OF COURSE, THE INTERESTING THING WAS THAT THE JAPANESE OPENED THEIR FACTORY LATER THAT YEAR AND TOWNELY'S NOW PROSPERED QUITE AMAZINGLY.
WHAT HAPPENED SEEMS TO HAVE BEEN SORT OF CATHARTIC IN A WAY.
WELL, YEAH, THAT'S WHAT I'M TRYING TO BRING OUT IN THIS PLAY.
YES, WELL...
ANYWAY... THANKS FOR THE MEAL, ALAN. HOPE YOU DON'T MIND ME HAVING TO RUN OFF LIKE THIS BUT I HAVE AN EDITORIAL MEETING...
LOOK FORWARD TO SEEING THE PLAY ON TELLY. I HOPE YOU'LL HAVE A DECENT ACTRESS PLAYING MY PART.
IT'S BEEN NICE TALKING TO YOU. I'LL...
MISS?
DON'T FORGET YOUR COAT.
WHAT?
THAT'S NOT MY...
MISS WOOLF, YES?
BUT IT HAS YOUR NAME INSIDE.
IT'S YOUR COAT, MISS WOOLF.
SEE?
IT IS YOUR COAT.
YES.

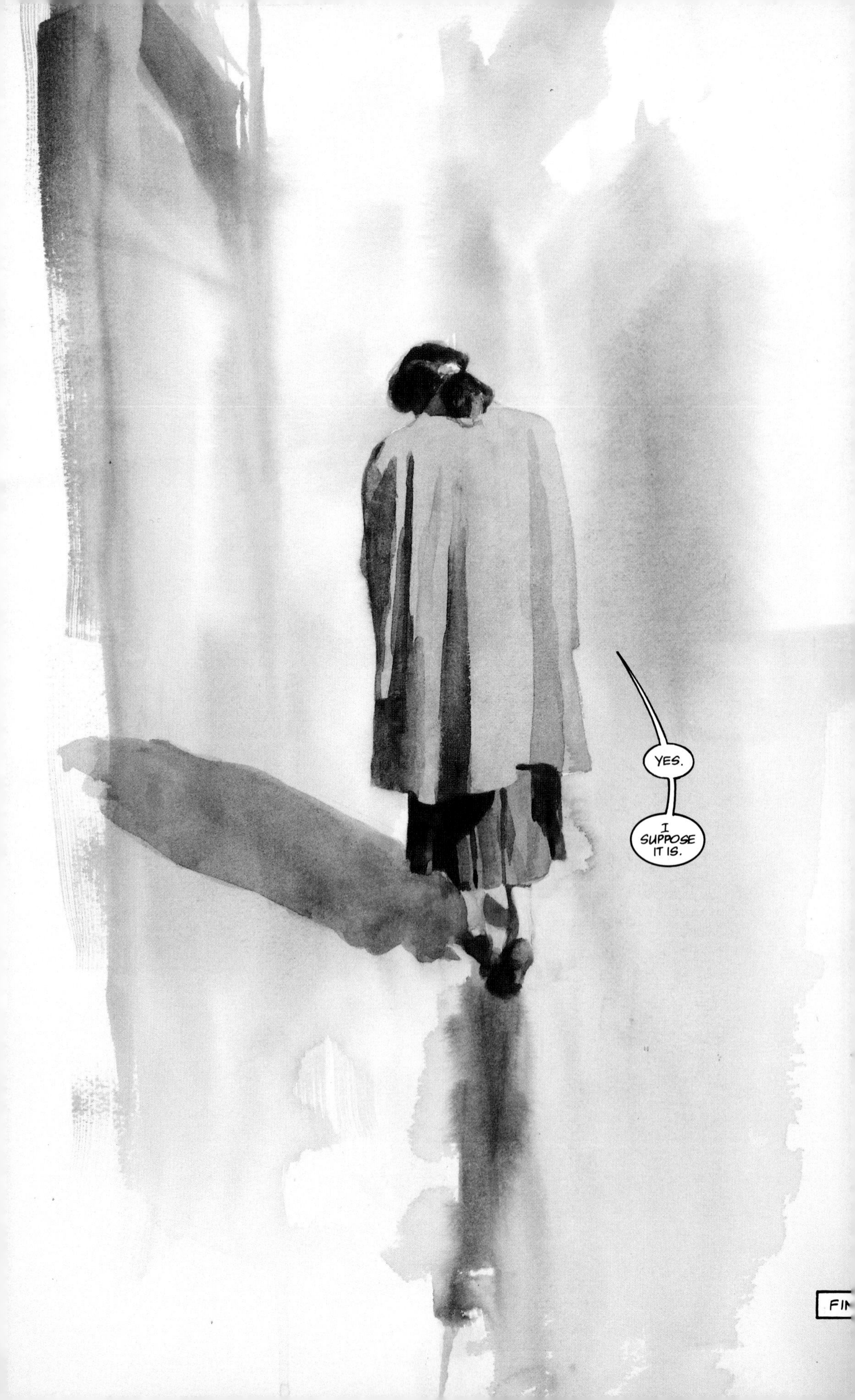
YES.
I SUPPOSE IT IS.

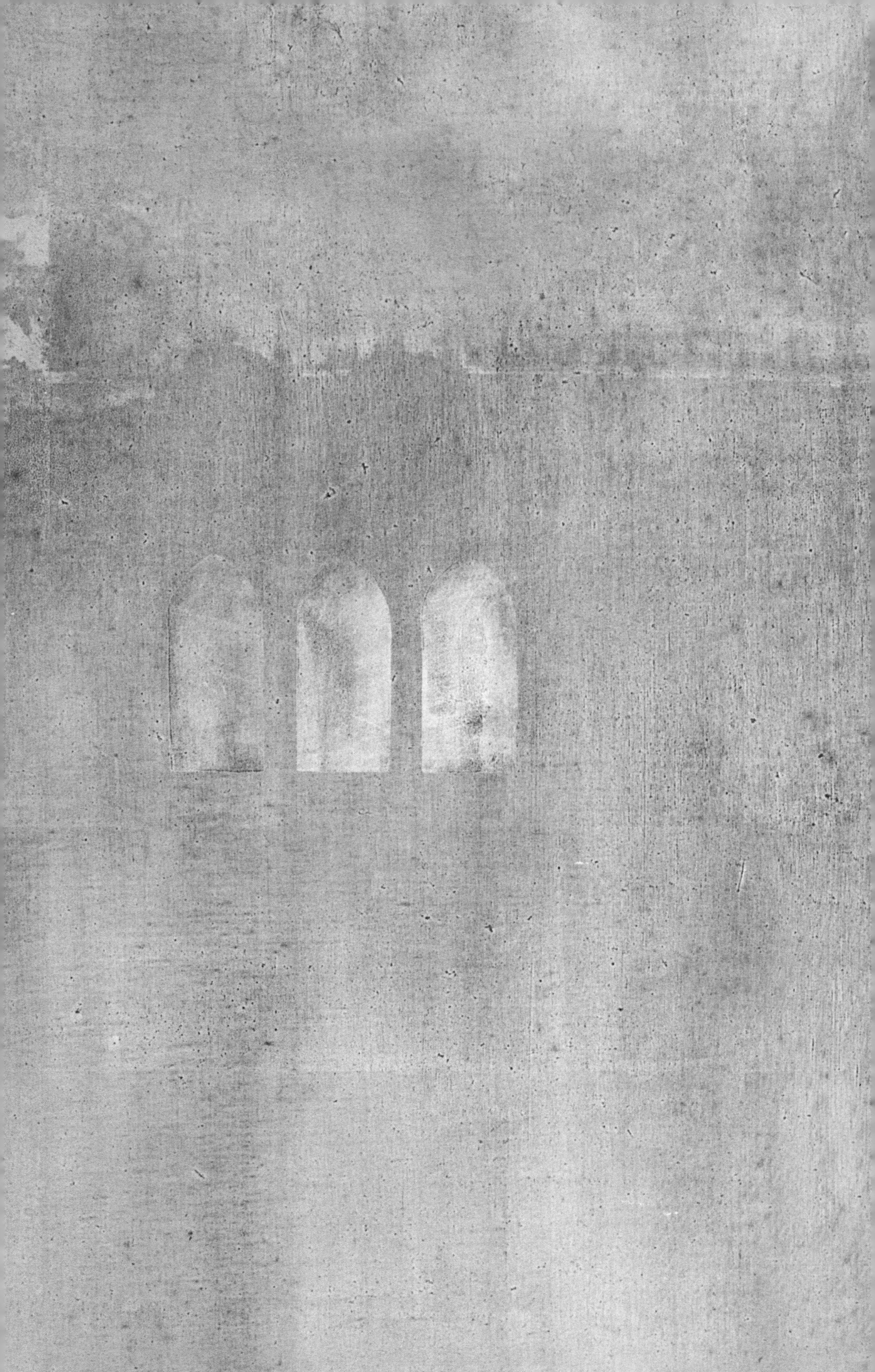

Dustjacket art by Jon J Muth for the original hardcover edition of THE MYSTERY PLAY

Grant Morrison has been working with DC Comics for more than 20 years, beginning with his legendary runs on the revolutionary titles ANIMAL MAN and DOOM PATROL. Since then he has written numerous bestsellers—including JLA, BATMAN and *New X-Men*—as well as the critically acclaimed creator-owned series THE INVISIBLES, SEAGUY, THE FILTH, WE3 and JOE THE BARBARIAN. Morrison has also expanded the borders of the DC Universe in the award-winning ALL-STAR SUPERMAN, FINAL CRISIS, BATMAN INCORPORATED, ACTION COMICS and the Grand DC Unification Theory that is THE MULTIVERSITY.

In his secret identity, Morrison is a "counterculture" spokesperson, a musician, an award-winning playwright and a chaos magician. He is also the author of the *New York Times* bestseller *Supergods*, a groundbreaking psycho-historic mapping of the superhero as a cultural organism. He divides his time between his homes in Los Angeles and Scotland.

Steve Yeowell's first professional collaboration with Grant Morrison was on the licensed toy feature "Zoids" in the pages of *Spider-Man and Zoids* published by Marvel UK; his second was on *2000 AD*'s superhero feature *Zenith*. SEBASTIAN O was his first work for DC Comics, for whom he went on to pencil issues of THE INVISIBLES, STARMAN, LEGENDS OF THE DARK KNIGHT and THE ATOM for DC's Convergence event of 2015. For Marvel Comics he pencilled *Skrull Kill Krew*, and for *2000 AD* he has also drawn *Judge Dredd*, *DeMarco*, *P.I.*, the long-running Harryhausan-esque pirate adventure *The Red Seas* and the Dark Age-era lycanthrope fantasy *Black Shuck*. He lives in northwest England.

After working in comics for 20 years (and receiving an Eisner Award along the way), **Jon J Muth** went into the desert on a camel and came out a children's book author and illustrator. (The camel did not return calls in time for this biography.) Over the past decade, Muth's picture books have received numerous awards (including a Caldecott Honor) and have been translated into a dozen or so languages. He has interests in music, stone and spending time with his family. Muth lives in New York with his wife and four children.